LIBRARY OF PHILOSOPHY

GENERAL EDITOR:

PROFESSOR J. H. MUIRHEAD, LL.D.

CONTEMPORARY
AMERICAN PHILOSOPHY
VOL. II

PROFESSOR JOHN DEWEY

CONTEMPORARY AMERICAN PHILOSOPHY

PERSONAL STATEMENTS

VOL. II

BY

J. DEWEY	A. K. ROGERS
C. I. LEWIS	G. SANTAYANA
J. LOEWENBERG	R. W. SELLARS
A. O. LOVEJOY	E. A. SINGER, Jr.
E. B. McGILVARY	C. A. STRONG
W. P. MONTAGUE	J. H. TUFTS
De W. H. PARKER	W. M. URBAN
R. B. PERRY	R. M. WENLEY
J. B. PRATT	F. J. E. WOODBRIDGE

EDITED BY

GEORGE P. ADAMS

AND

WM. PEPPERELL MONTAGUE

NEW YORK

THE MACMILLAN COMPANY

1930

FIRST PUBLISHED IN THE U.S.A. IN 1930

191.9
C767
v.2

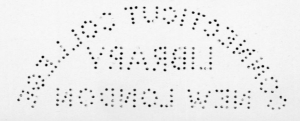

THESE ESSAYS ARE
AFFECTIONATELY DEDICATED TO
GEORGE HERBERT PALMER
THE FRIEND AND TEACHER
OF SO MANY AMERICAN PHILOSOPHERS

CONTENTS

FROM ABSOLUTISM TO EXPERI-MENTALISM

By JOHN DEWEY

Born 1859; Professor of Philosophy, Columbia University,
New York City.

FROM ABSOLUTISM TO EXPERIMENTALISM

IN the late 'seventies, when I was an undergraduate, "electives" were still unknown in the smaller New England colleges. But in the one I attended, the University of Vermont, the tradition of a "senior-year course" still subsisted. This course was regarded as a kind of intellectual coping to the structure erected in earlier years, or, at least, as an insertion of the key-stone of the arch. It included courses in political economy, international law, history of civilization (Guizot), psychology, ethics, philosophy of religion (Butler's *Analogy*), logic, etc., not history of philosophy, save incidentally. The enumeration of these titles may not serve the purpose for which it is made; but the idea was that after three years of somewhat specialized study in languages and sciences, the last year was reserved for an introduction into serious intellectual topics of wide and deep significance—an introduction into the world of ideas. I doubt if in many cases it served its alleged end; however, it fell in with my own inclinations, and I have always been grateful for that year of my schooling. There was, however, one course in the previous year that had excited a taste that in retrospect may be called philosophical. That was a rather short course, without laboratory work, in Physiology, a book of Huxley's being the text. It is difficult to speak with exactitude about what happened to me intellectually so many years ago, but I have an impression that there was derived from that study a sense of interdependence and interrelated unity that gave form to intellectual stirrings that had been previously inchoate, and created a kind of type or model of a view of things to which material in any field ought to conform. Subconsciously, at least, I was led to desire a world and a life that would have the same properties as had the human organism in the picture of it derived from study of Huxley's treatment. At all events, I got great stimulation from the study, more than from anything I had had contact with before; and as no desire was awakened in me to continue that particular branch of learning, I date from this time the awakening of a distinctive philosophic interest.

The University of Vermont rather prided itself upon its tradition in philosophy. One of its earlier teachers, Dr. Marsh, was almost the first person in the United States to venture upon the speculative and dubiously orthodox seas of German thinking —that of Kant, Schelling, and Hegel. The venture, to be sure, was made largely by way of Coleridge; Marsh edited an American edition of Coleridge's *Aids to Reflection*. Even this degree of speculative generalization, in its somewhat obvious tendency to rationalize the body of Christian theological doctrines, created a flutter in ecclesiastical dovecots. In particular, a controversy was carried on between the Germanizing rationalizers and the orthodox representatives of the Scottish school of thought through the representatives of the latter at Princeton. I imagine— although it is a very long time since I have had any contact with this material—that the controversy still provides data for a section, if not a chapter, in the history of thought in this country.

Although the University retained pride in its pioneer work, and its atmosphere was for those days theologically "liberal"— of the Congregational type—the teaching of philosophy had become more restrained in tone, more influenced by the still dominant Scotch school. Its professor, Mr. H. A. P. Torrey, was a man of genuinely sensitive and cultivated mind, with marked esthetic interest and taste, which, in a more congenial atmosphere than that of northern New England in those days, would have achieved something significant. He was, however, constitutionally timid, and never really let his mind go. I recall that, in a conversation I had with him a few years after graduation, he said: "Undoubtedly pantheism is the most satisfactory form of metaphysics intellectually, but it goes counter to religious faith." I fancy that remark told of an inner conflict that prevented his native capacity from coming to full fruition. His interest in philosophy, however, was genuine, not perfunctory; he was an excellent teacher, and I owe to him a double debt, that of turning my thoughts definitely to the study of philosophy as a life-pursuit, and of a generous gift of time to me during a year devoted privately under his direction to a reading of classics in the history of philosophy and learning to read philosophic

German. In our walks and talks during this year, after three years on my part of high-school teaching, he let his mind go much more freely than in the class-room, and revealed potentialities that might have placed him among the leaders in the development of a freer American philosophy—but the time for the latter had not yet come.

Teachers of philosophy were at that time, almost to a man, clergymen; the supposed requirements of religion, or theology, dominated the teaching of philosophy in most colleges. Just how and why Scotch philosophy lent itself so well to the exigencies of religion I cannot say; probably the causes were more extrinsic than intrinsic; but at all events there was a firm alliance established between religion and the cause of "intuition". It is probably impossible to recover at this date the almost sacrosanct air that enveloped the idea of intuitions; but somehow the cause of all holy and valuable things was supposed to stand or fall with the validity of intuitionalism; the only vital issue was that between intuitionalism and a sensational empiricism that explained away the reality of all higher objects. The story of this almost forgotten debate, once so urgent, is probably a factor in developing in me a certain scepticism about the depth and range of purely contemporary issues; it is likely that many of those which seem highly important to-day will also in a generation have receded to the status of the local and provincial. It also aided in generating a sense of the value of the history of philosophy; some of the claims made for this as a sole avenue of approach to the study of philosophic problems seem to me misdirected and injurious. But its value in giving perspective and a sense of proportion in relation to immediate contemporary issues can hardly be over-estimated.

I do not mention this theological and intuitional phase because it had any lasting influence upon my own development, except negatively. I learned the terminology of an intuitional philosophy, but it did not go deep, and in no way did it satisfy what I was dimly reaching for. I was brought up in a conventionally evangelical atmosphere of the more "liberal" sort; and the struggles that later arose between acceptance of that faith and

the discarding of traditional and institutional creeds came from personal experiences and not from the effects of philosophical teaching. It was not, in other words, in this respect that philosophy either appealed to me or influenced me—though I am not sure that Butler's *Analogy*, with its cold logic and acute analysis, was not, in a reversed way, a factor in developing "scepticism".

During the year of private study, of which mention has been made, I decided to make philosophy my life-study, and accordingly went to Johns Hopkins the next year (1884) to enter upon that new thing, "graduate work". It was something of a risk; the work offered there was almost the only indication that there were likely to be any self-supporting jobs in the field of philosophy for others than clergymen. Aside from the effect of my study with Professor Torrey, another influence moved me to undertake the risk. During the years after graduation I had kept up philosophical readings and I had even written a few articles which I sent to Dr. W. T. Harris, the well-known Hegelian, and the editor of the *Journal of Speculative Philosophy*, the only philosophic journal in the country at that time, as he and his group formed almost the only group of laymen devoted to philosophy for non-theological reasons. In sending an article I asked Dr. Harris for advice as to the possibility of my successfully prosecuting philosophic studies. His reply was so encouraging that it was a distinct factor in deciding me to try philosophy as a pro fessional career.

The articles sent were, as I recall them, highly schematic and formal; they were couched in the language of intuitionalism; of Hegel I was then ignorant. My deeper interests had not as yet been met, and in the absence of subject-matter that would correspond to them, the only topics at my command were such as were capable of a merely formal treatment. I imagine that my development has been controlled largely by a struggle between a native inclination toward the schematic and formally logical, and those incidents of personal experience that compelled me to take account of actual material. Probably there is in the consciously articulated ideas of every thinker an over-weighting of just those things that are contrary to his natural tendencies, an emphasis

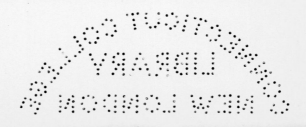

upon those things that are contrary to his intrinsic bent, and which, therefore, he has to struggle to bring to expression, while the native bent, on the other hand, can take care of itself. Anyway, a case might be made out for the proposition that the emphasis upon the concrete, empirical, and "practical" in my later writings is partly due to considerations of this nature. It was a reaction against what was more natural, and it served as a protest and protection against something in myself which, in the pressure of the weight of actual experiences, I knew to be a weakness. It is, I suppose, becoming a commonplace that when anyone is unduly concerned with controversy, the remarks that seem to be directed against others are really concerned with a struggle that is going on inside himself. The marks, the stigmata, of the struggle to weld together the characteristics of a formal, theoretic interest and the material of a maturing experience of contacts with realities also showed themselves, naturally, in style of writing and manner of presentation. During the time when the schematic interest predominated, writing was comparatively easy; there were even compliments upon the clearness of my style. Since then thinking and writing have been hard work. It is easy to give way to the dialectic development of a theme; the pressure of concrete experiences was, however, sufficiently heavy, so that a sense of intellectual honesty prevented a surrender to that course. But, on the other hand, the formal interest persisted, so that there was an inner demand for an intellectual technique that would be consistent and yet capable of flexible adaptation to the concrete diversity of experienced things. It is hardly necessary to say that I have not been among those to whom the union of abilities to satisfy these two opposed requirements, the formal and the material, came easily. For that very reason I have been acutely aware, too much so, doubtless, of a tendency of other thinkers and writers to achieve a specious lucidity and simplicity by the mere process of ignoring considerations which a greater respect for concrete materials of experience would have forced upon them.

It is a commonplace of educational history that the opening of Johns Hopkins University marked a new epoch in higher education in the United States. We are probably not in a condition as yet to estimate the extent to which its foundation and the development of graduate schools in other universities, following its example, mark a turn in our American culture. The 'eighties and 'nineties seem to mark the definitive close of our pioneer period, and the turn from the civil war era into the new industrialized and commercial age. In philosophy, at least, the influence of Johns Hopkins was not due to the size of the provision that was made. There was a half-year of lecturing and seminar work given by Professor George Sylvester Morris, of the University of Michigan; belief in the "demonstrated" (a favourite word of his) truth of the substance of German idealism, and of belief in its competency to give direction to a life of aspiring thought, emotion, and action. I have never known a more single-hearted and whole-souled man—a man of a single piece all the way through; while I long since deviated from his philosophic faith, I should be happy to believe that the influence of the spirit of his teaching has been an enduring influence.

While it was impossible that a young and impressionable student, unacquainted with any system of thought that satisfied his head and heart, should not have been deeply affected, to the point of at least a temporary conversion, by the enthusiastic and scholarly devotion of Mr. Morris, this effect was far from being the only source of my own "Hegelianism". The 'eighties and 'nineties were a time of new ferment in English thought; the reaction against atomic individualism and sensationalistic empiricism was in full swing. It was the time of Thomas Hill Green, of the two Cairds, of Wallace, of the appearance of the *Essays in Philosophical Criticism,* co-operatively produced by a younger group under the leadership of the late Lord Haldane. This movement was at the time the vital and constructive one in philosophy. Naturally its influence fell in with and reinforced that of Professor Morris. There was but one marked difference, and that, I think, was in favour of Mr. Morris. He came to Kant through Hegel instead of to Hegel by way of Kant, so that his attitude toward Kant was the critical one expressed by Hegel himself. Moreover, he retained something of his early Scotch

philosophical training in a common-sense belief in the existence
of the external world. He used to make merry over those who
thought the *existence* of this world and of matter were things to
be proved by philosophy. To him the only philosophical question
was as to the *meaning* of this existence; his idealism was wholly
of the objective type. Like his contemporary, Professor John
Watson, of Kingston, he combined a logical and idealistic
metaphysics with a realistic epistemology. Through his teacher
at Berlin, Trendelenburg, he had acquired a great reverence for
Aristotle, and he had no difficulty in uniting Aristoteleanism
with Hegelianism.

There were, however, also "subjective" reasons for the appeal
that Hegel's thought made to me; it supplied a demand for
unification that was doubtless an intense emotional craving, and
yet was a hunger that only an intellectualized subject-matter
could satisfy. It is more than difficult, it is impossible, to recover
that early mood. But the sense of divisions and separations that
were, I suppose, borne in upon me as a consequence of a heritage
of New England culture, divisions by way of isolation of self
from the world, of soul from body, of nature from God, brought
a painful oppression—or, rather, they were an inward laceration.
My earlier philosophic study had been an intellectual gymnastic.
Hegel's synthesis of subject and object, matter and spirit, the
divine and the human, was, however, no mere intellectual formula;
it operated as an immense release, a liberation. Hegel's treatment of human culture, of institutions and the arts, involved the
same dissolution of hard-and-fast dividing walls, and had a
special attraction for me.

As I have already intimated, while the conflict of traditional
religious beliefs with opinions that I could myself honestly
entertain was the source of a trying personal crisis, it did
not at any time constitute a leading philosophical problem.
This might look as if the two things were kept apart; in
reality it was due to a feeling that any genuinely sound religious
experience could and should adapt itself to whatever beliefs
one found oneself intellectually entitled to hold—a half unconscious sense at first, but one which ensuing years have deepened

into a fundamental conviction. In consequence, while I have, I hope, a due degree of personal sympathy with individuals who are undergoing the throes of a personal change of attitude, I have not been able to attach much importance to religion as a philosophic problem; for the effect of that attachment seems to be in the end a subornation of candid philosophic thinking to the alleged but factitious needs of some special set of convictions. I have enough faith in the depth of the religious tendencies of men to believe that they will adapt themselves to any required intellectual change, and that it is futile (and likely to be dishonest) to forecast prematurely just what forms the religious interest will take as a final consequence of the great intellectual transformation that is going on. As I have been frequently criticized for undue reticence about the problems of religion, I insert this explanation: it seems to me that the great solicitude of many persons, professing belief in the universality of the need for religion, about the present and future of religion proves that in fact they are moved more by partisan interest in a particular religion than by interest in religious experience.

The chief reason, however, for inserting these remarks at this point is to bring out a contrast effect. Social interests and problems from an early period had to me the intellectual appeal and provided the intellectual sustenance that many seem to have found primarily in religious questions. In undergraduate days I had run across, in the college library, Harriet Martineau's exposition of Comte. I cannot remember that his law of "the three stages" affected me particularly; but his idea of the disorganized character of Western modern culture, due to a disintegrative "individualism", and his idea of a synthesis of science that should be a regulative method of an organized social life, impressed me deeply. I found, as I thought, the same criticisms combined with a deeper and more far-reaching integration in Hegel. I did not, in those days when I read Francis Bacon, detect the origin of the Comtean idea in him, and I had not made acquaintance with Condorcet, the connecting link.

I drifted away from Hegelianism in the next fifteen years; the word "drifting" expresses the slow and, for a long time,

imperceptible character of the movement, though it does not
convey the impression that there was an adequate cause for
the change. Nevertheless I should never think of ignoring, much
less denying, what an astute critic occasionally refers to as a
novel discovery—that acquaintance with Hegel has left a permanent deposit in my thinking. The form, the schematism, of his
system now seems to me artificial to the last degree. But in the
content of his ideas there is often an extraordinary depth; in
many of his analyses, taken out of their mechanical dialectical
setting, an extraordinary acuteness. Were it possible for me to be
a devotee of any system, I still should believe that there is greater
richness and greater variety of insight in Hegel than in any
other single systematic philosopher—though when I say this I exclude Plato, who still provides my favourite philosophic reading.
For I am unable to find in him that all-comprehensive and
overriding system which later interpretation has, as it seems to
me, conferred upon him as a dubious boon. The ancient sceptics
overworked another aspect of Plato's thought when they treated
him as their spiritual father, but they were nearer the truth, I
think, than those who force him into the frame of a rigidly
systematized doctrine. Although I have not the aversion to system
as such that is sometimes attributed to me, I am dubious of my
own ability to reach inclusive systematic unity, and in consequence, perhaps, of that fact also dubious about my contemporaries. Nothing could be more helpful to present philosophizing
than a "Back to Plato" movement; but it would have to be
back to the dramatic, restless, co-operatively inquiring Plato of
the Dialogues, trying one mode of attack after another to see
what it might yield; back to the Plato whose highest flight of
metaphysics always terminated with a social and practical turn,
and not to the artificial Plato constructed by unimaginative
commentators who treat him as the original university professor.
    The rest of the story of my intellectual development I am
unable to record without more faking than I care to indulge in.
What I have so far related is so far removed in time that I can
talk about myself as another person; and much has faded, so that
a few points stand out without my having to force them into

the foreground. The philosopher, if I may apply that word to myself, that I became as I moved away from German idealism, is too much the self that I still am and is still too much in process of change to lend itself to record. I envy, up to a certain point, those who can write their intellectual biography in a unified pattern, woven out of a few distinctly discernible strands of interest and influence. By contrast, I seem to be unstable, chameleon-like, yielding one after another to many diverse and even incompatible influences; struggling to assimilate something from each and yet striving to carry it forward in a way that is logically consistent with what has been learned from its predecessors. Upon the whole, the forces that have influenced me have come from persons and from situations more than from books—not that I have not, I hope, learned a great deal from philosophical writings, but that what I have learned from them has been technical in comparison with what I have been forced to think upon and about because of some experience in which I found myself entangled. It is for this reason that I cannot say with candour that I envy completely, or envy beyond a certain point, those to whom I have referred. I like to think, though it may be a defence reaction, that with all the inconveniences of the road I have been forced to travel, it has the compensatory advantage of not inducing an immunity of thought to experiences—which perhaps, after all should not be treated even by a philosopher as the germ of a disease to which he needs to develop resistance.

While I cannot write an account of intellectual development without giving it the semblance of a continuity that it does not in fact own, there are four special points that seem to stand out. One is the importance that the practice and theory of education have had for me: especially the education of the young, for I have never been able to feel much optimism regarding the possibilities of "higher" education when it is built upon warped and weak foundations. This interest fused with and brought together what might otherwise have been separate interests—that in psychology and that in social institutions and social life. I can recall but one critic who has suggested that my thinking has been too much permeated by interest in education. Although

a book called *Democracy and Education* was for many years that
in which my philosophy, such as it is, was most fully expounded,
I do not know that philosophic critics, as distinct from teachers,
have ever had recourse to it. I have wondered whether such
facts signified that philosophers in general, although they are
themselves usually teachers, have not taken education with
sufficient seriousness for it to occur to them that any rational
person could actually think it possible that philosophizing should
focus about education as the supreme human interest in which,
moreover, other problems, cosmological, moral, logical, come to a
head. At all events, this handle is offered to any subsequent
critic who may wish to lay hold of it.

A second point is that as my study and thinking progressed,
I became more and more troubled by the intellectual scandal
that seemed to me involved in the current (and traditional)
dualism in logical standpoint and method between something
called "science" on the one hand and something called "morals"
on the other. I have long felt that the construction of a logic,
that is, a method of effective inquiry, which would apply without
abrupt breach of continuity to the fields designated by both of
these words, is at once our needed theoretical solvent and the
supply of our greatest practical want. This belief has had much
more to do with the development of what I termed, for lack of
a better word, "instrumentalism", than have most of the reasons
that have been assigned.

The third point forms the great exception to what was said
about no very fundamental vital influence issuing from books;
it concerns the influence of William James. As far as I can discover, one specifiable philosophic factor which entered into my
thinking so as to give it a new direction and quality, it is this one.
To say that it proceeded from his *Psychology* rather than from
the essays collected in the volume called *Will to Believe*, his
Pluralistic Universe, or *Pragmatism*, is to say something that
needs explanation. For there are, I think, two unreconciled
strains in the *Psychology*. One is found in the adoption of the
subjective tenor of prior psychological tradition; even when the
special tenets of that tradition are radically criticized, an under-

lying subjectivism is retained, at least in vocabulary—and the difficulty in finding a vocabulary which will intelligibly convey a genuinely new idea is perhaps the obstacle that most retards the easy progress of philosophy. I may cite as an illustration the substitution of the "stream of consciousness" for discrete elementary states : the advance made was enormous. Nevertheless the point of view remained that of a realm of consciousness set off by itself. The other strain is objective, having its roots in a return to the earlier biological conception of the *psyche*, but a return possessed of a new force and value due to the immense progress made by biology since the time of Aristotle. I doubt if we have as yet begun to realize all that is due to William James for the introduction and use of this idea; as I have already intimated, I do not think that he fully and consistently realized it himself. Anyway, it worked its way more and more into all my ideas and acted as a ferment to transform old beliefs.

If this biological conception and mode of approach had been prematurely hardened by James, its effect might have been merely to substitute one schematism for another. But it is not tautology to say that James's sense of life was itself vital. He had a profound sense, in origin artistic and moral, perhaps, rather than "scientific", of the difference between the categories of the living and of the mechanical; some time, I think, someone may write an essay that will show how the most distinctive factors in his general philosophic view, pluralism, novelty, freedom, individuality, are all connected with his feeling for the qualities and traits of that which lives. Many philosophers have had much to say about the idea of organism; but they have taken it structurally and hence statically. It was reserved for James to think of life in terms of life in action. This point, and that about the objective biological factor in James's conception of thought (discrimination, abstraction, conception, generalization), is fundamental when the rôle of psychology in philosophy comes under consideration. It is true that the effect of its introduction into philosophy has often, usually, been to dilute and distort the latter. But that is because the psychology was bad psychology.

I do not mean that I think that in the end the connection of

psychology with philosophy is, in the abstract, closer than is
that of other branches of science. Logically it stands on the same
plane with them. But historically and at the present juncture
the revolution introduced by James had, and still has, a peculiar
significance. On the negative side it is important, for it is indispensable as a purge of the heavy charge of bad psychology that
is so embedded in the philosophical tradition that is not generally
recognized to be psychology at all. As an example, I would say
that the problem of "sense data", which occupies such a great
bulk in recent British thinking, has to my mind no significance
other than as a survival of an old and outworn psychological
doctrine—although those who deal with the problem are for the
most part among those who stoutly assert the complete irrele-
vance of psychology to philosophy. On the positive side we
have the obverse of this situation. The newer objective psychology
supplies the easiest way, pedagogically if not in the abstract, by
which to reach a fruitful conception of thought and its work,
and thus to better our logical theories—provided thought and
logic have anything to do with one another. And in the present
state of men's minds the linking of philosophy to the significant
issues of actual experience is facilitated by constant interaction
with the methods and conclusions of psychology. The more abstract
sciences, mathematics and physics, for example, have left their
impress deep upon traditional philosophy. The former, in connection with an exaggerated anxiety about formal certainty, has
more than once operated to divorce philosophic thinking from
connection with questions that have a source in existence. The
remoteness of psychology from such abstractions, its nearness
to what is distinctively human, gives it an emphatic claim for
a sympathetic hearing at the present time.

In connection with an increasing recognition of this human
aspect, there developed the influence which forms the fourth
heading of this recital. The objective biological approach of the
Jamesian psychology led straight to the perception of the
importance of distinctive social categories, especially communication and participation. It is my conviction that a great deal of
our philosophizing needs to be done over again from this point

of view, and that there will ultimately result an integrated synthesis in a philosophy congruous with modern science and related to actual needs in education, morals, and religion. One has to take a broad survey in detachment from immediate prepossessions to realize the extent to which the characteristic traits of the science of to-day are connected with the development of social subjects—anthropology, history, politics, economics, language and literature, social and abnormal psychology, and so on. The movement is both so new, in an intellectual sense, and we are so much of it and it so much of us, that it escapes definite notice. Technically the influence of mathematics upon philosophy is more obvious; the great change that has taken place in recent years in the ruling ideas and methods of the physical sciences attracts attention much more easily than does the growth of the social subjects, just because it is farther away from impact upon us. Intellectual prophecy is dangerous; but if I read the cultural signs of the times aright, the next synthetic movement in philosophy will emerge when the significance of the social sciences and arts has become an object of reflective attention in the same way that mathematical and physical sciences have been made the objects of thought in the past, and when their full import is grasped. If I read these signs wrongly, nevertheless the statement may stand as a token of a factor significant in my own intellectual development.

In any case, I think it shows a deplorable deadness of imagination to suppose that philosophy will indefinitely revolve within the scope of the problems and systems that two thousand years of European history have bequeathed to us. Seen in the long perspective of the future, the whole of western European history is a provincial episode. I do not expect to see in my day a genuine as distinct from a forced and artificial, integration of thought. But a mind that is not too egotistically impatient can have faith that this unification will issue in its season. Meantime a chief task of those who call themselves philosophers is to help get rid of the useless lumber that blocks our highways of thought, and strive to make straight and open the paths that lead to the future. Forty years spent in wandering in a wilderness like that

of the present is not a sad fate—unless one attempts to make
himself believe that the wilderness is after all itself the promised
land.

PRINCIPAL PUBLICATIONS

The School and Society (University of Chicago Press, 1900).
Ethics (with James H. Tufts), (Henry Holt & Co., 1908).
Influence of Darwin and Other Essays (Henry Holt, 1910).
How We Think (D. C. Heath, 1910).
Democracy and Education (Macmillan & Co., 1916).
Essays in Experimental Logic (University of Chicago Press, 1916).
Reconstruction in Philosophy (Henry Holt, 1920).
Human Nature and Conduct (Henry Holt, 1922; London : George
    Allen & Unwin Ltd.).
Experience and Nature (Open Court Publishing Co., 1925; London:
    George Allen & Unwin Ltd.),
The Public and Its Problems (Henry Holt, 1927; London: George
    Allen & Unwin Ltd.).
The Quest for Certainty (Minton Balch & Co., New York, 1929).

LOGIC AND PRAGMATISM

By CLARENCE IRVING LEWIS

Born 1883; Associate Professor of Philosophy, Harvard University,
Cambridge, Mass.

LOGIC AND PRAGMATISM

THE most powerful single influence in my intellectual development was an old lady whom I met when I was fifteen. A year or
two earlier I had begun a period of the most intense and furious
thinking I shall ever experience. The combination of native
scepticism and an orthodox upbringing had proved to be an
explosive mixture: I had been plunged into doubts and questions
which went on and on until I faced the universe with something
of the wonder of the first man. The old lady, with compassionate
understanding, confessed that she too was a heretic, and after
establishing our agreements we went on to the much more
enticing matter of our disagreements. Our discussions continued,
at intervals, over a period of about two years, at the end of which
time I had worked out my own answers to the puzzles which
beset me. Some of these, I am sure, must have startled and amused
my mentor, but she always agreed solemnly to consider them.

As yet no book on philosophy had even fallen under my eye;
but about this time someone must have said the right word,
because I remember reading a short history of Greek philosophy
(Marshall's, I think), and then, following the references, looking
into Ueberweg and the Zeller books. My chagrin was enormous.
Much of my philosophy had been anticipated by two gentlemen
named Heraclitus and Anaxagoras, and the rest could be fairly
duplicated by a judicious eclecticism amongst the other pre-
Socratics. It was my first professional disappointment, and
quite the most grievous. I read Spencer's *First Principles* also,
and found there much of stimulus and much which broadened
my horizons—so much, in fact, that I cannot now recall any
sense of bewilderment or failure to understand. Very likely I did
not comprehend enough of it even to be properly puzzled.

Nothing comparable in importance happened after that until
I became acquainted with Kant. I was now safely under academic
auspices, and thinking was no longer a lone adventure. Kant
compelled me. He had, so I felt, followed scepticism to its inevitable last stage, and laid his foundations where they could not be
disturbed. I was then, and have continued to be, impatient of

those who seem not to face the sceptical doubt seriously. Kant attracted me also by his intellectual integrity and by the massiveness and articulation of his structure. The evidence of Kant in my thinking ever since is unmistakable, however little I may achieve the excellences which aroused my youthful admiration.

Of my teachers at Harvard, Royce impressed me most. His ponderous cogency kept my steady attention, even though I never followed to his metaphysical conclusions. James, I thought, had a swift way of being right, but how he reached his conclusions was his own secret. Royce was, in fact, my paradigm of a philosopher, and I was prone to minimize the difference from him of such convictions as I had. It was Royce himself, finally, with my doctor's thesis before him, who pointed out the extent of these differences. He concluded by saying, with his usual dry humour, "I thought you were principally influenced by Perry, but I find he thinks you are principally influenced by me. Between us, we agreed that perhaps this is original."

Royce was also responsible for my interest in logic, or at least for the direction which it took. In 1910–11 I was his assistant in two courses in that subject, and he put into my hands one of the first copies of *Principia Mathematica*, volume i, which came to Cambridge. It is difficult now to appreciate what a novelty this work then was to all of us. Its logistic method was so decidedly an advance upon Schröder and Peano. The principles of mathematics were here deduced from definitions alone, without other assumptions than those of logic. I spent the better part of a year upon it.

However, I was troubled from the first by the presence in the logic of *Principia* of the theorems peculiar to material implication, such as "A false proposition implies any proposition," and "A true proposition is implied by any." The theorems themselves, of course, were familiar; they went back to Peirce and Schröder. But in spite of Peirce's remarks on the topic, I had never taken them seriously, because of their obvious historical origin.

The investigations to which I was moved by this relatively small matter grew in scope and occupied such leisure as I had for the next six years. Moreover, my thinking on other philosophic topics has been much influenced by these researches, so that I must present, as briefly as possible, the gist of this problem.

Those logicians who were earliest interested in an exact calculus of logic had, all of them, turned first to the relations of concepts or classes. This necessitates a choice—as may be discovered by their mistakes—between the logic of intension and the logic of extension. The relations of class-names in intension are meagre in certain ways, and hardly afford a calculus. Boole founded the algebra of logic, where Leibniz and his Continental successors had failed; principally because Boole interpreted logical relations exclusively in extension. This is no particular merit of Boole's; it seems, rather, to result from the fact that he was born in Great Britain, and knew nothing about his Continental predecessors. British logicians, when really original, have always thought in terms of extension; Continental ones in terms of intension. (Some psychologist with an eye for history ought to investigate this.) So Boole took the universal proposition, "All *a* is *b*," to mean, "The class of things *a* is included in the class *b*," instead of "The concept *a* includes or implies the concept *b*," as a Continental would have done. This extensional point of view requires the special case that if there are no members of the class *a*, then "All *a* is *b*" will hold, regardless of the connotations of *a* and *b*. If Boole had any misgivings about this paradox, the arithmetical analogies which he followed in constructing his algebra would have compelled it in any case. The null-class is contained in every class just as o $<$ *x*, for any positive number *x*. The converse principle, that any class is contained in the class of "everything," is obvious.

The effect of these limiting cases is to restrict the interpretation of the algebra as a logic of class-terms to the relations of extension. If there are no centaurs, then all the centaurs there are will be Greeks; this is true regardless of the connotation or intension of "centaur" and "Greek." It does not follow that if there *were* any centaurs they *would be* Greeks.

Now Boole discovered a second application of his algebra,

to propositions (more correctly, to propositional functions). For this, he let the symbols a, b, c, . . . represent the times when the propositions A, B, C, . . . are true. Here the analogue of "All a is b" is, "Whenever A is true, B is true," or "A implies B." If the algebra is to have this second application, the properties of implication must be point for point analogous to those of classes in extension. Hence if $A = 0$—that is, if A is always false —then A must imply any proposition B whatever. And if B is always true—that is, if $B = 1$—then B must be implied by every proposition. Boole's principal successors, Peirce and Schröder, observed that a proposition, as distinguished from a propositional function, if once true is always true. Hence as applied to propositions, $A = 0$ may be interpreted simply as "A is false," and $B = 1$ as "B is true."

Thus the application of the algebra to propositions requires these two principles, "A false proposition implies anything," and, "A true proposition is implied by any." In the sense of "implies," which figures in the algebra, "A implies B" will hold if A is false or if B is true, and will fail only when A is true and B is false.

As the analogy with classes shows, this is the case only because the algebra must be restricted to relations of extension. The relation here designated by "implies" is such that a false proposition implies anything, but that throws no light on what it *would* imply if it *were true*.

A meaning of "implies" which is such that the implications of a proposition depend upon its truth or falsity is certainly not the usual one. And the peculiar properties of it are neither important logical discoveries nor absurdities; they are merely the inevitable consequences of a novel denotation for an old and familiar word, long used in common parlance in a different meaning. Thus the calculus of propositions which is historically continuous with Boole is not a calculus of implications, such as those with which logic and deduction generally have always been concerned. This new meaning of "implies" (now called "material implication") should be submitted to some examination before its laws are accepted as a canon of deduction. Such examination was lacking in *Principia*.

Two sorts of problems were before me. First and most obviously: Is there an exact logic, comparable to this extensional calculus, which will exhibit the analogous relations in intension? And is the intensional analogue of material implication the relation upon which deductive inference is usually founded? Second, there were larger and vaguer questions: Could there be different exact logics? If I should find my calculus of intension, it and material implication would be incompatible, on some points, when applied to inference. In that case, in what sense would there be a question of validity or truth to be determined between them? And what criteria could determine the validity of logic, since logic itself provides the criteria of validity used elsewhere, and the application of these to logic itself would be *petitio principii?*

Even the two questions of the first sort could not really be determined in separation from these more general problems. Yet I chose to begin with them. It seemed more promising to argue from exactly determined facts of the behaviour of symbolic systems to conclusions on more general problems than to attempt to reverse this procedure. Logicians who argue from "first principles" to the validity or invalidity of logistic developments find themselves in a weak position, since they dogmatize about a matter which they either have not investigated or have approached with an initial prejudice which commits the *petitio principii* just pointed out.

Leaving, then, the larger questions, I turned to the logistic development of the logic of intension. The results of this investigation may be briefly summarized, since it has been outlined in Chapter V of the *Survey of Symbolic Logic.*[1]

[1] A note should be added concerning the mistaken postulate, which I there assumed for the system of strict implication. This was later pointed out by Dr. E. L. Post, and corrected by me in a note in the *Journal of Philosophy*. In developing the system, I had worked for a month to avoid this principle, which later turned out to be false. Then, finding no reason to think it false, I sacrificed economy and put it in. It was because it thus entered the system so late in its development that I was able, when the mistake was discovered, to correct it in brief space.

The system of strict implication, as printed, contained no postulate logistically incompatible with a material interpretation, such as

The intensional implication relation (or "strict implication" as I called it) gives rise to a calculus as exact as the older logistic systems. It is also more inclusive; when the extensional relations are introduced by definition, it includes the calculus of propositions, as previously developed, as a sub-system. While there are ambiguities about the usual meaning of "implies," and the final issues are such as have seldom been faced at all, on the whole accepted deductive procedures and ordinary logical intuitions accord with strict implication and do not accord with material implication where it diverges.

The only implication relation upon which inference is likely to be based is this intensional or strict implication, for reasons which are fairly obvious. "The proposition A materially implies the proposition B" means precisely, "It is not the case that A is true and B false." This is necessary to ordinary deduction, since otherwise false conclusions could be derived from true premises, but it is not sufficient. To see this, let us inquire how this relation might be verified as holding. In a particular case, it could be verified simply by finding A to be false; but that would mean finding our premise false, so that the conclusion B would ordinarily not be drawn. Sometimes, however, we are interested to draw the inferences from false assumptions. But we should not do this on the basis of material implication, precisely because a false premise materially implies anything and everything. That A materially implies B, *because A is false*, throws no light on the question what A *would* imply if it *were* *true.*

We might also verify "A materially implies B" in a concrete instance by finding B to be true. But this would mean finding our conclusion to be true. Most frequently in such cases we should not "make the inference" because it would be superfluous. Sometimes, however, we are interested to discover what implies some known fact and what does not—for example, in the testing

$\Sigma p: -p. - (p < -p).$ To include this would have required a fundamental complication, undesirable in a book addressed to beginning students. I am lately in receipt of a proof, made by a Polish student, M. Wajsberg, that the principle $p < .q < p$ is independent of the amended postulates. This covers the same point.

of hypotheses. But a known fact is *materially* implied by *any* hypothesis. Amongst known facts, the material implications of all hypotheses whatever are identical.

Consequently no use can be made of material implication in drawing valid inferences, except in those cases in which the implication can be known to hold for some other reason than that the premise is false or that the conclusion is true. When we inquire how we can know that it is not the case that A is true and B false, without knowing that A is false and without knowing that B is true, the only answer is: By knowing that if A *were* true, B *must be* true; by knowing that the truth of A is inconsistent with the falsity of B; by knowing that the situation in which A should be true and B false is an impossible situation. That is to say, the only case in which any inference could be based on a material implication is precisely the case in which it should coincide (and *be known* to coincide) with the intensional or strict implication of B by A. This amounts to saying that the real basis of the inference is the strict implication. "A strictly implies B" means exactly "The truth of A is inconsistent with the falsity of B."

The so-called "formal implication," "For every x, ϕx materially implies ψx," would coincide, in its general deductive significance, with strict implication provided "For every x" be interpreted to mean, "For every possible or conceivable x." It will be obvious that "For every conceivable x, it is not the case that ϕx is true and ψx false," is a strict implication, differently phrased. But if "For every x" means "For every x that *exists*," then this formal implication represents the ordinary relation of classes, "Every existent thing having the property ϕ has also the property ψ." In *Principia* it is this second interpretation of formal implication which is chosen.

Various technical problems which came to light in the course of these investigations may be omitted here as probably of small interest to the general reader. However, there is one such matter which must be mentioned because it influenced the direction of my thinking outside the field of exact logic. Early in the course of these researches I formed the conviction that all valid inference, being a matter of intension, rests upon the analysis of meaning. The reasons for this will probably be evident from the foregoing. But the symbolic relations I was dealing with proved to have properties which I had not anticipated, and some of these gave me pause. In particular, while it would not be true, in the system of strict implication, that a merely false proposition implied anything and everything and a merely true proposition is implied by any, it *would* hold that a "necessary" proposition (defined as one which is implied by its own denial) is implied by any, and that a self-contradictory proposition (one which implies its own denial) implies anything.

Had I made a mistake in my assumptions so that the system was out of accord with the properties of analytic inference? Or did the implication relation of ordinary inference have these properties? The latter proved to be the true alternative. There was no way to avoid the principles stated by these unexpected theorems without giving up so many generally accepted laws as to leave it dubious that we could have any formal logic at all.

There were many corroborations. The simplest to set down is as follows: Suppose that a proposition A (say, "To-day is Monday") implies another, B ("To-morrow is Tuesday"). Then the premise A, together with any additional proposition, C (say, "Mars is not inhabited"), will likewise imply B—that is, "To-day is Monday and Mars is not inhabited" implies "To-morrow is Tuesday." According to another general principle, if two premises give a conclusion, but that conclusion is false while one of the premises is true, the other premise must be false. "All men are mortal" and "Socrates is a man" together imply "Socrates is mortal." Hence if all men are mortal, but Socrates is not mortal, then it follows that Socrates is not a man— that is, we have the rule: If "A and C" implies B, then "A but not B" implies "not C." Applying this rule to our first example, we have: "To-day is Monday and Mars is not inhabited" implies "To-morrow is Tuesday," hence "To-day is Monday, but to-morrow is not Tuesday" implies "Mars is inhabited." In this illustration, the last-mentioned proposition might have been anything you please without altering anything else. Thus ordinary logical conceptions require that the affirmation of a premise, together with the denial of its consequence (a case of contradiction), will imply anything and everything.

If, then, I had made no mistake, the line of division which marks off that class of propositions which are capable of corroboration by logic alone (necessary propositions) from merely empirical truths, and marks off the impossible or absurd, which can be refuted by logic alone, from merely empirical falsehood, is a division of major importance. Possible and impossible, contingent and necessary, consistent and inconsistent, such categories of intension are independent of material truth, and their distinct nature is founded in logic itself. Moreover, as is easily obvious, all the propositions of logic are truths of intension, and therefore certifiable without reference to the merely factual or empirical.

But I had further doubts. In particular it was not clear that if one should, by inadvertence, set out with incompatible assumptions, there would be no conclusion whatever which one might not draw from them by analytic inference. Nor was it clear that all necessary propositions are analytically derivable from any assumption you please. The facts of the symbolic system were inescapable, and ordinary practice corroborated them; but what did these facts mean?

In part, the answer was a simple one which should have been anticipated. These unexpected properties of implication did not mean that all necessary propositions are analytically derivable from any arbitrarily chosen assumptions whatever; they did represent the fact that implication is not a property of isolated propositions as such, but of systems. Necessary truths are all of them principles of logic, or such as can be certified on grounds of logic alone. Without logic, nothing is derivable from anything; the logic of it is implicit in every deductive system. All necessary propositions are thus, explicitly or tacitly, present in every system, and indeed in every assertion conceived as having logical consequences. Inference is analytic of the system rather than of its separate and bare constituents. If there is any exact logic

which is capable of representing inference as analytic in any
other sense, I have never been able to discover a clue to it. I
should but be dumbfounded to learn of such to-morrow, but I
have followed every lead that has occurred to me, always with
negative results.

If inference is analytic of systems, not of propositions in
isolation, does this mean that logic compels the acceptance of
a coherence theory of truth or the acceptance of that kind of
unity of the world which is maintained by logicians of the
"modern" or Hegelian school? I turned briefly to the consideration of this possibility—though, I must admit, without any conviction of the necessity of so doing—because while it had become
apparent to me that logic required the existence of necessary
propositions, it was not so apparent that it required the existence
of any truth which is *not* necessary. That the distinction of
necessary and contingent must finally fail and all truth reveal
itself as necessary, because inference depends on systematic
unity, is just what the modern logicians claim. The conclusions
which I reached are outlined in a little paper, "Facts, Systems,
and the Unity of the World." The thesis that all truths are
necessary, and none independent of any other, is hopelessly
implausible in the light of certain facts of mathematical systems
concerning which nobody (unless it be the modern logicians themselves) has ever entertained a doubt. The whole development of
modern geometry, for example, must be somehow invalid if they
are right.

The most general and important issue was still before me. I
had set out to determine a question of truth between two symbolic systems—material implication and a logic of intensional
implication. This had raised the further question what kind of an
issue of truth there could be in such a case, and what criteria
could determine it. I had found, in commonly accepted practices
and principles, corroboration of the characterizing features of
strict implication—the distinction of necessary from contingent
truth, the classification of logical principles themselves as necessary, and, as a consequence, the status of logic as self-affirming
or self-critical, its principles being implied by their own denial.

Could such necessity or self-affirmation be accepted as a final criterion of truth in logic?

There was unmistakable evidence that such was not the case. In the first place, both material implication and strict implication had this character, yet both could not be accepted as stating the truth about what can validly be inferred from what—the truth of logic. Also I found that other and somewhat similar systems could be devised, each of which would have the same general kind of mathematical precision and methodological integrity. These might be called "pseudo-logics" or "metalogics." Though I made no systematic investigation, it became evident that the number of such would be limited only by some criterion of "logistic system" or of the principles of derivation which should be allowed. Such a criterion would itself be an antecedent principle limiting "logical" truth. That such a system might be totally unacceptable as a "true logic" and yet be entirely consistent, and even self-affirming, in its own terms, is due to the curious involution which is peculiar and inevitable to logical truth. "Consistency" is the absence of an "implication": two propositions are consistent when neither implies the negation of the other. Hence if the meaning of "implies"—and consequently the methods of derivation—be allowed to vary, a "queer" logic may be "consistent" or "self-critical" in its own "queer" way.

Thus we revert to the previous question, which now assumes a somewhat complicated form. If formal logic is capable of any exact development at all, then we are confronted with the task of deciding which, amongst various possible and actual logistic systems, is such that its principles state the truth about valid inference. Internal consistency and "self-criticism" are not sufficient criteria to determine a truth which is independent of initial assumptions which are themselves logical in nature. Thus logic cannot test itself—or rather, such test does not prove truth in logic.

It was clear that such a problem has no solution in logic; I was carried beyond logic into the field of epistemology. Many other strands, not mentioned here, were, of course, already woven into my thinking. In particular it had been impressed upon me

that it is possible to take symbolic procedures both too seriously
and too lightly. To paraphrase Hobbes: Symbols are our counters;
they are the money of fools. But on the other hand, the behaviour
of symbolic systems is nothing more nor less than the behaviour
of the human mind, using its most characteristic instrument:
there is nothing in them which we have not put in ourselves, but
they teach us inexorably what our commitments mean.

Also, at just this time it became my duty and privilege to
turn over the numerous unpublished papers of Charles Peirce.
Though I was not specially conscious of it, this was perhaps the
means of stirring up old thoughts of the time when I had listened
to James, and reminding me also of what Royce used to call
his "absolute pragmatism." Again, I had long been attracted
to certain theses of Dewey's logic—if only he would not mis-
call "logic" what is rightly a much wider thing, the analysis of
the constructive thought-process! The study of exact logic itself
had revealed unmistakably that in every process of reasoning
there must be an extra-logical element. This cannot but be so,
since from any premise or set of premises whatever an infinite
number of valid inferences can be drawn. (This is an immediate
consequence of Poretsky's laws.) What is called *"the* conclusion"
must be selected from this infinity by psychological obviousness
or by some purpose or interest; certainly logic does not dictate
it. The *direction* of thought inevitably belongs, then, to such
an extra-logical factor. Finally, Peirce's "conceptual pragmatism," turning as it does upon the instrumental and empirical
significance of concepts rather than upon any non-absolute
character of truth, was at some points consonant with my own
reflections where James and Dewey were not.

Whatever it was that turned my thoughts in this direction,
at any rate I began to see that the principles of logic will answer
to criteria of the general sort which may be termed pragmatic,
and that where empirical verification is not in point, and logical
"necessity" itself is not sufficient, no other kind of criterion can
in any sense be final.

It had become apparent from my little experiments with
strange "logics" that two minds which followed different systems

in their modes of inference need not be unintelligible to one another—that, in fact, they might be so related that when their premises were common neither (outside of logic itself) would ever reach a conclusion which the other must repudiate as false. But, as between two such, the road from premise to conclusion would be more or less direct, more or less impeded. Fundamental psychological bent might here dictate a choice. Or again, if the general course of experience were other than it is—if, for example, all processes in nature should be reversible—then, although no different choice of modes of inference would be dictated, a different "logic" would apply with more facility. Thus the ultimate ground of accepted logical principles, as against other self-consistent modes, might be criteria of convenience (a poor word, but the best I can think of), somewhat like those which Poincaré suggested as determining our choice of Euclidean geometry.

This thesis, by itself, seems implausible and highly paradoxical; the stronghold of pragmatism supposedly lies in the empirical; logic is the citadel of rationalism. Nevertheless I became more and more convinced that this was right. Pragmatism, as ordinarily understood, seems to take things wrong end on; it is the element which mind contributes, in truth and knowledge, which may be pragmatic; the empirical brute fact of the given is absolute datum. Logic contains no material truth; it is independent of the given precisely because it dictates nothing whatever with regard to the content of experience, but determines only the mind's mode of dealing with it. This thought suggested others, which soon came to keep it company and mitigate the paradoxical air which it exhibited in isolation.

A variety of other problems, mainly in the theory of knowledge, had been in my mind for the past few years. Some of them were closely related to those already suggested as growing out of logic. I now sat down (this was in 1921) to the first draft of something concerning these, which I projected as "Studies in Logic and Epistemology." These will never see the light. They grew from one box to two, and then to several. But the yeast of the newly awakened pragmatic conceptions was working too strongly. My thought changed and widened as I attempted to formulate it, and the result, instead of moving toward some unity of subject and literary coherence, spread in widening circles through the whole field of philosophy. It was a most satisfactory period to me personally, because in the course of it I squared my account with many problems and brought them into touch with one another. What I shall venture to call "conceptualistic pragmatism" proved to be, for me, the key that opened many doors. But my notes I put away, except for a relatively small portion, and concentrated upon certain closely related topics which I found myself particularly interested to develop further. The attempt to outline some of these is the remaining task of this paper.

Logic, and that which is certifiable on logical grounds alone, constitutes the a priori element in knowledge. The Kantian cross-classification, by which *synthetic* judgments a priori become the foundations of science, has more and more clearly been proved to be without foundation, as mathematics and exact science have developed. Mathematics has been shown to be capable of purely logical development, by analysis alone, and without recourse to any synthetic element, such as geometric constructions, which represent an appeal from pure conception to intuition. *Principia Mathematica* represents the final stage of the movement in this direction: we see here the deductive development of mathematics merely from the logical analysis (definition) of the mathematical concepts. There is and must be a synthetic element in judgment about the *applications* of mathematics, about real space, or about concrete collections of things. At the same time that mathematics becomes purely logical and analytic, it becomes abstract. Which of the various abstract geometrics applies to space becomes a separate and extra-mathematical question, and, as Poincaré and relativity have shown, one which is to be determined either upon empirical grounds; in which case the answer is probable only, or by some pragmatic choice, or by some interplay between these two.

Hume was right in his somewhat wavering conviction that the truths of mathematics represent necessary connections of ideas, and likewise right that this by itself does not prove any necessary connection of matters of fact. The line between the a priori and the a posteriori coincides with the division between conceptual and empirical; and it likewise coincides with the distinction between what mind itself contributes or determines and what is given as datum of sense.

A priori truth is independent of experience because it is purely analytic of our conceptual meanings, and dictates nothing to the given. Logic, mathematics, and in general whatever has structure and order and system, may be developed in abstraction from all consideration of the empirical by purely logical analysis. It depends upon nothing but its own conceptual integrity for that kind of truth which is possible to abstract systems.

Such a priori truth is not assertive of material fact, but definitive. This is the clue to many problems. In the first place, it exhibits clearly the sense in which we can make stipulations applicable to experience but independent of its content. In the absence of definitive criteria, experience would be unintelligible; these are prerequisite to truth and knowledge, though not to mere givenness. The definitive principle is "necessary" truth; it cannot be false; it is prerequisite to intelligibility; it must be taken in advance of the particular experience; it dictates nothing as to the content of the experience.

In the second place, this solves the problem of the criterion between what mind contributes in truth and knowledge and what is independent of the mind. How should we know what mind does, if mind could do no different? I discover what I do solely by the difference in what ensues when I refuse to do, or do differently. If there should be immutable and "ungetoverable" modes of intuition or of thought, the mind could never discover that these belonged to itself and were not characters of the independent real; they would be absolute data, flatly given in experience, and the individual would find them as he finds his ears.

There must, then, in some sense or other, be conceivable alternatives to what is a priori. In those modes of our own intellectual activity which are exhibited in the criteria supplied by definitive principles, there are such alternatives. A definition may be laid down in one or another way; we classify and order and understand as we ourselves determine. Once our exact concepts are taken, the unfolding of them is an absolute truth: there is no alternative about that (unless we ascend to some higher choice of alternative modes of deductive order itself). But what concepts we shall formulate, and what we shall apply, admits of choice. The mind approaches the chaos of experience with its own intellectual instruments, which are independent of the given as the given is of them. Truth and knowledge represent the meeting of these two. That the particular truth and knowledge may reflect, in some part, a choice of such instruments, that the net of understanding may be stretched across the given in terms of one or another reference system of conceptual order, is a matter which might well be illustrated at some length, but will probably be evident without such exemplification. And the sense in which the truths of experience will be, on one side, determined by the presence of such definitive conceptual order, though the content of the given is not thus determined, will likewise be clear. The whole trend of exact science serves strongly to enforce the fact of this presence, throughout all knowledge, of an a priori element which enters through the simple fact that experience never supplies its own conceptual interpretation, but that conceptual systems, amongst which there may. be possible choice, serve as criteria of such interpretation, without imposing any limit on the empirical content. That in the presence of such alternative systems of order, pragmatic criteria, which may reflect on the one side human bent and interest, and on the other a facility determined by the general character of what is presented, will have their place in fixing the truths of experience, needs no special demonstration.

If, however, all truth which can be certain in advance of the experience to which it applies is of this purely analytic and definitive sort, then we might be led to remark that such abstract a priori truth tells us nothing of the nature of reality beyond our own minds, and is significant only of our own consistency of thought. This conclusion would be a mistaken one; paradoxical as it may sound, we can predict the nature of reality without prescribing the character of future experience. What the mind meets in experience is not independent *reality*, but an independent *given*; the given is not, without further ado, the real, but contains all the content of dream, illusion, and deceitful appearance.

In fact, the criteria of reality represent a peculiarly illuminating example of the a priori. The word "real" has a meaning, and represents a definite conception which, when applied to the content of experience, leads to the interpretation of this content sometimes as "real," sometimes as "unreal." The formulation of the criteria of the real constitutes a merely analytic or definitive statement, representing our interpretative attitude. Such criteria of reality can neither be supplied by experience (since direct generalization from an unsorted experience, not already classified as real, would not serve) nor can experience invalidate them. Whatever in experience does not conform to the criteria of reality is automatically thrown out of court.

We can and must prescribe the nature of reality. We cannot prescribe the nature of the given. The paradox of this is mitigated somewhat when we observe that the word "real" is systematically ambiguous. "Reality" is of different sorts, physical, mental, mathematical—the easily named categories do not cover the easily recognized distinctions. A mirror-image, for example, is its own particular kind of reality, neither "physical" nor "mental," as is also a mirage and "appearances" in general. Each category of reality has its own peculiar criteria, and what is unreal in one sense will be real in some other. *Any* content of given experience will be real in some category or other—will be that kind of reality which is ascribed to it when it is "correctly understood." The categories are neither a Procrustean bed into which experience is thrust nor concepts whose applicability depends on some pre-established harmony between the given and the mind. Rather they are like the reference system which the mathematician stretches through all space and with respect to which whatever positions and motions are there to be described will inevitably be describable. Categorial criteria are neither insignificant and verbal tautologies nor empirical prophecies, but exhibit definitive criteria of intelligent classification and interpretation.

The content of a properly conceived metaphysics is the analytic truths which exhibit the fundamental criteria and major classifications of the real; it is definitive of "real"-ity, not descriptive of the universe *in extenso*. In fact, all philosophy has for its task such analytic depiction of the a priori—to define the good, the right, the true, the valid, and the real.

It will be evident that the absoluteness of such a priori principles, whenever and wherever they are held, is entirely compatible with their historical alteration, just as modes of classification or alternative reference systems, expressible in definitive principles or initial prescriptions, would be absolute while adhered to, but might be subject to considerations of usefulness and to historical change. The assurance of perpetuity for our categories is no greater than the assurance that our basic human nature and the broad outlines of experience will never alter. There is an eternal truth about our abstract concepts—the given is absolute datum; but the chosen conceptual systems applied to the interpretation of the given are subject to possible change. In the field of metaphysical concepts particularly, such change would seem to be a fact—as the history of such concepts as "matter," "mind," and "cause," bears witness.

The categories differ in no wise from concepts in general except in degree of comprehensiveness and fundamental character. Every concept whatever exhibits criteria of its own little kind of reality. In so far as experience is intelligible and expressible only when grasped in some framework of conceptual interpretation, this a priori element of the definitive is all-pervasive.

It is the conceptual order of experience alone which is communicable or expressible. The given, apart from such conceptual interpretation, is ineffable. If, so to speak, one sensory quality could be lifted out of the network of relations in which it stands and replaced by another, the æsthetic character of experience might be altered, but everything which has to do with knowledge and with action would remain precisely as before. Community of thought and knowledge requires community of concept or of relational pattern, but if there should be idiosyncrasies of sense which do not affect discrimination and relation, these would be immaterial to our common understanding and co-operation. In fact, in the face of all those *verifiable* differences of sense which are evidenced by our different powers of discrimination, we possess a common understanding and a common reality through the social achievement of common categories and concepts. When the vast and impressive institution of human education— in its wider sense—is remarked, the assumption that such community is simply native or ready-made is seen to be superfluous. My world is my intellectual achievement; our common world, a social one. The frequent objection of the sceptic, that knowledge is implausible in view of the subjectivity of sense, is an *ignoratio elenchi*.

Knowledge grasps conceptual structure or order alone. It was Berkeley who, almost without noting it himself, first phrased this nature of our knowledge. One idea is "sign of" another in the order of nature. If it be a reliable sign—that is, if it bear constant and orderly relationships—one empirical *quale* is as good as another to serve this function of cognition. Knowledge of the external world consists of relations between one item of experience and another, not in the content of experience somehow matching the quality of an external real. Such qualitative coincidence of idea and object—if the notion means anything—would be extraneous to knowledge. This conclusion is quite independent of idealism.

There are not two kinds of knowledge; one of principles or relations, expressible in propositions, and another which we have by mere presentation of the object. The conceptual interpretation of the given is the implicit prediction of other possible experience. As Mr. Whitehead has pointed out, no object can be known without reference to some temporal spread. My knowledge of the object is not the mere having of this presentation, but the implicit prediction of the eventuation of other experience continuous with this. What is thus predicted is not at the moment verified, but it must be verifiable if the interpretative concept is veridically applicable. The mere naming of this thing I see as "desk" predicts eventualities of a specific sort, which, if they should fail to be realized, would lead to the repudiation of the concept "desk" (or perhaps even of "physical reality") as inapplicable to this which I see. The knowledge of any object transcends its given presentation and grasps a structure of experience. Without order, there can be no *thing*, no experience of *reality*. This, in brief, is the deduction of the categories.

That *if* this be a desk, it *will be* thus and so, is an analytic consequence of the concept "desk," not subject to any falsification by experience. That any given "this" is really a desk, is theoretically not completely certain. Thus there is an a priori element which is all-pervasive in knowledge and prescriptive of reality. Yet all empirical truth, without exception, is probable only.

One further note I should like to make in closing. As the word "knowledge" has been used above, it is narrowed somewhat from its usual meaning. It comprises what have sometimes been called the "truths of description" which, as it is here conceived, depend exclusively upon conceptual order. It excludes "truths of appreciation," the æsthetic quality of the given, and all that depends upon sympathy and upon that communion of minds which requires coincidence of immediate experience. Evaluation can hardly be indifferent to the quality of the given. Nor can the basis of ethics be laid without reference to the felt character of experience in another mind. And the religious sense, if it is to take reality as the matrix of human values, will likewise transcend the interests of knowledge in this restricted sense. There is, then, a line of division between such intérests and cognition of the type of science. And it is suggested that the foundation of these, not being found in knowledge alone, may rest upon some postulate.

PRINCIPAL PUBLICATIONS

A Survey of Symbolic Logic. (Univ. of California Press, Berkeley, 1918.)

The Pragmatic Element in Knowledge (The Howison Lecture, 1926). (Univ. of California Press, Berkeley, 1926.)

Mind and the World-Order. (Scribners, New York, 1929.)

PROBLEMATIC REALISM

By J. LOEWENBERG

Born 1882; Professor of Philosophy, University of California,
Berkeley, California.

PROBLEMATIC REALISM

PHILOSOPHICAL labels are necessary evils. How get on without them? How distinguish one doctrine from another? But there are two kinds of labels. Lazy labels—the felicitous expression is Professor Palmer's—are those which we affix to beliefs not our own: they are inert names for endlessly variable shades of opinion. Such naming is simply pigeon-holing. It is a facile way of lumping together under a single rubric incomparable visions and theories. Philosophers not unjustly resent having their doctrines so indolently amalgamated from without. Witness, for instance, the notorious disavowal by modern idealists of the epithet "Hegelian." The names under which we epitomize our own philosophies we take more seriously. They are creative labels. They are scrupulously designed to convey what is indigenous and characteristic. They are part and parcel of the creative activity to the products of which they are attached.

The label by which I here designate my own philosophic beliefs must be understood as intimately bound up with them. It has been chosen with care to express a fresh variation of an ancient doctrine. Realism is certainly venerable; and even those who qualify it as "new" are not ignorant of its antiquity. Realism was not born with "New Realism." The adjective "new" is here either pretentious or factitious. Its usurpation by a particular version of realism is to be deplored and resented. Novelty is a feature belonging to every genuine variant of a general theme.

The variation of realism which I label "problematic" shares with the variations distinguished by other names a central theme. What is the common thread that runs through the manifold forms of realism? To this question there is unfortunately no unambiguous answer. But when technical guises are laid aside all realism appears to consist in the conviction that reality is prior to the knowledge of it, and that consequently mind has a status which is derivative and not pivotal. It is misleading, I think, to state the case for realism by saying that reality is independent of being known. Why is reality independent of the cognitive relation? Is it because the cognitive relation is a *relation* or because it is *cognitive*? And what is independence? Independence is either too equivocal or too uncompromising a term through which to express the cardinal principle of realism. Every philosophy, to be philosophy at all, must rest on the supposition that between being and knowing there is some linkage. What distinguishes realism from other views is not insulation but emancipation of being from knowing. What is insulated is isolated and thus disconnected; what is emancipated is merely liberated, but not deprived of relation. Not in extruding from reality all relations consists the work of realism, but rather in investing it in respect to knowledge with a particular kind of relation, the relation of *priority*.

I share, then, the general view common to all forms of realism—namely, that reality is prior to knowledge, and hence to mind, if knowledge is impossible in the absence of mind. But what are we to understand by reality? And what by knowledge? To these two questions—surely second to few in philosophic importance—my version of realism hazards an answer.

I hold, for various reasons soon to be mentioned, that reality is a substantive qualifiable by human knowledge as problematic, if the qualification is to be regarded as final. In other words, the only adjective *ultimately* descriptive of reality is the adjective problematic. To this belief—big with implications—I have come by different routes. It is, of course, not possible to retrace them here in detail. I can only indicate a few salient landmarks.

One route leading me to Problematic Realism lies in following the ontological consequences of scientific methodology. Scientific knowledge is surely knowledge of the real, and the only kind of knowledge which is controlled by rigorous methods of observation and experiment. Hence the solidity and solidarity of scientific achievements. The results of scientific investigation are public, attained though they are through the toil or genius of individual men. It is hardly worth mentioning that no fact is a scientific fact, even though but one individual may claim the glory of having observed it for the first time, if it is inaccessible to observation by other individuals competent to observe it. And similarly no inference about the nature of things is valid, however justified in the light of numerous and meticulous observations, if it is contradicted by later discoveries of fresh and relevant data. Scientific observations and generalizations are seemingly handicapped by the very qualities to which they owe social prestige and logical exactitude. For if all that in science is certain is the result of actual verification, and if all that in science is established is modifiable through discovery of facts as yet unfathomed, then the limits of science—limits variable and extensible—are the limits of verification and discovery. As long as the need for verification is perennial, and as long as the unknown regions of fact are still undiscovered, an ineradicable scepticism must always cleave to the work of science. The method of science seems to be a method either of allaying or of confirming ubiquitous suspicion—suspicion that what for the nonce is certain and established may require revision and reconstruction. And the instruments through which such suspicion is either weakened or fostered are *endless* verification and *indefatigable* discovery. It would, however, be wrong to conclude that scientific suspicion which engenders the twin demands for *insatiable* verification and discovery involves merely scepticism of metaphysics. Science is indeed radically opposed to metaphysics, in so far as the latter is charged with the office of furnishing a description of the universe so final that further verification becomes otiose and further discovery negligible. Finality of this sort is obviously incompatible with the spirit and method of science. Yet metaphysical finality of another kind is clearly involved in the enterprise of science. The view that reality is such as to suffer no judgment concerning its nature to stay continual verification and discovery is itself a final view. I call this view, not scepticism of metaphysics, but metaphysics of scepticism. Suspicion of finality, one of the most characteristic traits of science, is born of the ontological insight that reality is full of surds—surds that pale the brilliance of all scientific achievements. In the last analysis, it is the metaphysical conception of the universe as the *inexhaustible* source of problems which forbids scientific assertions the enjoyment of security and completeness.

Another route towards Problematic Realism proceeds from the very idea of the "ultimate," which science is said to shun and which metaphysics is supposed to court. What are we to understand by the ultimate, a notion so very vague yet so much in vogue? It is ordinarily used with reckless inattention to the conflicting meanings it harbours. I find it employed as a synonym for notions bewildering in number and variety. Here are some of its equivalents—the absolute, the unconditioned, the inexplicable, the indescribable, the indefinable, the indiscernible, the fundamental, the basic, the primary, the final, the indubitable, the irreducible. Are these terms on a parity? Are they really synonymous? Apart from the obscurity of it, due to too much opulence of meaning, the ultimate as commonly employed suffers from incurable stiffness or rigidity. It is a state or condition or act or category so inelastic that any stretching or straining beyond it is assumed to be for ever precluded. And of the ultimate as something "unstretchable" philosophers are supposed to be the traditional champions and custodians. But there are two ways of regarding anything as unmalleable. The being or constitution of the thing itself may be such as to prevent stretching, and if so, then it is what I call *ontologically* ultimate; or it may be inflexible simply for our thought, in the sense that it defies further reduction or analysis or definition, in which case it is what I designate as *cognitively* ultimate. In metaphysics, all sorts of things have paraded as ultimate, either because of their own irrefragable nature or because of our inability to stretch our imagination beyond them. Atoms, monads, essences, events, space-time, experience—need I mention other "unstretchables"?—have been proclaimed by different philosophers as the irresilient constituents of being or the unbreakable terms of thought. Unfortunately, what in one system of metaphysics is viewed as ontologically or cognitively tenacious is in another considered constitutively or logically brittle. From system to system the ultimate changes its content. This is manifestly an intolerable situation. It can be relieved only by the recognition of what I venture to call *the elastic ultimate*.

The elasticity of the ultimate is certainly demanded by the

scientific method. Every science is able to reach something "unstretchable," when it pushes analysis as far as it will go, and when its inferences are such as to withstand the tests of consistent thought. Within the limits of human observation and generalization science is competent to traffic in things and ideas relatively irresilient; the accumulated evidence is for the time being so overwhelming in their favour that, if there is to be any science at all, no doubt can be entertained as to their *present* right to claim finality. But the state of the "unstretchables" in any particular science is a limiting state; if and when we have in any given science reached the limits of observation and inference we have reached what is inelastic *pro tempore*. The element of suspicion, such an essential part of the scientific method, casts its shadow upon everything. There is no guarantee that what now appears irrefragable will enjoy this privilege in perpetuity. The absolute to-day may become relative to-morrow. What at present is rigid and fixed may in the future, through continual analysis and experiment, exhibit astonishing plasticity. It must thus be said that science both vindicates and repudiates the ultimate—it needs it as an elastic concept, but it shuns it as something inherently unstretchable. The elastic ultimate, as furnished by science, is a singular instance of what I mean by the real which is problematic and the problematic which is real. For such an ultimate is describable by the two adjectives simultaneously and interchangeably: it is real, since it represents the actual limit of scientific verification and discovery; and it is problematic, since a later limiting state of observation and inference may render precarious the "ultimates" now in force. That the ultimate is but ultimate *in transitu*—that it has movable boundaries in the extension of which science is continually engaged—is indeed a powerful argument in favour of Problematic Realism.

Another way pointing in its direction lies in considering what is meant by the "given." What are we to understand by a concept doing such yeoman's service for science and philosophy? It is certainly a fundamental term, but is it unequivocal? I find the "given" as bewildering a notion as the notion of the "ultimate."

And here, too, we may profit by discerning the elastic from the inelastic uses of it. For the given may mean either that with which inquiry starts or that in which it terminates. It is important to render distinct these two meanings by giving them separate names. Accordingly, by "pre-analytical" I designate whatever functions as a source of analysis, and by "post-analytical" whatever is discovered as the limit of analysis. It is manifestly bootless to appeal to the given unless we distinguish in the most explicit manner between what is given *for* analysis and what is given *through* analysis. By a strange equivocation the given, without forfeiting the sense of something "primitive," is in philosophy frequently identified, not with that from which the *investigation* takes its start, but with the simple constituents to which the *investigated object* may by analysis be reduced. Givenness, in short, is viewed as belonging to post-analytical entities and relations, those at which analysis is obliged to halt, rather than to a pre-analytical situation inaugurating and prompting analysis. No such equivocation can be laid at the door of science. All scientific data are pre-analytical: they are literally points of departure, initial states or stages in any investigation. The given in science signifies any fact, event, situation, or circumstance capable of enticing inquiry and eliciting the operation of the scientific method. Thus democratic and accommodating is the scientific use of the given. Furthermore, if we distinguish between the object demanding description and the terms employed in describing it, the scientific datum signifies not that *by* which it is described, but rather that *to* which scientific description addresses itself. When a more adequate study of any "given situation" necessitates a different description of it, what happens is that we simply exchange one set of terms for another; the datum, however fluctuating the descriptive terms, is the same original situation at the behest of which the descriptive process is set in motion. It follows that the scientific datum, connoting for the most part something supple and provisional, coincides essentially with what we ordinarily mean by a "problem." The given from which scientific inquiry takes its start is neither an unquestioned fact nor the indubitable knowledge of it. As a whole or as an incident in a wider context, the given is for science a continual challenge, always remaining "pre-analytical," in the sense of never condemning as superfluous the task of more searching analysis.

What a contrast is the philosophic use of the given! The given, as, for instance, it figures in epistemology, is never a relative starting-point of analysis, but rather its absolute halting-place. The given in which analysis terminates is the termination of the analytical process itself. Although disclosed by the solvent work of analysis, the given once revealed is that which compels analysis to draw its last breath. For the given is ultimate, and the ultimate is in philosophy the unstretchable. Post-analytical data, unlike their pre-analytical cousins, are thus essentially aristocratic: they are privileged beings of an exclusive order. The data, which in epistemology the discerning work of critical analysis brings to light, are alleged to enjoy peerless predicates, such as "pure," "irreducible," "original," "immediate," "indubitable." These evidently are not the tokens of our plebeian objects of perception. It thus follows that the given, standing as it does for a restricted and favoured class of beings, designates the elements to which our complex objects may be reduced and not the reducible complexes themselves. The hard and inflexible terms, those resisting the stoutest assault of analysis, these alone are regarded as the legitimate and strait-laced data. And if this is the case, such post-analytical terms, incapable as they are of being reduced to anything more elementary or more primitive, partake of the nature of "solutions." There is supposedly nothing problematic about epistemological data. Repelling the need of further analysis, they have a finality which can obviously not belong to scientific data.

And yet, despite the contrast between pre-analytical and post-analytical data, is it not apparent that epistemological data are scientific in disguise? The signification of a datum as a "starting-point" is never lost sight of in epistemology. In the beginning is the given. This is a maxim for every discipline; but whereas in science the given is an initial state by which knowledge is carried *forward*, in epistemology the given is a primary state to which analysis carries us *backward*. Back of our knowledge of objects and the objects of our knowledge lies something aboriginal, and to this the tortuous work of epistemological analysis endeavours to return. The epistemological anomaly resides in the demand that the given be at once something "initial" and "terminal"—the Alpha and Omega of knowledge. It is endowed with precedence, sometimes genetic and sometimes evidential, but it is a precedence which coincides with the end of analysis. But how can we be sure whether the limits of analysis are not spurious limits, due simply to our present impotence to discern? Can epistemology, unlike any other science, evade the conception of elastic finality? Besides, the faith in the revelations of unstretchable data by *rigorous* analysis or *pure* intuition (and *pure* intuition is itself an analytical product, in the sense that neither its enjoyment nor its definition is possible without a process of abstraction or insulation from the mixed and impure states of ordinary knowledge) is a faith bound up with too simple a view of judgment and of truth. This, however, will occupy us later.

I have allotted so much space to a consideration of the "given" because the central thesis of Problematic Realism may by means of it be stated most succinctly. Is the real given, and is the given real? At first blush the question seems meaningless. With *both* of its terms so equivocal (the ambiguity of the "real" will be mentioned anon), how can the suggested equation be hazarded? Nevertheless we cannot avoid linking each to each the "real" and the "given," for to sever them is to leave both concepts naked of all possible meaning. For me the real is indeed the given, and given in both senses of this misused term. But the two senses of the given signify for me different aspects of a more fundamental notion—namely, the notion of the problematic. Accordingly, I state the equation thus: the real = the given and the given = the problematic. From one point of view, the real is a pre-analytical datum, as it figures in any scientific investigation, and as such it is problematic at both ends of the investigational scale. At one end the real is a problem productive of scientific inquiry, and at the other it is a problem which scientific inquiry itself produces: it is the real as ultimately described or explained, but in terms whose ultimacy is elastic in the light of progressive verification and discovery. From another point of view, the real is a post-analytical datum, such as it emerges on the highest or deepest reaches of philosophical discernment, and there its problematic character has a double face rather than a dual direction. Is the post-analytical datum a pure *what*, or is it a pure *that*? If it is a pure character or quality—and this seems to be the prevailing opinion—what is the *that* to which it is attached? For those who cannot envisage the possibility of "floating adjectives," such a datum is problematic with respect to the substantive it qualifies or characterizes. If it is a pure substantival entity—and as such it appears to me to be disclosed by analysis—what are its true predicates or attributes? I, for one, cannot readily dissolve the union of the *what* and the *that*. I can conceive neither of unanchored qualities nor of unqualitied (though, indeed, of unqualified or unqualifiable) substances. The post-analytical datum, the result of *final* analysis, has to be conceived either as a quality belonging to an unknown substantive or as a substantive of which the true description is uncertain. In either case the datum is problematic. For my own part I find nowhere in my experience anything corresponding to either abstraction. I have never encountered either loose qualities or characterless entities. Yet, if I take any concrete experience and remove by abstraction all that I can possibly detach from it, what remains is an indeterminate *this* or *that*. I find it quite possible to disengage by analysis the *that* from the *what*, but I cannot perform the opposite operation and take away the *that* from the *what*. The appeal to experience is here unavailing; never are bare qualities and unqualitied entities "given," if given be understood as "presented," they are "taken" by an act of difficult abstraction from a concrete situation in which they are always found together.

The analysis of concrete experience, when it culminates in the priority of the *that* over the *what*, brings us face to face with the notion of substance. Substance is indeed the absolute surd of all awareness and all analysis. I am not unmindful of the many meanings which the idea of substance connotes. I am using it here not as category or as thing. As category, its use is logical or formal, indistinguishable from that of the grammatical subject. As thing, its use is empirical or material, applicable to every cohesion of qualities and relations that exhibits relative individuality and permanency. What I here mean by substance is metaphysical self-existence. It is a name for the reality *underlying* whatever we encounter in concrete experience. It is the absolute ground of things, the nethermost root of them. It is that than which there is nothing deeper. Existing upon its own terms, it is the fertile source of all that appears. It asserts itself in all things, and can be known only through its manifestations, none of which, however, can define or exhaust it. *What* is its intrinsic nature? This is the perplexing question perennially present in every science and in every philosophy. The "ontological argument," in its traditional employment, has distorted a genuine problem by placing the cart before the horse. Taking for granted God's essence, partisans of this argument have by tortuous devices sought to demonstrate his existence. The problem lies in the opposite direction. It is easy enough to grant God's being, if God is (as in the case of Spinoza) but another name for substance or self-existence; but what save a verbal definition assures me of his nature? His essence (his *what*) is infinitely more problematic than his being (his *that*). I am ready, indeed, to accept as speculatively plausible all the "proofs" of God's existence, but who can tell me whether God is actually good and wise and powerful? The mystics are less perverse. Sure as they are of God's being, they consistently refuse to define his attributes. Theirs is the only proof entitled to be called *ontological*, since the assurance it vouchsafes is confined to the bare affirmation that "God is." The attempt to describe his intrinsic nature, they rightly hold, is enmeshed in snares and illusions. How extremes meet! The logic of mysticism—I am, of course, not speaking of its psychology —is the logic of modern science. It is the logic of what I have called the metaphysics of scepticism involved in scientific methodology. Science, too, is infinitely more certain of the being of things than it is of their inner nature. The "given" in science —the incipient occasion or generating condition of inquiry—

has being as a matter of course, for the question *what* the datum is, the question with which scientific description is primarily concerned, presupposes the presence of *that* which provokes the question. It is not the being of the datum which is ever doubtful, but the manner of its being, the circumstances under which it appears, the specific characters and qualities it owns, the detailed affinities to other appearances it enjoys. In short, science is description, and description means adjectival qualification of an antecedently present substantive. And since adjectival qualification of any scientific substantive can possess elastic ultimacy only, owing to the extensible character of verification and the ubiquitous possibility of discovery, the scientific object, though never surrendering its substantival status, has but a temporary title to the adjectives assigned to it. Scientific methodology is thus always dealing with indubitable substantives that are adjectivally problematic. Since this is true of all the sciences, the ontology common to them may therefore be described in terms of substance. All science presupposes the self-existent whose manifestations it notes; and since the manifestations of substance are relative to ceaseless discovery and the noting of them subject to endless verification, "scientific" description can never disown its problematic character. And is it otherwise with descriptions called "metaphysical"? Metaphysical systems, too, if Aristotle is right, are "sciences"; they are no less intent upon describing the essential attributes of being, limiting or qualifying by preferential adjectives an antecedently existing substance. It is the "same" substantive reality which in all the competing systems of metaphysics is subject to divergent descriptions. And what do these rival descriptions indicate save the priority of the *that* over the *what*? Of the substantival status of reality we are much surer than we are of its adjectival nature; this holds in the case of metaphysics as much as it does in that of physics. The possibility (sufficiently attested by the perennial strife of metaphysics) of ascribing to the same "world" or "universe" emulous predicates, all reeking with ultimacy, may justify two different positions. We may move in the direction of mysticism, refusing altogether to describe reality, on the ground of its being intrinsically unqualitied and hence unqualifiable. Or we may move in the direction of realism, describing the inner nature of things as problematic, on the ground that substance is so richly qualitied as to license the multiform qualifications of it by the different metaphysical systems. Any escape from Problematic Realism by a way other than the mystic seems to me to culminate in anthropomorphism, for what else than anthropomorphic is the identification of the inherently qualitied real with the preferential qualifications of it such as are embodied in the sundry systems of human judgments?

For the view that reality is always manifest substantivally but never adjectivally—and this is the essence of Problematic Realism—I find confirmation in the nature of judgment itself. What is judgment? No question is more crucial. For it is judgment which renders explicit by its work of predication the adjectival nature of reality, and it is judgment to which alone the distinction between the true and the false appears to be relevant. Judgment thus communicates at once with reality and with truth, being a sort of hyphen between them, separating and joining at the same time. A thing so fundamental—the vehicle of truth in pursuit of reality—must obviously be purged of its wonted confusion. The confusion from which judgment ordinarily suffers is due to the neglect of its manifold nature. Judgment is too commonly identified with only a fragment of its essence. I find judgment to be a composite term. Any judgment—the simple perceptual judgment that "this flower is red" may serve as illustration—is the expression of a man's *belief*; it is the discursive *statement* of such belief; it is what *awareness* prompts a man to believe and to assert that he believes; and it is a *description* of a real object or situation occasioning the awareness in question. These four aspects of judgment—the personal, the formal, the noetic, the material—I find distinguishable, but not separable. They are all present whenever any significant judgment is present.

This complex or composite nature of judgment, which in traditional theories tends to be violated either by the suppression or exaggeration of one or another of its aspects, is the source of two major paradoxes. (I shall briefly mention them and show how each points in the direction of Problematic Realism.) One paradox—the "ontological," as I may call it—centres around the so-called "existential" or "objective" reference of judgment. Reference is, of course, an indicative relation, but judgment, endowing whatever it indicates with a determinate nature, transforms ineluctably by its work of predication the act of reference into an act of description. In other words, the only mode of reference to its object which judgment can establish is by describing it, i.e. by asserting *what* it is. The objective reference *of* judgment and the description of the object *by* judgment are identical acts. And if this is so, the situation is indeed paradoxical: the object referred to by judgment is whatever judgment itself succeeds in describing. The absolute fusion of the referential and descriptive acts on the part of the judging process inevitably leads to the confusion of different ontological levels, as if the referred real and the described real, distinguishable by analysis, could ever be made to coincide: the referred real is the *subject* of characterization, the described real is the characterized *object*. The referred real is simply that boundless ontological realm to which we give the compendious name of "being." In this realm room is provided for everything imaginable or mentionable. Prior to the specifying work of judgment nothing is lacking in being; even "nothing," as a logical conception or as a term in discourse, has an ontological status. It is to the labour of attribution wrought by judgment that we owe the distinction *within* the sphere of being *between* one mode of being and another. While it is possible with the aid of specific attributes to distinguish the existent from the non-existent and the real from the unreal, it is not possible to *refer* to anything not rejoicing in being. The *reference* of judgment is never "existential"; it is merely "ontological." Existence, connoting as it does a *determinate* region within the area of being, has such determinations as judgment by its act of *description* ascribes to it. The nerve of the ontological paradox of judgment lies in the irremediable fact that its reference is identical with description, yet that to which it refers must be differentiated from what it describes. What judgment describes is some aspect or mode of being as disclosed in awareness. And since awareness may be of the unreal and the non-existent, what is "given" in awareness, never problematic as regards its being, is always problematic as regards its reality or existence, until judgment has determined by valid description its intrinsic qualities and relations. Judgment, therefore, when its composite nature is acknowledged and not mutilated, furnishes another road towards Problematic Realism. Judgment is always a mind's expression of a belief in simultaneous commerce with the two dimensions of "knowing" and "being." In so far as its noetic aspect can by analysis be detached from its material aspect, judgment simply refers to what a mind is aware of. And what it is aware of is something indubitable substantivally but problematic adjectivally. It is judgment, on its material side, which by its work of predication determines whether anything rejoicing in being is included also in the more restricted areas of reality and existence; but whether judgment's description of being corresponds with its intrinsic or qualitied nature involves the question how far we can validate judgment's claim to "truth."

This leads me to the second paradox with which judgment is burdened—namely, the "epistemological." This paradox resides in the fact that truth has a four-fold root. If truth is a property of judgment, it is a property of its four aspects; and truth is equally anomalous whether it is the property of the ingredients of judgment taken separately or jointly. If truth belongs to the components of judgment distributively, we have four kinds of truth; and if it belongs to them collectively, we may secure the unity of truth, but only through an arbitrary fiat that one component exercises control over the rest. If by analysis we isolate the four elements which together belong to the meaning of judgment, we may readily construct a different theory of truth appropriate to each of them. (1) Detaching belief as the primary element of judgment, the truth of it may be called *adverbial*, if the meaning of belief lies, not in its verbal assertion, but in its practical enactment, and if any distinction can be established between successfully and unpropitiously enacted beliefs. That belief, the enactment of which is functionally efficacious, is *truly* efficacious. The emphasis upon the adverb "truly" as fundamental seems distinctive of pragmatism. And since the adverb always expresses a way of acting, successful or satisfactory practice is obviously the standard to which adverbial truth must conform. (2) If we identify judgment with the formal expression of it, truth acquires a purely logical status. Truth is then pre-eminently a noun or substantive. It is a name for a self-generated concordance of propositions divorced from their psychological origin and actual application. Truth, consisting in agreement of discourse with itself, when discourse is carried on in accordance with certain rules laid down and recognized as coercive by discourse itself, may be called *substantival*: it is an independent "body" or "system" of pure propositions. And substantival truth, being a structure of harmonious discourse, is manifestly subject to the standard of consistency or coherence. (3) The definition of judgment as the exhibition in discursive dress of an act or state of awareness leads to the notion of truth as *adjectival*: "trueness" is an inexpungible quality of awareness itself, and may thus vicariously be attached to the judgment, if judgment is nothing but a case of awareness given articulate expression. My judgment can never be false if what it expresses is *merely* what I am aware of. The test of adjectival truth accordingly is the test of awareness itself. And what is this test but immediacy? Whatever I am immediately aware of is true, *if* I am immediately aware of it. (4) If judgment is primarily a description of something real or existential, truth is material—that is, truth is *about* that which somehow transcends belief and discourse and awareness. Neither the judgment as description nor the described "something" is true by itself; true is the relation between them. Material truth is a form-matter truth; truth resides in the link between the two and not apart from either of them. We may call this truth *bi-prepositional*, since it is the truth *of* the real and *by* discourse, or we may speak of it as *hyphenated*, since truth here is a span or bridge between the world of discourse and the world of things, and the test of such truth is evidently by correspondence or agreement between judgment as description and the described thing or event transcending it.

The mutilation of judgment thus leads to the growth of a separate kind of truth from each of its segmented roots. Is truth adverbial, substantival, adjectival, or prepositional? And is it tested by practice, coherence, immediacy, or correspondence? Whatever names we give to them—and I do not set store by the labels I have chosen—these four kinds of truth are as distinguishable as the four aspects of judgment with which they are correlated. The epistemological paradox is equally irremediable whether we regard each truth as a truth *sui generis* or whether we proclaim one as the genus and the remaining three as its species. Shall we confer plural sovereignty upon a quadrified truth, or absolute sovereignty upon a single overweening type holding in subjection whatever other truths may rebelliously assert their independence? In the former case, any judgment is in the anomalous position of being at once true and false, for it may be true substantivally (formally or rationally), but false prepositionally (existentially or materially), or true adjectivally (intuitively or mystically), and false adverbially (instrumentally or pragmatically), and vice versa. In the latter case, to which kind of truth shall we accord the place of genus enjoying exclusive sovereignty? If truth is the truth of judgment as composite, one only of the components being in the privileged position of mastery, to which shall we yield the sceptre? If the claim to such rule be based upon self-sufficiency and inclusiveness, has one element the advantage over the rest? As a matter of fact, each element has the power to annex and to control on its own level the other three ingredients of judgment.

The epistemological paradox of judgment, the analysis of which leaves us either with four unassimilable kinds of truth or with four different ways of assimilating them, affords another approach towards Problematic Realism. The truth-paradox is the heel of Achilles of human knowledge. Human knowledge can be neither true nor false until it passes through the crucible of judgment, but judgment has a composite nature with filaments stretching out in four different directions. The truth of judgment is relative to the way a man believes and thinks and experiences;

and since his ways of believing and thinking and experiencing can be distinguished but not separated from the descriptive function of judgment, the described real can never be identical with the real described. I am forced to the inference that the real as judgmentally qualified can never coalesce with the real as internally qualitied, which is to say that the inherently adjectival nature of reality is for human knowledge problematic. The truth of our descriptive judgments, if true at all, is a resultant of several factors, and some are induced by our responsive natures rather than by the nature of reality to which in our judgments we seek to respond.

Judgment for me is thus always the response of a mind to a problematic situation. The four constituents of judgment simply represent different levels of response. By truth I mean the response on each level conceived as consummated. On all the levels truth has thus the same "meaning": it is completely successful action or finally coherent discourse or absolutely immediate experience or ultimately relevant description. On all these levels judgment functions as one and whole, since its ingredients are mutually implicative; and its truth, if achieved, is simply the "solution" of such "problems" as are encountered in action, in thought, in experience, and in science. The truth-relation is in the end definable as a relation between a "problem" and its "solution." But is the "solution" ever attained? *Relatively*, yes. Our enacted beliefs enjoy the success which a dynamic ideal of "work-ability" is able for the nonce to guarantee; our deductive systems of propositions possess such actual coherence as the man-made rules of discourse permit; our intuitions and visions may achieve completeness and infallibility in conformity with the elusive or illusive standard of immediacy; and our sciences may indeed assume, in the light of *present* verifications and discoveries, that their descriptive versions of the real are ultimate, remembering, however, that such ultimacy is elastic. The standards in control of man's fourfold response embodied in judgment are all "regulative"—ideals to be striven for, not fixed ends ever attained or attainable. The truth-relation, being on all the levels of response a relation between a "problem" and a "solution," must thus be regarded as essentially plastic and variable.

The notion of levels of response, in which the analysis of judgment and of truth culminates, enables me to survey "the life of reason" from the point of view of incommensurable attitudes, to each of which I must assign a relatively autonomous character. The German expressions, *Weltanschauung* and *Lebensanschauung*, though verbally sonorous, are more or less factitious, as if the whole of our tangled world and confused life could be focussed and compressed into a single snapshot. What is there so disconcerting about a diversity of incongruous views? It does not worry me to look upon the world and life from different standpoints, and I do not feel abashed because I cannot combine them into a total and absolute perspective. Thus—to mention three divergent "views"—between "anthropomorphism," "solipsism," and "cosmomorphism," I do not feel the need of making a drastic choice or of uniting them into a "higher synthesis." I find them equally relevant and equally important.

In ethics and logic I am frankly anthropomorphic: I do not see how in action and in thought we can ever get out of the human skin. What is morally good and formally true for species other than the human we can either not assert at all or we must give to human postulates a cosmic range. The latter alternative is grossly impertinent and constitutes bad anthropomorphism. The *general* will (if there is such a thing) which expresses itself in human behaviour and the *universal* reason which asserts itself in human thinking are general and universal only for a particular species. To graft human ideals upon cosmic nature is a pathetic fallacy. Good anthropomorphism lies in the avoidance of this fallacy by giving unto Caesar what is merely Caesar's. If nationalism, for instance, is morally good for man, what folly to extend it to other animals or to angels! And if coherent discourse, whether mathematical or rhetorical, syllogistic or dialectical, is logically true for the human understanding, is it not likewise absurd to regard it as coercive for beings possessing different forms of thought and of speech? It is human action alone to which the morally good is relevant; and logical or formal validity is pertinent only to human discourse. What I have called adverbial truth and substantival truth are both inescapably anthropocentric.

Anthropomorphic as I am in ethics and logic, I am willing to be called a solipsist in art and religion. In so far as they are embodied in action and discourse, art and religion share, of course, in the anthropocentric nature of morality and logic; and in so far as they are held to make manifest, sensuously or pictorially, a trans-human world, art and religion are cognate with the explicitly cosmocentric endeavours of science and metaphysics. But when I strip away from art and religion those expressive and representative features which, being the defining characteristics of other modes of response, are but ancillary to them, I am left with intimate intuitions and ineffable feelings radiating from the inaccessible depths of solitary beings. The original seat of art and religion is in the inner recesses of each soul in perfect isolation and private "enjoyment." The inner life with which art and religion is primarily concerned is indeed the life of "windowless monads." And those who make light of solipsism because it is seemingly confined to the life of feeling and dreaming must be reminded of death as the most striking instance of it. I know that I shall die alone. The experience of dying will be endured by me in complete solitude. At that moment of supreme anguish or supreme joy the world will collapse for me like a house of cards. We shall all be solipsists when the flame of life flickers away from us. But dying is no exception. We are no less alone during all other moments of intense experience, when, insulated from other beings, we revel in our own ego-centric world. Such solitary moments come to their fullest fruition in art and religion. And if during the absorbing moments of æsthetic enjoyment and religious meditation we appear to be selfless, it is because no other selves intrude to give rise by contrast-effect to the consciousness of separate selfhood. To be absolutely alone is to be free from that oppressive loneliness born of social intercourse. Speculative mysticism has its *raison d'être* in the radical solitariness of all feeling: mysticism is emotional individualism distilled into philosophical solipsism. And if mystic self-absorption is the distinguishing mark of those experiences commonly called æsthetic or religious, the standard of their truth lies in the bosom of the self who has these experiences. Here if anywhere are comparisons odious. What I have called adjectival truth is but a pedantic circumlocution for solipsism. Every judgment has an inalienable verity if it is but a record of what a mind chances to experience. *A fortiori*, therefore, each æsthetic or religious judgment is indefeasibly true for him whose private feelings and intuitions it expresses. The anarchy which prevails in the case of the æsthetic and the religious judgments of mankind is thus not to be wondered at: it results from the sincere asseverations of idiosyncratic solipsists, one *ipse dixit* being as infallible as another.

Such anarchy we find justly intolerable in dealing with judgments designed to describe "the nature of things." In science and metaphysics we must seek to eschew—how far we can succeed in this is another question—solipsism as well as anthropomorphism. Here our *attitude* is deliberately cosmocentric; the centricity which on other levels of response belongs to the human species or to the single self is in science and metaphysics transferred to a wider sphere, to a sphere not coincident with the scene of human action and discourse or with the seat of idiosyncratic intuitions and feelings. What I call cosmomorphism exacts a conscious surrender of those perspectives which enable us to define judgment either as belief or as discourse or as awareness: all these differentiae of judgment tend to magnify the importance of the human or individual agent engaged in *judging*. It is only in relation to *subjects* functioning in certain ways that the three varieties of *immanent* truth—pragmatic or adverbial, formal or substantival, mystic or adjectival—can be rendered unexceptionable. But when stress is laid upon the descriptive office of judgment the centre of gravity shifts at once from the act of judging to the thing judged. A different designation is thus needed for the truth of descriptive judgments. Material truth is the name commonly given to it. Material truth is *transcendent* truth: it is *of* something transcending the forms in which we incase it under the pressure of anthropocentric and egocentric activities and experiences. Such truth (in my own terminology) is bi-pre-positional, but only one preposition plays here the dominating rôle. All truth is *of* reality *by* a mind employing the complex vehicle of judgment. But whereas in anthropomorphism and solipsism the importance lies in the fact that truth is truth *by* a mind, in cosmomorphism the accent falls on the other preposition, and truth is viewed exclusively as truth *of* the real or existential. In the interest of cosmomorphic truth I must be willing to sacrifice one preposition in favour of the other.

It is of the essence of Problematic Realism to recognize at once the necessity and the impossibility of such sacrifice. We long to be cosmocentric, yet it is a longing that cannot be satisfied. The choice of the term "problematic," by which my realism is to be distinguished, may now be seen to have a double implication. One implication is ontological: in suffering no adjectival limitation of being, wrought by judgment, the enjoy-ment of absolute certainty, the substantial status of the real is made impregnable against anthropomorphism and solipsism. The assertion that the adjectival nature of reality is for human knowledge problematic involves the most complete avowal of cosmomorphism, since it recognizes the disparity between the intrinsically qualitied real and the real as humanly qualified. The other implication is epistemological: the characterization as problematic of the results of our cognitive efforts to lay bare the inherently qualitied nature of being follows from the composite character of judgment whose cosmocentric direction can be distinguished but not separated from its anthropocentric (or egocentric) source and origin. In other words, judgments *of* the real, being ineluctably judgments *by* the mind, are peren-nially precarious. The refusal to accept as final the adjectival limitation of the real by human judgments—and scientific and metaphysical judgments are certainly human—is complementary to the ontological notion of a cosmomorphic substance. These two implications of Problematic Realism constitute the quintessence of scientific methodology. Scientific methodology, as I have shown, requires for its application a cosmomorphic reality, the descriptions of which, however ultimate, must remain elastic or problematic, for reasons at once objective and subjective. It is this conception of the elastic ultimate which furnishes the basis for a new sort of metaphysics—the metaphysics of scepticism. Problematic Realism is but another name for this kind of metaphysics. As for other brands of metaphysical generalizations—those that issue in accounts of the nature and structure of the universe presumably ultimate in a dogmatic or inelastic sense—the very divergences between them converge upon Problematic Realism. For what are they but the Procrustean translations of a cosmomorphic substance, differing from one another in accordance with the multifarious visions by which speculative minds are inspired? Whenever any one of these mighty generalizations will have been proved undeniably true—not as a national policy is pragmatically true, nor as one of the non-Euclidean geometries is formally true, nor as the æsthetic contemplation of a sunset is mystically true, but true cosmocentrically as a final description of the intrinsic nature of reality—then I shall gladly renounce Problematic Realism.

The salient features of my philosophy, to which I am here for the first time attaching a hazardous label, may be found elaborated in a number of essays and articles. The chronological order of these has determined the form of the present sketch. Although still in the making, my philosophy has deviated but little from its earliest inceptions and utterances. I find it difficult to state at what period in my intellectual development the philosophic insight which I now call my own came to light or took on definite shape. Various influences have contributed to its genesis; and some of these I shall now briefly indicate.

I confess to an early attachment to Kant's "thing-in-itself." I could never make head or tail of transcendentalism without its realistic underpinning. The cavalier neglect of Kant's realism by those who profess to follow in his epistemological footsteps has always seemed to me a scandal. It is the "thing-in-itself" which saves experience from being downright autogenous. An unknown ground of knowledge, though dialectically a baffling conception, is certainly more intelligible than the alternative we are bidden to countenance—namely, the conception of knowledge as self-generated or self-grounded. To escape from a cosmomorphic reality inaccessible to human knowledge, we are asked to accept the absurd apotheosis of anthropocentric sensibility and understanding. The reflection upon the necessity of some "thing-in-itself," without which knowledge has to be conceived as producing itself as well as its objects, first led me to the view I now designate as Problematic Realism. I soon perceived that the "thing-in-itself" is but an infelicitous name for substance or self-existence, and in that I soon recognized a cosmomorphic bulwark against the connivance and idolatry of human passion and logic.

To Josiah Royce, my first teacher in metaphysics, I owe a debt greater than can here be intimated. From him I first learned to suspect the "existential predicate" of being the bull in the philosopher's china shop. His Four Conceptions of Being showed me that nothing can apparently be characterized as "real" save in relation to the truth of this or that metaphysical theory. This soon led me to the following dilemma: either the "real" is so *neutral* a term that, prior to the validated truth of a particular ontology, it is applicable to anything and everything—in which case it is meaningless—or it is a *eulogistic* term, restricted by metaphysical fiat to favoured entities and relations—in which case it is useless until the fiat question has established its claim to exclusive validity. The reflection upon this dilemma has taught me to be wary of a term so strangely equivocal and to use it in the manner already proposed. The "real," to be initially free from the constraining influence of any special ontology, can obviously signify nothing more than the substantive occasion of metaphysical inquiry, the adjectival nature of which must remain problematic until judgment concerning it attains the degree of material truth supposedly inelastic. The "real" and the "problematic" thus gradually grew in my mind as inseparable as twins. In this direction Royce's examination of the "ontological predicate" inevitably led me. His own Idealism or Voluntarism, though logically formidable, could never elicit my assent. I could never escape the conviction that his massive edifice of dialectical construction rested on the parlous foundations of solipsism and anthropomorphism. The "internal meaning" of ideas, starting the sloping process up to God, to the "external meaning" of absolute or cosmomorphic bulk, could never lose for me its taint of idiosyncrasy or humanity. The "purpose" seeking fulfilment, which is supposed to constitute the "internal" life of every "idea," I could not take seriously as being anything else than uniquely egocentric or uniformly anthropocentric: purposes not *analogous* to my own solitary strivings or to the collective ends embodied in the stratified institutions of human society I simply could not fathom. To draw the universe within the orbit of "purpose" seemed to me tantamount to a denial of its cosmo-centricity. Royce's metaphysics, with which I earnestly wrestled with all my might, had the effect of establishing in my own mind as fundamental the distinction between reality as substantival or cosmocentric and the adjectival limitations of it inspired by will-attitudes either incommensurably individual or concurrently human.

My initiation into the mysteries of Hegel's philosophy, which played an important part in my intellectual development, I owe chiefly to Royce. Left to myself, I should have imbibed the hackneyed interpretations of Hegel repeated in a hundred text-books. Royce, however, taught me to look for the genius of Hegel in the neglected *Phenomenology* rather than in the exploited *Logic*. The *Phenomenology*, accordingly, has been one of my chief sources of philosophic inspiration. The dialectical method, as exhibited in that perverse but great book, strengthened immeasurably some of my spontaneous convictions. I soon discovered in Hegel's dialectic two distinct strains, one repelling and the other attracting me. What I found repellent was the view of the dialectic as a mode of rhythmic *experience*. This strain, which I call the *histrionic*, obliges us to equate the real with the totality of "parts," enacted and superseded by an Absolute Mind. The universe is thus made to proclaim the glory of a versatile genius in whose dramatic will and reason we must find the spiritual necessity of all the seemingly irrational gyrations in nature and history. The dialectic as a method of tragic experience is simply a sinister apology for the spirit of romanticism: Truth is lodged in the restless and insatiable mind of a Protean

Absolute. By a strange equivocation Hegel managed to impugn the romanticism of the human self while endowing with romantic traits his super-human "Subject." More to my liking I found the second strain in his dialectic, which I call the *comic*, because it is an impersonal mode of exhibiting the perpetual incongruities involved in all human ideas and attitudes. This side of the dialectic appealed to me as a weapon for laying siege to everything dogmatic by rendering its partisan claims logically ridiculous. Hegel's dialectical method, though impotent to win absolute knowledge, led me to see the absurd consequences that inhere in the attempts to lodge absolute truth in anything egocentric or anthropocentric. His *Phenomenology* thus became for me a comedy of errors, a vast playground of human ideas striving to be more than human. The impressive panorama of our typical attitudes and beliefs, all suffering from the illusion of perspective and the blindness of partisanship, taught me to turn Hegel's idealism into "its own other": the lesson I learned was to accept as absolute a realistically qualitied substance, of which all the human qualifications, Hegel's own included, must remain dialectically vulnerable—that is, problematic.

Fresh impetus in the direction of Problematic Realism I received later from Mr. Santayana. His books, the depths of which I did not gauge at first, became for me, as I read them over and over again, treasure-houses of sanity and wisdom. In melodious language, free from cant and sophistry, Mr. Santayana has richly variegated the only theme that really matters in all philosophy: the relation between substantive reality and the translations of it in the polygot terms of human reason and imagination. His naturalism, viewed as cosmomorphic description, seemed to me too positive, and his scepticism of existence, assumed to follow when knowledge by suspension of judgment becomes intuitive or disinterested, too transcendental. But the difficulty in understanding the relation between his naturalism and scepticism could never obscure the fact for me that for Mr. Santayana no identity can be established between the intrinsic nature of substance and the symbolic portrayals of it wrought by the human (or animal) psyche. Mr. Santayana taught me not to confuse the life of reason with the life of substance. The life of reason, being essentially egocentric and anthropocentric, being a life in which romance and fable are such potent organs, is incommensurable with the inner nature of what exists in itself, and what can only be understood through itself. The understanding of substance, beyond the fact that it exists, involves the impossible feat of seeing it from its own point of view: a feat as impossible for Mr. Sanatayana as apparently it was for Spinoza. Even the highest kind of knowledge to which Spinoza appealed—even the view of the universe *sub specie aeternitatis*—was powerless to reveal the *specific* nature of the *infinite* attributes belonging to substance. And since the indigenous attributes of substance (on the assumption that their number is infinite) are unfathomable —a view which for different reasons Mr. Santayana shares with Spinoza—the human "circumnavigators of being," to employ Mr. Santayana's striking phrase, in fathoming the universe, sound their own hearts and minds, and import into cosmic nature the illusory limits of their dreams and speculations.

These dreams and speculations, though no indices to the secret operations of substance, are precious as human responses to them. The recognition that in framing judgments about the cosmos we never leave the human plane does not detract from their "truth," if truth is a category pertinent to *all* the ingredients of such judgments. The notion that truth is a category ancillary to that of "response" I owe to the pragmatists, but I am reluctant to connive at their vernacular, which is either too psychological or too biological. I refuse to put my philosophical eggs in the basket of a *particular* science. The pragmatic element in my doctrine, which is speculative or dialectical, was inspired more by George Simmel than either by William James or by John Dewey. From these two great American liberals and liberators I imbibed, indeed, the spirit of rebellion against the pretensions of absolutism, but a constructive humanism, not enmeshed in exclusively psychological or biological terms, I first found in Simmel. The books of this subtle thinker played no inconsiderable part in shaping my view of "differential" metaphysics. It was perhaps through them that I first came to understand the positive implications in the perennial strife of systems. Metaphysical harmony is no more feasible than either religious harmony or political harmony. All the "humanities" exhibit incomparable responses to the same "problematic" reality, each at once universal and particular, unique yet perpetually recurring, like a musical theme which is capable of endless variations. Problematic Realism, though issuing in what I have called the "metaphysics of scepticism," which is nothing more than a speculative extension of the "elastic ultimate" involved in all scientific methodology, is on its positive side a philosophy of liberalism and tolerance. Just because the nature of reality is so everlastingly problematic every human effort to sound its depths becomes invested with indelible worth.

PRINCIPAL PUBLICATIONS

"The Metaphysics of Modern Scepticism," *Philosophical Review*, vol. xxxii, 1923.
"The Metaphysics of Critical Realism," *University of California Publications in Philosophy*, vol. iv, 1923.
"The Idea of the Ultimate," *ibid.*, vol. v, 1924.
"Is Metaphysics Descriptive or Normative?" *ibid.*, vol. vii, 1925.
"The Metaphysical Status of Things and Ideas," *ibid.*, vol. viii, 1926.
"Pre-Analytical and Post-Analytical Data," *Journal of Philosophy*, vol. xxiv, 1927.
"Subject and Substance," *University of California Publications in Philosophy*, vol. ix, 1927.
"The Paradox of Judgment," *Journal of Philosophy*, vol. xxv, 1928.
"The Fourfold Root of Truth," *University of California Publications in Philosophy*, vol. x, 1928.
"The Prepositional Nature of Truth," *ibid.*, vol. xi, 1929.

A TEMPORALISTIC REALISM

By ARTHUR O. LOVEJOY

Born 1873; Professor of Philosophy, The Johns Hopkins University,
Baltimore.

A TEMPORALISTIC REALISM

THE metaphysics of the philosophical teachers whose influence was dominant in most of the American universities thirty-five years ago had one common and fundamental premise which was supposed to be established beyond the possibility of reasonable doubt; to question it was simply to betray one's want of a genuine initiation into philosophy. It was the proposition that, in Bradley's words, "to be real, or even barely to exist, is to fall within sentience; sentient experience, in short, is reality, and what is not this is not real. There is no being or fact outside of that which is commonly called psychical existence." As my first teacher in philosophy, George Holmes Howison said, in summing up a memorable philosophical symposium in 1895: "We are all agreed" in one "great tenet," which is "the entire foundation of philosophy itself: that explanation of the world which maintains that the only thing absolutely real is mind; that all material and all temporal existences take their being from Consciousness that thinks and experiences; that out of consciousness they all issue, to consciousness they are presented, and that presence to consciousness constitutes their entire reality." With almost a whole generation of acute and powerful minds this passed for a virtual axiom. And with a great part of the succeeding generation of American and British philosophers the contradictory of this proposition has passed for a virtual axiom: viz., that "all experience"—or, at least, "all sensory experience"—"carries with it the guarantee of the extra-mentality of its object." To me neither of these propositions has appeared either self-evident or, on its face, particularly probable. It is, obviously, unpleasant and disillusioning to be compelled to believe so many of the teachers of one's youth, on the one hand, or so many of one's most eminent contemporaries, on the other, to be simply the victims of a specious pseudo-axiom concerning the primary issue of metaphysics; but this alternative, at least, has been unescapable for most of us who contribute to these volumes. It is, however, still more unfortunate, and still more productive of doubts about the way in which the business of philosophizing is conducted, to be compelled to regard both groups as basing their philosophies upon opposite and equally unconvincing pseudo-axioms. And in this latter position I regretfully find myself placed. I am unable, in short, to see any inconceivability in the supposition that "reality" may be of a mixed character, and that the "objects" apprehended in sensory or other experience may be in some cases purely "mental" and in others "extra-mental"—though I regard these traditional adjectives as not altogether happily chosen; and I find what seem to me strong reasons for regarding this supposition as probable.

The student of philosophy in our time, in other words, appears to me to have usually been confronted with the entirely gratuitous dilemma of an absolute idealism or an absolute realism (i.e., a "pan-objectivism"). To be unable to embrace either horn of the dilemma—to believe in a physical world, a most disreputable thing in the eyes of the one party, but also to believe in "ideas" in something like the Cartesian and Lockian sense, an equally disreputable thing in the eyes of the other party—is to be in a position which, among its other inconveniences, imposes upon one who has a natural wish to vindicate the reasonableness of his opinions the necessity of conducting a polemic upon two fronts at once, or, at the least, of meeting two convergent attacks. And to do both (not to say either) in a manner adequate to the importance of the issues and the number and undeniable plausibility of the considerations urged upon the two sides would obviously be impossible within the limits set for these papers. But there is, after all, one considerable advantage in an intermediate position: the object of convergent attacks may save himself some effort by stepping aside and permitting the attacks to converge upon one another. The result may be the destruction of one, if not both, of the assailants, or at least the weakening of one or both. And of this possible economy of effort I shall take advantage. Some of the reasons why the "great tenet" of idealism has ceased to appear to me evident or probable will, I imagine, be found clearly and forcefully expressed in other contributions to these volumes; and it would be a redundancy to repeat them here. Most—though by no means all—of us in America who were initiated into philosophy thirty or forty years ago have passed, up to a point, through much the same reflective experience; we have found the idealistic creed, in one or another form of which our philosophic youth was nurtured, untenable, and have done so in part under the pressure of the same considerations. But of those who have gone thus far together, the greater number (at all events until recently) have seen no permanent assurance for philosophy against a relapse into the error from which they have themselves, as they believe, escaped, unless the road be followed almost or quite to its opposite extreme—unless, that is, it be held, either that "consciousness" does not exist at all, or that, at most, it is a mere otiose awareness of objects in no way dependent upon it— that, in other words, there are *no* existences which "take their being from consciousness," or whose "presence to consciousness constitutes their entire reality." In my own belief the real danger of a relapse lies rather in passing to this alternative extreme; but I am glad to profit by such arguments as others have offered to show, at least, the necessity of abandoning the old position.

There is, however, one consideration, relevant to the question of the tenability of idealism, but also to many other philosophical issues, which has figured much more largely in my own reflection than it has, so far as I have been able to gather, in that of most American realists; and I shall be less likely to repeat what others will have better said if I dwell chiefly upon this. To all theories about the nature of reality or of knowledge I early began to apply one touch-stone before any other—that of congruence with the most indubitable fact of our experience, namely, that experience itself is temporal. That life is transition; that our existence is meted out to us in fragments which succeed and supplant one another; that there is a region of being—even though it consist only of our own past thoughts and deeds and emotions—of which the content and character are settled and unalterable, and a region of the not-yet-realized, which our volitional natures and our most irrepressible affective attitudes —hope and fear, resolution and hesitancy, purpose and planning— manifestly presuppose, and apart from the conception of which they would be meaningless: these have always seemed to me to be the first and fundamental *empirical* truths of which philosophical speculation must take account. It is in the degree in which it keeps steadfastly in mind the temporality of man's being and his knowing that a philosophy is faithful to the primary certitude of human consciousness about its own nature, and is relevant to human life. But it is precisely from this aspect of existence that philosophy has throughout the greater part of its history made haste to turn its gaze, to fix it upon things that are complete, self-contained, eternal, or immutable. That there are no such things, or even that our chief concern may not be with them, is not, indeed, implied merely by the fact that our *experience* is mutable and successive; but no assertion of any supra-temporal realm of being can, as it has seemed to me, be admitted into a philosophy which does not resort to the silly verbal subterfuge of illusionism, unless the reality of the eternal entities which are affirmed can be shown to be reconcilable with the elementary and immediately certain fact that we mortals *live*—that is, have a transitive, perpetually lapsing and yet continuing, mode of being under the form of time, and with what is implied even by the theory of eternal realities itself—namely, that the knowing of such realities by us occurs in time.

How many difficulties and paradoxes the notion of temporal process presents to the analytic understanding I am well aware; that philosophers, being for the most part eager and impatient rationalizers of the scheme of things, have often had little interest in that notion is only too easily comprehensible. Reality would, of course, be far more manageable intellectually if it were innocent of succession; some of the German Romanticists, and Bergson after them, were quite right in declaring that the natural and persistent tendency of the intellect is to translate temporal into quasi-spatial categories, to treat the flux as if it were stationary and the unrealized as if it were existent. But the embarrassments which the concept of time has created for philosophy are no justification for denying, ignoring, or slighting the strange yet unescapable fact which every man, and therefore every philosopher, is continually experiencing—the fact that his very thought is in process, that there lie behind him moments of being which

ARTHUR O. LOVEJOY

he can never in themselves recapture and before him a possible future which he can, perhaps, in some measure foreshadow, but which he assuredly does not yet in its living poignancy possess.

I came, then, to a conclusion which—along with much with which I should disagree—Bosanquet long afterwards expressed when he wrote: "The ultimate crux of speculation" is "the place of time, progress, and change in the universe. There is nothing so difficult as this problem and nothing so essential to reasonable thought or conduct." It was thus the fact of the reality of time, and the problems of the psychological nature of our experience of succession and the significance of the temporal process, that did most to arouse my dissatisfaction with the doctrines of some of my early teachers, and to set me upon the attempt to philosophize for myself; and when, later, it seemed necessary to have a label to attach to the way of thinking to which I inclined, I ventured to coin the word "temporalism" for that purpose.[1] The term still seems to me a desirable addition to the philosophical vocabulary as a means for setting off from all other doctrines those which regard the reality of time as among the irreducible ultimates of philosophy and as a crucial test of the tenability of metaphysical and epistemological theories. A "temporalist" philosophy, as I should use the term, would not necessarily assert that all that is is temporal; but it would insist that whatever empirically *is* temporal is so irretrievably—that its temporality can by no dialectical hocus-pocus be transubstantiated or *aufgehoben* into, or embraced within, the eternal.

Tested by this criterion, the whole scheme of absolute idealism, which had been so earnestly and impressively taught (with variations) by Green, the Cairds, Bradley, Bosanquet, and other British neo-Hegelians, and to which Royce was in the eighteen-nineties giving what seems to me its most coherent and adequate expression, at once broke down. The essence of that doctrine was the supposition that an eternal whole can be conceived to be

[1] The term has not, I believe, been extensively adopted; it is, however, frequently employed by Bosanquet in *The Meeting of Extremes in Contemporary Philosophy* to designate the view which he there chiefly attacks—and which is, in essence, the view that I hold and should so designate.

made up of temporal parts, that an absolute experience, which is incapable of alteration because it is for ever at the goal, can include within itself innumerable experiences of succession. This, even in my student days, seemed to me no better than a flat contradiction—and so it seems to me still. That there may be, apart from the temporal world, some reality corresponding to that Boethian definition of eternity which Royce loved to quote—*interminabilis vitae tota simul ac perfecta possessio*—in other words, to the Aristotelian and Scholastic Absolute—I will not deny, though, as a temporal creature, I find the conception, to say the least, difficult, irrelevant, and unappealing. But that such a reality should be identified with the *whole* of a world of which we temporal creatures and our present strivings, our lost yesterdays and hoped-for to-morrows, are declared to be genuine component parts—this I cannot but consider as preposterous a paradox as any which the history of philosophy has to show—and that, I think, is saying much.

I am, also, not unaware how strong and natural are the religious motives which make for this sort of metaphysics. It is a very soothing and comfortable self-contradiction—as is not surprising; for it is of the nature of self-contradictions to be comfortable, and conversely, I am not sure that there are any altogether comfortable views of the world which are not self-contradictory. The good which all men naturally desire is the privilege of eating their cake and having it too; and this human craving, which finds such small satisfaction in the world of physical experience and the logical world of the "mere understanding," many types of philosophy have sought to gratify in the matter of our beliefs. Psychologically considered, this has been one of the frequent historic functions of speculative philosophy; and psychopathologically considered, it has, perhaps, been a benign function. To escape somewhere from the exasperating factual and logical incompatibilities of things, from the necessity of choice between alternatives of which both are desirable, from the everlasting *entweder-oder des hartnäckigen Verstandes*—this, of course, is a grateful, and may to some temperaments be a needful, relief; and those philosophies which offer it, and especially those

which give what seem subtly reasoned justifications for it, have
always been assured, and probably always will be assured, of a
welcome. But of all such philosophies, and therefore, in particular,
of Hegelianism and its offspring, I early became suspicious—
chiefly, I think, under the influence of William James and of
the reading of Renouvier, to which he used to incite his students
in the 'nineties. Both helped me to realize that the lust to reconcile
the irreconcilable is one of the besetting temptations of the metaphysical temperament, one of the dangers against which the
philosopher needs most to be on his guard—a temptation the
greater and the more insidious in proportion to the many-sided-
ness of the philosopher's mind and the consequent diversity and
intensity of his intellectual sympathies.

This conviction, of course, settled no specific problem. There
obviously have been set up, in the history of thought, a number
of spurious contradictions which do disappear upon adequate
analysis. But the influences which I have mentioned helped to
create, or to sharpen, a predisposition which has, I suppose,
affected my conclusions on a number of problems, and in particular upon the tenability of absolute idealism. They freed me (I
hope) of any readiness to let the attractiveness or "nobility" of
any proposed reconciliation of opposites obscure contradictions
lurking in it or in the argument for it; and they led me to believe
that, in the main, the philosopher's business consists in making
choice between alternatives. I did not fail to examine with care
such acute and ingenious arguments as were offered by Bradley
and by Royce to prove that there is no contradiction in the notion
of a *totum simul* made up of successive parts. But Bradley's
argument, as Royce himself helped me to see, was only a roundabout way of saying that the Absolute Experience is *not* really
made up of the sort of relational (including temporal) experience
which is ours; and Royce's own attempt (especially in vol. ii of
The World and the Individual) to show how it conceivably may
be literally so made up seemed to me a failure. (To prove that it
was, in fact, a failure would, of course, require an analysis far too
lengthy to be presented here.) Nor, I may add, was my conclusion
shaken when, long after, Bosanquet, in his *The Meeting of*

Extremes in Contemporary Philosophy, endeavoured afresh to vindicate "the view that the foundational character of all that is, *while containing the infinite changes* which are the revelation of its inexhaustible life, not confinable within a single direction or temporal career, *is not itself and as such engaged in a progress and mutation.*"[1] The greater the dialectical resources bestowed upon the justification of such a conception, the more nakedly did the essential self-contradiction in it appear to me to stand out.

The form of idealism to which I had been introduced by Howison did not, indeed, present this contradiction. While it recognized an eternal as well as a temporal order of being, the eternal did not—for it—contain the temporal. Each finite mind was declared to be, "in one side of its being," an "empirical" existence in time, and, in another side, to "have an eternal reality that did not arise out of change, and that cannot by change pass away"—"eternal" here being expressly defined as the negation of "temporal."[2] That what is experienced as temporal is so genuinely and without any sublation into its opposite was therefore not denied by this theory. Yet even this less paradoxical sort of eternalism I was unable to accept. In the first place the proofs offered for it seemed to me unconvincing. It rested mainly upon Kantian premises. Our possession of a priori knowledge was supposed to imply the existence of an eternal or noumenal Ego as the "source" and ground of all these "connecting and inference-supporting elements in human consciousness." But I could never see the connection between the premise and the conclusion. That at each moment the contents of each individual consciousness have a "unique and not further analysable togetherness" I recognized; and that some factor of continuity, some element persistent or identically recurrent in consciousness from moment to moment, must be assumed, to make our experience of succession and duration conceivable at all, seemed to me evident. But why the fact—supposing it a fact—that we find certain specific judgments "necessary," and therefore are constrained to

---

[1] *Op. cit.*, p. 210; italics mine.
[2] *The Limits of Evolution*, 1901, pp. xv, xvi.

think them valid for cases of which we have not yet had experience, should be regarded as a reason for affirming the reality of a multitude of supra-temporal or eternal selves, was to me incomprehensible. The apprehension of the necessity is itself always an empirical event having a date in a temporal sequence; and if the necessity apprehended be something both objective and eternal, the eternity, surely, must attach to the logical order—to what Locke calls the "relation of connection and agreement, or disagreement and repugnancy between ideas"—to which the judgment, *quâ* necessary and universal, relates, and not to the function of judging nor to the psychological subject, or maker, of the judgment.[1] If, in short, *any* "eternal reality" is implied by the assumption that we have a priori knowledge, that reality is the world of noumenal objects of Platonic realism, not the noumenal Egos of Kantianism.

Not only did the proof offered for the latter seem unpersuasive, but the conception, when taken in its entirety, seemed impossible. How a temporal experience could be hitched on to an eternal self without infecting the latter with its temporality, I could not, and cannot, see—nor yet how an eternal self could be constantly engaged in temporal acts of cognition without impairment of its eternity. As little did the theory appear to me to have the ethical and religious consequences which were drawn from it, and which, as I could not but feel, were in reality its chief generating motives. It purported to vindicate both freedom and immortality. Because out of time all selves were also out of the causal nexus and thus

---

[1] Misconception of Locke's position is so prevalent that the quotation from him here will perhaps seem to some readers inapposite. But it should be patent that in the fourth book of the *Essay* his theory is essentially a sort of Platonistic rationalism. We "know," in the strict sense, only when we perceive a logically *inherent* "connection between ideas," and experience is not for him knowledge nor, properly speaking, a source of knowledge. The notion that Locke was an empiricist has arisen through reading his sensationalist account of the "origin of our ideas," i.e. of the way in which "ideas" get into our minds, into his theory of the nature and grounds of *knowledge*. His total doctrine is that the ideas, though they come to us through our senses, come bringing their eternal and necessary logical inter-relations with them; and "knowledge" consists exclusively in intuitively reading off these relations.

undetermined and independent; "relatively to the natural world they are free, in the sense of being in control of it: so far from being bound by it and its laws, they are the very source of all the law there is or can be in it." But even supposing this admitted, such freedom manifestly had no moral significance; it belonged to an abstraction, a noumenal Ego that never acted in time, in which alone moral good and evil subsist—or, if it did so act, became thereby enmeshed, along with all the temporal life of man, in necessity. And inasmuch as the distinctive "empirical character" of the individual was supposed—as it had already been by Kant[1]—to be somehow the expression or temporal unfolding of something unique in the "intelligible character" of each eternal self, this so-called freedom was indistinguishable from the most absolute necessity. Every man is and does what the differentiating *nuance* that makes his supersensible character distinct from all others requires; and this determination from all eternity, and apart from all volition, to be the kind of self that one is, is a blanker, more unexplainable sort of predestination than that implied by the postulate of causal uniformity in temporal phenomena. Similarly, any argument from the "eternity" of the noumenal self to the persistence in the future of an empirical individual existence—which, moreover, was supposed to have *begun* in time—appeared to me impossible. Either the "supersensible self" really was eternal—i.e., without duration or succession in time—or it was temporal. If the former, nothing could be inferred about the duration of the temporal self somehow incomprehensibly associated with it; if the latter, it appeared antecedently as conceivable that any individual entity of this kind should have an end as that it should have a beginning.

Thus both the pluralistic and the monistic type of idealism, though they were presented by teachers of such rare gifts and philosophic power as Howison and Royce, appeared to me equally unacceptable as wholes. Yet one essential contention of the former theory, as against the latter, I found convincing; and this consisted precisely in its pluralism. That there is in the

[1] I am referring to Kant's amazing reasoning about freedom in the *Kritik der praktischen Vernunft*, pp. 224–36.

experience of each individual at each moment something unique and unshareable—that to know about another's experience is never the same as having it—this seemed to me a truth upon which the "multi-personalist" rightly insisted. Monistic idealism —especially in the form which it had when Royce rid it of its usual foggy indefiniteness—seemed to imply that you could take a lump of experience commonly called John's, add to it another lump commonly called Peter's, another commonly called the experience of Peter's dog, and so proceed *ad infinitum*, and thereby could compound a total, called the Absolute Experience, in which nothing that had belonged to any of these component units would be lacking, though much might be added. But something, I think, would necessarily be lacking—namely, that which made the first experience John's, the second Peter's, the third the dog's. An experience, in short, appears to be always a centred or appropriated mass of ingredients; it may have elements in common with other experiences, may be directed upon identical objects, but the "unique togetherness" of the mass in the individual moment of consciousness is a togetherness from a special point of view; and *this* feature of any one experience, though it can be designated in general and abstract terms, cannot, so far as I can see, be actually and in its concrete particularity an attribute of any other experience. Even the limitations or dissatisfactions of my present thought or feeling are more than *mere* limitations. If the Absolute knows my error, but at the same time sees beyond it to the truth, it is not my experience of erring that he is having; and if he is aware of my grief, but at the same time knows that it is transitory and that some joy is to follow, he is not sharing my grief, since of that the very essence is its seeming finality. You can't, I am inclined to think, ever add to an experience without subtracting something; cannot enlarge without also omitting; cannot, even from what is called a more comprehensive point of view, see all the aspects which things present from a more contracted one. This, if true, confirmed the conclusion based upon the considerations respecting time which have been previously mentioned. Both the temporality and the individuatedness of our human experiences forbade the supposition that they can all be embraced as experiences in any single Whole or be in their immediacy and integrity possessed by any Universal Mind.

But the same two considerations which thus led me to reject absolute idealism seemed to contain a positive implication of great importance. They both assert the separateness, the mutual existential externality, of certain of the parts of reality—externality which in the one case may be called lengthwise, in the other case crosswise. Yesterday's experience is truly contained neither in my to-day nor in any eternal to-day of a Cosmic Consciousness; as little, even apart from the question of time, can my neighbour's life be integrally a part of mine or of that of a Cosmic Consciousness. But I was constrained to believe that I am capable of *knowing* (more or less imperfectly) both my own yesterday and my neighbour's life—not only that there *was* a yesterday, and that there *are* lives not my own, but also something of their content and character. These beliefs are not derived through reasoning; they are not "necessary" in the sense that their opposites are self-contradictory; and they obviously can never be, in the strict sense, "empirically" verified, because they consist in affirmations of the possibility of a knowledge of existents which are not, when known, immediate data *in* experience. But they are beliefs which underlie the whole of human life as it is actually lived by all of us; genuinely to disbelieve them appears to be impossible to man, certainly to those whom we are accustomed to classify as sane. The occasional lovers of philosophic paradox who have professed such disbelief seem to me merely to display an unconvincing affectation. In any case these beliefs were obviously implicit in the temporalism and the pluralism which I had already accepted; and at the same time, when explicitly construed from a temporalistic and pluralistic point of view, they manifestly entailed a definite theory about the nature of knowledge. If there is a real succession of experiences, and if, nevertheless, the experience of one moment may include, or consist in, a knowing of the existence of some prior or subsequent moment's experience, it follows that knowledge consists in somehow "apprehending" one bit of existence by means of another which is not identical with it. And, similarly, if my fellow's experience—at all events his experienc*ing*—may nevertheless be known by me, the same conclusion again follows.

The acceptance of a temporalistic and pluralistic metaphysics thus carried with it the acceptance of an epistemological dualism. Both intertemporal cognition and interpersonal cognition seem to me to show that, in its very essence, knowing, our most characteristic human function, is an organic process characterized by a potential reference to, an evocation and apprehension of, a Beyond. When we know in these ways we appear somehow to have presented in our experience at a given moment realities which we must at the same time conceive as existing outside of that experience, in the sense (at least) that they do *not* exist at that moment, or that they are experiences (or experiencings) of other selves. To be known (except in the way in which immediate sensory content is sometimes, but, as I think, unfortunately said to be "known") things must—to use a happy phrase of Professor Dewey's—be "present-as-absent"; but since—in the view of a temporalist and a pluralist—a given bit of reality cannot be literally *both* present and absent, knowing must be a function of a unique and anomalous (but not a self-contradictory) sort. It must consist (partly) in the existence, at a given time and within an individuated field of consciousness, of particulars which do duty for other particulars, extraneous to that time and that field; and the former particulars must have associated with them in consciousness, the peculiar—but, as I submit, empirically the perfectly familiar—property which some of the Schoolmen termed "intentionality" and later dualistic epistemology has called "self-transcendent reference." The "intentional" or referential quality of a given bit of content present *now* in *my* cognitive experience is itself an item in the same present experience. For example, the pastness of its date of reference is itself a present and directly experienced quality of a memory-image, which does not in the least mean that in memory the past is directly experienced. "We apprehend the various elements of our presented content as fitting into a framework of conceptualized temporal relations—which, in fact, appear in consciousness, at a given moment, largely by the aid of spatial imagery, as of a calendar or a time-table. And this temporal framework in which our images appear has a curious twofold relation to our present consciousness. As a datum for introspection, as an existent now given in experience, the framework is *included* in the present content; but at the same time, as a conceived scheme of relations, it logically includes the present moment and its content as a single unit in the larger system represented."

In cognition, in short, consciousness becomes, in Royce's phrase, "self-representative." A given moment of thought may consist in a representation of a whole world of objects in relations of many kinds—temporal, spatial, logical—in which it is itself, *as represented*, a mere fragment. Thus it is that a given experience, e.g. a memory can cognitively or representatively transcend itself without any existential self-transcendence. The memory-image exists as a transient bit of reality now and at no other time; but it exists in its place in a representation of a more comprehensive whole in which the now is an element consciously distinguished from the not-now. If the notion of "intentionality" seems to some a paradox and a mystery, I reply that, on the contrary, it is a notion obviously entertained by the plain man and by most philosophers in their normal moments. For—to leave the case of memory—when men conceive themselves to be knowing about a future event, or even so much as distinguishing the future from the past, they do not conceive of the future as existent in the same sense as the present. The whole point of the distinction lies in the conception of the future as something not now experienced or possessed; yet the conception of it *as not* now experienced manifestly *is* now experienced. And what is described by the formidable term "self-transcendent reference" is no more (and no less) mysterious than this common phenomenon in the functioning of any creature capable of looking before and after.[1]

My approach to realism was thus through a criticism of the

[1] The theme of this paragraph I have dealt with somewhat less inadequately in a paper on "The Anomaly of Consciousness" in the *University of California Publications in Philosophy*, vol. iv, from which a few sentences above are taken.

idealistic philosophies prevalent when my reflection on these matters began; but this criticism, when its implications were examined, turned out to require, as its positive corollary, a conception of knowledge as indirect and substitutional; it involved, in short, a theory of representative ideas, at least with respect to cognition of past and future events and of the experiences of other selves. And with this the epistemological basis of every sort of idealism collapsed. If knowledge was, in fact, mediate in certain cases, it might conceivably be mediate in others—for example, in the case of sense-perception. There might be reasons of other kinds for accepting a spiritualistic metaphysics; but the citadel of the idealistic position—to change the figure—had always been the epistemological assumption that only the immediate compresent content of a cognitive experience could be known through that experience; even in "objective" idealism this assumption had persisted, but its application had been transferred to the Absolute, who in that theory was the only knower in the strict sense, the sole possessor of genuine truth. But this citadel had now, as it seemed to me, been breached. In the usual epistemological sense of the term, a temporalistic or a pluralistic "idealism" would obviously not be idealism at all; for example, any consistent monadology is clearly a form of realism, since it implies that there are, between two monads, real relations which do not fall within the experience of either or of any third monad. If, then, a *particular* knower at a particular time can truly know realities which do not have their existence within, or in dependence upon, his consciousness at *that time*; and if there may subsist relations, even though they be relations between consciousnesses, which are not in *any* consciousness— then there is no decisive presumption to be drawn from purely epistemological considerations against even physical realism. Meanwhile, a vigorous revolt against idealism had been taking place in other quarters, motivated by other reasons. Some of these seemed to me valid, and therefore reinforced the argument based upon the temporalistic and pluralistic considerations I have mentioned. Especially sound and salutary seemed to me the attacks made by several writers upon the doctrine of the "internality" of all relations, which had been so important among the logical motives of post-Kantian idealism. This I had already rejected as incompatible with both temporalism and pluralism; but I had not subjected it to the separate and direct analysis which was now brought to bear upon it by others. Nevertheless the theses that were most distinctive, and in some sense "new," in the neo-realistic movements which became conspicuous in American and British philosophy during the first decade of the century, I could by no means accept; and the primary reason for this was the view about the nature of knowledge that was implicit on the grounds upon which I had rejected idealism. The new types of realistic theory were profoundly influenced either by William James's supposed discovery that "consciousness," as distinct from "content" or "objects," does not exist, or by G. E. Moore's supposed discovery, about the same time, that "consciousness" *does* exist, but is entirely distinct from content and is incapable of generating or modifying its immediate data. If either of these premises was adopted, it followed that all knowing is immediate, that the "content" (of consciousness, or the "content" without any consciousness) present in the cognitive experience is existentially identical with the object known. In the words of the authors of *The New Realism*, "there is no special class of entities, qualitatively or substantively distinguished from all other entities, as the media of knowledge. In the end all things are known through being themselves brought directly into that relation in which they are said to be witnessed or apprehended. In other words, things when consciousness is had of them become themselves contents of consciousness."[1] There was some wavering among neo-realists about following out this principle universally; but so far as it was consistently followed out it led to a sort of epistemological primitivism. What was proposed, as the same volume announced, was "a return to natural or naïve realism," which was defined as the "theory which makes no distinction between seeming and being," but holds that "things *are* just what they seem."[2]

Now it appeared to me, for the reasons previously indicated,

[1] *Op. cit.*, 1912, p. 35.   [2] *Ibid.*, pp. 10 and 2.

to be certainly false to say that when I recall an event of yesterday, or foreknow an event of to-morrow, or apprehend my neighbour's thought or feeling, these objects of my knowledge literally "become themselves contents of (my) consciousness," in the same way in which my own present sense-datum, or imagery, or feeling, is content of my consciousness. If yesterday's experience is past, it cannot be "numerically identical" either with the present event of my experiencing or with the content which is existent simultaneously with my present experiencing. Attempts have sometimes been made to meet this objection, either by suggesting that a present remembrance need have no compresent content —which seems to me an absurdity—or by conceiving of the past event as somehow actually persisting in the present. With respect to the latter way of evading the difficulty I am in agreement with the remark of Mr. Bertrand Russell: "This is mere mythology. The event which occurs when I remember is quite different from the event remembered. People who are starving can recollect their last meal, but the recollection does not appease their hunger. There is no mystic survival of the past when we remember merely a new event having a certain relation to the old one."[1] In short, a consideration of memory alone would suffice, if there were no other reasons, to lead me, as a "temporalist," to reject the epistemological monism, i.e. the generalized hypothesis of direct knowledge without intermediating "ideas," which is the essence of the "new" realism.

But there are many other reasons. The most important of these is the utter inability of any theory which regards knowledge as always an immediate apprehension of its intended object to account for error and illusion. The fact of error is the acid test for any epistemology; and the implication, in this regard, of neo-realism was all too truly indicated by the early American champions of that philosophy when they identified it, "broadly speaking," with the theory—so "naïve" that no one, I suppose, had ever previously asserted it—which "makes no distinction between seeming and being," but regards objects as "being precisely what they appear to be." The definition did not, it is

[1] *Philosophy*, p. 198.

true, prevent the authors of it from elsewhere recognizing clearly and candidly that the problem of error was for them crucial, and from attempting to find a solution of it which should be consistent with their hypothesis. These attempts are both too numerous —since nearly every adherent of the theory offers a different solution—and too ingenious and involved to be examined in detail here. I must be content, without repeating the reasons which I have tried to set forth elsewhere, to say that none of the attempts appears to me successful, and that any doctrine of direct knowledge must, I believe—precisely so far as it really *is* such a doctrine—be incapable of accounting for error or even of recognizing its possibility.

It is a further implication of the theory that knowing is always a direct apprehension of objects which would be just the same if no cognitive event had occurred, that all data of perception, whether those commonly regarded as veridical or those called illusory, are genuine parts of the physical world. To this conclusion the neo-realist is led, no doubt, by more than one logical motive. The desire to eliminate the duality of "mental" and "physical," at all events with respect to the content of consciousness (in distinction from a possible function of merely "being conscious"), is widely manifest in contemporary philosophy. It is, of course, a natural desire, since, if it could be satisfied, the result would be a great unification of our conception of the nature of things—a unification in realistic instead of idealistic terms. It is manifest, therefore, in other contemporary realists, such as Mr. Bertrand Russell, who reject epistemological monism. But here, too, I have been unable to follow the road which so many philosophical minds of my generation have found inviting and apparently satisfying. To explain the considerations which have deterred me from doing so would manifestly require, first of all, an attempt to define the nature of the "physical world," and then an examination of each of the classes of experienced content which seem to me to resist inclusion in that world, when so defined. It would also require, in order to be relevant to the latest phase of the controversy, a discussion of Mr. Russell's recent ingenious hypothesis that our percepts (and apparently all other content) are "in our heads," and that, e.g., the bit of what I call "blue sky" which is now present in my visual field is really a part of my brain—a task the more difficult because I find it hard to see how Mr. Russell's general theory permits us to suppose that we have any members properly describable as "heads." These are, of course, too large and complicated undertakings to be attempted here. But if I may assume that membership in the physical world means presence in a single, public, spatial, or spatio-temporal order, in which the laws of physics hold good, then I cannot see how the content of dreams, hallucinations, illusions, or even the contents of veridical perception as the epistemological dualist must conceive them, can be given a place in that world. This does not imply that the existence of these contents is not dependent upon processes themselves physical and conforming to the generalizations of the physicists. But physical science itself would be impossible if such entities as dream-monsters, the dipsomaniac's pink rats, or present memory-images of vanished objects—all with the qualities and behaviour which they are experienced as exhibiting—were placed upon the same footing as "scientific objects." The distinction between the "mental," in the sense of that which *merely* "appears" in an individuated private field of content, and the "physical," in the sense of an independent, orderly, perduring system of entities or "events" having dynamic or causal relations *inter se* of the kind which physical science hypothetically describes, was perhaps one of the earliest, and is still, I am disposed to think, one of the most indispensable of the philosophical acquisitions of mankind. The "bifurcation" of experience, if not of "nature" (the use of the term in this connection is question-begging), is the beginning of wisdom in metaphysics.

This will, perhaps, suffice to convey some very general notion of the primary considerations (though these are by no means all) which have brought me to that position mentioned at the outset, intermediate between the idealism accepted by most good philosophers when my acquaintance with philosophy began, and the type of realism enthusiastically adopted by so many good philosophers during the past quarter-century. Some steps in this *itinerarium mentis* have necessarily been omitted altogether. For example, any idealistic reader will have discerned that no *positive* reason has been given for accepting a physical realism; but that is one of the deficiencies which will, I hope, be abundantly made good by some of the other contributors to these volumes. And the temporalistic premise in which the whole process began needs, I realize, much further elucidation, alike with respect to the difficult concept of time itself, to its cosmological implications, the general world-view which it entails or suggests, and to its bearing upon the historic issues of religious belief. But both to express opinions on these further matters and also to present reasons for the opinions is plainly out of the question within the limits of space available here; and the statement of conclusions (on matters about which the views of reasonable men differ) without reasons is manifestly not philosophy.

PRINCIPAL PUBLICATIONS

"The Thirteen Pragmatisms," *Journal of Philosophy*, vol. v (1908).
"The Obsolescence of the Eternal," *Philosophical Review*, vol. xviii (1909).
"Reflections of a Temporalist on the New Realism," *Journal of Philosophy*, vol. viii (1911).
"William James as Philosopher," *International Journal of Ethics*, vol. xxi (1911).
Papers on Vitalism, *Science*, 1911, 1912.
"The Problem of Time in Recent French Philosophy," *Philosophical Review*, vol. xxi (1912).
"Realism *versus* Epistemological Monism," *Journal of Philosophy*, vol. x (1913).
"On Some Novelties of the New Realism," *Journal of Philosophy*, vol. x (1913).
"Error and the New Realism," *Philosophical Review*, vol. xxii (1913).
"Bergson and Romantic Evolution," *University of California Press*, 1914.
"On the Existence of Ideas," *Johns Hopkins University Circular* (1914).
"On Some Conditions of Progress in Philosophical Inquiry," *Philosophical Review*, vol. xxvi (1917).
"Pragmatism as Interactionism," *Journal of Philosophy*, vol. xvii (1920).
"Pragmatism *versus* the Pragmatist," in *Essays in Critical Realism*, 1920.
"Time, Meaning, and Transcendence," *Journal of Philosophy*, vol. xix (1922).
"The Paradox of the Thinking Behaviorist," *Philosophical Review*, vol. xxxi (1922).
"The Anomaly of Knowledge," in *University of California Publications in Philosophy*, vol. iv (1923).
"The Discontinuities of Evolution," *Ibid.*, vol. v (1924).
"Pastness and Transcendence," *Journal of Philosophy*, vol. xxi (1924).
"La théorie de la stérilité de la conscience dans la philosophie américaine et anglaise," *Bulletin de la Société Française de Philosophie*, 1926.
"Optimism and Romanticism," *Publications of the Modern Language Association of America*, vol. xlii (1927).
"The Meanings of 'Emergence' and its Modes," *Journal of Philosophical Studies*, vol. ii (1927).

A TENTATIVE REALISTIC METAPHYSICS

By EVANDER BRADLEY McGILVARY

Born Bangkok, Siam, 1864; Professor of Philosophy, University of
Wisconsin.

A TENTATIVE REALISTIC METAPHYSICS

My philosophical creed is that if ever we are to have an even partially satisfactory philosophy, we shall get it only by the use of scientific methods. The materials to which these methods are to be applied are supplied by experience, not the crude experience of everyday life, but this experience as interpreted by the various special sciences. The interpretation given by any special science to the material it investigates is relevant to that material; but the question of the adequacy of that interpretation when that material is considered as only one aspect of the world revealed to us in experience is one that the special science seldom raises. What the philosopher tries to do is to fit this interpretation into a larger scheme which embraces other aspects of the world as interpreted by other special sciences. Thus the self-imposed task of the philosopher is the integration of the scientific interpretations of the world in which he finds himself. Any step he takes in the accomplishment of his task is precarious; there are too many factors of uncertainty. The special sciences are themselves constantly changing their interpretations, and even at any time the interpretation any science gives to findings in its field cannot be fully understood unless all the facts it investigates are taken into account; and it is only the special scientist who has detailed knowledge of these facts. It thus behoves a philosopher to be quite humble in his attitude toward his results. He should never infallibly know that he is right, and should always suspect that he is wrong. He attacks his problem not because he believes that he can definitely solve it, but because he is interested in it and cannot keep his hands off. He merely hopes that he may perhaps contribute something to its solution; at best the contribution will be infinitesimally small in the ultimate reckoning—and perhaps there will be no *ultimate* reckoning.

For this reason it is wise for the philosopher to content himself with being a philosopher only within very narrow limits. He will attack only one philosophical problem at a time: he will attempt to integrate the interpretation of experience given in some special science with that given in some other special science, but he will not attempt a wholesale integration. This does not mean that he does not keep a weather-eye open for winds that may be brewing elsewhere. As a philosopher he must have that eye always functioning; but it cannot see everything. It is rather on the look out for something that may be at variance with what he thinks he sees in the immediate neighbourhood.

There are two philosophical problems that have most persistently interested me, the metaphysical and the moral problems. In a paper like this it seems better to confine myself to the former. In view of the direction in which the solution of this problem seems to lie, I am tempted to define metaphysics as the view of the world in which physics and psychology are satisfactorily integrated. Under such a definition behaviourism is metaphysical. The reason it has not recognized its metaphysical status is that for it only that metaphysics is metaphysics which is not its own metaphysics. Behaviourism is, I think, a one-sided metaphysics, which has managed somehow to lose its first two syllables with out thereby becoming identical with physics. The works of such men as Whitehead, Russell, and Broad would seem to show that a metaphysician can keep in close touch with physics without developing an evangelical fervour hard to reconcile with an impartial outlook upon the facts of experience. The metaphysics of lip-service to physics, including laryngeal ministrations, may consistently with itself prove to be neither physics nor philosophy, but mere *talk*.

Descartes and Santayana have tried to see how much of common sense they can doubt and yet have anything left. I have been trying for years to see how much of common sense one can *keep* and yet have anything scientific. As yet I have found no conclusive evidence that the space and time found in my experience are not the space and time of physical objects; of course not *all* of the latter, but at least parts of the latter. Whether any of the sensible qualities found in my experience can be regarded as belonging to physical objects is a question that I will touch upon later.

In saying that the space and the time in which I see things are actually and identically the space and the time in which physical objects have their being, I do not mean to prejudge the question of relativity in physics. Even if the relativist's conception of space-time be accepted, still the space and time of the system to which my *body* belongs are physical, and it is that space and that time that, I believe, can be shown to be the space and time of my *experience*; or rather they cannot be shown not to be. Even if one goes so far as Mr. Eddington in suggesting that "space and time are only approximate conceptions, which must ultimately give way to a more general conception of the ordering of events in nature not expressible in terms of a fourfold coordinate-system," [1] one need not despair of common sense. Four-dimensional space-time does not necessarily annul the difference between space and time; space and time each may keep within the higher unity its indelible character, and each is an order-system, even though each is an element in a more comprehensive order-system. If mathematical physics should ultimately find that space-time belongs to a more general ordering of nature, there is no reason to suppose that it will lose its character in the larger order. Just as the spatial character of a parabola is not lost when expressed in an equation with time as parameter, so if ultimately we shall find it necessary to express space-time in equations with an as yet unknown parameter, it is gratuitous to fear that the spatial and temporal character of space and time will be lost by reason of such equations. Mathematics mistakes its scientific function if it supposes that its equations undo the facts of the experimentalist; correlation is not annihilation.

As a preliminary to showing that the space and time of sensible experience can be identified with the space and time of physics, it is necessary to call attention to a classification of relations which has quite often been ignored. Relations may be *direct* or *indirect*. An example of a direct relation is similarity; an example of an indirect relation is brotherhood. When we say that A and B are similar, we do not *imply* any other relation in which A and B stand. When we say that A and B are brothers, we *do imply* that they stand in another relation, the relation of sonship

[1] *The Mathematical Theory of Relativity*, p. 225.

to shared parents, C and D. Only by reason of their common sonship to C and D are they brothers. Let us call any relational complex in which the terms are indirectly related an "indirect complex." Let us call the implied term or terms of the relation implied by an indirect complex the "condition" of the complex. Thus the condition of an indirect complex is not a member or term of *that* complex: the parents of A and B are not members of the complex "brothers"; they are members of the more comprehensive complex "family," of which the members of the indirect complex are members. The relationship of father-mother to son or daughter is by our definition the only *direct* relation found in a consanguine family.

Let us now take the indirect complex, "second cousins at common law." They are great-grandchildren of common great-grandparents. The latter are the "condition" of the relation of second-cousinship. In general, great-grandparents are not alive when their great-grandchildren are born. In such a case, the great-grandparents do not become great-grandparents until after they are dead, thus reminding one of Solon's happy man. The cousins before they are born do not have great-grandparents, and after they are born it would seem as if, by a logic often employed, they were too late to *have* them. What I mean can be illustrated by the possible answers to the question, "Have you a wife?" "Yes" means "I have a wife and she is *living*." "No" may mean "I haven't and never had one," or it may mean "I had one but she is dead" (or probably divorced). In these cases the present tense "I have" implies that the wife is living and is a wife at the time of the answer. On the other hand, ask a man how many great-great-grandfathers he has, and ten to one, if he likes to calculate, he will begin to count up without noticing the tense of the verb in your question. When it comes to accurate expression, tenses are difficult and treacherous; there are too few of them for precision, and what there are of them must often serve purposes for which they were not intended, with the result that a grammatical philosopher is misled or becomes sophistical.

The difficulty found by so many philosophers in my *seeing*

now what *now no longer exists* is, I think, exactly the same difficulty a man grammatically meticulous has in deciding whether he *has* any great-grandfathers. I postulate that a physical field of vision is an indirect complex whose condition is an organism with an optical nervous system normally functioning and whose terms are material surfaces. The surfaces of physical objects (or events if you prefer) from which light arrives at the same time at the normally functioning eyes of an organism form a collection indirectly related by virtue of their relation to the organism. Vision is the relation in which the organism stands to the indirect complex just described. Vision is not an *act* of the organism or of a mind; it is the converse of the relation in which the objects just identified stand to the organism. If vision were an *act* of the organism, it would indeed be difficult to understand how an organism could see *now* what antedates the seeing. But if vision is the relation in which an organism stands to what initiated (or reflected) the light that on arriving at the eyes of the organism sets up changes in it, it is difficult to understand how vision could fail to be later than the objects (or events) which initiated the light. Just as great-grandparents do not become great-grandparents until a great-grandchild is born to them, so physical objects do not become a field of vision until light from them has stimulated an organism through its eyes. Upon the arrival of light from objects, the organism has vision in relation to these objects, just as a child in being born is born having great-grandparents, not having had them before.[1] When I say "I see physical objects," the verb "see" does not name any act I perform on the objects that I say I see, any more than my having a great-grandfather is an act I perform toward him. I see, in having a

---

[1] The analogy fails in a point not relevant to our argument: my ancestors were instrumental in bringing me into the world; the objects that eventually have succeeded in stimulating my organism through my eyes did not play any such part, exceptional cases excepted. To see that all this is irrelevant, consider the case of a man who marries an orphan, thereby making two deceased persons his parents-in-law. By his act a posthumous relation comes to obtain between them, the relation of being *in common* parents-in-law. Here there is no question of an existential dependence on either side.

physical field of vision; I don't have it *because* I see. In other words, "to see physical objects" means exactly the same thing as "to have a physical field of vision."

To make this point clearer, let us take the case of a camera in act of photographing objects. Something is doing in the plate of the camera, something consisting in photo-chemical processes. Now the field of the camera may be defined as all the surfaces of physical objects, light from which eventually sets these photo-chemical processes afoot. If the camera be an astronomer's camera photographing a star-cluster, the objects in the field long antedated the processes they now have set going; and those objects did not all at the same time send out the light whose arrival at the same time as the camera makes the changes in the plate which we call photographing the stars. If it be objected that the field of the camera does not consist of the *stars* of long ago that sent out this light, but of the *light now arriving* from those stars, I reply that this is a matter of definition merely. If you wish to reserve the term "field of the camera" for the *light* arriving at the plate, this does not annul the fact that the dynamic relation starting from the stars and ending at the plate divides the objects of the physical universe into two classes, one consisting of the objects in this relation and the other consisting of all other objects. The camera stands to the former objects in a relation converse to that in which they stand to it; and in standing to those objects in that converse relation it has in them a *natural* group of correlata all of which long antedated its having them, and all of which presumably had various physical time-relations to each other. The time and place of its having these correlata are the time and place of the chemical changes occurring in it. The times and places of the correlata it has are not the time and place of the chemical changes it undergoes; each of the correlata had its own time and place.

Now in the theory I propose as to the physical field of vision, the objects "seen" are analogous to the objects photographed. "Seeing" is analogous to the relation in which the camera while photographing its objects stands to the objects it photographs.

In seeing an object, I do nothing to it; it has succeeded in doing
something to me. When I see, I am indeed doing, but this doing
is not my seeing. The analogy fails *linguistically*, only in that the
verb "to photograph" does not, except by implication, express
the relation in which the camera stands to the stars while it is
photographing them; it expresses the changes taking place in
the plate which will later result in a developed negative, whereas
the verb "to see" does express the relation in which my organism
stands to the stars, and does not express but merely implies
what is taking place in my organism.

If it be objected that we sometimes have vision of only one
object, and that therefore we may not properly define the
physical field of vision as the class of objects from which light
arrives at the eyes and starts physiological processes, I am
willing for the sake of argument to concede the point. I should
then define a vision of that object as the relation of an organism
to that *one* object, a relation which is the converse of the relation
in which that object stands to the organism in having started
processes which finally result in stimulating the organism.

Now a logical definition of a thing is not that thing itself.
So our proposed definition of vision is not vision itself. It is
possible to define many classes which as classes are artificial.
Thus I can classify all the events in the universe into two groups,
one consisting of all the events that occurred within the twenty-
nine minutes that began forty-seven hours and thirteen seconds
after the birth of any of Julius Caesar's ancestors, the events
having occurred at a distance from the relevant birthplace of
not less than two thousand three hundred fifty-three miles,
and of not more than fifty-two thousand three hundred
eighteen miles and eleven inches. There is *logically* such a class
of occurrences, which of course would have to be defined more
precisely if we accept the theory of relativity. But such a classification is wantonly capricious and so far as we know does not
correspond to any natural, i.e. dynamic, grouping in nature.
On the other hand, the class consisting of all the ancestors of
any person is a natural class, corresponding conversely to a
certain dynamic cleavage in nature, i.e. converging lines in the

"advance of nature" give rise to a grouping of points of departure *retrospectively* considered. So also it is with the class of surfaces of physical objects that have sent out light that reaches the eyes of an organism at any time.

But this is not the whole story of the naturalness of the latter class. So far as we have gone, the only difference between the physical field of vision and the field of a camera, as we have defined them, is found in the difference between a camera and an organism with eyes. Is this the only difference? *No!* In the case of the indirect complex whose condition is an organism with eyes, the group, in addition to being a natural class considered retrospectively, is a natural group from which all *consideration* of anything takes its departure. In fact, there would be no science of physics and no logical classification were there not in nature such a natural group. Whatever else the physicist is, he is an organism which under proper conditions has a physical field of vision as an integral natural group, and he begins his studies by starting from what is in that field of vision and in other fields similar in character. In other words, such sense-fields are the natural premises of all knowledge, and whatever later passes for knowledge may not contradict these premises. No other groupings which he later comes to recognize as natural may involve the denial of the epistemologically more fundamental natural character of such groups. Groups of this latter sort are first in the order of knowing even though they are late in the order of being: they are the most "primitive" and most natural groups we know. We do not discover them by logical construction; we start from them as the aboriginally given. Later we discover by logical construction how to classify them. Nature has been kind to us in sparing us the futile labour of making a physical universe out of whole cloth. To adopt and adapt a splendid personification from Mr. Santayana (*Scepticism and Animal Faith*, p. 191), Nature says to Knowledge: "My child, there is a great world for thee to conquer, but it is a vast, an ancient, and a recalcitrant world. It yields a wonderful treasure to courage when courage is guided by art and respects the limits I have set to it. I should not have been so cruel as to give thee birth if there had been nothing for thee to master, nor so fatuous as to think thy task could be accomplished by one who had no foothold in the world to be won. In giving thee senses I give and will continue to give thee parts of that world, as vantage ground from which thou art to advance to thy conquest."

A concept which has become familiar to all readers in the literature of relativity will aid us in formulating our theory, whether or not we accept the theory of relativity as valid. In this theory a spatio-temporal "interval" between any two events has zero-value if it is such that the same ray of light can be present at both events. Thus the event of the departure of a light-ray from the sun and the event of its arrival on the earth have a zero-interval between them, i.e. no interval at all. For relativity this interval is physically more fundamental than the time-lapse of eight minutes or the distance of ninety odd millions of miles separating the two events. Speaking relativistically, we may say that nature in our physical fields of vision includes surfaces which are separated by zero-interval; and the primitive unity of such fields is a unity that does not have to be undone when in physics we come to separate the events into time and space. Nature does not distort herself in giving us all these objects *at once in space-time*; it is we who are responsible for any mistake when later we come to the conclusion that what is thus given is all *at once in physical time*. The philosopher may find the greatest value of relativity in its insistence on the fact that the concept of physical simultaneity is a logical construction which comes about as a result of our operations of measurement of velocities. Physical simultaneity is a matter of definition; it is not a "datum" given aboriginally in experience. Any classification of events as physically simultaneous, if it is to have relevance to observation and experiment, may not make null and void the relation of spatio-temporal "at-onceness" in which events stand as they are given in the field of vision of the observer.

Now in the physical field of vision the events which are at "zero-interval" from the conditioning organism have the relation that

I shall name "visual simultaneity." When I see a star through the branches of a tree, the star and the branches are visually simultaneous, although in physical time they are separated by hundreds of years. There is no contradiction in this statement; those who find such contradiction either regard the seeing as a present *act* which has the star of *long ago* as its *present* object; else they fail to see that physical simultaneity is a matter of definition. Once recognize that the verb "to see" belongs to the class represented by the verb "to relate" rather than to the class represented by the verb "to strike," and the difficulty of the first group of puzzled thinkers disappears. Similarity and posteriority can relate a man to his great-grandfather; in thus relating them they do not do something to the *past now*. What similarity and posteriority can be in the way of relations, there is no logical reason why vision cannot be. It relates an organism to what has physically preceded it. When this relation occurs, the organism is said to "see" the physical objects to which it is thus related. As against those who fail to see that *physical* simultaneity is a matter of definition, perhaps nothing argumentatively effective can be said. They have a self-evidencing intuition that is proof against dispute.

A more mathematical way of stating what we have just said is to assert that what is called physical simultaneity is simultaneity treated mathematically, i.e. an event at any place is given a time-coordinate equal to the coordinates given to certain other events in other places. What I call visual simultaneity can be treated mathematically by a distribution of equal coordinates to a different set of events, the two distributions, however, retaining the same order of temporal sequence. The difference is analogous to the reference of points in a plane to two different frames of reference, one rectangular and the other oblique, both of them having their X-axes and their origins respectively coincident. Except for points on the X-axis, the abscissa of any point referred to one frame is different from that of the same point referred to the other frame; but the difference of reference does not disarrange the serial order of points in the X-direction. Even so the difference between physical time and visual time treated mathematically is a difference as to the events which at different places shall have the same time-coordinates as the events at the origin; it is not a difference as to the temporal order of the events. It is the same time-order that is visual and physical; but the same time referred to different temporal planes of simultaneity. By a plane of simultaneity is meant all the events at different places which are regarded as having equal time-coordinates. Any plane of simultaneity is logically as good as any other. The two planes of simultaneity, the one physical, the other visual, intersect at the physiological events that condition the physical field of vision. Just what these events are, it is not necessary nor is it as yet possible to state in detail. All that we need do is to say that somewhere along the line of physiological changes, beginning with the stimulation of the eyes and ending with muscular response, the planes of simultaneity of visual time and of physical time intersect.

Before going farther it may be of help to contrast our theory with some others now held. Behaviourists make vision consist in the muscular processes which take place in the organism; our theory recognizes these processes and also their relevance to vision; but it denies that the relevance is an identity. The processes are one thing, the vision another. Without the processes, no vision; but the vision is not the processes. The American critical realists (in general), together with the happily non-American Mr. Broad, distinguish, indeed, between vision and the physiological processes that condition it: for them what is in the field of vision stands in spatial and temporal relations, but the space and time in vision are *not* the space and time of physics; the world of each organism's visual experience is a world of its own, both as regards qualities and seen relations. Mr. Russell takes such a world with all its qualities and seen relations and puts the whole thing in the physical space of the brain of the organism concerned. The view I have been presenting of the physical field of vision is more closely allied to that of the new realist than to any of the others. For instance, Mr. Holt (*The Concept of Consciousness*, p. 182) says: "We have

seen that the phenomenon of *response* defines a cross-section of
the environment without, which is a neutral manifold. Now this
neutral cross-section outside of the nervous system, and composed of the neutral elements of physical and non-physical
objects to which the nervous system is responding, by some
specific response—this neutral cross-section, I submit, coincides
exactly with the list of objects of which we say that we are
conscious." Leave out reference to "non-physical objects" and
"the neutral manifold," and restrict the statement to the time
and space relations of the physical objects which initiate physical
processes that finally stimulate the organism through its end-
organs to response, and the statement would express our view
quite correctly. But when Mr. Holt goes on to say: "This neutral
cross-section . . . is consciousness," I fail to follow. I should
rather say that the consciousness in vision, for example, *is* the
vision, which, as we have repeatedly observed, is the relation in
which the organism stands to the objects in the cross-section
defined. This, however, may be a mere difference in terminology.

Before taking up the question of the qualities found in the
physical visual field, we must consider some other problems.
The physical field of vision is, of course, not our only sense-field.
Physical objects stimulate the human organism through many
sense-organs. When this occurs there is a physical field of sense-
objects including all the objects that have initiated the stimula-
tions. However it may be in infants, whose sense-fields I cannot
investigate, my adult sense-field is *unitary*. To call a physical
object in such a complex field a *seen* object and another a *heard*
object is to imply a belief that the former is in the field because
of my eyes, the latter because of my ears. *But the heard objects
are in the same space and the same time with the seen objects.* If
it is argued that this is the result of laboriously acquired co-
ordinations in infancy, the statement may be true; for the sake
of argument let us grant that it is true. From such a concession
it does not necessarily follow that the space of sight and the
space of hearing are originally different spaces. I suppose that
infants, as well as grown people, who go to sleep in a *seen* familiar
room and wake up in a *seen* unfamiliar one have to do a good

deal of coordinating to get the two *seen* spaces connected into one visual space; and if preliminary coordinating is proof of lack of original identity of the spaces ultimately coordinated, an infant begins life with a good many more spaces than he has sense-organs. Not finding it necessary to have quite so many different spaces and times, I agree with Mr. Russell when he says: "The direct logical importance of investigations into the origins of our mental processes is *nil*." [1] And on that account I find of no logical value practically all the chapter toward the end of which this sentence occurs. Much of this chapter is devoted to the thesis: "In physics there is only one space, while in psychology there are several for each individual"; the thesis is established by appeal to the fact that infants have to coordinate the originally different spaces of each sense-field. Mr. Russell admits that "an immense theoretical reconstruction was required" before the theory of relativity was achieved; and yet he himself accepts the objectively unitary character of the space-time of relativity. What was this theoretical reconstruction but a stupendous coordination. Coordination may result in the *discovery* of unity as well as in the *production* of unity.

When we take into consideration not merely the physical field of vision but any integral physical field of sense, say of vision and of audition, we have a sensible simultaneity of objects, as in the case of hearing the whistle of a not too distant locomotive while still seeing the steam coming from the whistle. In such a case the whistle heard is physically prior to the steam seen. This example shows that according to our theory the relativist's zero-interval cannot be identified with all sensible simultaneity. This is because the relativist deals almost exclusively with what Mr. Russell calls "sight-physics." [2] The correlation of sensible simultaneity with physical simultaneity requires consideration of the varying velocities of propagation from physical objects to the sense-organs of an organism.

But not all objects in a sense-field are sensibly simultaneous.

[1] *The Analysis of Matter*, p. 154. The next two quotations made above are from pages 144 and 195.
[2] *Op. cit.* pp. 160 ff.

Some are there as prior to others, even though some are there as simultaneous with others. The time therein is a stretch of time and not a durationless instant. The sensible stretch of time is what William James signalized as the "sensible present." [1] Unfortunately his description of it contained an inaccuracy which, I cannot but think, proved fatal in that it has led to many mistakes in recent philosophies. The passage in which this mistake occurred is so famous that full quotation is unnecessary. I will quote only one sentence, trusting to the reader to supply the context from memory. Speaking of this sensible present, James says: "We do not *first* feel one end and *then* feel the other *after* it." (I have italicized the words which seem to me to be mistaken.) It is generally just the other way around: we *do* first feel one end and then feel the other after it. For instance, in looking at an electric sign in which the bulbs are successively illuminated I see first one point of light and then another, and then another; while *still* seeing the first I come to see the second; while still seeing these two I come to see the third. The experience is *not* "a synthetic datum from the outset" in the sense that what I see when I see the third is exactly what I saw when first I saw the first. The seeing of all three *becomes* a synthetic datum when the third sign is seen as illuminated. The confusion perhaps arises from the fact that most specious presents follow upon other specious presents, each, when it is, being a synthetic datum.

An analogy will make my point clear. Take a short tube, open at both ends, and pass it lengthwise through water. At any time there will be water in the tube, but some of the water will be just passing into it, and some just passing out of it, while between the two ends there will be water all of which is unambiguously within the tube. But of this water that toward the forward end *entered* the tube after that toward the rearward end; but after it has entered, it is in the tube together with the rest that is in the tube. The water in the forward end is analogous to what is later in any specious present; that in the rear end is analogous to what is earlier in the specious present; all the

[1] *The Principles of Psychology*, I, 608 ff.

water in the tube at any time is analogous to the whole of the specious present at any time; the water lying in any perpendicular cross-section is analogous to what is sensibly simultaneous in the specious present. The priority of any object *in* a specious present with reference to any other object therein is due to its *earlier entrance into the field*. In general the specious present does not come by jumps, each replacing its predecessor *in toto*. There is continuity of sequence. This continuity is just the fact that there is at any time a hold-over to greet a new-comer. It is not continuity as defined by the mathematician. Royce and Santayana, each in his own way, has allowed himself to be misled by James on this point; thus the former got the *totum simul* of the Absolute Experience, and the latter the "speciousness" of the specious present and the changelessness of change.

This character of sensible continuity, with sensible priority, sensible simultaneity and sensible posteriority in the continuity, is doubtless due to the fact that the physiological processes that are the condition of the field have what is called an akoluthic character. They are not physically instantaneous, but have a duration in which they wax and wane. While these processes continue, the physical objects that through intermediaries initiated the processes remain in the field. Here, then, we have an important difference between sensible time and physical time, in addition to the difference we have already noted between physical and sensible simultaneity. The measured physical duration of the physical object may not be equal to its sensible duration. A light-flash that occupies at its source an infinitesimal fraction of a physical second may occupy a second in sensible time. Does this difference force us to say that the two times cannot be identical? Not unless we say that the time in which a dead man remains a father-in-law is not the same time as that in which he lived.[1]

Let us now consider the relation between physical space and

[1] A deceased father of a woman remains the father-in-law of her husband so long as she remains the latter's wife. The father-in-law may have died at the age of twenty-two, and may later *remain* a father-in-law for fifty years.

the space of a sensible field. The classic objection to a realistic theory of sensible space is based on the differences in shape and size a penny has as seen from different points. It is assumed by objectors that a physical penny in physical space is only circular; but the seen penny is rarely (if ever) circular; the conclusion is that the seen space of the penny is not the physical space of the penny. Mr. Broad [1] has stated this objection as forcibly as any one. He distinguishes between the "sensible form" of the penny, which is, of course, a variable, and the "geometrical property" which is exclusively circular, and which is an "intrinsic" property of the penny. The latter can be defined, the former can be identified only by exemplification. Now presumably a definition for Mr. Broad ties down what is defined to *exclusive* conformity with the definition. That the circularity of a penny is a geometrical property of it I do not deny. I cannot, however, concede the claim that it is an *intrinsic* property, if by that is meant a property the penny has without regard to relations in which it stands to other things, or a property it has in all relations to other things. The classical definition of circularity is most obviously a relational definition; the definition tells what a circle is *in terms of measurement by a rigid measuring-rod*, applied in the plane of the circle; Euclidean equality of distance has no meaning except in terms of measurement. The property thus turns out to be *extrinsic* with a vengeance. This is not to deny that the circle has the property Mr. Broad's definition gives it; it does have that property, but it has it only in a certain reference. Apart from that reference, the property is meaningless. Euclid's geometry was largely metrical; but there is a Euclidean projective geometry. The projection of a circle upon another plane is as much a geometrical property of a circle as its metrical properties within its own plane; and its projection on such planes is as much a *physical* property of a physical circle as its "circularity," as the amount of light reflected from a penny in different directions proves. Try it on the camera. As has been often pointed out, the shape of an object is the shape it has where it is, but it is not that shape just by itself without

[1] *The Mind and its Place in Nature*, pp. 170 ff.

reference to anything else; it has, where it is, different shapes from different places. What, for instance, is the "intrinsic" shape of a man's face? The shape it has in profile or *vis-à-vis*? Is a tube round or straight? These and many other similar questions lead one to be very suspicious of "intrinsic" geometrical properties. An "intrinsic" property is intrinsic only when one is so familiar with a standard reference that one uses it absent-mindedly.

What is true of shape is also true of size. Is the sun large or small as compared with the moon? In terms of linear measurement it is vastly larger; in terms of angular measurement made from some spot on the earth as the apex of the angle, it is about the same size. So it is with sizes in general. A man at any distance from you is *physically*, from where you are, twice as small in any dimension as he is when at half that distance. Again, try it on the camera. Our usual method of measurement of familiar objects is by superposition of a measuring-rod; but this is only one way of measuring; and the size got by any measurement is always relative to the way in which the measurement is made.[1]

What has been said in the last two paragraphs is not equivalent to the assertion that a thing has no properties. So far is it from having no properties, that it has many more than any standard description recognizes. It *has* all the properties that *in any relation* it has, but it has each only in the relevant relation. The contention that properties are relative is not the contention that properties are relations, as Thomas Hill Green apparently supposed. Just as a man is a father in one relation and a son in another, without being the relation of fatherhood or of sonship, so an object is big in one relation and small in another without being the relation of bigness or smallness. So much is anything what it is only in relation to other things, that I find it difficult to believe that any one thing *just by itself* could be even that one thing.

It has been urged against the view which identifies physical and sensible space, that when light comes to our eyes through a refracting medium the object is not, in the space of the field

[1] See Bridgman's *The Logic of Modern Physics*, especially pp. 66 ff,

of sense, where it is in physical space; hence the two spaces are not one space. Here we have in another form the same problem. A physical object as a source of light arriving at another physical object is for the latter something that electromagnetically was in the direction from which the light came. In other words, direction in physical space is not just one simple thing. We have accustomed ourselves to a standardized description of physical space conceived on Euclidean principles, and when we find that our description does not fit the facts, we say that the facts are not in physical space. The sensible brokenness of a "straight" stick in water is a case in point. The "new realists" have not wearied of pointing out that in the optical space of the camera the stick is just as much broken as it is in sensible space. Physical space is not a rigid container of physical objects. It is a system of relations, and what holds of physical objects in one of these relations does not necessarily hold of them in some other of these relations. There is no reason for believing that the visual space of physical objects for human beings differs from the optical space of the same physical objects for cameras placed where the human beings are.

We are now ready to take up the question of the seen qualities of physical objects. Is the seen redness of a physical object, for instance, a quality that belongs to the physical object when it is not in a field of vision? Most of the arguments used to prove that it does not so belong are based on the theory that a physical object, if it has any colour at all, can have only one colour at any one spot on it at any one time. That theory is a huge assumption. Colour is a relative quality; it is relative to the kind of light that is emitted or reflected from the coloured object. A "red" object is not red in the dark, nor in a room lighted only from without, whose windows absorb or reflect all the red rays. The same spot of a "red" object may be red from one direction and not from another according to the kind of light it reflects in the two directions. The experience of a jaundiced person proves nothing, since the crystalline lens of such a person may have become temporarily impervious to most of the light-rays. If redness is a physical quality, the red object is red where it is, but that is not the whole story; it is red where it is *from other places*, as Mr. Russell urges in another connection. The only facts that give me pause when I am inclined to assume that redness is a physical quality that an object would have from the place where an eye is even if the eye were replaced by some photo-sensitive object, are the facts of colour-blindness. If we only knew enough of the physiology of colour-blindness, we could in all probability resolve the question. But I understand that no theory of colour-blindness is adequate; meanwhile, is it not wiser to let the question remain unsettled than to settle it dogmatically?

If it be said, as it often is, that the physicist has proved that physically no object has colour, I should reply with the question: "When and how did he prove it?" In his mathematical treatment of the physical world he *ignores* qualitative redness and replaces it with frequencies of wave-length, *after he has got started* on his mathematical equations. If this be proof, then a surveyor, in ignoring the fertility of the soil or the mineral deposits underneath, proves that there are no such things, when his problem is only to find the boundaries and the area of a plot of ground. What the physicist is justified in ignoring in the physical world is not necessarily non-physical unless we adopt Mr. Russell's convenient definition of a physical object as what physics is concerned with. In this sense X-rays and many other things became physical objects only a short time ago; and so far as we know colours may some of these days become physical qualities.

I am content to leave the problem unsolved for the reason that, unlike the new realists, I do not think that we can successfully maintain that everything appearing in a field of vision is physical. It perhaps will have been observed that heretofore I have spoken of "physical fields of vision." This unusual turn of expression was purposively adopted in view of the fact that there are other fields of vision, as for instance in dreams and in delirium. While I believe that there is every reason to suppose that in normal waking experience the surfaces of physical objects are bodily in the field of vision, there is also every reason to

suppose that they are not always the only things in the field.
Visual images are frequently there. I am credibly informed that
in some fields of vision with an alcoholic organism as condition
there are snakes (or is it *rats*?) as well as physical pyjamas and
doctors and nurses, whereas from the fields whose conditions
are the organisms called doctors and nurses the snakes are
absent, but the pyjamas are present therein. From personal
experience I can testify that just now there is in my field of
vision a something (much like an old friend of mine) sitting in
a chair, and I am sure it would not appear in a field of a camera
placed anywhere in the room, although the chair could be made
to appear in it. Such a thing I call a visual image.

In such cases I find that the seen spatial and temporal relations between the image and physical things are just the kind
of relations that obtain between physical things and physical
things. I therefore say that images are in the same visual space
and time as physical objects. Why should I not? They are not
physical objects, but that is no reason why they should not be
where they are seen to be; in fact, it is a reason why they can
be there. In general, dealing macroscopically, we say that no
two physical objects are in the same place at the same time.
This is an empirically ascertained fact, not an *a priori* necessity.
But the very same empirical basis that justifies me in saying
that we cannot put a physical chair where a physical table is
without displacing the latter, justifies me in saying that an
image can be where a physical object is without displacing the
latter. Shakespeare was true to the kind of life Macbeth was
leading, when in Macbeth's field of vision he put Banquo's
ghost, shaking his gory locks at him, in the physical "place
reserved" for the living general. The difference between physical
things and images is not that they are in different spaces, but
that they behave differently in the same space. A physical
object is to be defined in terms of other relations than the
merely spatial and temporal ones. These other relations are
dynamical. This is the reason why we say that Banquo's ghost
was not physical. If it had been physical, it would have reflected
light and thus got into the field of vision of anyone whose

normally functioning eyes were directed toward the place
reserved. The question often asked of a holder of my theory,
"Why, if your image is where you say it is, do I not see it when
I look there?" is very simply and consistently answered by
saying that the reason is to be found in the fact that my image
is not a physical object and therefore does not send light to
your eyes. For the same reason my visual images cannot be
photographed and my auditory images cannot be phonographed.
The fact that they cannot be recorded by physical instruments
proves that they are not physical; it does not prove that they
are not where I see them. I cannot see any reason why the
space-time which physical objects inhabit may not have as
temporary denizens at seen places all the images that all the
gentle reveries and wild ravings of men (and of animals if
necessary) have found in it. "There may be more things in
heaven and earth, Horatio, than are dreamt of in your philosophy." The recognition of them as there does no harm if they
are recognized for what they are, such stuff as dreams are made
of. They are where they are *as the result* of physiological processes.
With regard to them it would seem as if an epiphenomenalistic
interpretation would hold. There is no physical reason why an
alcoholized physiological organism may not give rise to such
physically ineffective and therefore non-physical things as
hallucinated snakes or rats which, when they are, are where
they are seen to be.

But where did the dream-objects of last night find their place
in the space in which physical objects are? I don't know; but
if the unconscious victim of an accident is taken to an unfamiliar
hospital, can he say, when he comes to, where in physical space
he is? Is his inability to say a proof that he is not somewhere
in physical space? I rather suspect that the objects of a dream
are in the space neighbouring the dreamer's body; but there
are sometimes not enough data to make a good map of the
locality. An adequate account of the whole matter, including
the question as to the whereabouts of Shakespeare's Coast of
Bohemia, would take more space than we have left. We may
conclude our discussion of this topic by saying that while there

are many problems requiring more detailed treatment, a sense-field in general includes physical objects and objects not physical, all in the same space and time, and *none of them*, in general, *in the brain* of the organism which is the condition of the field. The latter are in the brain only by metonymy; what *is* in the brain is only the physiological condition of their being in the sense-field. They are "functions" of the nervous system, not in the sense that they are nervous processes, but in the sense that they depend on the nervous system for their being, and that they change with changes in the nervous system. They are not "functions" in the sense of being acts that the nervous system performs. The ambiguity of the word "function" has led to many mistakes.

Images are not the only transients in space-time which thus depend on the physiological organism. It is not necessary to list such "functions"; we may name a few. Desires and emotions belong to this class. Specific processes take place in an organism when it desires and when it has emotions; but these physical (physiological) processes are not the only "desires" or "emotions." Physiological hunger is different from hunger as it appears in the field of sense. Theoretically a physiologist with appropriate instruments could discover the former; only the organism itself discovers the latter. In this case certain nerves are stimulated by the processes taking place in the intestines as the result of lack of food, and at some time in the course of the nervous excitation thus arising the quality known as hunger appears in the sense-field. The hunger that I sense no one else can have in his field of sense; he may see my grimaces and my writhings; he may by proper devices discover glandular secretions. But none of these things nor all of them added together are the hunger as it is in my sense-field. There is no profit in discussing the question which of these things is *the* "hunger." That question is merely a lexicographical question; and lexicographically either the outwardly observable facts or the inwardly sensed fact is "hunger." The point is that the proposed reservation of the word "hunger" for what is outwardly observable, if adopted, does not abolish the quality of hunger as it is in the sense-field

of the organism whose physiological processes and secretions can
be detected by another.

Unfortunately it is not possible in this paper to deal with
perceptual fields as distinct from sense-fields, nor with thinking.
The rest of this paper, according to the specifications of the
editors, must deal with autobiographical details, stressing the
influences which, so far as I know, have been most powerful in
determining my philosophical thought. My first impulse toward
philosophy was a reaction against theology, in which I had been
schooled. Foremost among the positive influences I take pleasure
in naming the association I had with Professor G. H. Howison.
I have strayed far from the Kantian school in which in his day
he was a dominating personality; but, as Nietzsche said, one ill
requiteth a master if one remain merely a pupil. I owe to Professor
Howison my first living interest in philosophy, and also my
acquaintance with Hegel which has proved most useful. Anyone
who has studied Hegel sympathetically and thoroughly may
violently revolt against his system; but rebels often carry away
much that is positive from that against which they rebel. It
would be a hopeless task to name the philosophers of the past
to whom I owe much. For the last twenty-five or thirty years
the debts of which I am most conscious are to my colleagues
like Creighton and to my other contemporaries; those to whom
I owe most are those with whom I do not find myself in greatest
agreement. I had already begun to work toward a realistic
philosophy before I became acquainted with the collaborated
volume *The New Realism*, but the writings of the members of
this group and a paper by Woodbridge helped me very greatly
in my subsequent thinking. Perhaps it was William James,
whom I met in 1897 when he delivered in Berkeley, California,
his famous address, "Philosophical Conceptions and Practical
Results," who first of all set me to questioning the satisfactoriness
of idealism; at any rate I should name him as the most influential
factor in giving direction to my thinking for the next decade
and perhaps ever since. Naturally, John Dewey came next in
the order of time as well as in the order of power. The persistent
criticism with which I have confronted these two men in my

private thinking is the best proof of the influence they have
had on me. To pass by the name of Bergson would be to do
him a serious injustice without his knowing or caring. Einstein
and the relativists, Whitehead and Russell, have been the latest
influences. My greatest regret in my present philosophical work
is that I have not had an adequate training in the higher mathematics and in mathematical physics. If I mistake not, the metaphysics of the next generation, as that of the seventeenth century,
will be in the hands of those who have command of a knowledge
of mathematical physics.

In naming my creditors I should be ungrateful if I were to
omit mention of my former and present pupils from whom I
have learned more than they have learned from me. When
"blue books" come in, and I am tempted to assent to the
cynicism of the professor who said that a university would be a
glorious place to work in were it not for the students, I have
only to look back upon my former pupils to see that it is the
living contact with young minds that perhaps alone can keep
an older mind from growing hopelessly senile.

PRINCIPAL PUBLICATIONS

"Presupposition Question in Hegel's Logic," *Philosophical Review*,
vol. vi, 1897.
"The Dialectical Method," *Mind*, n.s., vol. vii, 1898.
"Altruism in Hume's Treatise," *Philosophical Review*, vol. xii, 1903.
"Realism and the Physiological Argument," and two other articles
on Realism, *Journal of Philosophy*, vol. iv, 1907.
"The Fringe in James's Psychology the Basis of Logic," *Philo-
sophical Review*, vol. xx, 1911.
"Relation of Consciousness and Object in Sense-Perception,"
Philosophical Review, vol. xxi, 1912.
"Time and the Experience of Time," *Philosophical Review*, vol. xxiii,
1914.
"Warfare of Moral Ideals," *Hibbert Journal*, vol. xiv, 1915-16.
"Times, New and Old," *University of California Publications in
Philosophy*, vol. vi, No. 4, 1928.

CONFESSIONS OF AN ANIMISTIC MATERIALIST

By WM. PEPPERELL MONTAGUE

Born 1873; Professor of Philosophy, Barnard College, Columbia University, New York.

CONFESSIONS OF AN ANIMISTIC MATERIALIST

THE first question of a philosophic kind that I can remember considering concerned the nature of the soul and its relation to the body. Having been informed by my mother that the soul was that which made you laugh and cry and think and move, I asked if you could get it out by boring very carefully up through the foot and leg until you reached it somewhere in the chest. To this question my mother was giving a hesitant and somewhat puzzled negative, when my father broke in impatiently with the warning that I must never think of the soul in that way, that it was not at all the kind of thing that had a place inside the body from which it could be fished out.

I mention this little incident of early childhood because the question I asked then is the kind of question I have been asking ever since, and the reproof for it administered by my father is the same reproof that I have received many times from my teachers and colleagues in philosophy.

I feel myself to be a thing in a world of things. And the thing that I am does not seem to me to be the thing that my body is. The two are alike in being substantive rather than adjectival. They are alike also in being agents and patients in space and time, but they are contrasted with respect to the laws and processes pertaining to them. The intimate union in existence of these entities so disparate in essence has become to me ever more mysterious. All my thinking has been oriented with regard to the psycho-physical problem. And blessed or cursed by this "animistic complex," and goaded on by it, I have sought continuously for an intellectual theory that will bridge a dualism imposed upon me by feeling or intuition and increasingly confirmed by the evidences of experience.

Next to the metaphysical question of mind and body there came, and continued, the religious problem. Church services in the early morning with my mother gave me a poignant sense of the beauty of the Christian doctrine. Sunday-school and the atmosphere of a small New England community gave me an equally poignant sense of the falsity and incredible ugliness of the authoritarian and ascetic aspects of that same doctrine. Cool, condescending approval or an equally cool and tolerant contempt, which are the usual alternative attitudes toward Christianity that are prescribed by the "genteel tradition" in American philosophy, have never done justice to its baffling mixture of what is best with what is worst. Love and enthusiasm for one half of the Church, righteous hate and contempt for the other, are sternly called for.

Somewhere between twelve and fifteen I read Bellamy's *Looking Backward*, Abbott's *Flatland*, and articles on theosophy by Blavatsky and others. Bellamy, in addition to making me a socialist, made me realize that the business of the good life was an institutional as well as an individual affair. *Flatland* and the theosophy stimulated and made more explicit what might be called my metaphysical interests. The characteristically theosophic attempt to explain the mind and its doings in terms of material or pseudo-material categories appealed to my animistic attitude, and seemed to me then, as indeed it does now, to be the most delightful of pastimes.

It was not until the middle of my sophomore year that my formal education took on significance. I suddenly found myself suspended from college, and very miserably I made visits to my various professors to get instructions for the enforced period of home work. Josiah Royce, whose course in the History of Philosophy I had been taking with some real interest, received me kindly, and inquired what I planned to fit myself for. I replied that I didn't know, but supposed that I should have to be a lawyer. Whereupon he asked me encouragingly if I had ever thought of the academic career. I never had, and I hardly knew the meaning of the phrase, but the fact that here was a great man showing me sympathy and faith in my dark hour stirred me unforgettably. By hard, eager study I passed well the final examination in his course. It had opened a new world to me. Everything was changed, and I was happy. In my Junior and Senior years in college, and in the three years in the graduate school that followed, I gave my whole time, so far as I was allowed, to philosophy. The classes suddenly ceased to be tedious interludes between parties, and became themselves the most exciting of parties.

Everyone knows the extraordinary company who dispensed philosophy at Harvard in the late 'nineties: Palmer, James and Royce, Münsterberg and Santayana. Each of them had a distinctive philosophy, and each of them preached it with the force of conviction. Their methods of teaching were almost as different as their viewpoints. Palmer's lectures were incomparably the most finished, both as to content and to form, of all that I have ever heard; and whether because of, or in spite of, their literary perfection, their pedagogical effectiveness was extraordinary. I had the good luck to be his assistant or reader, and so had an opportunity to see the progress in philosophic comprehension made by the large group of undergraduates in his course, each of whom was required to submit four papers during the year. Quite apart from this ideal of pedagogical technique, and in addition to many specific illuminations, I owe to Palmer the realization that a naturalistic relativism, as regards the varying *content* of the good, is quite compatible with a Kantian rigorism as regards the invariant *form* of right or duty.

The classroom lectures of James were in striking contrast to those of Palmer, and, indeed, to the polish of his own formal papers. He would utter his thoughts spontaneously, just as they came. As a result his talks were most uneven in quality. The roughness and irregularity were, however, more than balanced by the simplicity and directness of his conversational manner. It was an inspiration to see and hear a great man work out his own thoughts in the presence of his students. The informal and colloquial speech coming from a scholar and a genius possessed a peculiar piquancy. I have seen him stop in the middle of a sentence with some such remark as: "By George, Mr. Smith, perhaps you were right, after all, in what you said a few minutes ago; I had never really thought of that." Mr. Smith thus honoured, would, of course, become the envy of all of us and the devoted slave of his master. Nor would he realize that James, with characteristic and unconscious generosity, had probably read into his comment a richness and meaning of which Smith himself had been quite innocent.

The parts of James's philosophy that concerned his Pragmatism and Radical Empiricism left me uninterested or actually repelled, but to the more mystical and less explicitly developed phases of his thought I owe much. His conception of the subconscious and hidden energies of men, his Transmission hypothesis, his defence of indeterminism and of a finite God, I greedily accepted. Taken in connection with the Tychism of his friend, Charles Peirce, they furnished me with a large part of my philosophic faith. For Peirce himself I had a kind of worship. While his intellect was cold and clear, his metaphysical imagination was capricious, scintillating, and unbridled, and his whole personality was so rich and mysterious that he seemed a being apart, a super-man. I would rather have been like him than like anyone else I ever met. And on the two or three occasions in which he carefully criticized and then praised some of my student writing I was transported with happiness.

It is to Santayana especially that I owe my realization of Plato's truth. I took his courses at about the same time that I read Huxley's *Evolution and Ethics* and Stevenson's *Pulvis et Umbra*. In all three the teaching was to the effect that value did not depend on existence, nor right on might, nor ethics on religion. An atheistic nature red with tooth and claw could in no sense absolve man from his obligation to actualize ideals of beauty and goodness; nor could it deprive him of the consolation of knowing that those ideals were always and eternally there, be the world what it might. The fact that I did not share the pessimism of Huxley and Santayana as to the existing world in no way lessened my debt of gratitude.

Another thing I got from Santayana's courses was support and confirmation of my temperamental belief in a world of substances. Hegel's hideous slogan, "Not sub*stance*, but sub*ject*," so fertile in sterilities of every kind, had been pretty generally adopted by professional philosophers, and it was a relief to hear Santayana, who had gone through that epistemological hell with his common sense unscathed, talk delightfully and quietly about the various substances of which the world might conceivably be composed.[1]

It was, however, to Josiah Royce that my debt was greatest, though in another sense it was also least. He taught me almost all that I know about the world's great philosophers, and yet in his own philosophy there was hardly anything that seemed to me true. His lectures on the history of metaphysics were glorious affairs. He not only made the various systems clear in themselves, but he portrayed their inter-relations so luminously and with such originality and depth of insight that the whole course of speculative thought was presented in a series of magnificent vistas and then given the unity of a single great picture of the human mind objectified. He had an unexampled power of making abstract ideas concrete and almost sensuously vivid. It was the ideas themselves rather than the biographical details or even the identities of their authors that he emphasized; and I think all his students were impressed with the fact that, however it may be in other history, in the history of philosophy, at least, it is not the *who's who* but the *what's what* that really matters. I not only got from Royce my knowledge and appreciation of philosophy, but I got from him the kindest and most painstaking assistance in working out my own philosophic problems. He gave me this technical help through my five years of advanced study, and he accompanied it with continuous personal interest and affectionate counsel. He had, moreover, started me going, and trusted me when I was down and out. I owed everything to him, and it seemed mean and disloyal for me not to become his disciple. He was my dear teacher, and I longed to call him master, but I couldn't because his idealistic premises seemed to me false. Despite this I felt the tug of the will to believe wherever I could find elements within my teacher's philosophy that did not seem definitely false. And in a system so rich there were, of course, many such elements. I remember particularly the hypothesis about the varying time-spans in

[1] My first philosophic article, "A Plea for Soul Substance" (*Psychological Review*, November 1899), was written with his kind advice and encouragement.

nature put forward in the second volume of *The World and the Individual,* and how I jumped at it with almost tearful gratitude as a clear good thought that might even be true. For it was a new and interesting contribution to the great pan-psychist tradition. It could be studied and appraised on its own merits in the light of what was known and guessed about the world. And it did not in the least depend upon the monstrous premise on which the rest of the book was based, that that great nature, in which we are such recent and humble participants, is itself the product of our social consciousness and of the funny little techniques of communication which we have developed.

My doctor's thesis, formidably entitled *An Introduction to the Ontological Implicates of Practical Reason,* was suggested by Kant's *Critique* and by Hegel's *Phenomenology.* Sheldon and I worked a great deal together, and we each felt that the principle of *negativität* was inadequate to the great enterprise of categorial deduction which, translated into modern terms, meant the search for a principle of hierarchical organization in the domain of subsistence or essence. We were cheerfully confident of being able to remedy the defect. Sheldon took the principle of the *Self-Repeater* and I took the principle of growth or increase, perhaps suggested by Bergson's *durée* to which James had introduced us. Royce christened my principle the *Pleon,* and helped me with his customary generous kindness to lick the thing into shape. I supplemented my revision of the Hegelian deduction of the categories with an adaptation of Kant's treatment of the sense of duty as revealing a reality more ultimate than anything contained in the world of sense-perception, and attempted to show that in the experience of moral obligation the Pleon revealed itself in its true colours as the principle of reality itself. The thesis was long, and must have been pretty awful as judged by contemporary standards; but it was fun to write, and it got me the degree.

The following year I secured my first regular job under Professor Howison in the University of California. Howison, like Royce, had a variant of post-Kantian idealism, but it was more original than Royce's, though not nearly so well organized and supported. It was a sort of Fichtean monadism in which God was no Absolute, but merely *primus inter pares*, and the world was the phenomenal manifestation of the society of eternal persons who, by timelessly recognizing one another and one another's recognitions of one another, etc., *à la* Leibniz, created the time process and generally kept things going. The pluralism was in refreshing contrast to the anthropophagous absolutes of Royce and Bradley, and to its author, at any rate, it had come as a genuine *apperçu*. He preached it with fiery and unflagging earnestness, and so great was the force of his personality that people all over the Pacific Coast began and have continued to study the philosophy of German Idealism. The spirit at Berkeley was very different from that at Harvard. Under Howison, philosophy was not a fencing-match in which friendly gentlemen exchanged playful thrusts and courteously applauded their adversaries. It was a grim thing of life and death for the soul, a veritable religion in which either you were orthodox (Howisonian), or you were damned. I with my realism was mostly damned, and would have been completely had it not been that Howison was really two persons—a grand inquisitor who would burn your body to save your soul and also one of the kindest men alive. I was lucky enough to win his affection and not only his professional condemnation, so for four years he kept me on, scolding me angrily for my rotten views and even warning his students against my courses, and then, together with dear Mrs. Howison, showering me and my family with every sort of friendly kindness and material help.

It was for me a strange, hard-working time, and in striking contrast to the dreaming and brooding years at Cambridge. I learned to teach, and found I could do it all right, which was a great relief, because both I and my Harvard teachers had had grave doubts about my being able to. I formed a friendship with Overstreet, who was at that time devoted to the study of Plotinus and in high favour with Howison, and that helped me as it has ever since. I took two interesting courses, one with Professor Slate in physics and one with Professor Stringham in mathematics. The course with Slate was a splendid one, and started me reading hard such books on science as I could understand. Stringham's course had an even stronger effect. He was a man much like Peirce. He had a Pythagorean sense for the things that really count, and a Lewis Carroll humour. I had no ear for music, but I think I got from his functions and series the kind of experience that musicians must get from their music. The numbers had always had for me an almost pathological fascination, and an almost tangible objectivity. To regard the number 37, for example, as the product of a human mind, a result of the counting activity by which we reached it, seemed not only false but idiotic. The numbers stand in vast and infinite array with all their still more multitudinous inter-relations full of unending and delightful surprises. They are what they are, and must through all time be what they have been, more steadfast than the stars and more clear and beautiful than existing things can ever hope to be. It would be easier and less absurd to suppose that Baedeker had by his descriptions created the Jungfrau at which I am now looking than to suppose that the ephemeral mathematicians of this planet create by their technique of procedure the timeless truths which they discover.

Stringham's course revived all my old interest in mathematics, and the result was disastrous, for I became an addict and began to neglect my philosophy in order to play amateurishly with the new problems. Cardan's solution of the Cubic seemed intolerably complicated, and I got the feeling that the ease with which equational knots of any degree could be tied must mean that an equally general formula for untieing them must exist. On that presumably hopeless quest I spent days and nights undissuaded by the kindly warning of my mathematical colleagues that the general equations of even the fifth degree had been actually proved to be insoluble by the ordinary methods which I was using. Then also there were the several simple-seeming series for the summation of which no formula had yet been found; and always, and best of all, there was the ancient lure of the primes. I suppose it was vanity or laziness or an unacknowledged distrust of my own competency to master the real stuff I needed that prevented me from fitting myself by serious study for this new game. I preferred instead to wait until the house was quiet, and then like a secret drinker unlock my cupboard and take out with guilty joy, not the good little black bottle, but the nice blank book in which I kept my scribblings, and hold high revel with myself through the night, exploring the lovely grottos in which the roots of my equations lurked, bound by mysterious threads to combinations of the known and visible coefficients on the surface up above. In the more than twenty-five years in which I have indulged this vice I have discovered—at least I think I have discovered—a few odd and pretty things, though certainly not enough as yet to justify the hours filched from philosophy.

In spite of this disastrous by-product of my work with String- ham, and perhaps partly because of it, but still more because of the course with Slate and the reading which grew out of it, I began to take realism with a new seriousness. Science was discovering most exciting things. With the atoms being not only arranged in families, but actually caught and counted, it seemed a piece of pedantic insolence for philosophers who knew nothing of the new work, and cared nothing for it, to label the atoms and their electronic constituents as "vicious abstractions from the organic unity of experience," or similar barren nonsense. If philosophy was to play its historic rôle it must acquaint itself with the new truths and exploit whatever speculative possibilities they con- tained. Idealism began to seem to me, not just a falsity to be neglected, but a positive menace debauching the minds of the youths who studied it. There was need for a definite campaign to deliver philosophy from the fog of confusion that threatened to obliterate it. This feeling as to the increasing importance of getting the epistemological situation properly cleared up, not as an end in itself, but as an indispensable prerequisite to a worth- while philosophy, made me glad to accept the call to Columbia in 1903.

The new place was quite different in atmosphere from either Harvard or Berkeley, and wonderfully stimulating. Sheldon was there, and we could resume both our golf and our duets in ulti- mate romantic metaphysics. Woodbridge was as realistic as I was myself—perhaps more realistic—at least as concerned the world of concrete existence. And it was almost disconcerting to find that what had for so long been my daring and dangerous heresy was now taken by the head of my department as a mere matter of course. And yet there were moments even in those early days when I had misgivings that the new realistic accord was itself not so close as it appeared and as I wanted it to be. For Woodbridge seemed to have nothing of that inner veil of sensation through which we all must pass to reach the outer world. When a distant star would hit him in the eye with its light, his body would bow or gesture in the direction from which the light had come; and he would say in effect: *"That* is my perception of the star—*voilà tout!"* What could it mean to identify the publicly observable bodily antecedents and consequents of an experience with the experience itself, the latter being obviously private and not observable by others?

It was the first case of acute behaviourism that I had seen, and the first, I believe, that existed. To believe in the outer world was indeed very good, but to purchase that belief at the cost of denying the inner world was too high a price even for realism. The baby had been emptied out with the bath. But even though the theory were as queer as it seemed it was original and never put forward before. And in philosophy, at least, we should do everything once. So I was not very much troubled if my friend, for some unaccountable reason, chose to make believe that his own sensations were non-existent. Moreover, Descartes had tried this theory on the animals, and it was a pretty sporting thing for a man to be willing to try it out on himself.

Under the stimulus of this new and, to me, delightful association I changed from the representative or dualistic theory of perception to a presentative or monistic theory. Not that I ever doubted the existence of my own mental states and their location inside my skull, but I got to believe that the objects immediately present in perception were not those states but their meanings or implicates, which as such could coincide (though they need not), not only in essence, but in position and date with the things and events in the extra-cranial world. The states that do this revealing are not themselves revealed. They are not motions, but they are describable in physical terms. What kind of event it is that can reveal events at other places and times than its own is one phase of the psycho-physical problem. That intra-cerebral states can and do reveal without creating such events is sufficient for epistemology.

Beginning about 1910 there came the association with Perry, Holt, and the others which resulted in the publication of *The New Realism*. We set out with high hope of success, confident in one another and in the sympathy of our big brothers in Europe, Russell, Moore, and Meinong. We wanted, first of all, to introduce into philosophy the two methods that had been so profitably employed in science: the method of co-operative work and the method of isolating problems and tackling them one by one. And in addition to these methodological policies we had (at least so I thought) several epistemological theses which we all believed to be true and which we intended to establish.

To me, at least, these theses committed us to no decision as to the more properly metaphysical issues concerning the ultimate nature of the world, or even of the nature of mind and its functions. On these latter questions I was pretty sure that I was not in agreement with my confrères, except possibly with Pitkin. Our realism was thus not a philosophy; it was rather a prolegomenon to philosophy and a declaration of independence that would make it possible to investigate the nature of things on their own merits without dragging in the tedious and usually irrelevant fact that they could be experienced by us.

But even within the domain of epistemology, or closely connected with it, there were incipient differences that were destined soon to loom large. The cognitive function was interpreted by Perry and Holt, as by Woodbridge and Watson, to be nothing more than a "specific response," i.e. a motion of the organism, or some part of it, elicited by a stimulus. For reasons already stated this seemed to me preposterously false. Magnify the importance of bodily movements as much as we please, they can never be other than north or south, east or west, up or down, or in directions intermediate to these. But the peculiar *rapport* between an individual and the objects of which he is aware extends to past and future and to the realm of the abstract. And it is impossible for the body to move in the "direction" of such entities. But what is perhaps an even more serious difference between my neo-realist colleagues and myself has developed in recent years. The objects which appear in distorted illusory and hallucinatory experience, which were always for me, not existential, but merely subsistential complexes of essences that could not on reflection be believed to be in real space, however vividly they might appear there at the moment of perception, have been given an existential status by most of those calling themselves neo-realists. The result is to make of the space in which we live and move a dumping-ground for all the contents of dreams and illusions, actual and possible. Any space would crack under such a strain, and of course "neo-realist" space has cracked and broken up into a series of "private spaces" and a "public space" as a construct of each individual. Are there as many public spaces as there are individuals who construct them? Do they interpenetrate completely or partly? Or are they mutually external and side by side in a super-public space which is not a construct? These last questions must also be asked about the private spaces. And *where* were the individuals who construct public space before they did their constructing, i.e. when they were babies or embryos? I would rather be an idealist, at least a Kantian idealist, than swallow any such mess. For Kantian space, even when reduced to an a priori form of perception, could still keep up, though in straitened circumstances, a semblance of Euclidean respectability and enjoy a dignified priority to its own contents.

It seems to me to be a certainty that the things of which the existing world consists must at each instant have ultimately univocal positions, regardless of all of the conflicting perspectives in which they may appear. And if we make temporal cross-sections of these things, as we always can, and thus treat them as histories or continuous series of events, and accept in addition the Special Theory of Relativity, the situation is not essentially altered; for though in that case space and time will have become interdependent aspects of the single four-dimensional continuum of "space-time," yet even so each event will enjoy a univocal "date-locus" or absolute "position" in the new continuum. How otherwise could the events be unambiguously inter-related by the Eddington "intervals," which are to remain invariant, regardless of the perspectives which vary with the motions of the systems from which they are taken? Nor do the spaces and times of even these varying perspectives include places for hallucinatory contents. Relativity to the photographic plates on moving systems is not relativity to the apperception-masses of the men suffering from nightmares or delirium.

If neo-realism is to mean an ontological equalitarianism in which existential status is to be accorded to every content of perceptual experience, whether veridical or illusory, then such a theory is not *realism* at all. We may give new names, such as "sense-data" or "sensa" or "sensibilia," to the rabble of experiential contents, and insist piously on calling them "physical" in every sentence; but they are not properly physical, for they are not properly things at all. They are not agents and patients; they cannot go under their own power; and, worst of all, they are totally incapable of orderly arrangement in a single *milieu*, whether a space or a time or the space-time of Relativity. They are, in fact, nothing but the well-known adjectival sense-impressions of Hume and Mill and Mach and Pearson masquerading under fancy appellations. And in treating them as the sole constituents of the world of existence, the New Realism has surrendered unconditionally to the old phenomenalism.

These sad trends of behaviourism and positivism, which have taken place in the last ten years and which I have attempted to describe, spoiled my interest in the movement from which I had hoped so much good would result; and once more, as in the old days at Harvard and at Berkeley, I am left without a party.

My general ethical theory had developed smoothly into an articulate conception of what I had always vaguely longed for. The good life was the most abundant life. Happiness was increment of psychic substance—fulfilment of tendencies and capaci-

ties. We should seek a maximum of it and a minimum of
its opposite for all. Courage and sympathy were the means to
that end. They were the intensive and extensive coefficients of
righteousness and the only primary virtues.

As to the religious question which had from the beginning
been my second philosophic interest, I felt that my views were
crystallizing into a fairly coherent structure. And this structure
was based upon two postulates:

1. The Problem of Good is insoluble in terms of the traditional
Atheism.

2. The Problem of Evil is insoluble in terms of the traditional
Theism.

There seemed to be too much of goodness and purposiveness
in the world to be the outcome of blindly or mechanistically
determined particles; but also too much evil and inconsequenti-
ality to be compatible with any power at once omnipotent and
benign. There must be a God, a force or trend upward, to account
for the more than casual amount of goodness in existence, and
there must be a tremendous limitation in such a power to account
for the evil. The finite Deity of Mill and James was thus indicated, both on grounds of metaphysical plausibility and of
ethical satisfaction.

When, however, we consider, not the processes of the Universe,
but its structure, we must recognize that the only chance for
the existence of anything worthy the appellation of Deity must
turn on the possibility that the cosmos has a life and mind of its
own over and above the lesser beings included within it. In
the old and unattractive words we may ask: Is there any likeli-
hood that the world is an animal? Can the sprawling galaxies
conceivably possess that degree of integration and organicity
which would constitute them an adequate vehicle or external
manifestation of a unitary and personal experience? To this
question I could give an affirmative answer. Not with certainty,
but yet with high probability, we may believe that the enduring
unity of the whole is more rather than less than the transitory
unities of its parts. Such a Being would, like other beings, possess

an "environment" which would, however, be internal rather than external, and would consist of its own confused and recalcitrant constituents: "that in God which is not God." Encompassing this unitary totality of existence there would abide the eternal Logos, or totality of subsistent possibles, of which the actual world is itself but an infinitesimal fraction—an indeterminate and ever-changing precipitate of compossibility, the resultant, so to speak, of a struggle for existence on the part of the essences. The will to good, or the tendency toward harmony, would be but one essence among many; but its intent to inform the stubborn and warring parts of the universe with the harmony and unity of the Logos would give it an advantage over all other less eirenic tendencies. And the epic of cosmic evolution would consist in the uncertain, imperfect, and interrupted, but generally progressive, leavening of an infinite chaos by the element in it of divine love and good. This little yet perfect thing working in the heart of all things we can symbolize as Prometheus or as Christ, the finite will of a God whose essence and substance are all-comprehending and infinite.

I am painfully aware, not only of the inadequacy of my language to express this Leibnizo-Peircian theory, but of what will appear to my colleagues as the antiquated and fantastic character of the theory itself. And I am equally well aware that no such theological system of hazardous and far-flung speculation, were it a thousand times more skilful and plausible, could constitute more than the intellectual husk of religious experience itself. The feelings of loneliness, insufficiency, and terror are the real drives that generate religion. The ancient and pathetic hope that the world is somehow kin to us, and that the things for which we care most are not ultimately at the mercy of blind and indifferent forces, impels the search for God. And when this hope is reinforced by a mystic sense of being sustained by something sweet and quick, not of us, but very close to us, we have enough to justify the attempt to reconcile the need of our heart with the cold and meagre knowledge of the facts of existence.

Of far greater importance to me than the beliefs on epistemology, ethics, and religion, the nature and genesis of which I have been describing, was a certain conception of the nature of the mind and its relation to the body which came to me in a curious way, and which has seemed to me to constitute the solution of the problem which of all problems had interested me most. I have tried in four or five articles to present and defend the hypothesis in question, but my failure to convey to my friends my own conviction of its truth and importance warns me that I shall probably fail also in this new and necessarily brief account of the nature of the theory and the manner of its genesis.

In my second year of teaching at Berkeley I had been using as textbooks Höffding's *Psychology*, Pearson's *Grammar of Science* and the *Critique of Pure Reason*. In Höffding I had come across a reference to Lotze's comment on Herbart's doctrine of degrees of intensity in mental states. I do not remember the exact point of the matter, but it had been haunting my mind, and I had commented upon it to my class. In Pearson I had been struck with a statement to the effect that whether the analogy between sense-impressions and forms of strain was anything more than a mere analogy he would leave undetermined. In my course on Kant we had been dealing with the "Analogies of Experience," particularly the one concerned with intensive quantity. At the close of a morning in which the discussion in the Kant class had been especially lively and profitable, I was walking home to lunch in fine spirits and full of satisfaction with the students and with the work that we were doing together. Suddenly I got the strangest experience; and if in my attempt to describe it I make it seem silly or even meaningless, I can only ask the reader's patience on the ground that, however preposterous he may find it, it has meant more to me than anything else that has happened in my life. The feeling came as I was crossing a little brook; and it was as if I could look into and down through each point of space and perceive a kind of well of indefinite depth. The new realm was like a fourth dimension in that it was perpendicular to the three dimensions of space, and yet as contained within each point it seemed to be a lesser thing than a spatial dimension. I described it to myself as a "hypo-space," a realm of negative dimensionality or essential fractions of the punctiform units of an extensive manifold. It seemed to be the domain of intensity and density, so that if I thought of a continuous solid being diminished in its extent until it had shrunk to a point, that would not be a zero of mass magnitude, for each point of a solid must be as different from a point of empty space as a finite sphere of solid is from the same sphere of empty space. After you reduced matter to points, each of those solid points would have to *wane* or *fade down* in density or intensity in order to reach the true zero of mass. The first implication or application of my *apperçu*, if I may dignify to that extent my novel experience, was the realization that there was room inside a point for a whole microcosmic intensive replica, though in a curious inverted form, of the extended macrocosm outside; and that the elements of that intensive replica would have, on the one hand, a privacy and invisibility, and, on the other hand, a unity and organicity which, while preserving the plurality of specificities, would permit of their being superposed upon one another rather than placed side by side as in extensive pluralities. The different elements would occupy the same place just as a shape and its colour, or a tone-magnitude and its pitch. The second reflection it occurred to me to make on the new conception was that whenever a motion or stream of kinetic energy was checked and transformed into a potential state of strain or stress, the place of that strain and of an indefinite number of further strains that could be successively superposed upon it was the new dimension that stretched in and "down" through each point of space. It was because of this beautiful and unsuspected hiding-place for energies that they were enabled to pass into the seeming nothingness of mere potentiality and emerge again with all their specificities unscathed. And then, putting these two sets of reflections together, it came over me suddenly that I had discovered the real nature of the psychical and the manner of its relation to the cerebral matrix in which it was so elusively located. I had found the way in which sensations were produced at the points in the brain where the neural currents were transformed into potential energy prior to their re-issuance as motor responses. I had found the place where an indefinitely rich system of memories could be piled up as traces left by the sensory currents during the potential stage of their journey. I had found how it was that a sequence of successive moments, mutually exclusive in the physical order, could nevertheless be felt as a solid chunk of duration extending back and down into the past, the "specious present" or *durée real* of Bergson, which more than anything else differentiates the mental from the moment-to-moment reality of a physical system. I had, in short, discovered the soul in its hiding-place, and not indirectly through dialectical inference, but concretely through an intuition. I walked off the little bridge on which I had stopped when the thing came on me and went home in a daze of ecstasy.

The ideas initiated by the strange experience that I had undergone have persisted up to the present, and despite the epistemological, sociological, and religious interests to which I have referred, my dominant philosophic purpose has been to make clear to myself and others the full meaning of what had been revealed in my intuition while crossing the brook. To the fulfilment of this purpose there have been obstacles—in particular, my own self-distrust. I knew that I had the taint of the circle-squarer deep in me, and that fantastic analogies were apt to seize on my mind and gain an importance and a fascination far beyond their logical value. Perhaps it was because of my weakness and tolerance for the fantastic that the various pseudo-philosophic cranks, who are always appealing to universities for academic endorsement of their wild schemes, were usually referred to me by my colleagues in philosophy and psychology. I recall one poor lady who had accepted as a commonplace and established fact the crazy notion that every name had a "vibration rate" which, by a sort of sympathetic magic, controlled the object named. Her own original addition to this nonsense was the great theory that the word "vibration" must itself have a vibration-rate which, could it only be discovered, would be a potent control over the whole universe. I proceeded, as in less acute cases, to disillusionize her gently but firmly as to any hope of academic encouragement for her theory. As at last she turned

to go, I noticed the stricken look begin to fade from her face
and the horrible secret smile of the paranoiac gradually triumph
over the hurt. I felt an eerie goose-flesh shudder on my own part,
and suddenly the memory of John Bunyan came to mind, and
I thought, "There, but for the Grace of God, go I"—and perhaps
there I do go anyway. Was it not terribly possible that my own
gorgeous intuition might turn out to be of the same pitiful
tinsel stuff as that of the vibration-lady whose idea I had just
sentenced to a well-deserved death?

In the more than twenty-five years that have elapsed, my
theory has developed through four successive stages, psychological, epistemological, biological, and cosmological. I will try
to set down briefly and in turn the principal conclusions in each
of these fields.

1. *Psychological.*—Sensations are the modes of intensive or
potential energy into which the afferent currents of motion
or kinetic energy are transformed at those points in the nervous
system (presumably the synapses) in which they are re-directed
into efferent currents of muscular and other responses. When
and where the energy of the stimulus ceases to be externally
observable as motion, there and then the new kind of energy,
purely private and internally observable as sensation, comes into
existence. What from the standpoint of the physicist is mere
potentiality of future motion, is in and for itself the actuality
of feeling and sensation. These intensive energy-forms fade out
rapidly, though never completely, into their appropriate motor
responses; but their traces in all their specificity are retained,
accumulated, and superposed on one another after the fashion
of the successive twists imposed upon a rope or spring. They
constitute the memory-system of the individual, and like a
faint but pervasive field of force they modify in accordance with
their structure and pattern the responses to later stimuli. There
thus grows up an organism within the organism, an enduring
and ever-present register of the succession of past sensations, not
externally observable yet causally effective upon the visible
cerebral matrix. Unless we are to assume that a complex system
of motions could pass at their moments of re-direction into

complete nothingness and emerge unscathed in magnitude and in form, we must believe that those energies in their latent or so-called potential phase possess, though invisible, all the richness and definiteness of structure that characterizes their visible antecedents and consequents. The character of such a field of potential energy as indirectly inferred from without possesses all the essential characters of the mind as directly experienced from within. Looked at from either standpoint, we find privacy, unity, "extension in time," or duration of the past in the present, and variety of content without divisibility or side-by-sideness. In any extensive aggregate of particles in motion, the unity is factitious and secondary, and the behaviour is the sum of behaviours of the separate elements. The forms and relations of the system are not, as such, primarily effective. But a field of force is like a mind in that the organic unity and pattern of the whole dominates the behaviour of the constituents, which are thus distinct phases rather than separate parts. And the forms and relations or *gestalten* within such an intensive system become what they never are in an extensive aggregate—namely, primary and effective determiners as such.

These, in briefest summary, are some of the reasons in support of the theory that the potentiality of external motion is the actuality of internal experience. Furthermore, such a theory has what seems to me a very important methodological advantage over other theories of the relation of mind to body. It enables us, in the first place, to accept as true the various points which psycho-physical dualists, from Descartes to Bergson, have urged so effectively as revealing the impossibility of the kind of structure which we know as mind, being a mere concomitant or inseparable aspect of the very different and essentially contrasting kind of structure which we know as brain. But in the second place the theory enables us to express these truths of dualism without departing from the physical categories which constitute the strength and fruitfulness of the mechanistic conception. To treat mind as a field of potential energy is to do justice both to its uniqueness of structure and to its homogeneity with the material world of which it is an integral part.

2. *Epistemological.*—Turning from the psycho-physical problem of the relation of mind to brain to that quite other though related problem of the relation of the individual as knower (whatever else he may be) to the object as known (whatever else it may be), we find an extraordinary situation—a situation in which an organism or system of events is in a curious and unique *rapport* with other events whose *loci* and dates are different from its own. Consciousness may, indeed, be defined as a situation in which certain events (the objects) enjoy a vicarious efficacy in spaces and times other than their own—namely, those of the brain that knows them. For when my conduct is controlled by my awareness of spatio-temporally distant objects, to that extent those objects are causally efficacious in positions other than their proper ones. And again, from the side of the knower or subject, the internal states by means of which he apprehends are controlled by their external and objective meanings rather than by their sensory content. The psycho-physical theory that the mind is a system of potential energies enables us to understand how and why its objects are other than itself. For potential energy has a double self-transcending reference. As the determiner of future motions it is an agent and faces future-ward, but as the "determinee" of past motions it faces past-ward, and is a patient. It is this retrospective reference of potentialities to their causes that constitutes the curious cognitive function. We live forward, but we experience backward. Facts are what we apprehend, and every fact is a *factum*, something done, a *fait accompli*. This explains the curious relativity of objects known to the subject that knows them, a relativity that is "selective" but never constitutive, like the relativity of historical events to the words that describe them. *Which things* we shall know at any moment depends on our internal states at that moment, but *the things* thus known are independent both in essence and existence of the states that reveal them. And as a potentiality viewed as a forward-facing tendency may be counteracted and fail to produce its characteristic effect, so may that same potentiality, in its backward-facing or cognitive reference, fail to reveal its true cause. This is the explanation of error. Our cognitive states

reveal their normal or most probable implicates, which may be, but need not be, identical with existing objects.

3. *Biological.*—The outstanding mystery of organic life is the peculiar capacity of a fertilized germ to embody in its own material structure—apart from the truth or falsity of the Lamarckian theory—the structures of its myriad of ancestors. These present embodiments of an enormous past certainly do not exist side by side or within one another, as the "Encasement" theory would have it, nor can they be accounted for in terms of the number of possible combinations and permutations of their atoms. These various possible arrangements would, of course, be more than sufficient numerically, but they would not persist in any definite order through the intercourse with the environment. Their definiteness of arrangement would be washed out through successive interactions. In order to account for the persistence of the heredity-structure through all the vicissitudes of ontogeny and later growth, it is necessary to allow to the germ tremendous causal prepotency over its environment. The latter is only a releasing and sustaining condition, and by no means an equal partner in the interactions. Now, if the ancestral past of a germ is present in it as a system of potential energies superposed to any degree upon one another in an intensive hierarchy, then we have an adequate system of causal determiners of the process that ensues, and the reason for its persistence with unaltered specificity is plain. Pre-formation becomes reconciled with epigenesis. For the constellation of atoms in the material structure of the chromosomes can be meagre and without resemblance to the structures that are to ensue (epigenesis), while at the same time the hierarchy of intensive energy forms may embody in their own invisible and temporally ordered structure an infinitely rich system of all, and more than all, of the forms of past ancestry and of possible future posterity. This is a sort of pre-formationism, but it is "energic" rather than materialistic.

4. *Cosmological.*—The Einstein Theory of Relativity might appear at first sight to have no relevant bearings upon my hypothesis as to the nature of mind and life, and yet it has seemed increasingly to be congruent with it. The Einstein-Minkowski

world is a four-dimensional continuum of space-time. As usually conceived, that world is in a queer sense static. The time aspect of it is like time that is past. The present flowing of time, what Whitehead calls the fact of *Passage*, is not provided for. It is a world whose objects, when temporally considered, are histories; but as in the world of Spinoza they are histories that *sub specie aeternitatis* have been always completed. Now, if we amend this world to provide for its life as well as its shadowgraph, we may fancy it as a space-time hyper-sphere, not static, but growing or expanding cumulatively, and (if the Special Theory of Relativity is true) non-Euclideanly—in a direction perpendicular to its "surface." The three-dimensional "surface" of this growing hyper-sphere is the spatial or material world. The electrons and protons may be thought of as the hills and hollows, or pimples and dimples, which are opposite and unequal fourth-dimensional displacements in the three-dimensional "surface" of our space. They would be produced by equal and opposite corkscrew "twist-thrusts." If the "surface" were *not* expanding, the equal and opposite "twist-thrusts" would give protuberances and depressions that also were respectively equal. But in an *expanding* spherical surface equal *twists* would be correlated with unequal *thrusts* or displacements in the direction of the perpendicular. If these displacements represent the mass of the hill or hollow and the twists represent the electric charge, then we could understand how the degree of the depression (protonic mass) could be greater (1,845 times greater) than the degree of elevation (electronic mass), though their degrees of twist or electric charge were equal.

If material particles can be thought of (following Clifford) as the permanent four-dimensional departures from the three-dimensional surface of the ether on which they float, then the associated vital and psychical systems of potential energy, registering the actual past and so foreshadowing the probable future of the bodies with which they are connected, can be conceived as the temporary and more tenuous four-dimensional extensions (or durations) that are the invisible appendages of their visible matrices. Thus I believe that the mind, as a system of potential energies in the cerebrum, is a real soul, thick or deep in the direction of the past from which the world has moved. The world is a true "pleon," a self-increaser, and the vital and mental structures contained in it are moving all together with a cumulative growth-motion in a fourth-dimensional direction. That motion we perceive, not as such, but as the *passage of time*. The inner part of the world-hyper-sphere constitutes its definite and still enduring past, while the as yet unoccupied space outside, into which it will grow, constitutes its indefinite future, filled only with the possibilities which are the shadows thrown forward by what already is. The world-soul, like the souls of men, hangs down in time, extends into the past. Its material existence and ours at each present instant is but the three-dimensional cross-section, the fighting-front of a four-dimensional spiritual reality.

I have made a desperate attempt to express in a few paragraphs the broader implications or applications of my theory of the character of mind and organic life. My philosophic speculations have brought me to the goal of a cosmological spiritualism, but a spiritualism that in a sense can be expressed in physical categories. And so with equal propriety it may be termed a spiritualistic or animistic materialism. The hopes and fears of one's heart exert such hidden and potent influences on one's intellect that it is hard for anyone to be sure whether his conclusions in matters of life-and-death importance are intellectually honest. At times I feel a sort of shame and self-mistrust that I should have come out with a philosophy so optimistic. That the world is a spirit, and that we are; and that perhaps we share even the immortality of a Life that contains and sustains us is a creed almost too happy and too good to be true. And yet I do believe that if not true it is something very like the truth.

PRINCIPAL PUBLICATIONS

"A Theory of Time Perception," *American Journal of Psychology*, October 1904.

"Consciousness a Form of Energy," *Essays Philosophical and Psychological in Honor of William James*, New York, 1908.

"May a Realist be a Pragmatist?" *Journal of Philosophy*, August, September, and October 1909.

"A Realistic Theory of Truth and Error," *The New Realism*, New York, 1912.

"The Antinomy and its Implications for Logical Theory," *Studies in the History of Ideas*, vol. i, New York, 1918.

"Variation, Heredity and Consciousness," *Proceedings of the Aristotelean Society*, 1921.

"The Einstein Theory and a Possible Alternative," *Philosophical Review*, March 1924.

"The Missing Link in the Case for Utilitarianism," *Studies in the History of Ideas*, vol. ii, New York, 1925.

"Time and the Fourth Dimension," *University of California Publications in Philosophy*, 1925.

The Ways of Knowing (Allen & Unwin, London, 1925).

"Truth Existential and Subsistential," *University of California Publications in Philosophy*, 1928.

"A Materialistic Theory of Emergent Evolution," *Essays in Honor of John Dewey*, New York, 1929.

EMPIRICAL IDEALISM

By DE WITT H. PARKER

Born 1885; Professor of Philosophy, University of Michigan.

EMPIRICAL IDEALISM

My interest in philosophy dates exactly from the moment when, in the little public library of Summit, N.J., a mere boy of eleven years, I chanced upon White's *History of the Warfare of Science with Theology* and read on through the afternoon until closing hour; then hastened home to announce to my astonished sisters that Adam and Eve never existed, that Noah never gathered the animals "two by two" into the Ark, that Jonah was never swallowed by a whale. Years of fervid quest followed, during which, without teachers and without fellow-inquirers, I tried to discover whether the 'faith of my fathers' was or was not true. Small wonder that, with a brain seething with such thoughts, I lost interest in the more usual pursuits of boyhood, so unexciting by comparison! I read all the books relating to the subject I could lay my hands on, making use later, on the family's removal to Boston, of the ample resources of the Public Library there; first, books of 'higher criticism,' beginning with Renan and Strauss; then books of popular philosophy, like those of Fiske, Haeckel, and Carus, dominated by the concept of evolution, and even weightier works, such as Martineau's *Seat of Authority in Religion* and Spencer's *First Principles*. Under the influence of all this reading I passed from orthodoxy to Unitarian 'theism' (fortified incidentally by Felix Adler's *Creed and Deed*, a book that I know has left a permanent impress on my mind); thence to a mystical pantheism and nature worship; and, finally, after reading Matthew Arnold's *God and the Bible*, Darwin's *Descent of Man*, and books of Spencerian and Comtean positivism, to entire rejection, as I thought, of all theological beliefs.

When I entered Harvard in 1902 I had, therefore, lived through six years of lonely and unguided reflection, with a purely negative result. Yet I came with a tremendous eagerness to discover, if possible, the real nature of things, and a profound conviction that philosophy, and philosophy alone, could inform me. My life's purpose was henceforth fixed. In my Freshman year I elected History of Philosophy, ancient philosophy being given by Santayana and modern philosophy by Professor R. B. Perry.

Few of my later experiences will stand comparison in vividness
and freshness of joy with my first readings in genuine philosophy
in connection with this course—the reading of Plato's *Republic*,
Aristotle's *Ethics*, Descartes' *Meditations*, Spinoza's *Ethics*,
Hume's *Treatise*, Berkeley's *Dialogues*. How trivial by contrast
all my previous reading seemed, as the shadow to the substance!
Later on I was to listen to Royce lecture on Kant and Symbolic
Logic, Santayana on Plato, Palmer on Goodness, Muensterberg
on Eternal Values, James on Tychism and Radical Empiricism.
To me and to my fellow-students, philosophy, as represented by
these men, whom we deemed immortal, was still in the making,
and "to be alive was very heaven" in their company. Yet I was
not able to count myself a disciple of any one of them. A regret-
table shyness, and a too great reverence for my professors,
prevented me from seeking them out and getting personally
acquainted with them; and besides, there were always, in the
case of each one of them, important matters of theory, with
regard to which I could not follow them. To my thoroughly
unpractical self, James's pragmatism was meaningless as philosophy; in his proofs for the existence of the Absolute, Royce
seemed to be always 'working for an answer,' like the small
boy who has peaked into the back of the exercise book and
already knows the solution of the problem; Santayana's materialism could not stand in my mind against Berkeley and Hume;
the new realism of Holt and Perry I thought incapable of accounting for subjectivity, for knowledge, error and illusion; Palmer's
ethical pietism seemed inconsistent with the fact of evil, and
Muensterberg's contrast between science and life too sharply
drawn. Yet from each of my Harvard teachers I learned things
invaluable for my philosophical development: from Royce my
interest in Symbolic Logic; from James the standpoint of
radical empiricism and a bias towards pluralism and indeterminism; from Santayana an awakening to the problems of value
(I still think Santayana's whole metaphysics, with its artifices
of matter and essence, however original and beautiful in
expression, a sad mistake, while his interpretations of culture
remain incomparable in our generation); from Perry and Holt a

discontent with traditional solutions. Aside from my debt to my teachers, I owed most, during my student days, to Berkeley and Hume; to Hegel and Nietzsche; to Bradley, Mach, and Avenarius, and outside of the field of philosophy, to my study of Greek and mathematics.

Since leaving Harvard I have taught at the University of Michigan for nearly twenty years, with the exception of two years spent at the University of California. During these years I have made a special study of aesthetics, both historical and theoretical, falling successively under the influence of Santayana, Lipps, and Croce, but eventually working my way to an independent standpoint, as represented in my books, *The Principles of Aesthetics*, 1920, and the *Analysis of Art*, 1926. Plato and Aristotle, whom I teach, have persistently occupied my thought; my knowledge of the German idealists and of Leibniz and Spinoza has been intermittently renewed and extended; Bergson and Peirce, both strangely neglected during my student days, have influenced me powerfully. Like most of my contemporaries, I fancy, I have been tantalized and stimulated by the writings of Russell, so fresh and mercurial; and through his work largely I have maintained my interest in symbolic logic, a subject which I teach occasionally to minute classes of advanced students. My book, *The Self and Nature*, 1917, represents the impact of all these influences for the first ten years of my professorial career. The book is merely an impressionistic sketch, full of inconsistencies and other shortcomings; but I still adhere to its essential positions. Very recently, as a result doubtless of ethical problems raised by the Great War, I have become interested in the problems connected with the general nature, classification, and criticism of Values. With reference to these problems I have derived the greatest help from Hegel, Nietzsche, Freud, and the Austrians, and more recently from the protagonists of the *Gestalt* concept. Throughout my career at Michigan I have profited exceedingly from the friendship and intellectual companionship of my colleagues, Professors Wenley, Lloyd, and Sellars. From Sellars I am sure I have borrowed some points in theory of knowledge, while dissenting vigorously from his disguised materialism.

With the above as an autobiographical introduction, I shall now attempt to give a sketch of my philosophical position, confining myself mainly to metaphysics.

For me the proper standpoint of philosophy is what James called 'radical empiricism,' which is, as I understand it, the demand that the philosopher shall use only concepts representing concrete experience. This point of view was already occupied by Hume when, for every idea, he sought the corresponding impression. Hence, I should say, Hume's method remains essentially sound, while his results are often defective owing to faulty analysis of experience. The key to the understanding of reality lies within experience, and to find the metaphysical meaning and validity of such concepts as cause, law, stuff, substance and the like, we must look to their experience-equivalents. Moreover, since experience is a part of the system of the universe, it is reasonable to believe that it provides us with a fair sample of the whole. I see no reason for believing that there is any other stuff or substance except experience; hence, to my thinking, materialism, naturalism—evolutionary or not—epiphenomenalism, and the like, are the *proles horrenda* of philosophic perversion. In philosophy we must start from ourselves, and I would quote Goethe's verses as applying not only to happiness but to truth:

> Willst du immer weiter schweifen
> Sieh, das Gute liegt so nah.

If it be objected that this is too introverted a standpoint, my reply is that following the other path has led to the contemporary impasse. In so far as the great systems of idealism built upon concrete experience rather than upon the abstract and problematic concepts of natural science, they were, I believe, on the right track; they were wrong, however, in neglecting such humble problems as the relation between mind and body; in accepting too uncritically the background of ideas supplied by Christianity, and in paying too little heed to science and its problems and major results. My own thinking is in line with the more empirical type of idealism represented by Berkeley and by Schopenhauer in his saner moments, and among recent thinkers, by the Bergson of *Les Donnés Immédiates* and the little masterpiece on Relativity. But now for some results following this method.

The analysis of experience reveals two types of facts, percepts, and activities. By activities I mean such facts as desiring, judging, appreciating; to call them activities is already to characterize them in a fashion, and to distinguish them from percepts which are given to us as relatively passive. Emotions, pleasures and pains, and the like, have an equivocal status, partaking of the nature of both. The activities, in their order and connections, constitute the self. I distinguish the self from the mind, for by mind should be meant the whole complex of activities and associated percepts. It is clear that each self is associated with a group of percepts in a way not further describable, and not associated in the same way with the activities and percepts of another mind. So far as our knowledge goes, there are no percepts without activities, and no activities not associated with percepts.

Following the method of radical empiricism and granting the existence of minds other than our own, we can define the nature of physical things. Let us begin by inquiring into the nature of the body of one of our fellow-men. In the first place, his body consists of certain percepts of mine, of his own, and of other minds that may be acquainted with him. These percepts resemble each other, and are connected together in a certain order in time and in space. To the old question whether a thing exists when I do not perceive it, the answer is always possible that it does, so long as there are any percepts of the type in question in the mind of someone else. But we can go farther than this, and in so doing we reach an enlarged notion of the reality of the thing. For it is possible to show, by a process of reasoning easily divined, but into the detail of which I have no space to enter, that all the percepts in question proceed from a single centre. For example, many men in a concert-hall get percepts of the violinist drawing his bow; but all these percepts proceed from an activity of the violinist—his interest, drive, wish, or whatever you choose to call it—which expresses itself in his playing. This activity is the real thing-in-itself, the true physical object, the focus of the thing, of which all our percepts may be called phenomena. (My dependence upon Schopenhauer, at this point, is obvious.) Of course, further knowledge of the body shows that most of its phenomena are not conditioned by the activities of the violinist; or, if so conditioned, are determined by other factors as well; so that, in the end, we come to see that the organism is a complicated system, of which the self is only a small part, co-governing only such phenomena as voluntary muscular action, and to a lesser degree, glandular and other 'autonomic' facts. What, then, is the reality corresponding to our percepts of the more purely somatic processes of the body? If we accept the principle which I am employing, that the self is a sample of nature, we shall be committed to believing that the other elements in the system of the organism are of the same character as the self, that they, too, are activities, associated as ours are, with percepts.

The inorganic world should be interpreted in the same way. For the organism is not essentially different from inorganic nature; from the point of view of the chemist, it is built of the same materials; metaphysically, also, it must be of the same kind. Every physical thing consists, in the last analysis, most immediately of percepts, which have no existence apart from minds; these I shall call the circumference of the object; and secondly of activities, which do exist independently of a perceiving mind; these I shall call the centre or focus of the object. The percept may be viewed, causally, as the reaction of one mind to the activities of another mind, and, epistemologically, as the symbol or awareness of the presence and efficacy of the other mind. Nature is a vast system of such centres of activity with their associated percepts. What in the contemporary philosophy of science are called events, are, in my view, happenings within such centres. The aim of science, as Russell puts it, is to give the chrono-geography of these events.

The activities are not only part of the stuff or material cause in the Aristotelian sense—the rest of the stuff being percepts—they are also substance, essence or 'continuant' (to borrow

W. E. Johnson's term), in the sense of that which remains identical despite change. There is nothing in the universe substantial except plan, purpose, wish, meaning. These facts are given to us as identical; indeed, the very import of the concept of identity can be shown to be dependent upon them. Sense data, on the other hand, come and go, are qualitatively alike, perhaps, but are never identical. My plans and interests, on the other hand, remain observably the same through the years. This sameness is, of course, not incompatible with difference; in fact, sameness, as Hegel insisted, is meaningless apart from difference; to affirm that "A is A" is to say no more than just "A." Essence is always immersed in change and growth. It has been objected to the type of metaphysics which I advocate that it provides no place for conservation, which is so important a fact in science; since mind, it is alleged, is by nature evanescent, new every day, following sleep, and perhaps every few moments, with each pulse-beat of attention. To this I would make reply that there are two important ways in which there is conservation in mind: first, in the identity of the activities, just referred to; and second, in memory and tradition, through which something out of the past is carried on into the present. And when one inquires narrowly into just what science teaches concerning conservation, one finds that it knows of no conservation except of types of behaviour, of laws. But laws are precisely the plans, the habits, the purposes, the memories of nature; or, more exactly, the ways in which these things manifest their invariances in our percepts.

The chief difficulty, however, in the way of accepting substance as pertaining to mind comes from false views of time. And since, in my opinion, almost everything of importance in metaphysics depends upon getting this matter straight, I shall give to a consideration of the category of time what might otherwise be a disproportionate number of pages of this essay. But even so, I shall be able to report only those radically empirical facts which seem to me of basic consequence for metaphysics.

Decisive for any conception of time is the definition of the 'present.' Now by the 'present' can be meant nothing short of the whole of reality of which *this*, whatever this is which I perceive, is a part. The present and reality are co-extensive, not to be sure in connotation, but in denotation. For reality can be defined only through relation to the perceived, as the conceived system to which the perceived belongs; it is the whole of which 'this' is a part. But the 'this' is not only the determining basis for the construction of reality, but also for the construction of the present; for the present is precisely the given, or the whole of which the given is a part. Hence the extension of the two concepts, 'present' and 'reality,' coincide. This might seem to reduce reality to a bare point, but only because of mistaken views of past and future, as we shall see. However, since percepts are shifting, new ones emerging and old ones disappearing, the present, and by the same token reality, as the whole of which this percept is a part, is a variable. Yet the shift is never total; for if my assumptions regarding substance are well-grounded, some elements or parts of reality are always conserved. If this were not so, then, since the present is the whole of reality, past and future would coincide with non-existence. But since it is so, and since, as I think may be taken for granted without argument, time by itself has no reality, but only its 'filling' is real, it follows that at least part of the past exists as part of the present. It so exists in two ways: First, all the identical elements of reality, since they did exist as well as now exist, *are themselves the past*; in them past and present overlap. Second, the past exists as memory and history. The shift within the mind is not merely a shift to new contents, but to the *preservation* of the old in memory and conceptual reconstruction.

Consider the matter with reference to yourself. What is your past? Surely your enduring interests are your past—this interest in philosophy, that affection, that belief, that habit—without all of which your past would never have been what it was. These facts are of your past, part and parcel of it, quite as much as they are of your present. When you look back over your past, you find them there, just as you now find them here. The only reason one might have for denying their pastness would be a false use of 'past' as a contrast term to 'present'; but there is no total difference between past and present; for precisely over the area of our persisting interests, they coincide. Our memories and records of the past are also bits of the past. As intuitive, memory contains at least a part of what it knows; and if record is true, its logical form or structure must be identical with the form of the things it records. But so far as memory and record are parts of the living mind, they not only contain a portion of the past, but are themselves a portion of the present. Whether some part of every past fact is conserved in the present through memory or record, or whether, in Plato's language, existence has a leak in it and there are elements which disappear entirely, is a question which, in my opinion, cannot be answered with certainty. So far as our own experience takes us, we know neither the riches nor the poverty of memory: we remember much more than we think we do, and, on the other hand, we have reason to believe that there were many things which we have forgotten, and of which there is no record. Yet that there exists no record of any fact anywhere in the universe cannot, of course, be known. But however this matter be settled, it remains true that not all of the past is conserved; for in the transition from primary experience to memory and record, something is lost. We have a direct experience of the breaking up, loss, and destruction of things. The vase that I hold in my hand will not be wholly conserved in my recollection of it if I drop and break it; nor will the deed that I do be wholly preserved, but only its pale echo of memory in my mind.

The theory of the status of the future can readily be constructed from the theory regarding the past. The future is real, as the past is, so far as it is a part of the present. It is real as the permanent interests, plans, and affections which, existing now, will exist also then, are real. As expectation and prophecy, it is also real. It has no more—and also no less—reality than this. And it, too, like the present, is a shifting reality, only the shift is in the opposite direction. Instead of beginning as primary experience and then shifting to idea, in which it is then partly conserved, it begins on the plane of idea and passes to the plane of primary experience; and again, instead of there being a loss as the result of the shift, there is a gain. The deed that I am about to do does not exist in some region remote from the present called the future; it exists not at all except as my present purpose and expectation, which are, however, also future. Hence through the shift towards the future, when the plan is fulfilled in the deed, there is compensation for what is lost through the shift to the past; and, as a result of both processes, there is a growing complexity in the present, which is reality; since something of the new that comes in at the future end of the process is not lost, but is conserved as memory or history, at the past end.

If this view is correct, it follows that past, present, and future are not exclusive; that to exist, which is always to exist in the present, is also to exist in the past and the present. There are no momentary existences. There are certainly no momentary selves. The self is a system of habits and memories; but habits and memories are 'the past over again,' and when I act in accordance with some habit or recollect some former deed, I am relieving a fragment of my former self. Yet, in thus reaching back into the past, I do not cease to live in the present; for my action and my memory are occurring *now*. Moreover, I never act without a plan, clear or vague; and when, reckoning with all relevant conditions, I 'dream on things to come,' my dream is more than mere prophecy; it is 'anticipation,' a taking before of the experience to which I am moving: hence, while my dream lasts, I am actually in the future. Nevertheless, I do not thereby cease to be in the present, for the dream is here and now. I am always at once past, present, and future, a threefold reality, but my past and my future lie within the present. Or consider a series of geological strata. The rock formations are dated in the past, yet they all lie here together in the present. And if I can predict what will overlie them as a new stratum, there must be something real of the future that even now makes my prediction true; otherwise, my judgment would be mere hypothesis, not truth. In general, whenever prediction is possible, there must be something of the future in the present which *makes* my predictions true: in the present reality of the comet, something which makes me certain of its return; in the earth, something which makes me certain of its continued revolution; nature, like man, must have its plans and its habits. The present is, therefore, no knife-edge, nor even of the limited breadth of a saddle-back, but as broad as history and prophecy.

The considerations adduced are fatal to the view of time as a series of instants comparable to the series of points on a line, and might serve to reinforce Bergson's critique. And it does not help matters at all to multiply the number of points to infinity, so long as the points and correlative instants are taken to be exclusive and repellent of their neighbours. Yet because time is not a series like that of the points on a line, it does not follow that it is no series at all, and that there is not a very definite order among its parts. In my book, *The Self and Nature*, I suggested that time might better be viewed as a series of overlapping areas, of which a series of concentric circles is the simplest illustration. Adopting this analogy for the moment, it is clear that the area of the outermost circle would represent *the* present, and the area of each inner circle would represent the parts of further presents which have been conserved; and since some part of each present always is conserved, there would be as many circles as there are 'moments' of past time, each moment containing within itself parts of all preceding moments. There would be no first moment (circle), and there would be a part of the total area contained in all circles or moments, namely the point that would be the limit of the series of diminishing circles. This point would represent the eternal part of reality. This analogy, like all static images of dynamic reality, is, of course, defective in that it does not provide for new presents, for growth. To remedy this defect, it is necessary to conceive of new circles being continually added on. However, this defect does not touch the main points of the discussion—the serial character of time and the non-exclusiveness of moments, for the laying down of new circles would occur in ordinal fashion, and the later circles would include the earlier. There is, nevertheless, one serious defect in the analogy, the failure to represent the inclusion of the future in the present; but, with some ingenuity, this could be remedied. The important fact of 'leakage' is represented by the diminishing area of the inner circles, while the growing area of the outer circles represents the increasing complexity of the present as compared with the past. Moreover, if the theory of relativity is true—I do not think that philosophy can *yet* assume that it is true—there would have to be as many circles as there are centres of experience, overlapping, to be sure, but never quite identical.

Space, no more than time, is a substance; but, as Leibniz asserted, a relation between substances. Moreover, as Guyau already knew, and as we are certain from the work of Minkowski and Einstein, space cannot be understood apart from time. Naturally, I can merely sketch what I believe to be the true picture of space. For example, the location of a thing is clearly ambiguous, if the entire thing, circumference as well as centre, is taken into account; for each percept of the thing is in a different place. For this reason, it is best to restrict the place of the thing to the place of its focus. Thus restricted, to choose the most interesting case, the place of the human mind turns out to be the same as the place of the brain, as Sellars has maintained. But, of course, place is nothing in itself, and one place can be defined only in relation to other places. A place is an office, and just as men may exchange their offices, as when two professors exchange their chairs for a year, so they may exchange their places; that is, the relations which A had are now had by B, and vice versa. Not all relations are relevant, but only the relation which may be called by a variety of names—influence, determination, communication. To be in the same space with another thing is to be able to influence, determine, communicate with that thing. In terms of this relation we can define what is meant by one thing being between two other things: A is between B and C, when, in terms of a certain type of process, if B is to influence C, it must first influence A; and conversely, if C is to influence A, it must also influence B. Three things have this order 'on the same straight line,' when a light signal, in order to reach C from B, must first pass through A. Again, one thing is in the neighbourhood of another, or is close to another, when, in order to communicate with that other, it can do so without first communicating with relatively many other substances. The dependence of space upon time is shown by the necessity for using the concept of temporal sequence in order to make these definitions. Distance can also be defined through the concept of communication in union with the concept of sequence. For one thing is nearer than another to a third, if in terms of a given process you can communicate with the one sooner than you can communicate with the other, starting from the third. Since, finally, metrical geometric relations can be reduced to ordinal relations, all spatial relations can be reduced to temporal relations, with the use of the concept of communication. Distance, 'spreadoutness,' voluminousness, etc., are secondary, not primary qualities of the world. Owing, however, to the tri-dimensionality of space, the carrying out of these definitions is extremely complicated; and if the theory of relativity is true, order itself, and therefore distance and location, are not determinate in certain cases.

Are space and time continuous or discontinuous, or is there some meaning in which they are both? Contemporary physics seems to answer, Both; and with regard to the special problems of science, metaphysics, standing in the position of humble learner, has nothing to say of her own. Yet in view of the fluctuating character of opinion in physics to-day, it is hazardous to accept any result as final; and, on the other hand, if the method of radical empiricism is acknowledged to be true, metaphysics has, I believe, something to contribute to the general problem. For if we are in earnest in taking the mind as the 'type-phenomenon,' we shall be inclined to accept as generally valid, the sort of continuity and discontinuity exemplified there. And what do we find when we examine experience? We find a basic continuity in the two fundamental dimensions of experience, its flow and its extension (the one corresponding to time and the other to space), and upon this continuity there is superposed discontinuity. Thus the 'advance' into the future of my experience is sensibly continuous, yet is broken by the discontinuity of the strokes of the campus clock as I hear them during the day; thus my visual field is sensibly continuous in the sense that there are no parts of it empty of colour, yet this continuity is overlaid with the discontinuities of the differences in colour between one patch and another.

The empirical continuity is, however, far from being continuity in the Cantorean sense, but rather in the sense of Aristotle, of unbrokenness and wholeness. In the empirical continuum there are no Dedikindean cuts, but party walls. In history, for example, there are no division lines between one age and another—say between the Middle Ages and the Renaissance; in the growth of the man, there is no point of time before which he is a child and after which he is a youth. A little way before, we can say, now he is a child, and a little way after, now he is an adolescent; but there is a stretch of time during which it is impossible to distinguish child from youth. So in space; some distance this side, I can say, now I am in this object; and some distance that side, now I am in that object, but there will be a stretch of space within which the objects are one. Empirically, things fuse at the edges, and at the edges the principle of excluded middle does not apply. It is a mere dogma to insist that it must apply everywhere; whatever validity the principles of logic have is empirically grounded. Nevertheless, I would not go the whole way with Bergson; for while insisting on the wholeness and unbrokenness of the empirical continuum, I believe that distinctions exist within it, except at the edges, where one thing shades off into another. The principle of excluded middle has a limited, and only a limited, validity. I am therefore not surprised to learn that contemporary physical theory does not seek to define the position of a particle at an instant, but merely a certain range within which it may be known to exist. This is not, I should think, a purely 'epistemic' difficulty (to borrow the convenient term of W. E. Johnson), but a metaphysical state of affairs. Following the guidance of the radically empirical facts, we shall expect the universe to contain an enormous number of centres of experience, of varying degrees of complexity, communicating with each other, some more directly, some more indirectly, through few or many intermediaries; and finally constituting as a whole a continuous unbroken substance, for the reason that there is direct contact between foci nearest to each other, in a next to next fashion. Thus, while there is discontinuity and only indirect communication between one man and another, there is direct and continuous communication between a man's mind and his body; or what is the same thing, between the nervous system and the somatic processes of the body: no one knows where the mind begins and the body ends. Certainly in the sensory processes, at the point where stimulus and reaction meet, and perhaps in many an obscure impulse, the mind of the nervous system and the 'mind' of the 'soma' *overlap*.

Once the non-empirical and approximate character of the Cantorean continuum is recognized, there remains no reason for believing either that there are an infinite number of foci or that each is infinitely complex. Empirically, we have what may be called an Aristotelian continuum, with a finite number of individuals enmeshed within it, both in extension and in flow; and while it is true that the success of physics in applying the differential calculus to nature seems to be a good argument for belief in nature's infinite complexity, two considerations on the other side are relevant. First, the application of the calculus is never more than approximate; and, second, recent researches into the foundations of the theory of functions, notably by such men as Brouwer and Weyl, have at least cast doubt upon the soundness of the structure completed by Cantor. It is my own opinion that the familiar paradoxes of the infinite have never been satisfactorily explained away, and that, viewed as an existence, an infinite collection is a self-contradictory notion. (I once ventured this opinion to Mr. Russell, who told me that if I had studied the matter for thirty years as he had, I would reach a different conclusion; I have to confess that I have studied it for only twenty years, and that not continuously.) It is again my personal opinion, which, however, I now hold with less diffidence than a decade ago, that the whole notion of existence should be abandoned in the philosophy of the infinite, and rules of construction substituted. Thus, instead of postulating in a dense point set that there exists a point between any two points, it should be postulated that I may construct one between any two whenever I want to; and, of course, I shall never get more than a finite number. In Aristotelian phraseology, the infinite is at best potential, never actual. This is certainly true of time; obviously of the future, the stages of which are not, as such, actual; but it is no less true of the past, for, as we have seen, the past exists either as persisting substance, within which no stages can be distinguished, since it is identical both in the present and in the past, or as memory and record, which never reveal more than a finite number of events.

These considerations relative to continuity and discontinuity are incompatible with an atomistic interpretation of mind and nature. The fact that, judging from history, atomism seems to be congenial to science, cannot weigh against its falsity from a radically empirical point of view. And to-day the inadequacy of atomism is receiving wide recognition; in psychology, notably by the members of the *Gestalt* school, and in the philosophy of science, by Whitehead, who recognizes that point, instant, and even event, when conceived atomistically, are constructions, not facts. Whole and part, not element and complex, are the metaphysically valid categories. Atomism has, to be sure, a last refuge to-day in the 'logical atomism' of Russell and Wittgenstein; but, once more, the *facts* require a different interpretation. There is no living philosopher who is not in debt to these thinkers —none more than I am—nor do I suppose that one can refute this doctrine in a paragraph; but, to my thinking, the unity or wholeness of the proposition is falsified by atomism; the assumed 'simples' are constructions, not facts; and a logic that has no room for general facts as such and denies the logical connection between present and future is clearly inadequate. But to return to the exposition of my philosophical *credo*.

Every centre of experience is in communication, directly or indirectly, with every other. (If the theory of relativity is true, there are exceptions to this, when the separation between centres is space-like.) This implies mutual determination, but allows for the relative isolation of systems. Moreover, every event that occurs is a response, determined partly from within its own centre, and partly by its 'neighbourhood.' There is no absolute spontaneity; for without the relations between one centre and another, nothing would happen; yet there is freedom in the sense that every event is determined from within its own relatively isolated home. Every fact is a co-operative deed. We think of a painting as the work of the artist, but his mind would be in-effective without his hand, his paint, and his canvas; these must lend themselves to his effort, and the product is their joint act. Every event is, therefore, multiply determined and richer in its significance than immediately appears. In the end, the entire universe is implicated; yet, for all this, there is freedom; for if the world has made me what I am, I in turn have made the world.

One reason for the denial of even so limited a spontaneity as this, is a false view of time. For if, as according to old views of time, the past were discontinuous with the present, and the present were its mere effect, there could obviously be no self-determination anywhere in the universe. But if, as I would maintain, the past exists in the present, its control over the present is the present's own control of itself. We cannot, for example, shift the blame for our conduct upon our hereditary past; for our heredity exists and operates within ourselves; hence in blaming it we blame ourselves. If we say, 'The past has made me what I am,' the answer is, 'You are that past that made you.'

Any statement of a philosophical *credo* to-day must include some stand with reference to the subject of evolution, especially as interpreted in the sense of 'emergence,' creative evolution, discontinuity of levels. And here my stand is far from the con-temporary orthodoxy. In the first place, I am unable, with Bergson and Alexander, to regard evolution as a category of the universe. Evolution, I believe, is an affair of the part, not of the whole of reality. Individual systems rise, flourish and decay, but the universe 'has no seasons.' Moreover, it is my conviction that what we call the inorganic physical world is a higher system than either the vital or the human. This is, I admit, a matter about which it is difficult to offer demonstrative arguments; but such reasons as I have are the following: First, a negative argu-ment. The superior complexity of biological facts from a chemical point of view is not an argument against my belief, since if you take the larger physical systems as wholes, like the solar system, for example, with all the phenomena they include, they are undoubtedly more complex than the organism. The philosophy of evolution has made the mistake of comparing the atom with the cell; instead of comparing the cell with, for example, the sun. This procedure is as false as it would be to judge the capacity of the organism as a whole with the capacity of the cell. Without doubt the atom is lowlier than the cell, but atoms are members of vast physical systems, possessed of their own individuality and way of existence, and these systems are incomparably higher in the scale than a man. Second, the more recent philosophy of physics tends to break down the sharpness of the distinction between the physical and the biological, in extending the concept of organism to the atom and the electron, and in recognizing a realm of physical chemistry. Last, physical systems are more permanent and stable than vital organisms, and with me, at any rate, this is an argument for their superiority. The contemporary mind does not feel the force of this consideration because of its romantic predilection for the transient and wayward—in short, for the pathetic. The Greek worship of the stars and Plotinus's notion of emanation represent, I believe, a truer conception of man's place in the universe than contemporary naturalism, which places man at the pinnacle of reality.

I find, however, a single valuable idea in the contemporary concept of emergence, namely a recognition of a strain of irrationality in existence. I have already insisted on this from other points of view. Here the emphasis is on the irrational element in causation. We are told that at certain 'critical' points in the world process, namely in the transition from physical to chemical action, from chemical to vital, from vital to mental, new types of behaviour and new qualities emerge, which, while determined by the earlier phases of existence, in the sense of growing out of them and being impossible without them, are nevertheless unpredictable from the earlier and irreducible to the system of the earlier phases. This concept of emergence is, by the way, not new; for one finds it in Schopenhauer long before Lloyd Morgan, Boutroux, Alexander, or Sellars. My chief point of criticism, and the only one I shall make here, is that the restriction of this irrational aspect of causality to a few spots is unwarranted. Our greatest American philosopher, Charles Peirce, had the truer vision in recognizing the presence of irrationality in all causality; and in what I am about to write I am following the spirit, if not the letter, of his thought. What I have in mind is this: law, and hence predictability, are secondary, not primary. It is true that, as we have seen, every event is determined as growing out of some system; but how it shall grow when the system contains novel elements can never be known beforehand; and there always 'emerges,' therefore, something unknown to the world hitherto. It is only after such an event has once happened that we can predict that, under the same circumstances, it will happen again; for by reason of its very happening, a habit or tendency to happen thus again has been established. Every new habit grows out of an old one, but when the old habit functions under novel conditions, its new development is never subject to exact formulation. Moreover, no situation in the world is ever quite new or quite old; hence everything that happens is at once subject to law and also beyond law. Law defines only the limits within which an event will take place, and these limits are precisely fixed; but within their bounds there is free play.

In contrast to all forms of materialism and naturalism, descended from the ancient line of Leucippus, Democritus, Epicurus, and Lucretius, which hold that value is a mere accident, incident, or epiphenomenon in the world, confined to certain so-called 'high level' regions, and that, therefore, there might well have been a world without value, I would maintain that value and existence are always correlative. This was the supreme insight of the counter-tradition of Pythagoras, Socrates, Plato, and Aristotle. There are certain facts within experience which are, I should say, obviously impossible apart from value: the song of the *prima donna*, the deed of love, the wine shared with friends. To suppose, as materialism does, that these things could be without their value is plain topsy-turveydom in philosophy. And such facts reveal clearly the nature of all value, as satisfaction of wish, or anticipation or memory of satisfaction of wish, usually all three together, since a wish fulfils itself in stages, looking before and after. Yet experience contains other things that are not so obviously values: the green colour and smell of grass, the pattern of a crystal, the shape of a cloud. Wherever in the mind the activities function and give form to percepts, there is value undeniable; but in the case of other percepts, where our experience is determined, not so much from within as from without, there is no obvious value. Yet even such facts, I should claim, are correlative with value; and I take my stand on the type-phenomenon, which is for me the key to the interpretation of the universe. For consider the song that I hear; this is a percept that no wish of mine has determined; yet some wish has determined it, for without some stirring in the breast of the singer, not only not she, but also not I, would hear it. Every percept is, similarly, determination from without, and also communication of value. Even the shape of the cloud, the pattern of the crystal, the smell and scent of grass, are the expression of some wish, somewhere in the world. I admit that I have no sympathetic understanding of these values; yet—to use the example of James—neither has the cat any understanding of the sonata that wakes her slumber. And while the value of some percepts is not a value for me, it is a value for me that I have all the percepts that I do have, because the whole structure of my own values is made secure only by working in cooperation with the external forces that control my percepts, and of which my percepts are a sign.

It has been the assumption of certain forms of religious sentiment that we are able to understand the values expressed in what we call the forces of nature, and that these forces are biased in our favour. But this is, I believe, a great mistake. There is no reason to suppose that man plays more than an insignificant part in the cosmic drama. The more mystical types of religion have recognized this in conceiving the glory of God, rather than the welfare of man, as the highest good. The passion of love, which, like religion, has often claimed a supermoral justification, is also a witness to this in its high contempt for prudential and conventional values, as if it knew itself to be serving larger interests that work themselves out in the biological, as distinct from the

DE WITT H. PARKER

183

human and social facts of the organism. However this be, it is
certain that no easy optimism regarding man's destiny follows
from the recognition of the union of value and existence. For the
values of one centre of experience are too often bought at the
cost of the values of other centres. The universe is the theatre
for a mighty conflict of wills, and without sacrifice there can be
no good anywhere. There is, nearest to us, the conflict of wishes
within each self; there is man's conflict with his fellows; the
disharmony, as exemplified by death, between himself and the
purely biologic facts of his organism; and finally, the conflict
between the human mind and its inorganic 'environment.' This
last—the inorganic world—is the final arbiter of our fate, and
to its will all other wills must bow. Nevertheless, it is possible
to exaggerate these conflicts, forgetting the inner peace of the
good man and the equilibrium of wishes attained in the imagination through art; forgetting mutual aid among men and the fact
that it is nature herself that, having permitted the new manner
of existence we call life, and later the human mind, still sustains
us. Our adaptation to the environment is also its adaptation to
us. Nature is ever the Great Mother. Yet this we know, that
whatever harmony is attained either by man or by nature is no
'easy beauty,' but a beauty founded upon conflict, the 'difficult'
beauty of tragedy.

PRINCIPAL PUBLICATIONS

The Self and Nature. (Cambridge, Mass: Harvard University Press,
1917.) Pp. 316.
The Principles of Aesthetics. (Boston: Silver, Burdett & Co., 1920.)
Pp. 366.
The Analysis of Art. (New Haven: The Yale University Press, 1926.)
Pp. 190.
"L'Esthétique de Kant: Une Appréciation," in Hommes (published
at Etichove, Belgium. No. 1, January, 1927, pp. 16–34.)
"Introductory Essay on Schopenhauer," in Selections from Schopen-
hauer. (The Modern Student's Library, Charles Scribner's Sons,
1927.)

REALISM IN RETROSPECT

By RALPH BARTON PERRY

Born 1876; Professor of Philosophy, Harvard University,
Cambridge, Mass.

REALISM IN RETROSPECT

I. THE CAMPAIGN AGAINST IDEALISM

I UNDERSTAND that the purpose of the present book is to deliver its authors from the bonds of reticence, or from that canon of literary taste which limits the use of the first person. I therefore begin with the pronoun "I," and shall use it with reckless frequency. I shall also speak out the faith that is in me, allowing my beliefs to override my critical conscience. To begin with, let me confess that when, for the purpose of recovering the past, I re-read my earliest writings, they impress me as extremely convincing, affording an unexpected confirmation of my present philosophical bias. Myself of twenty-five years ago committed blunders, no doubt, but his faults were the faults of youth and inexperience. His heart was in the right place.

Such philosophical nourishment as I received in early youth was derived from Emerson and Carlyle. From them I caught no hint of transcendental metaphysics, but only a desire to be heroic. This influence, together with an intense adolescent religious experience, brought me to the threshold of manhood with a vague eagerness "to do good," or to contribute something to the triumph of that cause of righteousness which I identified with Christianity. My pre-natal philosophical experience was obtained at Princeton, where an emeritus McCosh still walked the campus, and where "Jeremy" Ormond, ponderous, high-minded, and unintelligible, accustomed the ear and the pen to a polysyllabic vocabulary. Migrating from Princeton to Harvard in the middle 'nineties was for me a perilous spiritual adventure, an abrupt transition from faith to criticism. Here, for the first time, something happened to my *mind*, and the vocation of the ministry was gradually transformed, without reaction or bitterness, into that of the teacher and scholar. Creeds and dogmas having become impossible, I thought that I had found a way in which I might think freely and still "do good." It is that naïve hope that has sustained me ever since.

At Harvard in the late 'nineties it was, for most of us, a choice between James and Royce. Palmer taught us ethics, and by his example taught us how to teach. Santayana was historical and critical, Münsterberg schematic, and Everett learned. These were important elements in the configuration, and they generated both heat and light. But as regards fundamentals, whether of doctrine, method, or temper of mind, there was the way of Royce and the way of James. Royce was the battleship, heavily armoured, both for defence and offence. James combined the attributes of the light cruiser, the submarine, and the bombing aeroplane. It was natural to suppose that Royce was impregnable and irresistible. To surrender to him was as easy and as unexciting as to be a fundamentalist in Arkansas. James provided the rallying-point for those in whom the youthful spirit of revolt was stronger than tradition and prestige. Royce was the latest and nearest of a mighty race. His philosophy was powerfully reinforced by the texts of Bradley and Green, and by the great cult of Kant. His was the party of law and order, of piety and decency. This was not Royce's fault, nor did it at all adequately express his personal traits; but he suffered, none the less, from the taint of established things. So when James, overcoming his earlier fears, had the audacity to make jokes about the Absolute, there were Athenian youths who laughed with him. Many of us have, since that time, become sadder, and, I hope, wiser. But the spell of absolute idealism was irreparably broken. There arose a generation of younger philosophers who were, as Creighton expressed it (speaking more in sorrow than in anger), "flippant, like James."

James's right to flippancy was well earned. In the year 1896–97 he conducted a group of us through the text of Kant, and when, after months of intense effort and profound discouragement, he told me that I might sometimes attribute my difficulty to the author's obscurity or pedantry, rather than to my own feebleness, he conferred on me the title to a canine bark of my own even when Sir Oracle had spoken. James's example did not suggest an ignorance of philosophical literature, but it did beget in all of his students the habit of checking every text, no matter how authoritative, by their own experience. The question "What does the text say?" was incidental to the ulterior questions,

"What does the author mean?" and "Is it so?" I was not surprised, therefore, that upon receiving a copy of my maiden effort on "The Abstract Freedom of Kant,"[1] James should have written me expressing the hope that I might now feel justified in casting off the Kantian "ball and chain" which had for many years hampered the movements of philosophy.

To specify my indebtedness to James is as impossible as it would be to enumerate the traits which I have inherited from my parents. In view of contemporary developments in philosophy, I should like, however, to record the most vivid of the doctrinal impressions which he left upon me in the early days. I can remember even the stage-setting—the interior of the room in Sever Hall, the desk with which the lecturer took so many liberties, and the gestures with which James animatedly conveyed to us the intuition of common-sense realism. From that day I confess that I have never wavered in the belief that our perceptual experience disclosed a common world, inhabited by our perceiving bodies and our neighbours, and qualified by the evidence of our senses.[2]

It was the controversial atmosphere of my early studies that led to my preoccupation with the shortcomings of idealism, and to my sustained interest in the classification of contemporary philosophical tendencies.[3] European and American Philosophy, as I saw it at the close of the nineteenth century, was a dispute between the extravagant claims of the party of science (naturalism) and the equally extravagant claims of that post-Kantian idealistic philosophy, which, invigorated by its transplantation from Germany to a foreign soil, had become the bulwark of English-speaking Protestant piety.

It is unprofitable to quarrel over the diverse meanings of the term "idealism." That idealism which I went out to slay was

[1] *Philosophical Review*, 1900.
[2] The substance of this teaching was afterwards embodied in the article entitled "How Two Minds Can Know One Thing," which James published in the *Journal of Philosophy, Psychology, and Scientific Methods*, 1905.
[3] "Professor Royce's Refutation of Realism and Pluralism," *Monist*, 1902; *The Approach to Philosophy*, 1905; *Present Philosophical Tendencies*, 1912; *Present Conflict of Ideals*, 1918; *Philosophy of the Recent Past*, 1926.

born of the marriage of subjectivism and universalism. Its proof seemed to me then, as it seems to me still, to consist in an unseaworthy subjectivism rescued from the shipwreck of solipsism by the miraculous intervention of absolutism. The first premise is subjectivism, the doctrine, namely, that to be = to be perceived or thought. The second premise is universalism, the doctrine, namely, that being cannot be a product of human perception or thought, because man is a part of nature, and because the truth is a standard by which human perception and thought are themselves to be judged and corrected. The conclusion is absolute idealism, the doctrine, namely, that to be = to be perceived or thought (or willed, or felt, or otherwise manifested) by a transfinite, all-containing and infallible mind, commonly called *"the* Absolute."

The argument is dialectical and a priori, and its force depends on the truth of both premises. The critics of this reigning doctrine are readily divisible into two groups: those commonly called "realists," who have attacked the first premise; and those variously called "pragmatists," "instrumentalists," and "humanists," who have attacked the second premise. The former group being united by their rejection of subjectivism, are divided among themselves on the question of universalism; the latter, being united by their rejection of universalism, are divided on the issue of subjectivism. Both groups reject absolute idealism, but while one rejects this doctrine on the score of its idealism, the other rejects it on the score of its absolutism.

For the realist, then, the Absolute, construed as an individual mind or spirit, in which the imperfections of humanity are overcome and its prerogatives maximated—construed, in other words, as a being qualified to serve at one and the same time as the metaphysical reality, the moral standard and the object of worship—is the offspring of subjectivism. Such a being is not merely absolute: it is mind conceived as absolute. "I perceive," or "I judge," or "I will," or some similar act of conscious mind, is first supposed to be the inescapable form of reality; and since to identify this "I" with you or me or any or all finite creatures is palpably absurd, it is then inferred that there must be an "I" which is no creature at all, but the Creator. And, as Bradley has put it, what must be, is. Hence in so far as the realist refutes subjectivism he at the same time destroys the meaning and the ground of the Absolute in this idealistic sense.

An idealist of the post-Kantian school resents being called a "subjectivist," but this is because he takes the term to imply that the "subject" in question is the natural or psychological subject. If "subjectivism" be used to mean that all being is the dependent creation of *some* subject, or self, or mind, whether finite or absolute, then, I think, the term can be applied to the idealist without offence. In accordance with this usage absolute idealism is that species of subjectivism in which the unconditioned and all-conditioning subject has, over and above such properties as make it a subject, those other properties of infinity, perfection, and systematic unity, which the term "Absolute" is intended to convey. With this understanding I shall hereinafter use the terms "subjectivism" and "idealism" interchangeably.

The wide prevalence of subjectivism has always seemed to me to be due, in the first place, to excessive insistence on a relation which the reflective habits of the philosopher dispose him to magnify. Subjectivism exploits the relation, namely, which the world indubitably has to the human subject whenever he perceives it, or thinks about it, or otherwise concerns himself with it. He exploits this him-ward aspect of things *metaphysically*—that is, he construes it as fundamental, or takes it as affording the deepest insight. The realist, on the other hand, calls attention to the fact that this emphasis, natural as it is, may be misleading. Thus when Pistol says, "Why, then the world's mine oyster," we recognize that he is taking liberties with the world. It is true that the world is, among other things, Pistol's oyster, and Pistol is excusable for having mentioned the fact. But if, as a philosopher, one were interested in making the most significant possible statement about the world, it would scarcely be pertinent to remark that the world is that which is opened by Pistol's sword. This is not one of those central and pregnant characteristics of the world of which the metaphysician is in search. In the course of its career the world does meet Pistol, but this conjunction does not determine its orbit or destiny, nor does the bivalvular aspect which it presents to Pistol's sword afford the best clue to its essential structure.

In a sense that is at least superficially similar to Pistol's oyster, nature is Berkeley's percept and Kant's thought, or the idea of any philosopher who applies his mind to it. And it is not strange that sooner or later some philosopher should have taken this fact as the key to metaphysics. But the realist is one who is disposed, until more decisive evidence is advanced, to construe this indubitable relationship of the world to the mind that deals with it, as an accidental or subordinate aspect of the world. He refuses to assume [1] that knowing the world implies proprietorship. It is still open to him to suppose, with common sense, that the world *lends* itself to being known without surrendering itself wholly to that use. Such a view has its support in experiences that are no less authentic than Pistol's sense of ownership. If the idealist is justified in saying with Margaret Fuller, "I accept the universe," the realist is equally justified in remarking with Carlyle, "By gad, she'd better."

The question of the place of knowing mind in the universe, whether central or peripheral, is complicated by what I have called the "ego-centric predicament."[2] This was a successful bit of phrase-making, if one is to judge by the frequency with which it has been misunderstood. My purpose in introducing the phrase was to call attention to the fact that idealists have used as an argument what is, in fact, only a difficulty. The difficulty or predicament consists in the fact that the extent to which knowledge conditions any situation in which it is present cannot be discovered by the simple and conclusive method of direct elimination. I cannot see what things look like when my eyes are shut, or judge the effect of extinguishing my thought. If I cognize *a* in any way, shape, or manner, I am not cognizing *a* in the absence of that way, shape, or manner of cognition. This is, of course, a

[1] Arbitrarily to assign the leading rôle to a predicate merely because it happens to come first in the order of discovery or of discourse, has been called the "Fallacy of Initial Predication" (*The New Realism*, 1912, p. 15).

[2] "The Ego-Centric Predicament," *Journal of Philosophy, Psychology, and Scientific Method*, 1910.

truism, and in itself of no significance whatever. It does, however, bring to light the fact that the question which subjectivism raises is unique. In order that the question shall be *answered* at all, it is necessary to introduce the very factor, namely, the answering mind, which in examining this question it would be convenient to exclude. It follows that either the question must remain unanswered or that it must be attacked in some more indirect and perhaps less conclusive manner. If, for example, one can find out what the cognizing mind is and what it does, one can then discount its presence, or learn how much of the situation to ascribe to it.

Idealism has been guilty, historically, of arguing from what is only a methodological difficulty. It has created the appearance of a significant affirmation by concealing a redundancy. No one would think it worth while to say, "It is impossible for me to discover anything which is, when I discover it, undiscovered by me," or, "It is impossible that anything should remain totally unknown after it has become known"; but to say, "It is impossible to discover anything that is not thought," or, "It is impossible to find anything that is not known," has seemed to many idealists to be the beginning of philosophical wisdom—in spite of the fact that the self-evidence of the last two propositions consists entirely in the fact that "discover" and "thought," "find" and "known," are taken as meaning the same thing.

My contention has been, then, that the "ego-centric predicament" creates not the slightest presumption either for idealism or for realism. It is equally compatible with either alternative, although it has been, and still is, very generally supposed to nourish idealism and to stick in the crop of realism.

So far idealism is seen to rest on bias or ambiguity. The other arguments which have been advanced in its behalf are deserving of more respectful consideration, since they appeal to material facts for which any alternative theory must provide.

The oldest of the idealistic arguments are those which idealism shares with scepticism. Idealism has been held sometimes to be scepticism, sometimes to furnish the only authentic *escape* from it. Arguments of this general class may be summarily treated under the heads of "physiological relativism" and "psychological relativism."

Physiological relativism rests on the fact that sensation is doubly conditioned: externally, by a physical stimulus; and internally by the position, properties, and state of the organism. Sensation is then construed as the joint product or appearance created by these factors. At this point of the argument three alternatives diverge. The confirmed sceptic will hold that sensation, untrustworthy as it is, affords the only knowledge we possess, since thought is only its paler reflection. This is idealism of a sort, but a bankrupt, insolvent idealism—patently self-contradictory. The two remaining alternatives are realistic. The physicochemical realist credits scientific thought as a way of escape from the subjective relativities of sensation. The agnostic realist, holding with the sceptic that physico-chemical concepts are only reproductions of sense-experience, and equally subjective, still credits the residual reflection that sense-experience is produced by the action *of* something he knows not how *upon* something he knows not what. It is clear that, whatever their validity, arguments from physiological relativism afford small comfort to the idealist.

Psychological relativism is a scepticism of thought rather than of sense; indeed, it is often used as an argument in support of sense. The argument rests on the fact of prejudice. Thought is held to be an effect of emotion, will, habit, imitation, historical development, or social *milieu*; and reality, as man thinks it, to be a mere projection of human bias. Here, again, three paths diverge. If, in the first place, one appeals from thought to sense on the ground that sense is externally controlled, one moves in the direction of the scepticisms and realisms already considered. The second alternative is to rest in the relativity of thought, or to accept psychological scepticism as the last word. This view, that the world is what man thinks it, and that man's thinking of it varies from individual to individual and from time to time, is a widespread doctrine in modern philosophy; but it is not that idealism with which I am here concerned. The third alternative, the absolute idealism which modern realism seeks to slay, is an idealism which has already slain and devoured scepticism, and which rests its claim to acceptance largely upon that conquest. Psychological relativism is held to be intolerable, because it gives equal credit to contradictory human assertions, and because, since it places nature inside of a mind which is itself inside of nature, it is viciously circular. Realism and absolute idealism here take the same ground, and both attribute to thought a power to recognize and transcend its own relativities. The difference lies in the nature of this corrective thought. For realism its nature lies in its more perfect fidelity to fact, or in its more dispassionate and colourless objectivity. For idealism its nature lies in its profounder and more authoritative subjectivity. For realism thinking truly is a conformity of mind to the given reality, while for idealism thinking truly is a conformity of the finite mind to a universal mind.[1]

This resort to absolute idealism as the way of escape from psychological relativism involves two steps, both of which the realist refuses to take. The first step is to discredit sense-perception. The relative passivity of this mode of experience, instead of being construed as a mark of cognitive superiority because it suggests a deference of the knowing mind to its objects, is construed as a mark of inferiority because the genius of the mind itself is too imperfectly manifested. Sense becomes a virtual, incipient, or degraded form of thought. The absolute idealist can usually be recognized by his insistence that pure sensation is a myth, but pure or impure he can hardly deny it, and it still remains as one of his most serious stumbling-blocks.

The second step is to construe thought as essentially creative. There is a widespread disposition (a disposition connected, no

[1] Since this universal mind may be itself governed by will or emotion, as well as by cold logic, absolute idealism does not necessarily imply the rejection of moral, æsthetic, or religious experiences as sources of metaphysical insight. Any idealizing activity of mind, in which man recognizes the gap between aspiration and present attainment, may be taken as a revelation of that standard spiritual being whose self-realization furnishes the motive force of creation.

doubt, with the common-sense dogma that if things are not physical they must be mental) to suppose that the objects of thought, such as laws, mathematical quantities and forms, principles, categories, concepts, universals, necessities, possibilities, relations, and systematic unities, are the *creatures* of thought. Since the orderly structure of nature, as exhibited in the sciences, would fall to pieces without such connective tissue, this supposition is of decisive consequence, and is chiefly responsible for the hold of modern idealism upon those "tougher" minds which are not affected by its sentimental appeal.

Hence the rejection of a subjectivistic logic, and mathematics is one of the major arguments in the realistic polemic. Claiming the support of Socrates and Plato, and alliance with the whole stream of philosophical doctrine down through the Scholastics and Cartesians, modern realism distinguishes between the imaginative play of speculative thought, on the one hand, and, on the other hand, those moments of insight, acceptance, or contemplation in which the mind is confronted by a being not of its own making. Thought has moments in which its own caprice is superseded by specificities, connections, and consequences as intrusive and inexorable as the resistance of material bodies. One may think what one will, but having thought one finds oneself involved in natures and relations which have a way of their own, a way which must now be loyally followed if one is to think truly. The realms of mathematics and logic are not governed by psychological laws, but by laws intrinsic to themselves. Idealists recognize this autonomy, and thereupon extend and exalt the meaning of mind to embrace the larger domain. But to confer the term "mind" upon the intelligible features of the world, whether viewed abstractedly in hierarchies of categories, or concretely in the systematic unity of nature, can serve no useful purpose. It adds nothing to our understanding of that specific mode of natural existence associated with animal bodies from which the term "mind" derives its original meaning, while at the same time it invests the intelligible features of the world with an aspect of complaisance to man, and thus flatters hopes that it does not really justify.

No summary of idealistic arguments would be complete without mention of that argument which idealism shares with spiritualism. The distinctive mark of modern idealism is, I believe, its annexation of the object to the act or state or mode of knowledge, whether in the Berkeleyan or in the Kantian manner. But modern idealism also absorbs and continues a strain of metaphysical speculation which is much older. According to this older or spiritualistic view, the metaphysical demand for a substantial being and an originating cause can be met only by self-consciousness, which, as intuitively apprehended, dissolves the dialectical difficulties which beset the time-worn topics of the "one and the many," "the thing and its qualities," "identity and difference," "freedom and necessity," and "infinity." Mind, so it is alleged, is superlatively and exclusively qualified for reality. This view rests, however, on the assumption that the nature of mind is self-evident. Modern realists, for the most part, reject this alleged revelation in the name of patient observation and rigorous analysis. They regard the nature of mind, not as the primal insight, but as a highly complicated and baffling problem which possesses in an eminent degree whatever difficulties beset the problem of reality in general.[1] The first personal pronoun is felt to resemble a question-mark more than an exclamation point.

To these counter-arguments, by which realism has disputed the claims of idealism, I should like to add the difference of philosophical method and attitude which has often divided these opposing schools. It was not an accident that realists should have formulated a platform and attempted collaboration. Anglo-American idealism, impregnated as it is with the romantic tradition, has encouraged the individual to regard himself as an authoritative organ of truth, or a fountain of lyric self-expression.

[1] I have argued that the idealist's position rests here upon a confusion between the apparent simplicity of the familiar or the innocence of the eye, and the objective simplicity which survives the effort to distinguish an internal multiplicity. I have termed this error "the fallacy of pseudo-simplicity." Cf. "Realism as a Polemic and Programme of Reform," *Journal of Philosophy*, vol. vii (1910), p. 371.

To members of such a cult every attempt to define terms or to organize research must necessarily be abhorrent. Realists, on the other hand, cling to the naïve view that in the presence of common objects two philosophical minds should be able to find some area of agreement, or at least to localize and formulate their disagreement. The realist is baffled and annoyed by what seems to him the arrogant obscurity of idealism, which appears to claim the licence of poetry without assuming its artistic responsibilities. For the same reasons the realist is attracted by the use of the mathematical method, as a possible means of rendering philosophical discourse genuinely communicative, and philosophical discussion profitable and conclusive.

There is another incompatibility of temper which has divided idealists and realists. Idealistic metaphysics is essentially an a priori doctrine. Its central reality is inferred and not experienced. Indeed, the whole realm of human experience is disparaged as appearance. There is a tendency to solve problems in principle rather than in detail, or merely to read them by title. Since truth consists in the light shed by the whole on the part, since the Absolute is thus by definition the supreme solver of problems, and since all other minds are tainted with finitude, there is a temptation to rest cheerfully in the midst of unconquered difficulties, even when they are difficulties of the philosopher's own making. But pious resignation is not fruitful in philosophy. Whatever be the reasons, it seems to me in any case to be a fact that the idealist has contributed nothing to our understanding of infinity and continuity comparable with the contributions of the mathematical logician; and nothing to our understanding of the nature of consciousness, perception, matter, causality, or the relation of mind and body, comparable with the contributions made by their contemporaries of the pragmatist and realist schools. Idealists have been system-builders and have staked all on the monumental perfection of the whole. James, Bergson, Russell, and Whitehead, on the other hand, pay as they go. You do not have to be converted to their gospel in order to profit by them. They abound in suggestive hypothesis, shrewd observation, and delicate analysis which you can detach and build into your own thinking. The newer philosophy which has grown up in opposition to idealism, and which has set a fashion which even idealism is now adopting, has something of the fruitfulness of empirical science. It is achieving results which, because of their factual basis, may survive the decline of the systematic theories in which they are presently embodied.

Such, in brief, is the train of argument by which I have justified my own dissent from idealism, and in which for the most part I have been in agreement with those of my American colleagues who in 1910 formulated a "Programme and First Platform,"[1] and in 1912 wrote in collaboration the volume entitled *The New Realism*. The defence against the idealistic argument is only a part of the realistic polemic, but it is the most indispensable part—the declaration of independence, by which a new philosophy has sought to gain diplomatic recognition. This war of liberation has, it is true, been supported by an invasion of the enemy's territory. But here the chief weapon employed has been that charge of solipsism which is as familiar to idealists as to their opponents. Realism has, furthermore, been compelled in turn to consolidate and defend its own position. But the historic significance of the American movement at the opening of the present century will, I think, lie in its having revived and modernized a way of thinking which, in spite of its antiquity and its agreement both with science and with common sense, had at the close of the previous century been consigned to the obituary columns of the most authoritative philosophical organs.

Absolute idealism, at the very moment of its seeming triumph over naturalism, was attacked on both flanks: on the one by pragmatism, and on the other by the new realism. The former attack came first and had already lowered the morale of the idealistic forces when the realistic onslaught occurred. The issue of the battle is decisive only in the sense that the supremacy of idealism is destroyed. The hopes of naturalism, as well as of

[1] *Journal of Philosophy*, vol. vii (1910), p. 393.

medieval scholasticism, have revived owing to assistance received from unexpected quarters. The idealists, though checked, have rallied. Pragmatists and realists have fallen afoul of one another at the point of their convergent attack. Former enemies are fraternizing. Ranks are broken and regimental colours are abandoned on the field. What have realists to contribute to the reconstruction that now promises to follow after war?

The answer to this question is too long and too recent a story to find a place in this brief retrospect. Furthermore, it does not belong, in any exclusive sense, to an account of realism. Still less does it belong to my own personal philosophical autobiography. Indeed, that which is most characteristic of the present moment in philosophy, as I understand it, is a confluence of currents which have hitherto run in separate channels. We are (and I am glad, as well as convinced, that it is so) less inclined than formerly to pride ourselves on partisan loyalties and polemical victories. A contemplative observer of the times would have great difficulty in describing its characteristic philosophical activity in terms of the doctrinal cleavages that were so well marked at the opening of the century. Its most conspicuous feature is, I think, an avoidance of the dualisms and disjunctions with which the influence of Descartes is associated. This attitude is due in part to recent changes in science, in part to a revival of interest in ancient and medieval philosophy, and in part to a growing sense of the inadequacy of any of the sharply antithetical alternatives which divided the thought of the last century. Conceptions such as "pattern," "aspect," "pure experience," "essence," "emergence," "event" owe their present vogue to the hope of healing the breach between mind and matter, soul and body, religion and science, teleology and mechanism, or substance and attribute. Viewed in the light of this conjunctive or reconciling motive, there is a recognizable strain of similarity in the thought of James, Bergson, Husserl, Alexander, Bosanquet, McTaggart, Stout, Whitehead, Russell, Broad, Dewey, Santayana, Strong, Montague, and Holt. It would be pretentious and unwarranted for realism to claim the credit for this tendency, but it would be blind to deny that the

Anglo-American realism of the first decade of the century helped notably to prepare the way.[1]

II. A Practical Creed and the Reasons Why

That element in my composition which inclined me in earlier years to the Christian ministry is accountable, no doubt, for my sustained interest in moral philosophy,[2] an interest which in recent years had broadened to embrace the whole realm of "value." The passing of years, the habit of philosophizing, and, perhaps, the changed atmosphere of the times, have combined to give this interest more of reflective detachment and less of that reforming zeal which once burned within me.

At the foundation of my moral philosophy lies a temper of mind which I take to be the same as that which has led me to the rejection of idealism in other fields. Knowledge I regard as essentially a facing of facts, the conforming of a belief to that which, relatively to the belief, is antecedent and fixed. As between knowing and the object-to-be-known, it is the latter which, under the rules of this particular game, makes the first cast of the die. It is a case of "I match you," or, to use a better analogy, the lock is prior to the key. If the cogitans-key does not fit and unlock the cogitandum-lock, then it is the key and not the lock which has failed, and for which a better must be found. One who identifies himself fundamentally with this view of the rôle of cognitive mind, finds himself committed to a certain fundamental attitude in practical philosophy. He will endeavour, in taking account of his cosmic fortunes, to purge himself of preconceptions and of emotional bias. He will not ignore the human tendency to fashion reality after the human heart, or in accordance with human ways of thinking; on the contrary, he will be peculiarly alive to these disturbing factors in order, if possible, to correct the findings of his compass. Nor will he, merely because he does not wish to be blinded by the emotions, be in the least inclined to disparage them. The love of a fellow-creature may be the most sacred and

[1] Cf. my article entitled, "Peace without Victory in Philosophy," *Journal of Philosophical Studies*, vol. iii. (1928), p. 300.

[2] Cf. *The Moral Economy*, 1909.

the most powerful thing in a man's life, and yet, like a good physician, he may most scrupulously refuse to allow his hopes and fears to colour his judgment of the facts. He may realize that if his knowledge is to serve his passion, it must first be dispassionate. To the realist it is not even necessary that belief should be limited to evident facts. The man who can best afford to indulge in "over-beliefs," or in a faith supported by love and hope, is the man who is aware of the difference between cash and credit or between science and poetry. It is confusion, and not feeling, imagination, or conviction, which the knowing mind has most to fear.

In this context there is one specific doctrine that I should like to single out for special emphasis. It is essential to realism that a fact should not be construed as the creation of that act of mind which we designate as the knowing of it. But this does not at all imply that the fact in question should be non-mental. It would, of course, be palpably absurd for a realist, as for any other philosopher, to deny that there are mental facts. That which at any given moment I undertake to know may even be an act of my own cognition. In such a case there are two acts of cognition —the act-of-cognition-to-be-known, and the superadded act-of-knowing-it, both acts falling within that complex unity which the first personal pronoun is used to designate. What is true of cognition is *a fortiori* true of emotion. While emotion must not deflect knowledge, or substitute its own fond imagining for the intended object, an emotion is itself a kind of fact. Hence it is in no wise inconsistent with a fundamental realism to suppose that good and evil are emotionally conditioned.

Let me restate as simply as possible a view for which I have elsewhere argued at length.[1] The value of any object, in the most inclusive sense, as distinguished from its indifference, consists of that object's *moving* quality. Positive value (good) embraces the various modes of *attractiveness*, such as "desired," "loved," "joyous," "charming," "alluring," "auspicious"; negative value (bad) embraces the various modes of *repulsiveness*, such as "odious," "alarming," "portentous," "distasteful." In taking

[1] *General Theory of Value*, 1926.

this view, I dissent from those who hold that the positive value of an object consists in its colour, shape, unity, harmony, or universality—its negative value in the absence of these characters, or in their opposites; and I dissent from those who hold that "good" and "bad" are terms for which there are no equivalents, referring to unique qualities other than such as are mentioned above. I do not, of course, mean to deny that unified, harmonious, or universal objects are good, but only that if this be so it means that unity, harmony, and universality are attractive.

In the next place, attractiveness consists in attracting, and repulsiveness consists in repelling. In taking this view I dissent from those who hold that the various modes of attractiveness and repulsiveness can inhere in objects unrelated to minds. Attractiveness and repulsiveness are not those elements in an object *by virtue* of which it evokes feeling or will, they *are* the evoking of will and feeling and mean nothing apart from motor-affective response.

Finally, in order that a given individual may know that an object possesses the moving quality which constitutes value, it is not necessary that *he* should be moved by it; any more than, in order to know that an object is destructive, it is necessary that he should be destroyed by it. In the knowing of value the knower's own will and feeling is no more involved than in his knowing of anything else. It is true that in so far as I am conscious of being attracted or repelled by an object I know that that object is good or evil, but such evidence is no more authentic than the consciousness that somebody else is attracted or repelled by it. In taking this view I dissent from those idealists who hold that the knowledge of an object's value is inseparably one with the emotional response which makes it valuable. According to idealism, there can be no such thing as the discovery or recognition of a value already there, nor can a value possess that character of independence which facts are assumed to possess when they are cited in proof or disproof of judgments made about them.

Idealism seems to me, here again, to reduce to the same untenable alternatives solipsism, relativism, absolutism. The solipsist says, "Only what I approve is good, only what I disapprove is evil." Idealistically he cannot be argued from his position, because it has been conceded to him in advance that he can know values only in the approving or disapproving act of making them. Relativism is the illegitimate generalization of this position— doubly illegitimate: first, because the generalization itself claims to be true about values, despite the fact that it is neither an approval nor a disapproval; second, because solipsists contradict one another. One solipsist is justified in saying: "This, since it attracts me, is good"; another, in saying: "Since it does not attract *me*, it is not good." Thereupon idealism enters and redeems a situation for which it is itself responsible. The prerogative of creating values in the act of knowing them is now reserved for a universal Approver and Disapprover, alleged to be the *real* will and feeling of all finite individuals, or their will and feeling when they will and feel as they ought. An original idealistic sin is atoned by a tardy idealistic repentance. The remedy is gratuitous, since the disease was avoidable; and it is ineffectual, since the resulting problem of the relation between the Absolute and finite man is only a new name for the old problems with which the whole inquiry began.

The issue is central to ethics and the social sciences, since it touches the question of the logic of moral reasoning. Realism transcends moral egoism from the outset, judgments of right and wrong being attested, not by the will and feeling of the judge, but by wills and feelings generally. Similarly, authority, whether of conscience, State, or God proceeds from the greater goods which these powers represent. If the judgment of conscience is authoritative over the judgment of appetite, it is because conscience affirms truly that the integral good is better than any of its parts, which the appetite blindly denies. If the State, speaking for the nation, is authoritative over the individual, speaking for himself, it is because the good of all members of a nation *is* better than that of one of its individual members, all being greater than one. The authority of God has to be justified in the same way as the judgment which correctly sets the claims of a universe above those of either individual or nation. Authority, in other words, attaches to a true judgment as to what is best—true, namely, as agreeing with the nature of what *is* best.

Idealism, on the other hand, must hold that as nothing can be known to be good save in the very act of feeling it or willing it, so nothing can be known to be better or best save in the act of *preferring* it. You cannot, by this logic, argue with the egoist except in terms of his existing bias. There is no fulcrum of fact by which you can dislodge him. You may seek to arouse his "higher self," or to appeal to his "collective will," or to quicken his "divine spark." If, as unfortunately happens, you find none of these things in him, the matter ends there; for you have conceded in advance that so far as *his* judgment is concerned *his* preference shall be final. You cannot even argue that a unified self, or a social will, or a divine Love *would* be better than his present disposition, for on your idealistic premises he can have no evidence of their being better until he already possesses them.

Such a philosophy tends to a confused psychology as well as to an impotent logic. Clinging to the common belief that personality, sociality, and humanity *are* objectively better, or that their betterness possesses a validity that is binding on all individual judges, the idealist imputes to all individual judges a disposition to prefer them. In default of observable facts, he appeals to latencies and virtualities. Logically, the result is to destroy the force of moral reasoning. An obligation cannot be said to be binding until it is acknowledged, but then the time for its argument is past. If there is any virtue in moral reasoning, it must lie in its power to prove the claims of the ideal upon one to whom the ideal as yet makes no appeal: the claims of conscience upon the creature of passion, the claims of society upon the selfish individual, the claims of the State upon the lawless rebel, of international accord upon the chauvinist, or of piety upon the worldling. There is but one method by which this can be done, by assuming, namely, that a certain projected course of action is intrinsically superior, because of the greater value which it embraces or promotes; that it would be superior, though no man should adopt it; that it is really superior, though no man deems it so, or actively prefers it. Only in this way is it possible to legitimate the title of an authority when it is refused allegiance.

I have emphasized this question of the logic of the moral sciences, not only because it furnishes the link between these fields of inquiry and a man's general philosophical position, and distinguishes, as I believe, between the way of the realist and the way of the idealist; but also because it deeply underlies the practical creed with which I should like to conclude this personal confession. I suspect egoism, opportunism, dictatorship, militarism, theocracy, and mysticism (strange bed-fellows) of being the practical sequel to a theory which finds the ground of authority in the will or feeling of the judge rather than in the correctness of his judgment. I myself am one of those lonely beings who used to be called "liberals," and who are now viewed with suspicion both from the left and from the right. I have always held, and do still hold, to that view of life which I have always supposed, and do still suppose, to be Christian and democratic. The best way, I think, is the way that provides for the happiness of mankind, severally and in the aggregate. All individuals without exception are "equally" entitled to so much happiness as their multiplicity and differences, their inherent capacities, their common environmental resources, permit. The major problem of life is to promote sentiments and devise modes of organization by which human suffering may be mitigated, and by which every unnecessary thwarting of human desire may be eliminated.

If I am asked *why* I define the goal of endeavour in these terms, my answer is simply that if happiness be good, then the happiness of all is better than the happiness of one, and an innocent or radiant and fruitful happiness is better than a happiness which is produced at the cost of unhappiness. The pre-eminent good of the general happiness of sentient beings I hold to be a fact which is independent of judgment or sentiment, in the same sense as is the fact that a pair is greater than one of its members, or that a century of history embraces a greater span than one of its included decades. This greatest good may meet with neglect or cold indifference, without being in the least invalidated thereby. It is *there*, to be pointed out for the illumination or edification of mankind. From this stubborn objectivity the faculties, sentiments, maxims, and institutions of men derive such legitimate authority as they possess; legitimate, not in the sense of any law formulated and enforced by God or men, but in the sense which the philosophers of the seventeenth and eighteenth centuries obscurely intended when they spoke of "natural law" or the "law of reason."

It is this first principle, with its irrevocable force and its indifference to human ignorance or weakness, which justifies to me the major tenets of the Occidental and American tradition. Evil is as stubborn a fact as good, and there is no metaphysical sleight of hand by which the worse may be *made* the better course, however much it may *appear* to be. Hence the final truth of moral dualism. The greater good is not the mere outcropping of the deeper natural propensity, but can be attained only by the procrustean fitting of plastic materials to a mould defined by reason. Hence the profound truth of moral rigorism. Convinced as I am of the indefeasible, though partial, truth of dualism and rigorism, the contemptuous dismissal of Puritanism strikes me as atavistic or sophomoric rather than as evidence of philosophic emancipation.

This same criterion of the universal happiness of individuals justifies the Christian doctrine of love, not merely as poetry, but as science. Judged by the same criterion, the ideal polity must be that in which the happiness of citizens is the end, and their enlightened consent the seat, of sovereignty; or that form of society in which men rule themselves by discussion, persuasion, and agreement, for the sake of their common and maximum happiness. Hence democracy strikes me as Utopian only in the sense in which the best is always beyond the reach of present attainment; and the sceptics of democracy appear to me, not as shrewd political discoverers (for the failures of democracy are as old as human history), but as shallow opportunists, or victims of circumstance, or blind fanatics, or rhetorical adventurers, who are unconsciously retracing more primitive stages of political development.

By this same principle, I judge some general concord among the nations of the earth to lie ahead on the upward path by which men have painfully ascended from the condition of beasts who prey upon their own kind. I can understand those who believe that such a concord lies upon a remote, or even an inaccessible, summit. I can understand its discouraged or even its despairing devotees. But in the cynical or gleeful enemies of international peace, in those who refuse even their homage to such a cause, I can see only a recrudescence of original sin.

Finally, it is by the same principle that I find myself compelled to judge of religion. I would not belittle the comforts and compensations yielded by religion, but a *true* religion must be that which confirms man's humanity to man; or which, like Christianity, conceives the object of worship as compassionate and beneficent. The Father who pities his children is the superlatively appropriate symbol of God, not because the worshipper, being one of the children, may hope to profit by paternal indulgence, but because all-reaching and infinitely patient love is the one thing supremely worshipful. Nietzsche's rejection of Christianity strikes me, therefore, as intelligently and absolutely false; while the little Nietzscheans assume in my eyes the rôle of bad boys who have happily found an adult to justify their incorrigible naughtiness.

It is evident, then, that in practical matters I am old-fashioned —that is to say, Christian and democratic in the historic senses of these terms. Much of what is now taken to be prophetic appears in my eyes as a tedious revival of old errors, not infrequently prompted by juvenile delinquency. Or, since Christianity and democracy were once revolutionary, and are still regarded with suspicion by the friends of tyranny and established privilege, I might describe myself as one who is revolutionary enough to remain loyal to the great revolutions of the past.

PRINCIPAL PUBLICATIONS

The Approach to Philosophy (Scribner's, 1905).
The Moral Economy (Scribner's, 1908).
"A Realistic Theory of Independence," in *The New Realism* (Macmillan, 1912).
Present Philosophical Tendencies (Longmans, 1912).
The Present Conflict of Ideals (Longmans, 1918).
The Free Man and the Soldier (Scribner's, 1916).
Philosophy of the Recent Past (Scribner's, 1926).
General Theory of Value (Longmans, 1926).

PERSONAL REALISM

By JAMES BISSETT PRATT

Born 1875; Professor of Philosophy, Williams College, Williamstown, Mass.

PERSONAL REALISM

THE first call that I heard to the philosophic life—in addition to my mother's influence—came to me, I suppose, through the reading of Emerson, Epictetus, and Marcus Aurelius. That was probably when I was about sixteen. I have read but little of Emerson since I was twenty; but during those four impressionable years he came to mean so much to me that as I look back over my life I think his was the greatest literary influence I have ever felt.

The seed he had to sow fell on soil well prepared; for on my mother's side I come from a line of Scotch Protestants who were deeply interested in ultimate problems. My mother's father, Dr. David Murdoch, was a Presbyterian minister who left Scotland to help evangelize Canada, and eventually was led, by his love of democracy, into the "States." My father, Daniel R. Pratt, though born in New York State, came from Connecticut Yankees on both sides, who traced back their line to the early days of Massachusetts Bay. I was born in Elmira, New York, on June 22, 1875, and educated in the Elmira Schools, till I went to Williams College. It was in part through the influence of my beloved teacher, Professor John E. Russell, that the attractions of philosophy grew upon me, till I determined to give my life to it.

A year of graduate study at Harvard (1898–99), with the very confusing experience of hearing James, Royce, Palmer, Münsterberg, Everett, and Santayana, each refuting in large part what the other taught—made me temporarily satiated with philosophy, and in deference to my father's wish that I should give up philosophy for law, I left Harvard and spent a year at Columbia Law School. The old call of philosophy, however, still sounded in my ears, and after one year at Columbia and two years of teaching Latin in the Elmira Free Academy, I returned to my first love, and went to Berlin (in 1902–3) for further study. I must confess to having been rather disappointed with what I found. Paulsen and Pfleiderer were indeed inspiring teachers, but on the whole I found the courses at Berlin much more elementary and much less thorough than those at Harvard. Therefore, after some months of travel in Europe and the Near East, I returned to America and in the autumn of 1903 went back to Harvard, where I remained two years, receiving my doctor's degree in June 1905.

The philosophical influences I felt at Harvard centred around two foci, the one James's realistic pluralism, the other the idealistic monism of Royce and Palmer. James's influence was at first supreme, and his concrete manner of thinking, his empirical point of view, have been, I suppose, more potent than anything else in the development of my intellectual life. Royce's influence was at first much less strong upon me. But when in my last year at Harvard, James was no longer giving courses, and Royce was reinforced by Palmer (in the Seminary on Kant and Hegel), the lure of idealism began to grow.

My doctor's thesis at Harvard was not in the field of philosophy in the narrower sense, but in that of the psychology of religion. In writing it I took Professor James as my chief guide. The general subject of the religious consciousness occupied most of my attention, not only during my last year at Harvard, but for a number of years after coming to Williams College as instructor (in 1905). My first book (*The Psychology of Religious Belief*) was on this subject, as was also the book to which I gave more years of work than to any other I have yet written, the *Religious Consciousness* (1920). All sorts of influences shared in making this work possible—the continued influence of James's thought, much reading and considerable study of religious conditions in Europe and India, and the helpful insight of my wife. I should add that though my work in this field led me rather aside from the main stream of philosophic thought, it was not without its influence on my more fundamental philosophy: for it steadily strengthened my confidence—as apparently a similar study strengthened James's —in the ultimate significance of the religious consciousness.

The growth of my epistemological and metaphysical views, during these early years at Williams, tended for a while away from James. I had never been able to go all the way with his Pragmatism, and the anti-intellectualism which under his leadership and that of Dewey and Schiller carried so large a part of the philosophical world with it in the first decade of this century seemed to me perilous for the life of the mind. Hence my little book *What is Pragmatism?* (1909), in which I attacked my beloved master with as much violence as my affection would permit—an attack which he received in the large and understanding way which so characterized William James. But it was not only negatively that I was tending away from the position of James. For several years I made an earnest attempt, in my thought and in my teaching, to mould my philosophy on the model of Royce or Hegel, and I may at least say that I made an honest and prolonged attempt to be an idealist.

I did not succeed. The epistemological arguments of idealism had never been really convincing to me, and the conceptual methods of the Hegelians never had for me (I knew it in the bottom of my heart) the ring of reality. The lessons of William James had been learned too well. I cannot say that I ceased being an idealist, for I never really had been one; I ceased trying to be one. I admitted frankly that while probably neither side of the controversy could fully prove its point, the realistic version of the epistemological situation seemed to me immensely more probable than the idealistic. Neither of the attempts, however, to resuscitate realism, which were being made at the time on the two sides of the Atlantic—the English New Realism and the American Neo-Realism—appealed to me: and my earnest search was for a realistic view which would neither commit itself to the impossible positions (as they seemed to me) of the new schools, nor yet return merely to the Lockean form.

It was at this rather critical moment in my thinking that the American Philosophical Association determined to devote a large part of its 1916 meeting to a discussion of the physical and the psychical: and, fortunately for me, I was asked to act as one of the leaders of the discussion. Each of the leaders was requested to publish a paper before the meeting, expressing his position on the topic to be discussed, and in conformity with this request I wrote "The Confessions of an Old Realist," which appeared in the *Journal of Philosophy* for December 7, 1916. My paper at the meeting of the Association was entitled "A Defence of Dualistic Realism" (published in the *Journal of Philosophy*, May 10, 1917).

The discussion at the 1916 meeting was in some ways disappointing; but for a few of us it did one important thing. There were four or five of us at the meeting whose thoughts had been developing along parallel lines, and there we discovered each other. Thus was formed a little group which met once or twice a year for several years, and which through these meetings and a rather lively correspondence at length formulated the epistemological point of view known (rather inappropriately, I think) as Critical Realism. The conclusions we finally reached in this attempt at cooperative thinking were published toward the close of 1920 under the title *Essays in Critical Realism.*

The reasons which led me to this realistic position have been stated at length in more places than one and can hardly be repeated here. Very briefly I will say that I find it impossible to construe my experience satisfactorily without recognizing the fact of transcendence. In the act of perceiving and conceiving the mind *means* more than it *is*: it refers to, intends, makes assertions about, other realities than its own states. The assertion of Locke that "the mind hath no other immediate object save its own ideas" not only is false, it is the root of many hopeless vagaries in both epistemology and ethics. For one who denies this power of transcendence on the part of the mind, the only logical position would seem to be the extreme form of solipsism, or else the denial of the subjective altogether. But if one is unwilling to take either of these extreme courses, it would seem difficult to avoid the assertion that the object which the mind refers to need not be existentially identical with any of its mental states. This last assertion, rather than the "essence" doctrine, I regard as the central thesis of Critical Realism. But it must not be forgotten that this assertion involves the principle of transcendence. And transcendence is a principle of wider import and application than Critical Realism. For me, at any rate, it is as fundamental to ethics as to epistemology: and once recognized there it undermines the whole psychological argument for egoistic hedonism.

Critical Realism was intended and is maintained as a purely epistemological doctrine. It would be strange, however, if it had no bearing on the problems of ontology. There is, to be sure, little agreement among critical realists as to what this bearing may be. Several of the members of the group that wrote the "Essays" have developed out of their epistemological realism a naturalistic metaphysic. As I view the question, the logic of the thing runs quite the other way. The concept of a mind that can and does transcend itself—which is the very centre of Critical Realism— would seem to me to imply a uniqueness on the part of mind such as to separate it rather sharply from the physical world and from mechanistic nature. This view of the mind I have to some extent developed in the little book, *Matter and Spirit*, published in 1922, in which I tried to show that the relation of body and mind is a question that cannot be dodged, and that among the solutions offered since the rise of Western thought, interaction is by far the most satisfactory. Now if this be true, if the mind can both transcend in its meanings its own states and can also affect the activities of the body, we would seem to be faced with the fact of a *dualism of process* in our world, the one mechanistic, the other teleological; the one the processes of unconscious "matter," the other the activities of selves. And I may add that the direction of my thought during the six years since the completion of *Matter and Spirit* has been ever more confidently toward some form of personalism. I cannot (as yet, at any rate) go the whole length of the "personalist" school and interpret Reality as a whole or in all its parts in personal or panpsychic terms; but I do feel that the reality and efficiency of our own human selves is one of the hard facts which philosophy is bound to reckon with. The acknowledgment of this fact, moreover, would seem to be of grave significance. If there are selves, if in knowing and willing they can and do transcend their own psychic states, if they can act upon their bodies and through their bodies in such fashion as to change the outcome of the mechanistic laws of "Nature," then this is a fact which characterizes not only the selves in question but the universe in which they live. The world we live in is the kind of world which continually produces selves.

One more influence that has contributed to the shaping of my metaphysical attitude must be mentioned before I close these personal confessions—the influence, namely, of Oriental thought.

My interest in the history of religions, and especially the religions of India, was aroused during my first year at Harvard by Charles Carroll Everett, of blessed memory. This interest was deepened by the lectures of Otto Pfleiderer in the University of Berlin; and my own serious and detailed study of the non-Christian faiths was begun under the guidance of George Foot Moore. Ever since I came to Williams College in 1905 I have given a course on the history of religions and my interest in the subject, particularly in the religions of Indian origin, has steadily grown. In order to gain more immediate contact with and first-hand knowledge of these religions I spent the larger part of two sabbatical years in the East, particularly in the study of Hinduism and Buddhism, and my two longest books[1] have been devoted to them. They are to me matters of much more than antiquarian interest. During all the years that I have spent developing a pluralistic realism, the undertone of the Upanishads has, strangely enough, never been long out of hearing. The monistic idealism of the Vedanta and the Mahayana has a kind of emotional and poetic charm for me in spite of my intellectual adhesion to a pluralistic and possibly dualistic philosophy. My long study of mysticism and the religious consciousness reinforces, I suspect, the influence of Oriental thought; and I cannot say with the assurance I should have felt some years ago that Hindu and Buddhist Monism are quite mistaken. Is my personal realism necessarily incompatible with the ancient insight of the East?

As yet I do not know. It may be that some day I shall have to resign one or both of them altogether. It may be I shall yet find some kind of synthesis that shall transmute and save them both. Most likely of all I shall never come to any definite conclusion, but shall continue to wonder to the end of my days. At any rate I trust I shall cling to reason and experience as my guides, and, with Socrates, shall "follow the argument." And if that course still leaves me wondering, I am not at all sure that this will be an evil fate. Long ago we were told that our human philosophy begins with wonder; and it may be best that it should end with it. As I view the matter, Philosophy is a persistent attempt to get

[1] *India and Its Faiths*, 1916; and *The Pilgrimage of Buddhism*, 1928.

at the most probable explanation of our experience, to draw the most persuasive and inclusive picture of the world we live in. Just for this reason it is an investigation that can never be complete, a question that can never be finally answered, a path that has no ending. It would be sad if the path ended with my last footprints. And for my own part, I have found the lure of the journey growing all the way.

PRINCIPAL PUBLICATIONS

The Psychology of Religious Belief (1907).
What is Pragmatism? (1909).
India and Its Faiths (1915).
The Religious Consciousness (1920).
Matter and Spirit (1922).
The Pilgrimage of Buddhism (1928).

EMPIRICISM

By ARTHUR KENYON ROGERS

Born 1868; late Professor of Philosophy, Yale University,
New Haven, Conn

EMPIRICISM

In accordance with what I understand to be the intention of the present volumes I shall make no effort here to argue at length the right or wrong of my philosophical opinions; and I submit without regret to the restriction. I have long been of the belief that the only possible hope that philosophers may get together lies in dropping their logic temporarily and telling one another frankly and in plain terms the human interests that engage them. An interest or point of view is much less easy to demolish than a piece of reasoning, and also it is more difficult to brush aside without leaving one open unpleasantly to the charge of narrowness; and with the habit once started of considering sympathetically the point of view of others there is a sporting chance that a man's own outlook on the world may be enlarged.

My first interest in philosophy goes back to the fairly remote days when religion and science were still facing one another with considerable asperity. Though I could not remain entirely unaware of a measure of superior intellectual integrity and realism in the opposing camp, by temperament and training my natural leanings were toward the former side. The current disposition to turn naturalism into a final and comprehensive creed left me dissatisfied. The dogmatic forms of a naturalistic metaphysics did not impress me greatly; I thought then, and I still continue to think when I see the same predilection re-emerging in a more modern dress, that they are sufficiently exploded by relatively clear and simple considerations. But the more fluid agnosticism of scientists like Huxley worried and irritated me. I wanted to know, to find something solid and substantial into which I could get my teeth; and I saw no compelling reason to suppose that this natural desire was incapable of satisfaction.

At the end of nearly forty years I have a good deal more fellow-feeling with the state of mind which faced by the riddle of existence is content to give it up. I have never quite understood how philosophers who have spent their lives in pointing out the absurdity of all metaphysics save their own could retain so placid a faith in the infallibility of one residual line of reasoning; and while I usually seem to detect too easy a yielding to emotional or aesthetic prepossessions in those members of the younger generation who have abandoned the quest for ultimate truth before they have really set upon it, I nevertheless have ceased to look as coldly as I once did on the periodic outbreaks against all forms of metaphysics. The very recent revelation of a widespread distrust of abstract speculation which accompanied and partly accounted for the success of Mr. Durant's *Story of Philosophy* ought, I should say, to set the philosopher thinking, and lead him to ask himself anew what significance, if any, can fairly be established for his trade. And I do not know that I can better start my present undertaking than by putting this question to myself, and considering what I should have to say to one who urged that metaphysics is an unnecessary waste of human time and energy.

There is one answer that has no need to give rise to serious controversy. Systems of philosophy have sometimes been justified as works of art, and I am in fact myself inclined to fancy that, as systems, this is their strongest claim. Since they are in large measure mutually exclusive, it is plainly impossible to regard them all as true. But whether he accepts it or not, a philosopher can still take pleasure in an historic system as a beautiful piece of methodic reasoning. Spinoza, for example, will always arouse in the mind that is capable of following him much the same sort of appreciation that another man will find in an epic or a symphony. It is true the number of those who derive enjoyment from this particular sort of thing will always be strictly limited; but that is no reason for disparagement. The aestheticist in particular, who nowadays is most in evidence as a reviler of metaphysics, has no possible ground for condescension except his own incapacity for grasping a complicated intellectual construction, any more than I should have the right to exclude from works of art a fugue of Bach's because it held no message for my untrained ear.

As an answer to one sort of attack on metaphysics this admits, I should say, of no rebuttal; but of course it will not satisfy the real philosopher. I recall many years ago the appearance of a book made up entirely of mathematical formulas which—so I was informed—would to the expert prove highly diverting as a piece of mathematical humour. Such a display of ingenuity no one could reasonably object to as the by-product of a serious discipline, but it is not the kind of thing that would explain the zeal of the everyday mathematician. And philosophers could not long keep up an active interest if they thought of their labours only as an exercise of logical dexterity. The metaphysician must believe that he has a chance to reach objective truth if he is to take any permanent satisfaction in his work.

There is one such value in terms of truth which the unsympathetic critic almost always overlooks, but which may go a long way toward reassuring the philosopher when beset by disturbing doubts. Whatever else he may or may not be accomplishing, he can console himself with the conviction that it must be worth some pains to clear up the logical meaning of the terms and ideas which constitute the stock-in-trade of humankind, but which the average man makes use of with little or no critical understanding. To the philosopher must go a very large portion of the credit for rendering precise the terms of intellectual discourse and bringing them into something like an intelligible connection; apart from that subtle and technical tracing of the links of logical relationship which so irritates the unfriendly critic, the mind of man would be ruled even more universally than it is by a mass of desultory catchwords. Here lies, I think, a sufficient and perhaps the only answer to the perennial charge that historic philosophy is no more than a rabble of conflicting schools each trying to displace the rest and none actually succeeding. In so far as philosophy is identified with systems of philosophy, this charge is hard to meet, and there seems no special reason to suppose that the addition of more systems will materially change the fact. But every such attempt is likely to contribute something to a clearer understanding of this or that idea in which the author of the system feels a special interest; and other philosophers may profit by this even though its larger context is rejected.

Is it possible to go a step farther and to justify metaphysics not merely as a clearing up of the intellectual tools of thought but as an effort to understand what Being actually is like? Here more controversial questions will arise; and in taking note of them I come back to my proper theme.

Of course in a sense the alternatives just alluded to are not exclusive. We cannot separate an analysis of terms from a knowledge of reality unless we are prepared to say that the relationships which enter into terms stand themselves for nothing real; and while philosophers have held out for this at times, it is not the most natural conclusion. It is simpler and easier to suppose that any verifiable thread of connection which the mind perceives reveals in so far a character belonging to the real structure of the world. But a strictly metaphysical curiosity assumes something in addition; and this brings me to the first of the dogmas that have had most influence in shaping my own attempts at speculation.

The terms empiricism and rationalism, so far as I know, have never received an authoritative definition, and consequently I shall ask the privilege of giving them the sense that seems to me most useful. By a rationalist I shall mean a philosopher who believes not only that logic is a valid process but that the content of logic, the relational network which mind traces, is itself conterminous with reality or being. The more rigorous of the metaphysical systems have commonly gone on this assumption, tacit or expressed, and it is this alone that renders plausible their persuasion that the intellect is competent to reach an authoritative account of things impervious to logical attack. Hegel is the most thoroughgoing and consistent master of the method, for Hegel alone has tried explicitly to do what on such a showing plainly should be done—bring every human concept into a single articulated whole.

That no one has succeeded up to date in propounding such a system of metaphysics capable of more than a limited appeal might, I suppose, be taken to mean that the philosopher is to look for some new system in the future which will be more fortunate. I prefer instead to think that the cause of failure lies not in any inadequacy of performance but in the method itself.

And the thing which so disposes me is not merely the historic strife of systems, though I should say this ought to arouse a healthy scepticism, but the conviction that there is something of which the method does not take account. And accordingly the distinctive note of empiricism I discover in the recognition that reality possesses a dimension which logical relationships fail to make intelligible. Call it stuff or matter or sensation or what not, *something* is there which is not reducible to conceptual thought; and since deductive certainty has no meaning save in terms of concepts, it follows that any attempt at strict demonstration, whether in the name of idealism or of science, must as applied to the universe at large be marked for failure. There is a factor in experience which we simply find, and whose necessity no conceivable logic can show.

But in calling myself an empiricist I am compelled immediately to supplement my meaning. Traditional English empiricism never appealed to me as highly plausible, for the reason that it is not empirical enough. A technical criticism which nowadays is generally allowed is that the non-conceptual stuff of historic empiricism is thought of in an altogether too disjointed way, which fails sufficiently to recognize that relationships are also real. In this criticism I acquiesce, provided it does not try to say that reality consists of sensations *and* relations. If when we set out to scrutinize the objects of experience we are led to note two distinguishable elements, well and good. But to take such components as more real than the concrete facts from which they were dissected is equally non-empirical and abstract whether the outcome is in terms of particular sense qualities or of relational connections. A genuinely empirical view will get its data from the things that come home to us in first-hand experience, and any metaphysics which results in disrupting these and leaving them without final significance, whatever its claim as metaphysics, at any rate is not empiricism.

What then are the data that common experience presupposes? I do not see much chance of dispute about the general facts. Most unmistakable and closest to man's most deeply rooted instincts is the assurance that we are persons in a community of persons, actuated by a variety of concrete motives to conduct in which these beings similar to ourselves are very much concerned. In the second place, there exists as a field of action common to us all alike a world on which the satisfaction of our interests is dependent, and which as human beings we can "know" only through the medium of ideas that are not identical with the objects to be known. About this world science has in detail many astonishing things to tell us, and many interesting and curious opinions have been held about its intrinsic nature; but in any case it is a thoroughly real and substantial sort of world, which to all appearance would not be very much put out were the human race to vanish altogether. It is this second item among the prejudices to which I have confessed about which I should perhaps feel most apologetic. Systems of metaphysics have pretty generally hesitated to concede it to the common sense of mankind, and I have always in consequence found myself excluded from that comforting sense of philosophical security that comes from membership in an established and reputable school of thought. It may, of course, be that some way exists of escaping this taint of dualism, but I have never found it; and the rather common practice of escape through closing one's eyes to the break involved alike with our everyday and with our scientific ways of thinking does not attract me.

Of the two main sets of problems that emerge from such a starting-point it was the more strictly metaphysical one that first engaged my interest; what is the nature of Reality *par excellence*? It seemed rather obvious to me, as I have said, that here was a question to which logic was not fully adequate. Since the field of reality pushes far beyond man with his limited capacities, there is an excellent chance that his guesses here may go astray; this leaves agnosticism always open as a last resort, which is no doubt the reason why I was disposed to be scandalized by the agnostic. But I nevertheless thought, nor do I see in the abstract any reason now to change my mind, that a more or less convincing theory might conceivably be devised to meet the needs of speculation once the pretence to demonstrative certainty was abandoned.

There were two reasons in particular which led me to look for such a theory in the general direction of what traditionally has been known as theism, and the first of these, at any rate, has no necessary connection with religiosity. It very early struck me that the condescension displayed by philosophy toward theism was due quite as much to a sentimental prejudice as to any inherent plausibility. It is not surprising that the temper of the theologian should provoke a reaction in the critical mind which leads it to turn away from notions that have a religious connotation as unworthy our intellectual respect. But I do not see that an anti-theological bias has any more right than a theological bias to determine the results of speculation; and the dislike of philosophers for theism appeared to me a little arbitrary. Mind, thought, consciousness—if these are not the most important things in the world, they are at any rate not the least intelligible; and such terms are all abstractions apart from *our* mind, *our* thought, *our* consciousness. The one reality which for the business of living is least open to sceptical distrust is the reality of ourselves; and if knowledge can only proceed by interpreting the problematical in terms of what is known, then the prevalent disposition to hold cheap the notion of personality for speculative purposes might readily be taken as a sign less of superior insight than of that innate preference for the abstract over the concrete which has always put empiricism on the defensive in the metaphysical game.

I must remark again that in my own case I was pointed toward theism less from motives that could properly be called religious than from such logical considerations, and from the lack of persuasive quality in competing brands of metaphysics. In all of these I was impressed by difficulties even more serious than those I found in theism. At the same time it is possible I might have been less firm in my preference for gnosticism had it not been for a second motive.

Along with the philosopher's predilection for the abstract, a further reason has existed for the disrepute of concepts connected with religion in the higher intellectual circles. This is the increasing leaven of utilitarianism in modern society, and the displacement of ideology and an interest in values by the gospel of material progress and success. Such a tendency has acquired a lustre not obviously due in its own right from an alliance with the most important intellectual movement of the day. Not that the scientist is himself a practitioner of the gospel of success; he is more apt to be an idealist of sorts. But whatever the spirit that guides his own activities, his subject-matter is expressly in terms of means or instruments rather than of ideals and ends, and his enormous prestige has lent utilitarianism and pragmatism of the practical variety a standing which offers some excuse for the impression that science and religion are opposed.

Now if, as I suppose to be the case, the central note of religion is the need man has of finding the human values that particularly appeal to him rooted in the more ultimate structure of the universe, a new compulsion will be added to that desire to know which animates the metaphysician; and in this new motive I seemed to find a reinforcement of the special type of doctrine to which independently I had been led. For I have never been able to make the least sense of value terms except as they connect themselves with persons. I do not propose to enter here on an analysis of value. But for my own thought a value in the last resort invariably leads to some concrete feeling of approval such as persons alone experience, and apart from which nothing would be left but bare existence. And accordingly I found logic and motivation both pointing toward the notion of personality as the most likely key to an understanding of reality.

As I have advanced in philosophical maturity if not in wisdom, has the key proved permanently useful? I hardly know how to make an unequivocal reply. Such reason as I own still tells me that on the whole it probably offers fewer difficulties in logic and in fact than any rival hypothesis I have met; and when I am rationally inclined I continue to find my arguments moderately convincing. But I confess that if I set aside ratiocination, as the best of philosophers at times must do, and lay myself open to spontaneous impressions from the encircling world, questionings arise that make them seem rather puny weapons. The sort of fact that casts the deepest shade of suspicion I pass by for the moment;

but just the immensity of things, the pressure of the everlasting and the infinite, is enough in man's humbler moods to give him cause to ask himself whether it may not be presumption rather than sound reason that leads him to think he has the slightest chance of measuring the interminable reaches of existence. Personally I get no kick out of sheer mystery and unintelligibility. The aesthetic cult of pure wonder as a substitute for religion is not for me; unless I could retain a modicum of faith that something in the nature of human meaning lies behind the veil of the unknown, I should feel I was making myself ridiculous by bowing down before mere weight and mass of being. But I am less ready to deny that faith may have to stand alone without logical crutches; and I find some consolation in the thought that perhaps this is not without its gain. Rationalization passes over too readily into talk, and religion that has grown vocal tends nearly always to be cheapened; possibly it would stand a better chance if philosophers and theologians and preachers would let it more alone. At any rate, the impulse to plot out the universe is not as strong as it used to be, and more and more my major interest has shifted.

Whether or not man's thought is robust enough to understand his cosmic dwelling-place, at least he can hope to know something about himself and his own experience; ethics and sociology—I use the latter term apologetically—still leave a field in which philosophy will have scope for some time to come. In point of fact, my empirical bias leads me to suspect that metaphysics here has usually succeeded in muddying the waters; man's life stands a considerable chance of being falsified if it is run into moulds created by the logic of a cosmic principle. I may pause a moment to disclaim any particular sympathy with current positivisms which draw the inference that an interest in human life ought to supplant and lay at rest the urge to any more pretentious form of metaphysics. Man is plainly too small and the world too big to compress reality within the confines of "experience"; and if we are constrained to recognize that reality exists beyond the regions on which the searchlight of experience plays it is an affront to man's natural curiosity to forbid him to let his imagination loose on such remoter and aesthetically more exciting themes. It is not for me to tell my brother philosopher how he should apportion his time and effort, or to despise him because he does not voluntarily limit his interests to mine. But for the empiricist it will nevertheless be true that the only safe propædeutic to any metaphysics is the unbiased consideration of what man himself is like; and the results will retain their value—their cardinal value doubtless—even in case he has to stop with man and his terrestrial affairs.

This is not the place to do more than set down dogmatically the three or four general conclusions which have been borne in upon me as having the most significance, for a further metaphysics if such a thing be possible, but in any case for the actual business of man's life. First, man is a being who lives in time, or perhaps I should rather say whose experience is incurably and fundamentally a temporal one. In the next place, he is an *individual,* and whatever the ties that bind him to his fellow-man—and these, of course, are numerous and exceedingly important—he also has a life and nature of his own with which he is most intimately concerned. Society is logically subordinate, not primary, and any attempt to make individual man a mere item in some comprehensive social programme or some abstract or concrete universal will have unhappy consequences alike for theory and practice. Again, the most distinctive part of man's nature is to be found in ideals and not in given facts. The things to which he extends a deliberate approval, and not the unthinking demands of his animal constitution, are what determine the ends belonging to his proper human status; and these approvals come home in terms of feeling rather than of sense or intellect. And it follows from this, lastly, that the essence of the ideal is not to be looked for in absolute principles or superhuman virtues, and least of all in those abstract catchwords through which convention or the self-interest of classes attempts to make men submissive to some form of pretended good which carries so little personal appeal that it has to be imposed from the outside. An ideal is simply an end still to be attained which one finds himself desiring, and which also he is able on reflection to view with admiration and esteem. And the only proper instrument consequently for securing the good or ideal life is man's individual intelligence—a personal and experimental intelligence unawed by glittering phrases or by claims to expert moral authority, whether by the best minds or by custom and historical prestige. It is intelligence moved by a sole desire to know the fact, on the one hand the utilitarian means to the attainment of man's wishes, and on the other his genuine good in the Socratic sense, his veritable preferences and approvals, to the intent that utility may not mislead him and cause him to substitute proximate and pedestrian goals for a permanent satisfaction.

And now one final word about metaphysics and religion. My conviction still persists that any whole-hearted exercise of the practical intelligence in terms of an ideal must needs be backed for most men by a belief, or at least a hope, that the universe is friendly to man and ready to meet him half-way. Were the human race content with material goods, this need would disappear with the increasing conquest of nature by science and industry; and the predominant concern of institutional religion with such blessings has, rightly and naturally, led the modern world progressively to lose interest in what there has been so much historic reason to think of as a mere device for insuring better crops, the dominance of one's own nation over others, and personal success in business or enjoyment. We know by the certain test of experience that man has a reasonable chance of wresting a livelihood from nature without the need for supernatural assurances. But the subtler values are vastly more precarious; and in proportion as one's intelligence is realistic is it likely that as he looks about him he will be tempted to doubt whether natural forces, and in particular the forces that lie in human nature itself, are not too strong for these incipient strivings after a more humane and lovelier career for man, unless we can be permitted to trust that something not ourselves is at work to supplement human efforts.

But now this new and final doubt, I have to grant, is double-edged. My best instincts seem to need cosmic backing if I am to look forward with much hope to their eventual satisfaction; but have I any real ground for thinking that the need is in the way of being met? Or is not the more realistic inference this, that

234 CONTEMPORARY AMERICAN PHILOSOPHY

human ideals are sports that arise sporadically in the evolutionary
process with no real relevance to its direction or final outcome?
I am afraid my early faith in the supremacy of man's finer tastes
has not worn quite as well as I could wish. As I survey the human
scene my eye is caught by so many things that offend my sense
of fitness—oil scandals and diplomatic lies and Massachusetts
justice, the cowardice and stupidity of men in office and their
influential backers, the hypocrisy and greed of business, the
difficulty of stirring the mass of men to an assertion of their own
clear rights and interests, to say nothing of any real generosity
of spirit or sense of impartial fairness, the inability even of nobler
minds to rise above moral obsessions and shibboleths, the determination of nearly everyone to prevent his neighbours from
embarking in their own way on the quest for life and happiness—
all this and much more counts heavily when I ask myself whether
the ideal of a democratic community wherein each man is allowed,
and encouraged, to seek his best good along lines of intelligent
and noble living which satisfy the test of reflective approval is
indeed an ideal which reality is prepared to gratify.

If the scales do not rest even, and if I still retain some measure
of faith in the fundamental soundness of the world in terms of
human notions of the good, it is due chiefly to one last consideration for which I do not pretend to offer proof. My own attitude
I find varying with my mood; but it is just the recognition of
this fact that for my reflective consciousness inclines the balance.
It is in the rôle of passive observer that evils overweigh me
most, whereas the times when I am least uncertain that man
may hope for a satisfying life in a world that is not unfriendly to
him are the times when my instincts are in active eruption; and
if I ask myself which mood carries with it the greater impression
of reality I do not have to hesitate about the answer. I may
on occasion be minded to discard ideals and resign myself to
salvaging such personal benefits as come my way, among which
a sardonic interest in the spectacle of human folly will perhaps
not prove the least enduring. But I do not find it in my heart
particularly to like or to admire such a temper. It is the man
who, without shutting his eyes to unpleasant facts, still trusts

his instincts and goes ahead to make them count who calls forth my spontaneous applause. And to free this last attitude from the suggestion either of sentimental bravado or of unintelligence, I need to contemplate it, not as a forlorn hope inspired by the courage of despair, but as the outgrowth of a confidence that the goal it sees to be desirable the world is so framed as to put within our reach. This, as I say, is less a reasoned conclusion than an intuition. But it will have a certain rational grounding also in so far as experience makes plausible the claim that *all* our human assurances rest in the end on just such an ultimate and unreasoned prompting of human nature. And at least metaphysics has left me with the firm persuasion—perhaps its most substantial service—that whether or not my own favourite arguments are sound, there is no logical compulsion in rival speculations to force me to abandon them.

PRINCIPAL PUBLICATIONS

A Brief Introduction to Modern Philosophy (1899).
A Student's History of Philosophy (1901).
The Religious Conception of the World (1907).
"The Problem of Error" (in *Essays in Critical Realism*) (1920).
English and American Philosophy since 1800 (1922).
The Theory of Ethics (1922).
What is Truth? (1923).
Morals in Review (1927).
"Instrumentalism and Ideals" (in *Essays in Philosophy,*) (1929).

BRIEF HISTORY OF MY OPINIONS

By GEORGE SANTAYANA

Born 1863; formerly Professor of Philosophy, Harvard University,
Cambridge, Mass.

BRIEF HISTORY OF MY OPINIONS

How came a child born in Spain of Spanish parents to be educated in Boston and to write in the English language? The case of my family was unusual. We were not emigrants; none of us ever changed his country, his class, or his religion. But special circumstances had given us hereditary points of attachment in opposite quarters, moral and geographical; and now that we are almost extinct—I mean those of us who had these mixed associations—I may say that we proved remarkably staunch in our complex allegiances, combining them as well as logic allowed, without at heart ever disowning anything. My philosophy in particular may be regarded as a synthesis of these various traditions, or as an attempt to view them from a level from which their several deliverances may be justly understood. I do not assert that such was actually the origin of my system: in any case its truth would be another question. I propose simply to describe as best I can the influences under which I have lived, and leave it for the reader, if he cares, to consider how far my philosophy may be an expression of them.

In the first place, we must go much farther afield than Boston or Spain, into the tropics, almost to the antipodes. Both my father and my mother's father were officials in the Spanish civil service in the Philippine Islands. This was in the 1840's and 1850's, long before my birth; for my parents were not married until later in life, in Spain, when my mother was a widow. But the tradition of the many years which each of them separately had spent in the East was always alive in our household. Those had been, for both, their more romantic and prosperous days. My father had studied the country and the natives, and had written a little book about the Island of Mindanao; he had been three times round the world in the sailing-ships of the period, and had incidentally visited England and the United States, and been immensely impressed by the energy and order prevalent in those nations. His respect for material greatness was profound, yet not unmixed with a secret irony or even repulsion. He had a seasoned and incredulous mind, trained to see other sorts of excellence also: in his boyhood he had worked in the studio of a professional painter of the school of Goya, and had translated the tragedies of Seneca into Spanish verse. His transmarine experiences, therefore, did not rattle, as so often happens, in an empty head. The sea itself, in those days, was still vast and blue, and the lands beyond it full of lessons and wonders. From childhood I have lived in the imaginative presence of interminable ocean spaces, coconut islands, blameless Malays, and immense continents swarming with Chinamen, polished and industrious, obscene and philosophical. It was habitual with me to think of scenes and customs pleasanter than those about me. My own travels have never carried me far from the frontiers of Christendom or of respectability, and chiefly back and forth across the North Atlantic— thirty-eight fussy voyages; but in mind I have always seen these things on an ironical background enormously empty, or breaking out in spots, like Polynesia, into nests of innocent particoloured humanity.

My mother's figure belonged to the same broad and somewhat exotic landscape; she had spent her youth in the same places; but the moral note resounding in her was somewhat different. Her father, José Borrás, of Reus in Catalonia, had been a disciple of Rousseau, an enthusiast and a wanderer: he taught her to revere pure reason and republican virtue and to abhor the vices of a corrupt world. But her own temper was cool and stoical, rather than ardent, and her disdain of corruption had in it a touch of elegance. At Manila, during the time of her first marriage, she had been rather the grand lady, in a style half Creole, half early Victorian. Virtue, beside those tropical seas, might stoop to be indolent. She had given a silver dollar every morning to her native major-domo, with which to provide for the family and the twelve servants, and keep the change for his wages. Meantime she bathed, arranged the flowers, received visits, and did embroidery. It had been a spacious life; and in our narrower circumstances in later years the sense of it never forsook her.

Her first husband, an American merchant established in Manila, had been the sixth son of Nathaniel Russell Sturgis, of Boston (1779–1856). In Boston, accordingly, her three Sturgis children had numerous relations and a little property, and there she had promised their father to bring them up in case of his death. When this occurred, in 1857, she therefore established herself in Boston; and this fact, by a sort of pre-natal or pre-established destiny, was the cause of my connection with the Sturgis family, with Boston, and with America.

It was in Madrid in 1862, where my mother had gone on a visit intended to be temporary, that my father and she were married. He had been an old friend of hers and of her first husband's, and was well aware of her settled plan to educate her children in America, and recognized the propriety of that arrangement. Various projects and combinations were mooted: but the matter eventually ended in a separation, friendly, if not altogether pleasant to either party. My mother returned with her Sturgis children to live in the United States and my father and I remained in Spain. Soon, however, this compromise proved unsatisfactory. The education and prospects which my father, in his modest retirement, could offer me in Spain were far from brilliant; and in 1872 he decided to take me to Boston, where, after remaining for one cold winter, he left me in my mother's care and went back to Spain.

I was then in my ninth year, having been born on December 16, 1863, and I did not know one word of English. Nor was I likely to learn the language at home, where the family always continued to speak a Spanish more or less pure. But by a happy thought I was sent during my first winter in Boston to a Kinder-garten, among much younger children, where there were no books, so that I picked up English by ear before knowing how it was written: a circumstance to which I probably owe speaking the language without a marked foreign accent. The Brimmer School, the Boston Latin School, and Harvard College then followed in order: but apart from the taste for English poetry which I first imbibed from our excellent English master, Mr. Byron Groce, the most decisive influences over my mind in boyhood continued to come from my family, where, with my grown-up brother and sisters, I was the only child. I played no games, but sat at home all the afternoon and evening reading or drawing; especially devouring anything I could find that regarded religion, architecture, or geography.

In the summer of 1883, after my Freshman year, I returned for the first time to Spain to see my father. Then, and during many subsequent holidays which I spent in his company, we naturally discussed the various careers that might be open to me. We should both of us have liked the Spanish army or diplomatic service: but for the first I was already too old, and our means and our social relations hardly sufficed for the second. Moreover, by that time I felt like a foreigner in Spain, more acutely so than in America, although for more trivial reasons: my Yankee manners seemed outlandish there, and I could not do myself justice in the language. Nor was I inclined to overcome this handicap, as perhaps I might have done with a little effort: nothing in Spanish life or literature at that time particularly attracted me. English had become my only possible instrument, and I deliberately put away everything that might confuse me in that medium. English, and the whole Anglo-Saxon tradition in literature and philosophy, have always been a medium to me rather than a source. My natural affinities were elsewhere. Moreover, scholarship and learning of any sort seemed to me a means, not an end. I always hated to be a professor. Latin and Greek, French, Italian, and German, although I can read them, were languages which I never learned well. It seemed an accident to me if the matters which interested me came clothed in the rhetoric of one or another of these nations: I was not without a certain temperamental rhetoric of my own in which to recast what I adopted. Thus in renouncing every thing else for the sake of English letters I might be said to have been guilty, quite unintentionally, of a little stratagem, as if I had set out to say plausibly in English as many un-English things as possible.

This brings me to religion, which is the head and front of everything. Like my parents, I have always set myself down officially as a Catholic: but this is a matter of sympathy and traditional allegiance, not of philosophy. In my adolescence, religion on its doctrinal and emotional side occupied me much more than it does now. I was more unhappy and unsettled; but I have never had any unquestioning faith in any dogma, and have never been what is called a practising Catholic. Indeed, it would hardly have been possible. My mother, like her father before her, was a Deist: she was sure there was a God, for who else could have made the world? But God was too great to take special thought for man: sacrifices, prayers, churches, and tales of immortality were invented by rascally priests in order to dominate the foolish. My father, except for the Deism, was emphatically of the same opinion. Thus, although I learned my prayers and catechism by rote, as was then inevitable in Spain, I knew that my parents regarded all religion as a work of human imagination: and I agreed, and still agree, with them there. But this carried an implication in their minds against which every instinct in me rebelled, namely that the works of human imagination are bad. No, said I to myself even as a boy: they are good, they alone are good; and the rest—the whole real world—is ashes in the mouth. My sympathies were entirely with those other members of my family who were devout believers. I loved the Christian epic, and all those doctrines and observances which bring it down into daily life: I thought how glorious it would have been to be a Dominican friar, preaching that epic eloquently, and solving afresh all the knottiest and sublimest mysteries of theology. I was delighted with anything, like Mallock's *Is Life Worth Living?*, which seemed to rebuke the fatuity of that age. For my own part, I was quite sure that life was not worth living; for if religion was false everything was worthless, and almost everything, if religion was true. In this youthful pessimism I was hardly more foolish than so many amateur mediævalists and religious æsthetes of my generation. I saw the same alternative between Catholicism and complete disillusion: but I was never afraid of disillusion, and I have chosen it.

Since those early years my feelings on this subject have become less strident. Does not modern philosophy teach that our idea of the so-called real world is also a work of imagination? A religion—for there are other religions than the Christian—simply offers a system of faith different from the vulgar one, or extending beyond it. The question is which imaginative system you will trust. My matured conclusion has been that no system is to be trusted, not even that of science in any literal or pictorial sense; but all systems may be used and, up to a certain point, trusted as symbols. Science expresses in human terms our dynamic relation to surrounding reality. Philosophies and religions, where they do not misrepresent these same dynamic relations and do not contradict science, express destiny in moral dimensions, in obviously mythical and poetical images: but how else should these moral truths be expressed at all in a traditional or popular fashion? Religions are the great fairy-tales of the conscience.

When I began the formal study of philosophy as an under-graduate at Harvard, I was already alive to the fundamental questions, and even had a certain dialectical nimbleness, due to familiarity with the fine points of theology: the arguments for and against free will and the proofs of the existence of God were warm and clear in my mind. I accordingly heard James and Royce with more wonder than serious agreement: my scholastic logic would have wished to reduce James at once to a materialist and Royce to a solipsist, and it seemed strangely irrational in them to resist such simplification. I had heard many Unitarian sermons (being taken to hear them lest I should become too Catholic), and had been interested in them so far as they were rationalistic and informative, or even amusingly irreligious, as I often thought them to be: but neither in those discourses nor in Harvard philosophy was it easy for me to understand the Protestant combination of earnestness with waywardness. I was used to see water flowing from fountains, architectural and above ground: it puzzled me to see it drawn painfully in bucketfuls from the subjective well, muddied, and half spilt over.

There was one lesson, however, which I was readier to learn, not only at Harvard from Professor Palmer and afterwards at Berlin from Paulsen, but from the general temper of that age well represented for me by the *Revue Des Deux Mondes* (which I habitually read from cover to cover) and by the works of Taine and of Matthew Arnold—I refer to the historical spirit of the nineteenth century, and to that splendid panorama of nations and religions, literatures and arts, which it unrolled before the imagination. These picturesque vistas into the past came to fill in circumstantially that geographical and moral vastness to which my imagination was already accustomed. Professor Palmer was especially skilful in bending the mind to a suave and sympathetic participation in the views of all philosophers in turn: were they not all great men, and must not the aspects of things which seemed persuasive to them be really persuasive? Yet even this form of romanticism, amiable as it is, could not altogether put to sleep my scholastic dogmatism. The historian of philosophy may be as sympathetic and as self-effacing as he likes: the philosopher in him must still ask whether any of those successive views were true, or whether the later ones were necessarily truer than the earlier: he cannot, unless he is a shameless sophist, rest content with a truth *pro tem*. In reality the sympathetic reconstruction of history is a literary art, and it depends for its plausibility as well as for its materials on a conventional belief in the natural world. Without this belief no history and no science would be anything but a poetic fiction, like a classification of the angelic choirs. The necessity of naturalism as a foundation for all further serious opinions was clear to me from the beginning. Naturalism might indeed be criticized—and I was myself intellectually and emotionally predisposed to criticize it, and to oscillate between supernaturalism and solipsism—but if naturalism was condemned, supernaturalism itself could have no point of application in the world of fact; and the whole edifice of human knowledge would crumble, since no perception would then be a report and no judgment would have a transcendent object. Hence historical reconstruction seemed to me more honestly and solidly practised by Taine, who was a professed naturalist, than by Hegel and his school, whose naturalism, though presupposed at every stage, was disguised and distorted by a dialectic imposed on it by the historian and useful at best only in simplifying his dramatic perspectives and lending them a false absoluteness and moralistic veneer.

The influence of Royce over me, though less important in the end than that of James, was at first much more active. Royce was the better dialectician, and traversed subjects in which I

was naturally more interested. The point that particularly
exercised me was Royce's Theodicy or justification for the existence of evil. It would be hard to exaggerate the ire which his arguments on this subject aroused in my youthful breast. Why that
emotion? Romantic sentiment that could find happiness only in
tears and virtue only in heroic agonies was something familiar to
me and not unsympathetic: a poetic play of mine, called *Lucifer*,
conceived in those days, is a clear proof of it. I knew Leopardi and
Musset largely by heart; Schopenhauer was soon to become, for
a brief period, one of my favourite authors. I carried Lucretius
in my pocket: and although the spirit of the poet in that case was
not romantic, the picture of human existence which he drew
glorified the same vanity. Spinoza, too, whom I was reading under
Royce himself, filled me with joy and enthusiasm: I gathered at
once from him a doctrine which has remained axiomatic with
me ever since, namely that good and evil are relative to the
natures of animals, irreversible in that relation, but indifferent
to the march of cosmic events, since the force of the universe
infinitely exceeds the force of any one of its parts. Had I found,
then, in Royce only a romantic view of life, or only pessimism,
or only stoical courage and pantheistic piety, I should have taken
no offence, but readily recognized the poetic truth or the moral
legitimacy of those positions. Conformity with fate, as I afterwards came to see, belongs to post-rational morality, which is
a normal though optional development of human sentiment:
Spinoza's "intellectual love of God" was a shining instance
of it.

But in Royce these attitudes, in themselves so honest and noble,
seemed to be somehow embroiled and rendered sophistical: nor
was he alone in this, for the same moral equivocation seemed
to pervade Hegel, Browning, and Nietzsche. That which repelled
me in all these men was the survival of a sort of forced optimism
and pulpit unction, by which a cruel and nasty world, painted by
them in the most lurid colours, was nevertheless set up as the
model and standard of what ought to be. The duty of an honest
moralist would have been rather to distinguish, in this bad or
mixed reality, the part, however small, that could be loved and

chosen from the remainder, however large, which was to be rejected and renounced. Certainly the universe was in flux and dynamically single: but this fatal flux could very well take care of itself; and it was not so fluid that no islands of a relative per- manence and beauty might not be formed in it. Ascetic con- formity was itself one of these islands: a scarcely inhabitable peak from which almost all human passions and activities were excluded. And the Greeks, whose deliberate ethics was rational, never denied the vague early Gods and the environing chaos, which perhaps would return in the end: but meantime they built their cities bravely on the hill-tops, as we all carry on pleasantly our temporal affairs, although we know that to-morrow we die. Life itself exists only by a modicum of organization, achieved and transmitted through a world of change: the momentum of such organization first creates a difference between good and evil, or gives them a meaning at all. Thus the core of life is always hereditary, steadfast, and classical; the margin of barbarism and blind adventure round it may be as wide as you will, and in some wild hearts the love of this fluid margin may be keen, as might be any other loose passion. But to *preach* barbarism as the only good, in ignorance or hatred of the possible perfection of every natural thing, was a scandal: a belated Calvinism that remained fanatical after ceasing to be Christian. And there was a further circumstance which made this attitude particularly odious to me. This romantic love of evil was not thoroughgoing: wilfulness and disorder were to reign only in spiritual matters; in govern- ment and industry, even in natural science, all was to be order and mechanical progress. Thus the absence of a positive religion and of a legislation, like that of the ancients, intended to be rational and final, was very far from liberating the spirit for higher flights: on the contrary, it opened the door to the pervasive tyranny of the world over the soul. And no wonder: a soul rebellious to its moral heritage is too weak to reach any firm definition of its inner life. It will feel lost and empty unless it summons the random labours of the contemporary world to fill and to enslave it. It must let mechanical and civic achievements reconcile it to its own moral confusion and triviality.

It was in this state of mind that I went to Germany to continue the study of philosophy—interested in all religious or metaphysical systems, but sceptical about them and scornful of any romantic worship or idealization of the real world. The life of a wandering student, like those of the Middle Ages, had an immense natural attraction for me—so great, that I have never willingly led any other. When I had to choose a profession, the prospect of a quiet academic existence seemed the least of evils. I was fond of reading and observation, and I liked young men; but I have never been a diligent student either of science or art, nor at all ambitious to be learned. I have been willing to let cosmological problems and technical questions solve themselves as they would or as the authorities agreed for the moment that they should be solved. My pleasure was rather in expression, in reflection, in irony: my spirit was content to intervene, in whatever world it might seem to find itself, in order to disentangle the intimate moral and intellectual echoes audible to it in that world. My naturalism or materialism is no academic opinion: it is not a survival of the alleged materialism of the nineteenth century, when all the professors of philosophy were idealists: it is an everyday conviction which came to me, as it came to my father, from experience and observation of the world at large, and especially of my own feelings and passions. It seems to me that those who are not materialists cannot be good observers of themselves: they may hear themselves thinking, but they cannot have watched themselves acting and feeling; for feeling and action are evidently accidents of matter. If a Democritus or Lucretius or Spinoza or Darwin works within the lines of nature, and clarifies some part of that familiar object, that fact is the ground of my attachment to them: they have the savour of truth; but what the savour of truth is, I know very well without their help. Consequently there is no opposition in my mind between materialism and a Platonic or even Indian discipline of the spirit. The recognition of the material world and of the conditions of existence in it merely enlightens the spirit concerning the source of its troubles and the means to its happiness or deliverance: and it was happiness or deliverance, the supervening supreme expression of human will and imagination, that alone really concerned me. This alone was genuine philosophy: this alone was the life of reason.

Had the life of reason ever been cultivated in the world by people with a sane imagination? Yes, once, by the Greeks. Of the Greeks, however, I knew very little: the philosophical and political departments at Harvard had not yet discovered Plato and Aristotle. It was with the greater pleasure that I heard Paulsen in Berlin expounding Greek ethics with a sweet reasonableness altogether worthy of the subject: here at last was a vindication of order and beauty in the institutions of men and in their ideas. Here, through the pleasant medium of transparent myths or of summary scientific images, like the water of Thales, nature was essentially understood and honestly described; and here, for that very reason, the free mind could disentangle its true good, and could express it in art, in manners, and even in the most refined or the most austere spiritual discipline. Yet, although I knew henceforth that in the Greeks I should find the natural support and point of attachment for my own philosophy, I was not then collected or mature enough to pursue the matter; not until ten years later, in 1896–1897, did I take the opportunity of a year's leave of absence to go to England and begin a systematic reading of Plato and Aristotle under Dr. Henry Jackson of Trinity College, Cambridge. I am not conscious of any change of opinion supervening, nor of any having occurred earlier; but by that study and change of scene my mind was greatly enriched; and the composition of *The Life of Reason* was the consequence.

This book was intended to be a summary history of the human imagination, expressly distinguishing those phases of it which showed what Herbert Spencer called an adjustment of inner to outer relations; in other words, an adaptation of fancy and habit to material facts and opportunities. On the one hand, then, my subject being the imagination, I was never called on to step beyond the subjective sphere. I set out to describe, not nature or God, but the ideas of God or nature bred in the human mind. On the other hand, I was not concerned with these ideas for their own sake, as in a work of pure poetry or erudition, but I meant to consider them in their natural genesis and significance; for I

assumed throughout that the whole life of reason was generated
and controlled by the animal life of man in the bosom of nature.
Human ideas had, accordingly, a symptomatic, expressive, and
symbolic value: they were the inner notes sounded by man's
passions and by his arts: and they became rational partly by their
vital and inward harmony—for reason is a harmony of the passions
—and partly by their adjustment to external facts and possibilities
—for reason is a harmony of the inner life with truth and with
fate. I was accordingly concerned to discover what wisdom is
possible to an animal whose mind, from beginning to end, is
poetical: and I found that this could not lie in discarding poetry
in favour of a science supposed to be clairvoyant and literally
true. Wisdom lay rather in taking everything good-humouredly,
with a grain of salt. In science there was an element of poetry,
pervasive, inevitable, and variable: it was strictly scientific and
true only in so far as it involved a close and prosperous adjustment to the surrounding world, at first by its origin in observation
and at last by its application in action. Science was the mental
accompaniment of art.

Here was a sort of pragmatism: the same which I have again
expressed, I hope more clearly, in one of the *Dialogues in Limbo*
entitled "Normal Madness." The human mind is a faculty of
dreaming awake, and its dreams are kept relevant to its environment and to its fate only by the external control exercised over
them by Punishment, when the accompanying conduct brings
ruin, or by Agreement, when it brings prosperity. In the latter
case it is possible to establish correspondences between one part
of a dream and another, or between the dreams of separate minds,
and so create the world of literature, or the life of reason. I am
not sure whether this notion, that thought is a controlled and
consistent madness, appears among the thirteen pragmatisms
which have been distinguished, but I have reason to think that
I came to it under the influence of William James; nevertheless,
when his book on *Pragmatism* appeared, about the same time
as my *Life of Reason*, it gave me a rude shock. I could not
stomach that way of speaking about truth; and the continual
substitution of human psychology—normal madness, in my view

—for the universe, in which man is but one distracted and befuddled animal, seemed to me a confused remnant of idealism, and not serious.

The William James who had been my master was not this William James of the later years, whose pragmatism and pure empiricism and romantic metaphysics have made such a stir in the world. It was rather the puzzled but brilliant doctor, impatient of metaphysics, whom I had known in my undergraduate days, one of whose maxims was that to study the abnormal was the best way of understanding the normal; or it was the genial author of *The Principles of Psychology*, chapters of which he read from the manuscript and discussed with a small class of us in 1889. Even then what I learned from him was perhaps chiefly things which explicitly he never taught, but which I imbibed from the spirit and background of his teaching. Chief of these, I should say, was a sense for the immediate: for the unadulterated, unexplained, instant fact of experience. Actual experience, for William James, however varied or rich its assault might be, was always and altogether of the nature of a sensation: it possessed a vital, leaping, globular unity which made the only fact, the flying fact, of our being. Whatever continuities of quality might be traced in it, its existence was always momentary and self-warranted. A man's life or soul borrowed its reality and imputed wholeness from the intrinsic actuality of its successive parts; existence was a perpetual re-birth, a travelling light to which the past was lost and the future uncertain. The element of indetermination which James felt so strongly in this flood of existence was precisely the pulse of fresh unpredictable sensation, summoning attention hither and thither to unexpected facts. Apprehension in him being impressionistic—that was the age of impressionism in painting too—and marvellously free from intellectual assumptions or presumptions, he felt intensely the fact of contingency, or the contingency of fact. This seemed to me not merely a peculiarity of temperament in him, but a profound insight into existence, in its inmost irrational essence. Existence, I learned to see, is intrinsically dispersed, seated in its distributed moments, and arbitrary not only as a whole, but in the character and place of each of its parts. Change the bits, and you change the mosaic: nor can we count or limit the elements, as in a little closed kaleidoscope, which may be shaken together into the next picture. Many of them, such as pleasure and pain, or the total picture itself, cannot possibly have pre-existed.

But, said I to myself, were these novelties for that reason unconditioned? Was not sensation, by continually surprising us, a continual warning to us of fatal conjunctions occurring outside? And would not the same conjunctions, but for memory and habit, always produce the same surprises? Experience of indetermination was no proof of indeterminism; and when James proceeded to turn immediate experience into ultimate physics, his thought seemed to me to lose itself in words or in confused superstitions. Free will, a deep moral power contrary to a romantic indetermination in being, he endeavoured to pack into the bias of attention—the most temperamental of accidents. He insisted passionately on the efficacy of consciousness, and invoked Darwinian arguments for its utility—arguments which assumed that consciousness was a material engine absorbing and transmitting energy: so that it was no wonder that presently he doubted whether consciousness existed at all. He suggested a new physics or metaphysics in which the essences given in immediate experience should be deployed and hypostatized into the constituents of nature: but this pictorial cosmology had the disadvantage of abolishing the human imagination, with all the pathos and poetry of its animal status. James thus renounced that gift for literary psychology, that romantic insight, in which alone he excelled; and indeed his followers are without it. I pride myself on remaining a disciple of his earlier unsophisticated self, when he was an agnostic about the universe, but in his diagnosis of the heart an impulsive poet: a master in the art of recording or divining the lyric quality of experience as it actually came to him or to me.

Lyric experience and literary psychology, as I have learned to conceive them, are chapters in the life of one race of animals, in one corner of the natural world. But before relegating them to that modest station (which takes nothing away from their spiritual prerogatives) I was compelled to face the terrible problem which arises when, as in modern philosophy, literary psychology and lyric experience are made the fulcrum or the stuff of the universe. Has this experience any external conditions? If it has, are they knowable? And if it has not, on what principle are its qualities generated or its episodes distributed? Nay, how can literary psychology or universal experience have any seat save the present fancy of the psychologist or the historian? Although James had been bothered and confused by these questions, and Royce had enthroned his philosophy upon them, neither of these my principal teachers seemed to have come to clearness on the subject: it was only afterwards, when I read Fichte and Schopenhauer, that I began to see my way to a solution. We must oscillate between a radical transcendentalism, frankly reduced to a solipsism of the living moment, and a materialism posited as a presupposition of conventional sanity. There was no contradiction in joining together a scepticism which was not a dogmatic negation of anything and an animal faith which avowedly was a mere assumption in action and description. Yet such oscillation, if it was to be justified and rendered coherent, still demanded some understanding of two further points: what, starting from immediate experience, was the *causa cognoscendi* of the natural world; and what, starting from the natural world, was the *causa fiendi* of immediate experience?

On this second point (in spite of the speculations of my friend Strong) I have not seen much new light. I am constrained merely to register as a brute fact the emergence of consciousness in animal bodies. A psyche, or nucleus of hereditary organization, gathers and governs these bodies, and at the same time breeds within them a dreaming, suffering, and watching mind. Such investigations as those of Fraser and of Freud have shown how rich and how mad a thing the mind is fundamentally, how pervasively it plays about animal life, and how remote its first and deepest intuitions are from any understanding of their true occasions. An interesting and consistent complement to these discoveries is furnished by behaviourism, which I heartily accept on its positive biological side: the hereditary life of the body, modified by accident or training, forms a closed cycle of habits and actions. Of this the mind is a concomitant spiritual expression, invisible, imponderable, and epiphenomenal, or, as I prefer to say, hypostatic: for in it the moving unities and tensions of animal life are synthesized on quite another plane of being, into actual intuitions and feelings. This spiritual fertility in living bodies is the most natural of things. It is unintelligible only as all existence, change, or genesis is unintelligible; but it might be better understood, that is, better assimilated to other natural miracles, if we understood better the life of matter everywhere, and that of its different aggregates.

On the other point raised by my naturalism, namely on the grounds of faith in the natural world, I have reached more positive conclusions. Criticism, I think, must first be invited to do its worst: nothing is more dangerous here than timidity or convention. A pure and radical transcendentalism will disclaim all knowledge of fact. Nature, history, the self become ghostly presences, mere notions of such things; and the being of these images becomes purely internal to them; they exist in no environing space or time; they possess no substance or hidden parts, but are all surface, all appearance. Such a being, or quality of being, I call an essence; and to the consideration of essences, composing of themselves an eternal and infinite realm, I have lately devoted much attention. To that sphere I transpose the familiar pictures painted by the senses, or by traditional science and religion. Taken as essences, all ideas are compatible and supplementary to one another, like the various arts of expression; it is possible to perceive, up to a certain point, the symbolic burden of each of them, and to profit by the spiritual criticism of experience which it may embody. In particular, I recognize this spiritual truth in the Neo-Platonic and Indian systems, without admitting their fabulous side: after all, it is an old maxim with me that many ideas may be convergent as poetry which would be divergent as dogmas. This applies, in quite another quarter, to that revolution in physics which is now loudly announced, sometimes as the bankruptcy of science, sometimes as the breakdown of materialism. This revolution becomes, in my view, simply a change in notation.

Matter may be called gravity or an electric charge or a tension in an ether; mathematics may readjust its equations to more accurate observations; any fresh description of nature which may result will still be a product of human wit, like the Ptolemaic and the Newtonian systems, and nothing but an intellectual symbol for man's contacts with matter, in so far as they have gone or as he has become distinctly sensitive to them. The real matter, within him and without, will meantime continue to rejoice in its ancient ways, or to adopt new ones, and incidentally to create these successive notions of it in his head.

When all the data of immediate experience and all the constructions of thought have thus been purified and reduced to what they are intrinsically, that is, to eternal essences, by a sort of counterblast the sense of existence, of action, of ambushed reality everywhere about us, becomes all the clearer and more imperious. This assurance of the not-given is involved in action, in expectation, in fear, hope, or want: I call it animal faith. The object of this faith is the substantial energetic thing encountered in action, whatever this thing may be in itself; by moving, devouring, or transforming this thing I assure myself of its existence; and at the same time my respect for it becomes enlightened and proportionate to its definite powers. But throughout, for the description of it in fancy, I have only the essences which my senses or thought may evoke in its presence; these are my inevitable signs and names for that object. Thus the whole sensuous and intellectual furniture of the mind becomes a store whence I may fetch terms for the description of nature, and may compose the silly home-poetry in which I talk to myself about everything. All is a tale told, if not by an idiot, at least by a dreamer; but it is far from signifying nothing. Sensations are rapid dreams: perceptions are dreams sustained and developed at will; sciences are dreams abstracted, controlled, measured, and rendered scrupulously proportional to their occasions. Knowledge accordingly always remains a part of imagination in its terms and in its seat; yet by virtue of its origin and intent it becomes a memorial and a guide to the fortunes of man in nature.

In the foregoing I have said nothing about my sentiments

concerning æsthetics or the fine arts; yet I have devoted two
volumes to those subjects, and I believe that to some people my
whole philosophy seems to be little but rhetoric or prose poetry.
I must frankly confess that I have written some verses; and at
one time I had thoughts of becoming an architect or even a
painter. The decorative and poetic aspects of art and nature have
always fascinated me and held my attention above everything
else. But in philosophy I recognize no separable thing called
æsthetics; and what has gone by the name of the philosophy of
art, like the so-called philosophy of history, seems to me sheer
verbiage. There is in art nothing but manual knack and professional tradition on the practical side, and on the contemplative
side pure intuition of essence, with the inevitable intellectual or
luxurious pleasure which pure intuition involves. I can draw no
distinction—save for academic programmes—between moral and
æsthetic values: beauty, being a good, is a moral good; and the
practice and enjoyment of art, like all practice and all enjoyment,
fall within the sphere of morals—at least if by morals we understand moral economy and not moral superstition. On the other
hand, the good, when actually realized and not merely pursued
from afar, is a joy in the immediate; it is possessed with wonder
and is in that sense æsthetic. Such pure joy when blind is called
pleasure, when centred in some sensible image is called beauty,
and when diffused over the thought of ulterior propitious things
is called happiness, love, or religious rapture. But where all is
manifest, as it is in intuition, classifications are pedantic. Harmony,
which might be called an æsthetic principle, is also the principle
of health, of justice, and of happiness. Every impulse, not the
æsthetic mood alone, is innocent and irresponsible in its origin
and precious in its own eyes; but every impulse or indulgence,
including the æsthetic, is evil in its effect, when it renders harmony
impossible in the general tenor of life, or produces in the soul
division and ruin. There is no lack of folly in the arts; they are
full of inertia and affectation and of what must seem ugliness to a
cultivated taste; yet there is no need of bringing the catapult of
criticism against it: indifference is enough. A society will breed
the art which it is capable of, and which it deserves; but even in

its own eyes this art will hardly be important or beautiful unless it engages deeply the resources of the soul. The arts may die of triviality, as they were born of enthusiasm. On the other hand, there will always be beauty, or a transport akin to the sense of beauty, in any high contemplative moment. And it is only in contemplative moments that life is truly vital, when routine gives place to intuition, and experience is synthesized and brought before the spirit in its sweep and truth. The intention of my philosophy has certainly been to attain, if possible, such wide intuitions, and to celebrate the emotions with which they fill the mind. If this object be æsthetic and merely poetical, well and good: but it is a poetry or æstheticism which shines by disillusion and is simply intent on the unvarnished truth.

PRINCIPAL PUBLICATIONS

The Sense of Beauty (1896).
Interpretations of Poetry and Religion (1900).
The Life of Reason, 5 vols. (1905–6).
Three Philosophical Poets (1910).
Winds of Doctrine (1913).
Egotişm in German Philosophy (1915).
Character and Opinion in the United States (1920).
Soliloquies in England (1921).
Scepticism and Animal Faith (1923).
Dialogues in Limbo (1925).
Platonism and the Spiritual Life (1927).
The Realm of Essence (1927).

REALISM, NATURALISM, AND HUMANISM

By ROY WOOD SELLARS

Born 1880; University of Michigan, Ann Arbor.

REALISM, NATURALISM, AND HUMANISM

I

BIOGRAPHICAL

I HAVE been given to understand that the essays included in this volume are supposed to present an exposition of the writer's philosophical creed—if he has a definite one—and, at the same time, to indicate some of the influences which have affected his thought. There is, I presume, no assumption that his thought is a mere effect of these influences, but rather the quite justified belief that it can be better understood in relation to them.

Because it will be easiest to consider first the influences which I can note in my life I shall begin in this way and so preface the systematic part of my essay with some remarks upon the development of my thought.

I was brought up in a small village in an almost pioneer community in north-eastern Michigan. Actually I was born in Canada of typically mixed stock, in which I can trace Scot, English, Welsh, Irish, and German ingredients, the Scot predominating. My father, who was a physician, was a man whom I have always regarded as of exceptional natural ability. He had struggled for an education, becoming a country school teacher in Canada at an early age, in a period when schools were attended by pretty rough boys and girls often older than the teacher. His stories of his life undoubtedly influenced my attitude to many things. Forced to give up school work by bad health after he had made a success, he attended the University of Michigan while a small family, myself the youngest, was dependent upon him. Economic pressure then forced him to find a place where practice would quickly come, and the new country of the North was chosen.

It was here that my formative years were spent, for I did not leave the little village until I was seventeen. Here my companions were farmers' boys, and my chief pleasure was reading what books I could lay my hands on and roaming through the woods. It was a simple life in its way, but one that would lead a sensitive and self-conscious boy to much introspection and meditation. Of philosophy I knew little as yet except the name, though I read Carlyle and Emerson assiduously. My father was almost a zealot in his insistence upon education, and I owe him much for his stimulation of my interest in history and science. His library was literally the only one in the whole neighbourhood, and consisted largely of the books dating from his days as a schoolmaster. As I grew older, we used to talk together in his office about medicine. It is an interesting coincidence that I, who have stood in this country for naturalism, realism, and humanism in a rather aggressive fashion, should have been brought up in this atmosphere. I recall this small point of agreement with Aristotle with pride.

I arrived at the University of Michigan at the age of nineteen, an undoubtedly queer freshman, with a large amount of self-education mingled with my schooling. In the sophomore year I started my work in philosophy. Here I came under the influence of Wenley, Lloyd, and Rebec. While I afterwards struck out on a path of my own, which they never entirely approved, I can see how they gave me perspective and awakened me intellectually. It was my contact with a fuller and deeper culture. Another teacher who affected me in many ways was Craig, who was head of the Semitics department. I have always regretted that the mathematics department had no outstanding men at the time. There was no vision in it. I laboured on to calculus and then stopped.

A year spent as Fellow at the University of Wisconsin brought me into contact with Sharp and Bode. This was in 1904. It was Sharp who called my attention to G. E. Moore's essay in *Mind*, entitled "A Refutation of Idealism." I frequently talked entire evenings with Bode, who was just then swinging to pragmatism. Called to Michigan the next year as an instructor, I devoted myself to teaching and to securing my doctorate. With the exception of two periods spent abroad, chiefly in France and Germany, my life has been passed in the little city of Ann Arbor, in the usual academic fashion.

A philosopher's thought is roughly distinguishable into his

technical investigation and the larger background of reflection and experience which makes up his life. These, of course, interact, but they are not exactly identical. It is the larger play of reflection and experience that constitutes the individual's intellectual and emotional adjustment to the world, his growing imaginative insight into the texture of reality. His technical analysis of traditional problems is an affair of detail, and it seems to me to proceed step by step with the growth of his outlook upon things.

Now I can plainly see that my general outlook has been dominated by the *set* of my own personality, which is strongly self-conscious and individualistic. I note that I have always rejected any theory which did not do justice to the uniqueness of each centre of consciousness, to doctrines of fusion and mysticism. I mean by this that I always held to mental pluralism while recognizing that the individual is part of a larger world which plays upon him. Thus, while in sympathy with the general fight of pragmatism against absolute idealism, I could never accept the tendency of the Chicago School to a social consciousness.

I began to work out my own view of things in connection with a course which I gave on the fundamental concepts of science. Here it was my method to start with natural realism and advance step by step to what I called scientific realism. Readers of my first book, *Critical Realism*, published in 1916, though sent to the publishing house in 1913, will recognize this method. I still regard it as the proper approach to theory of knowledge.

Accompanying this interest in science was a revolt against traditional religion and an increasing interest in human beings and in social movements. I discarded supernaturalism completely and decided that the heart of religion lay in the effort of man to safeguard what he conceived as valuable. Religion, I felt, was a reflection of man's strategy in the face of the world as he understood it. And this understanding varied. What, I asked myself, would happen to religion as the belief in supernatural agencies and controls gave way to naturalism. It seemed to me that religion would be transformed and become a philosophy of life dominated by a frank realization of man's place in nature and a keen sense for what was worth while in life. In the little book, *The Next Step in Religion,* I called this transformed religion humanism, a loyalty to human values. When I undertook to publish it, I was told by many that I was foolish, that such a frank suggestion of naturalism would get me into trouble, slow up my promotion, prevent my being called elsewhere. Perhaps it has had some of these effects, but there is compensation in freedom of self-expression. Besides, what was pioneer work ten years ago is almost commonplace already, so quickly does thought move in the United States. I do not think that foreigners sufficiently realize what opposing tendencies are at work here. Philosophy and psychology have been lifting themselves out of traditional perspectives more rapidly in America than elsewhere.

In social matters my development was analogous. I saw an unawareness of social problems and maladjustments, a constant whipping-up of the acquisitive instincts. Of course, this was not all that I saw, for there are many admirable sides to American life. Any criticism I had to pass was, I felt, applicable to modern civilization as a whole. Had the industrial revolution and modern finance concentrated power and nourished false ideals? Could we have faith in the coming of automatic readjustments? Or was it time for social planning and criticism? Becoming acquainted with the literature of social reform, I inevitably came into contact with the world-wide socialist movement. I tried to see what was valuable and what was outworn in Marxianism. The result was my *The Next Step in Democracy,* which fell into line with much of the English writing on the subject. It stressed the value of social experimentation in co-operation, profit-sharing, limitation of inheritance, and increased participation of employees. It is my desire to come back again to this field before long and do really systematic work in it.

These general remarks in regard to my intellectual development show that I was a child of the twentieth century, forward-looking and not too much impressed by intellectual and social traditions. I believed that man was slowly gaining insight into himself, into the texture of society, and into the general structure of the universe. My thought has thus been intertwined with the discoveries, generalizations, and valuations of the period. And yet I was never a mere child of the present. The history of philosophy brought to me the life of distant cultures and other times. Thus my knowledge of Greek thought confirmed me in my humanism and naturalism. It seemed to me that, in its brief period of splendour and success, Greece was working toward the same blend of humanism and naturalism that I had in mind. In spite of my admiration for Plato, I could not but regard him as the gifted advocate of a vicious trend in Greek thought which prepared the way for dualism and mysticism. My sympathies were more with Aristotle's attempt to keep his feet on the ground.

As I look back on my own development, I realize that a philosophy is not created in an isolated mind, but in one open to the currents of doctrine. I count myself peculiarly fortunate to have come to maturity in a period of reconstruction. What I brought was a very persistent mind with a keen sense for realities.

I come now to my technical inheritance. My teachers stressed the historical approach to philosophy so characteristic of the idealist movement of the latter part of the nineteenth century. This was valuable, but could easily be overdone. There was need of analysis as well and of a clear formulation of actual problems. From the very first I focussed my attention upon the mind-body problem as crucial, and quickly saw that it could not be solved apart from a mastery of theory of knowledge. My first publications were along this line.

Like all American thinkers of this period, I was strongly influenced by James's *Principles of Psychology*. James Ward, also, exercised his influence upon my psychology and thence upon my theory of knowledge. These men brought out the continuity of the field of experience and the discriminative and selective activity of the mind. In this I believe that they anticipated much of the *Gestalt* movement and certainly moved far away from strict associationism. I felt that they had analysed the actual flow of experience more adequately than had either Hume or Kant. What was needed was a fuller appreciation of the part played by the organism in all this. In both there lingered too much of the tradition of psycho-physical dualism. It is my belief that recent work in psychology shows a better sense of the response of the conscious organism and the part played by this in the construction and selection of percepts. Seeing the organism in its setting, I was led to think of perception as a selective interpretation of external things and to break away completely from the subjectivistic tradition that ideas are the objects of knowledge. I tried to work within the knowledge-claim and to make it pass from perception to critical judgment. From the very first, I found it impossible to find satisfaction in any form of the new realism. Knowledge could not be the actual givenness of the object; the field of consciousness was not a passive collection of things capable of entering and leaving it. No; knowing was a unique activity involving mediations and claims and pointing beyond itself. It was as near to the things known as we could get. Representative realism must be re-analysed and cut loose from Cartesian dualism. It was in this fashion that my particular brand of critical realism was born.

The eager mind absorbs and responds after its own fashion and in accordance with its own insights. Those we differ from are often of more value to us than those who vaguely agree with us. As time went on, I read chiefly in connection with the problems upon which I was at the moment working. But I have tried to make up for this by covering a wide field.

As I have already indicated, the problem of knowledge fascinated my mind jointly with the mind-body problem. It seemed to me then, as it seems to me still, that these two problems are in large measure inseparable. Make mind intrinsic to the organism, and you are at once forced to some kind of mediate realism. How can one think it out? The weaknesses of Locke must be avoided by laying more stress on an interpretative activity of the mind and upon the direct claim to know things and not ideas. Ideas must be seen as ingredients in knowing. Moreover, while the causal conditions of knowing an external object must be recognized, they must not be allowed to get in the way of the actual knowing, however much they underlie it. It has taken me a very

long time to deepen my insight into all these problems. I have
worked on the same hypotheses with confidence and obstinacy
these many years, but they have grown and become more delicate
and adequate.

So much for the biographical side and for the influences which
I can clearly recognize. I hope that this very brief survey will
give the reader some appreciation of the temper and content of
my mind and of my natural mode of approach to things. Now
to my position in philosophy. I have headed my contribution
"Realism, Naturalism, and Humanism," because I do think these
terms describe fairly well my outlook in theory of knowledge,
cosmology, and values. It is not because I am fond of labels that
I have always adopted a term to characterize my position, but
because definite positions deserve specific terms. In what follows
I shall describe and seek to justify critical realism in theory of
knowledge, evolutionary naturalism in cosmology, and humanism
in the field of values and human activities. After presenting them
separately, I shall try to bring them together as a whole to show
how they fit together in one *Weltanschauung*.

II

PHILOSOPHICAL CREED

Theory of knowledge is a tantalizing, as well as a fascinating,
field for reflection. The thinker must bear in mind the empirical
nature and conditions of human thinking as well as the claim
which knowing obviously makes to reveal its object. There has,
I think, been of late a growth of insight in regard to both of
these points. What is needed is the power to put them together.

It has frequently been pointed out that the purely scientific
approach is naturalistic and postulates a conscious organism
stimulated by things and responding differentially to these
stimuli. But such a point of view really takes knowing for granted
and is therefore incomplete. But I do not think that such a
standpoint is vicious, for knowledge is a fact which theory of
knowledge seeks to explain and interpret.

A study of the growth and conditions of knowledge uses the

results of psychology and logic. It is then seen how the external, physical thing is made the object of attention, and how a patterned content arises before the individual's awareness and is automatically identified with the object meant and reacted to. A careful study of perception would show how the content of perception is built up and discriminated, and how meanings, beliefs, and selections arise along with this content to give it a reference to an external object. We are at a fairly high mental level in perception, and there is a configuration here which must be acknowledged. This perceptual situation can, perhaps, be best described by saying that the category of thinghood has been achieved and operates at this level. Frankly, I would make much of categories, but I think of them as arising in experience naturally under the stress of the give-and-take of the conscious organism and the suggestions and pressures of conscious living. In this way, they are responsible achievements under the control of the external world rather than secretions of an inner self. The elementary categories are, if you will, natural ways of interpreting the world to which the organism is responding.

There is another feature of the field of perception which demands stress, and that is the presence in it of temporal and spatial order or arrangement. Here, again, I would differ from Kant and still more from the older English tradition. We do not begin with a chaos of sensations, but with a *patterned field*; and there is good reason to hold that the pattern is controlled in us by the actual arrangement of the stimuli coming to the organism. The activity of the organism helps to bring out this order, and such mental operations as comparison and discrimination further this end. The analogy of the camera has point, for the sense-organs operate after the same general plan, but we must not forget that the organism has inner resources which the camera does not possess.

But in this naturalistic and scientific way of approach to perception we are stressing conditions and processes as known, and we are not, in the strict sense, analysing perception as a claim to knowledge. This approach is not irrelevant, but it cannot take the place of the internal study of perception and judgment as claims to know which must be criticized. The philosopher must undertake this supplementary investigation which works *within* the experience of perceiving and judging and tries to determine the nature and claims of knowing. And since the idealist has long maintained that the results of such an internal investigation conflict with the naturalistic assumptions of science, the work of analysis must be thoroughly done.

I need not go into the history of this internal analysis of knowledge and its claims. Were Berkeley, Hume, and Kant right in arguing against a frank physical realism? In my opinion they were wrong. The dualism between mind and matter, the assumption that we know ideas rather than things, the clumsy scheme of qualities inhering in a substance—all these unmastered traditions got in the way.

The total act of perceiving with its beliefs, categories, and discriminations is the most elementary unit of knowing the external world. Reflection shows that this complex is mental and intrinsic to the active organism. I beg to point out that, when I use the word mental, I have in mind no dualistic assumption, but only the recognition that we have here a peculiar activity of the individual. In taking the act of knowing seriously, we must realize that we are on the inside of this act and that the logical discriminations used in it are not self-sufficient atoms to be called mental entities. We have here a structure which must be taken at its face value. The mind is interpreting an object in terms of characters. It is thinking the characteristics of the object. Shift the point of view quickly from a knowledge-claim to a survey of what is given in and to consciousness, and these characteristics of things become characters of a logical sort undoubtedly sustained by the mind. But then we are ceasing to claim to know external objects. The direction of the mind has altered.

How does this position differ from naïve realism? In three main ways. First, it is more aware of the conditions of knowing; second, it is ready to admit the mediate, or interpretative, nature of knowing; and, third, it holds that reflection must work within perceptual knowing to lift it to more adequate knowledge of the object. It sees that perception is dominated by practical interests and bodily perspective, and passes to science.

Let me summarize my results. In the first place, knowing is regarded as more than the awareness of abstracta to be called logical ideas. It is an interpretation of objects. Thus objective reference is intrinsic to the very nature of knowing whether perceptual or explicitly judgmental. This analysis rids us of the subjectivistic bias of traditional representative realism. In the second place, logical ideas are discriminations within a complex mental activity in which objects are selected and interpreted. We must not drop back to an atomistic psychology of sensations and images which ignores empirical facts. Our mental activity sustains for us an experienced structure in which we sense ourselves as interpreting objects in terms of predicates revealing their characteristics. This bit of redness, this instance of squareness, are logical characters enabling us to grasp the characteristics of the object. They are to be classed as mental only when we raise the question of their ultimate nature as related to the mental act of knowing to which they are intrinsic. In the act of knowing, it is their logical content which occupies our interest. We look through them at the object. Yet reflection, I believe, forces us to hold that the whole complex mental act to which they are intrinsic is a temporal affair expressive of the brain-mind. The only alternative is to hold them to be essences belonging to a realm of being other than that of physical existence. But this alternative theory seems to me less simple than the one I defend and more traditionalistic, more a reflection of Platonism.

The comment of the reader at this point may be somewhat as follows: Granted that the logic and psychology of this position is an advance upon Locke's and Kant's, due to the progress in both domains, does it not still hold that the characters held as predicates before the mind must resemble the qualities of the external thing? Yes and no. Sense-qualities fall away as we pass from naïve to critical claims and the appreciation of structure and relations increases. Now the structure conceived in the mind does, I believe, correspond to the structure of the object. It is because of this correspondence that the knowledge-claim is justified; the logical idea does reveal the characteristics of the object. These characteristics must not be conceived in the old fashion as properties inhering in an unknown substance, but as the nature of the physical system known. An object does weigh so much, is so large, has such and such a texture, will do certain things under certain conditions. We must simply move away from the literal assignment of passive sense-qualities.

A few words on a point which has been misunderstood is desirable. I was led to deny the reality of a cognitive relation. This did not mean that I did not supply what the cognitive relation stood for—reference to an object and the claim to know it. The expression "cognitive relation" was connected in my mind with the conflict between neo-realism and idealism. In the English form of the controversy, at least, there was assumed a sort of tenuous relation between the mind and the object called awareness. Was this internal or external? Now my own analysis forced me to maintain that a physical object known is never literally present in the field of consciousness; the mind makes no existential contact with it except through the sense-organs. Knowing is a claim and reference to an external object mediated by meanings in consciousness. It is a sort of mental pointing and not a literal transcendence. This fact but brings out more clearly the unique nature of knowing. This mental pointing, however, is founded on the attitude and response of the organism in perception and the reflection of this in consciousness. Conceptual pointing but carries on this structure and develops it in terms of frames of reference. Knowing handles objects through internal substitutes which are supposed to reveal the nature of the external object.

But, it may be replied, while you rightly avoid a gross interpretation of a cognitive relation by means of stress upon internal reference and claims attached to ideas, does it not remain a fact that the nature of the object is present to the mind? This query demands a reply. I do not think that, existentially, the nature of an object ever separates itself from the object. It can, however, be reproduced in the mind as an achieved abstractum and be held by that mind as a revelation of the nature of the object. We have here a logical, or better, a cognitive, identity between idea and object.

This problem brings out the fact that knowing is a kind of operation for which we can find no ordinary physical analogies. It depends upon the growth and use of distinctions, beliefs, and categories in consciousness. An object is cognitively present to the mind when it is known, but such knowledge does not involve the literal givenness of the object as an entity within the field of consciousness. Knowing is a looking at objects through the windows furnished by ideas. It is *sui generis*, though made possible by the situation and capacities of the organism.

In this very brief survey of some of the high points of epistemology we have now arrived at a stage which demands the discussion of truth. In order to secure clarity it will be better to limit ourselves to the question of what we mean by the trueness of a proposition. But, first of all, let me say that a proposition is to me a complex idea used in an act of knowing. It is a belief. Taken in this sense, a proposition seems to me to be called true when we consider it to give knowledge of its object, to reveal its object. Hence, I have always maintained that knowing is the basic idea which underlies truth. An idea which gives knowledge of its object is true. But, if this is the meaning of truth, what are the criteria or tests? It is often averred that critical realism has special difficulties here because of its doctrine of transcendence. How can you check up on the idea if the object is not given? And if the object is given, what need have you for ideas?

The proper approach is to ask what casts doubt on the truth-claim of a judgment. The doubt must be motivated and specific, otherwise we are merely doubting the ability of the human mind to know. When I come to analyse the situation, I find that the human mind begins in perception to interpret objects and that difficulties merely force a critical reinterpretation of this first interpretation. The basic postulate is the claim to know or, what amounts to the same thing at this level, the revelatory nature of our predicates. This postulate, if challenged, is confirmed by the success of our critical thinking. In other words, thought cures its own difficulties by showing how new distinctions satisfy old conflicts. The manner in which perceptual illusions are shown to result from our position and from the nature of our sense-organs illustrates what I mean. Critical thinking is the only remedy for specifically motivated doubt. And this success of critical thinking can be indicated under four headings: (1) the consilience of established facts; (2) the logical coherence of ideas; (3) agreement of investigators; and (4) guidance and control over nature. These headings have been so often discussed that there is no need to go into detail. It will be noted that I assign a place to both the logical and the larger pragmatic tests. But I am convinced that the very advance of thought rests on the belief that sense-perception is revelatory of nature and that the proper use of it enables us to penetrate into the characteristics of the world. The logic of science gives, I think, the proper use of sense-perception.

As conclusion of this summary account of critical realism, let me point out what I think is important about it as a direction of thought. It represents a deeper insight into the nature of human knowing and a greater awareness of its conditions. In place of knowing as a semi-magical intuition or compresence of mind and object, it grasps knowing as an achievement in which ideas function, ideas being distinctions within the field of consciousness used in accordance with slowly evolved meanings and beliefs. In this way it shows how organic activity flowers into knowing. It can be regarded more as a deepening of natural realism than its complete rejection. What, then, can we know about the external world? Essentially what science has worked out—structure, relative dimensions, relative mass, energy-content, behaviour. Theory of knowledge does not so much dictate to science as interpret it.

In the next section I shall pass to cosmology and defend naturalism. In anticipation I would point out that we must not forget that we have a double knowledge of our own organism and, aided by communication and analogy, other organisms. To forget this would cause unnecessary mistakes in cosmology.

III

Perhaps the best way in which I can introduce my exposition of naturalism is to tell why I adopted it as a term when it was largely in disrepute. What are the essential things for which naturalism has always stood? As I saw it, they were the following: (1) the self-sufficiency of nature as against popular supernaturalism or the sublimated sort called transcendentalism; (2) the basic significance for our world of space, time, and causality; (3) the denial of concentrated control in the universe and, in this sense, the acceptance of pluralism; and (4) the rejection of the primacy of mind. Now I was convinced of the essential truth of these cosmological principles and felt that their acceptance could best be summarized by the term naturalism.

On the whole, too, naturalism was a much more plastic term than materialism. To free it from its temporary disrepute did not seem impossible. Perhaps the ultimate result would be a new form of materialism capable of including mental activity and human motivation by values, but naturalism was clearly a step in the right direction.

The rejection of idealism in theory of knowledge, which had been coming apace, was already shaking objective idealism and spiritualism to their foundations. Critical realism implied physical realism, and physical realism is at least half-way to naturalism. Only the mind-body problem stood in the path. Achieve the idea of mind as intrinsic to the living organism, and naturalism is full-fledged. And, as I pointed out, I had always carried this problem in mind while I was working at theory of knowledge. Physical realism, plus the rejection of dualism, spelt naturalism.

Physical realism had hitherto gone with a strictly mechanical view of all physical processes and with the assumption that knowledge gives a penetrative vision of the stuff of the physical world. Could both of these assumptions be challenged? If we know only the structure, behaviour, and relative masses and energies of things by means of scientific investigation, it follows that we cannot intuit physical systems in some more direct way. Any static, sensuous representation betrays the habits of naïve

realism. For this reason, it is suggestive to say that we have
knowledge about nature rather than acquaintance with it. It is
illuminating knowledge, but it falls short of that intimate vision
which forever haunts us. Again, reflection seemed to show me
that the mechanical ideal was a hasty dogma set up in opposition
to final causes and that the character of physical changes had to
be discovered empirically.

Working along these lines, I was more and more convinced
of the significance of organization in nature. Do not physical
systems respond as wholes, and is not the nature of this response
a function of the kind of organization achieved? Mechanism in
the strict, traditional sense meant external relations, so that each
event expressed a specific impact, or complex of impacts, upon
some unit. For such an interpretation of nature, a physical
system was in no sense an actual unity. Instead, it was a constellation of movements.

But, if we take organization seriously, we must accept the
rise in nature of *natural kinds* with specific properties expressive
of the system. From this it would follow that we must expect
novelty and origination in nature and what may be called levels
of causality. Uniformity of process would no longer be the
scientific ideal. To reduce everything to one type would now be
looked upon as a false and impossible objective. Careful study
must replace dogmatism.

A comment upon the logic of this approach may be worth
while. It seems to me clear that such a stress upon the *specificity*
of physical systems is empirical rather than mystical. It does not
cast doubt on the value of analysis, for surely it is impossible to
conceive a physical whole which is not a togetherness of parts.
What it does accomplish is the clearer distinction between logical
analysis and physical analysis. In logical analysis, we seek to
see parts *in* their relations by constructive discrimination; in
physical analysis, we seek to break down a physical system into
simpler systems which we are apt to call parts. Really, these
simpler systems are not parts in a literal sense, for that would
imply that disintegration made no change, a view expressive of a
mechanical dogma. Now physical analysis often aids logical

analysis, and is so used by science, but it is not to be identified with it. In logical analysis of a physical system, we must have a sense of the whole as constituted by its parts and of the parts in their relations in the whole.

The frank acceptance of the significance of organization led me to reject what I called reductive materialism and to advocate the outlook, called evolutionary naturalism, which held that new physical systems arise in nature under favourable conditions, and that these new physical systems have properties which are functions of their organization. It was thus that I was led to interpret vital systems and, a still higher stage of the same, mental or intelligent systems. Life is not a non-natural force coming from outside, but a term for the new capacities of which nature has found itself capable. When certain intimate chemical relations and arrangements are achieved, the system can maintain itself under certain conditions of heat and light. And, upon this foundation, a new, experimental process goes on which gradually achieves those capacities of behaviour which we call intelligent.

Thus far it will be remembered that I am looking upon nature in that external way which behaviourism has emphasized. When I come to the mind-body problem, I must bring in, as supplementary, the fact of self-observation. And, of course, both science and human life in general involve *communication*, something not found at the lower levels of nature.

While I was working on these lines, the books of Alexander and Lloyd Morgan were published. It would seem wise to contrast my own distinctions with theirs while acknowledging how much we have in common.

Emergence has become the accepted term for novelty or origination in nature. If properly qualified, it seems to me as good a term as any other. Clearly it stands for epigenetic evolution with stress upon the significance of organization or relatedness.

For me the basic fact is the reality of change in physical systems. Properties are not stuck on to physical systems from the outside, but are expressions of their particular structure and method of 'go.' Much has been made of the epiphenomenal character of new properties. Such objections seem to me to apply to Alexander's system more than to Lloyd Morgan's or mine, for qualities simply appear as additions to the old to the immediate realist, however critical he may be in his epistemology. Colour bobs up in space-time in some mysterious fashion. But if the physical system is always the unit of activity, a change in the physical system means a new mode of activity. Properties are not entities, but expressions of the changed nature of the system. And it must be remembered that, for Lloyd Morgan and me, all sensory data are in the brain of the observer, itself a unique kind of physical system. It is the pattern of these data which reveals the logical character of the external system perceived and critically known.

Another point. I take the famous expression, natural piety, to signify nothing more than the part played by observation and experimentation in science. It is another term for empiricism as against deductive rationalism. The world is what it is, and we must study it. The object dictates to us as knowers.

It does not seem to me, however, that such empiricism precludes explanation or subordinates it to description. To connect a property with the particular organization of a thing is to explain it. To show how one organization passes into another is to explain it. All scientific explanation, so far as I can see, is the gaining of insight into the structure, relations, and operations of nature so that particular events can be interpreted. Explanation is knowledge and cannot demand more than knowledge can give. And it is clear that science passes beyond mere empirical description and summary of events to the discernment of the structures and processes in nature in which these events are embedded. In short, in the logic of science, description and explanation are terms for stages in explanation, and explanation can never go beyond the insight which knowledge gives.

As a frank naturalist, physical systems are for me ultimate, and I have seen no reason to postulate an extra-physical *nisus* of the sort that Morgan and Alexander acknowledge. Nature is for me intrinsically dynamic. I would express this by saying that causal uniformity reflects causality and causality is the 'onward go' of physical systems. In fact, such postulated *nisus* seems to me a shadow of dualism resembling the *élan vital* of Bergson. Evolutionary naturalism is a monistic, and not a dualistic, outlook.

We are now ready to consider the mind-consciousness-body problem. I am persuaded that this problem is simply being outgrown by reason of the vanishing of old traditions and assumptions. The disappearance of reductive materialism, the growth of behaviourism, the arrival of a clearer realistic episte-mology are all factors. Intelligence can be studied from the outside and turns out to be a capacity for certain modes of behaviour which involve memory, integration, and novel com-bination of response. Defined objectively, it is a term for modes of operation which emerge at a certain level of evolution, modes of which there are degrees which must be considered qualitative. But self-observation gives additional knowledge of the operation of intelligence as it appears within consciousness at a level of awareness—that is, conscious attention. It is at this point that basic metaphysical questions force themselves upon us.

Naïve materialism was dominated by two things, against which the evolutionary naturalist is on his guard: (1) atomic mechanism, and (2) a confident vision of the very stuff of the world as some-how inert, internally homogeneous, solid, and alien to those qualitative events which we call feelings, sensations, and thoughts. Without fully realizing it, naïve materialism was built upon the traditions of dualism. But we must surely challenge this whole perspective. What do we know from outside of that pulsing, integrated system the brain? Very little. We can guess, at most, about the action-patterns which are built up within it under tensions and which discharge into the motor-nerves and thence into the muscles. We know that past-experience is somehow conserved in this delicate organization and past facilities pre-served. The brain in its organic setting of muscle and gland *is* the mind. But, from the outside, we cannot catch a vision of this system as it is for itself. And to modern thought it is less a collec-tion of wooden atoms than a web of activities pulsing in a system which, though spatial, is organic. There is no cognitive vision of its intrinsic nature which forbids us to say that consciousness is there running its course.

But what is consciousness? To say that it is the concrete flow of the field of experience is not enough, though, I believe, correct so far as it goes. Here, again, we must avoid the traditions of dualism and refuse to consider it an immaterial kind of stuff. It would seem to be better conceived as a qualitative web of events intrinsic to the operations of the brain-mind. To appreciate this statement to the full we must realize that in consciousness, and in it alone, we are as conscious selves on the inside of reality. In knowing, we seek to transcend our own being and grasp the characteristics of the object known; but in feeling and thought we are our feelings and thoughts.

What prevents us, then, from holding that, in our consciousness, we are literally on the inside of the functioning brain-mind? As we discriminate in consciousness, so does our brain-mind discriminate and differentially respond to situations. Here is a *dimension of being* which external knowledge could not reveal to the observer, and which we therefore find it hard to think as intrinsic to the brain-mind, so long as we are dominated by an external approach to organisms. That is why a critical epistemology is so necessary for a clear insight into the mind-body problem.

It may be well to point out that I sharply distinguish between awareness and consciousness. Awareness is a characteristic function and contrast within the field of consciousness. It expresses anticipation, interpretation, and attention. Thus I am aware of the postman who is coming up the walk whistling. This awareness is complex and mediated in all sorts of ways, and it constitutes an active configuration within the field of consciousness. I am more and more impressed by such condensed accumulations as meanings, which are built around verbal symbols and attitudes. Clearly the field of consciousness reflects integrated mental systems which themselves are the activities and situations of the organism. There is mediation and originative integration all through it. The field of consciousness of any one moment is part and parcel of the functioning brain-mind.

It follows from this interpretation that I am not sympathetic to pan-psychism. It seems to me just the contrary error to naïve materialism. It is an attempt to find a stuff open to inspection. But consciousness seems to me a web of patterned, qualitative events rather than a stuff. It is not conserved but evanescent, coming and going, but sustained by a slowly evolved system of propensities, habits, and mind-brain systems. It falls under the category of event rather than under that of substance. The ultimate fact which I must accept is that the brain-mind system, when functioning, has this qualitative dimension. And since here alone are we on the inside of a physical system we have no antecedent with which to contrast it and cry miracle. Novelty there is, but a novelty undoubtedly prepared for in the very nature of organic systems. It is our inevitably small acquaintance with the inside of physical systems and our broad knowledge of their revealed structure and behaviour, as mediated by our sense data, that makes the assignment of consciousness to the brain-mind so startling. In short, I am not persuaded of the necessity of either pan-psychism or of the Spinozistic postulation of universal concomitance of the psychical and the physical. Neither view seems to me to take organic evolution seriously enough.

One other question in cosmology I must touch upon before I pass to the locus and nature of values in the new naturalism. It is the attitude to be adopted to the traditional opposition between monism and pluralism. Perhaps it would be better to say singularism and pluralism, since monism has been so frequently employed as a term in opposition to Cartesian dualism.

It is, I take it, obvious that singularism has been primarily a feature of objective idealism. The motives for it there are logical and appear in both Hegel and Bradley. I am persuaded that a realistic epistemology and a naturalistic cosmology change the venue entirely. Since I take space and time as significant categories in our knowledge of nature, this distinction between singularism and pluralism becomes simply one of the *degree* of interdependence in nature. Singularism seems to me to stand for homogeneity and tightness of union, while pluralism means heterogenity and *degrees of freedom*. If pluralism is interpreted in this way, I am a pluralist. Let me explain.

Take an organism. Clearly it is subject to the same gravitational relations as a stone. There is one kind of physical nexus binding the physical world into one system. And if the physical world were homogeneous, not much more would need to be said. But if we take organization seriously, we must admit the development of systems within this basic continuity, systems responding in accordance with their internal nature. While more complex and more highly integrated levels are reared within the system of nature and cannot violate its demands, they can yet add capacities for which these demands give permission and latitude. Thus human behaviour does not violate any of the demands of the inorganic world, but merely explores and expresses possibilities left open. It is this openness to novelty which evolution signifies. Thus singularism stands for general relatedness of the sort that physics investigates, or for a mystical unity, while pluralism stands for differentiation.

There is another aspect of this question which interests me. If we take the universe as a space-time system more organic than mechanical, there still remains the problem of control. Is control a function of the whole? If so, the control of a particular system must be dominantly lodged outside itself and thus external to it. Why? Because it is so small a part of the system. Now I do think that this argument holds for a homogeneous system, but I am not so sure that it holds for a heterogeneous one. In a heterogeneous system, self-control increases among the parts as these gain relative autonomy. External control sets a problem for self-control by giving its conditions. To make the matter short, I do not think that control is a mere function of the whole, but a struggle between the parts in a whole. The part may achieve new ways of doing things which give it new degrees of freedom. Thus human freedom means what intelligent and social organisms can do within the kind of a world we find ourselves in.

I can only indicate the bearing of this analysis upon the age-old antithesis between freedom and necessity. It implies—or so it appears to me—that freedom stresses the side of pluralism and calls attention to the possibilities relative to actual conditions. It stands for relative self-determination as against a control

282 CONTEMPORARY AMERICAN PHILOSOPHY

exercised from outside by force of numbers and magnitude. It is a declaration of the significance of quality, integration, and kind. And such freedom is rather the expression of the system undergoing change than a claim for a dualistic free will. Surely what happens has its conditions and soil. Freedom is a protest against mechanical determinism and in favour of the admission of activity and creativeness in nature, a creativeness whose range and quality varies with the level attained. Of course, this is only a hint of my way of approach to this thorny subject. When applied to man, there would be need to grasp the rôle of intelligence and the meaning of choice.

IV

Can humanism and values find elbow-room in naturalism? It was the common thesis of ethicists of the last generation that this was impossible. And, granted a naturalism wedded to mechanical, or reductive, materialism, I do not think that they were far wrong. If mechanical relations are the sole determinants of conduct, our values must be epiphenomena at least, if not illusions. What are the new possibilities in the field of value-theory?

The first thing to do, surely, is to find out what we mean by values. The next thing is to determine how values become effective in reality.

Axiology is certainly a fascinating field, but one which has not yet cleared up. It has seemed to me that part of this mistiness has been due to the fact that epistemology and cosmology lagged. In what follows I shall content myself with indicating what seem to me the fruitful distinctions to be made.

I would, first of all, distinguish between explicit valuations directed toward objects and what may be called implicit valuations, or value-experiences. It is out of the second that the first crystallize through concentration upon some object.

Implicit valuations are, of course, positive or negative, and, taken over a time-interval, may even be a mixture of plus and minus. We can have a good time, an unpleasant time, or something of a mixture of the two. These value-experiences may be simple or complex, elementary or sophisticated. In them is reflected the demand of the situation and the level of the person ality. The psychology of value-experiences needs study. Feeling and desire are obvious ingredients, and of these feeling is an invariable psychical matter. Desire is an interesting variable affected by all sorts of conditions which play upon the propensities of the individual. But I am inclined to hold that intellectual insight enters as an ingredient in value-experience and gives it what I would call perspective and a framework. I quite admit that desire and feeling are essential ingredients, but I hold that human value-experiences would be entirely different but for the depth and breadth which ideas give. All these factors are, of course, organic to each other.

These value-experiences are resident in consciousness, and their existential status is that of consciousness itself. Hence our solution of the mind-body problem gives us guidance here.

Let us turn next to what I have called explicit valuations directed toward objects. These may be called value-judgments in that they express an interpretation of an object. The problem before us is to decide how value-interpretations differ from strictly cognitional interpretations.

At the level of practical life, our interpretations of objects are both cognitional and valuational at the same time. Value-predicates mingle with descriptive predicates. Is it not clear that, at this level, the meaning of an object for ourselves dominates our effort at interpretation? Knowledge is an instrument, in the main, for our response to, and use of, things. We are agents facing life and trying to make the most of our surroundings. We are seldom interested in objects in a calm and objective way, but link them up with our interests and purposes.

Out of this practical attitude there has gradually differentiated all those specialized attitudes which we call economic, moral, and political. In all of these the significance of objects for our individual and social lives dominates. We are not trying to get at the object itself out of curiosity, but we are seeing how the object bears upon us and what we can make of it.

It is the gradual rise of pure cognition as an *ideal* that has made all this clear. In pure cognition our aim is to think the object as it is in itself and in its context of objective relations. We seek to decipher the characteristics of objects; our aim is to be intellectual spectators. The object is our standard.

Does this not throw our explicit valuations into relief? We now see that in valuation we are interpreting the object as it bears upon our lives, upon our desires, feelings, purposes. The meanings which now arise are value-meanings and are very different from the descriptive meanings explicit in pure cognition. In the two cases we are not trying to do the same thing.

Value-predicates are, then, objective in that they are interpretative of objects, but they are not cognitional. They make explicit what the object means to our lives and not what the object is in itself.

It has seemed to me that this analysis makes the situation clearer than the traditional term relative does. Values are relative to human needs and demands because these are active in their determination. But the significant point is that in valuation we are not trying to do the same kind of thing as in explicit cognition. In both cases we are dealing with objects, but not in the same way.

A value-predicate is a function of (1) the nature of the object, (2) the nature of our interest, and (3) the situation which is relevant to that interest. We may, accordingly, speak of these three factors as conditions of value.

Again, we may distinguish in explicit valuation between end and means. We have, then, instrumental values—that is, objects valued as instruments, and telic or end-values.

But I must hurry to my conclusion. If values are as I have analysed them, they are either predicates or objects as valued. When we raise the question of the efficacy of values, all we should mean is the part played in our volitional decisions by the value which we assign to objects. It is in this way that values secure a grip upon reality. The concrete agent is the self; apart from the self values are abstractions. And, if our analysis has been correct, values are expressions of the self in its relations and inevitably pass over into action. It is only for those who look upon values as eternal and transcendent that the question of the efficacy of values becomes puzzling. They must postulate a power in these values to attract our souls. But is this not metaphor? Is not self-expression the thing? Are we not integrations of tendencies, so that attraction expresses the stirring of some impulse in ourselves when exposed to stimuli interpreted to our souls by our minds? Our values are human values.

PRINCIPAL PUBLICATIONS

Critical Realism (1916).
The Next Step in Democracy (1916).
The Essentials of Logic (1917); revised edition, 1924.
The Essentials of Philosophy (1917).
The Next Step in Religion (1918).
Essays in Critical Realism (with others) (1921).
Evolutionary Naturalism (1921).
The Principles and Problems of Philosophy (1926).
Philosophy To-Day (with others) (1928).
Religion Coming of Age (1928).
Also articles in various philosophical magazines.

CONFESSIO PHILOSOPHI

By ⌊EDGAR A. SINGER, Jr.

Born 1873; Professor of Philosophy, University of Pennsylvania,
Philadelphia.

CONFESSIO PHILOSOPHI

I⊤ has been said, boyhood is religious, manhood forgets. But not all men forget; of those who cannot, part is able to follow in the old, part must try new ways. From the first come our priests, who know; from the second our philosophers, who seek—for philosophy either is, or else involves, the search for a religion. This search is of a nature to try men throughly and sort them; of those who set out on it some end in a finding, some endure till the end, some faint by the way. The last is the easiest solution, and in the toilsome way through experience to religion, few endure for all the length of their days; most resolve themselves into good citizens—having learned at last to follow, or learned at least to forget. And who shall say the world has not been gainer by these, philosophy's losses? But must we suppose the "lost ones" also to have won?

I wish I knew; for then this confession might have been a religion—might have been a creed in the hand instead of one in the seeking. But then, it would not have been written; not at least by a philosopher, that unaccepted lover of wisdom; nor yet for philosophers, who cannot be moved to accept. It is not for such as we to offer creeds to one another, who cannot afford them ourselves. We formulate in order to revise, and when one of us is asked (as on this occasion) to account for his creed in terms of his life,[1] what is left for him to do (if he would do his best to comply) but to recall the dissatisfactions that have pushed him on and are pushing him? His life will come before him as an education not yet complete; and if he would make a story of it, his only way can be to lend fictitious sequence to a play of influences dividing, not his life, but his fairly continuous attention. Thus may anyone, however blurred the memory of his own unimportant days, say with a certain truth, he has been to school to his century (itself a learner from others)—a school whose lessons he can now recall

---

[1] "To accord with the plans of the Committee, each article should embody its author's philosophical creed, together with the circumstances in his life history which influenced him in reaching it. We are asking in short for an intellectual autobiography. . . ."—COMMITTEE.

only in the order of their offering, not of his receiving. Where his own reflection on this experience of the years has found some formulation, of this he may speak by the book; but the only part of his "life" that can seem to himself living is the part that is being lived. Here ferments a lively discontent in all that has gone before, from which if from anything must come his hope of bettering the work of his hand.

In some such way as this your philosopher would order the story he is invited to tell: however little it may profit his comrades in the cause, it must, one feels, have its comfort for the "lost ones" of the last paragraph—from all such restless philosophy *they* at least are at rest. If besides it convey to any the singular satisfaction there is in that other repose, that dynamic content in the endless task of building and building always anew—why, then it will not have fallen far short of what was asked for; it will have revealed the psychology of a philosopher, though of one no different from another.

But first, by way of preface, what has held this philosopher from joining the majority, those who have come to rest? Of these we counted two classes: such as had found their religion, and such as had left off the search. The first, though lost to philosophy, have in no wise defected from its cause: never have they forgotten, nor is it for us to say they have lost what critical faculty once left them discontented with the finished things of the past. Now they are content again; and we who are not toil on: they perhaps are the blest; and whether their inability to hand the blessing on comes from their want of reason or ours of understanding, how shall we surely know? Where, indeed, they have given reasons for the various faiths that are in them, we may touch on these as we go and hint at our own reasons contra. But where they have offered none, where they have come to contentment in mystical "creeds outworn"—as once they judged of creeds—why, there we can neither contemn nor envy what we so little understand. We can only know that as yet such things are not for us.

But the second class of those who have found rest—in forgetfulness, namely—what shall we say of these? I believe I was about to say something very stupid, very respectable therefore: that we could learn nothing of religious interest from those who had forgotten religion. But when I came to think on this which I had always thought, a difficulty discovered itself I had never discovered before: how in the world are we to distinguish between a surrender of religion and a religion of surrender? Is not a "philosophy of forgetting" itself a religious achievement, a story carried to its end, and ending in a creed? No sooner has one put the matter to oneself in this way than one realizes how long a chapter might be written on the "religion of forgetting." Nor could this chapter be unimportant; it, too, would consider how men had found peace—or thought they had, for reasons well expressed or readily divined. No, I repent me of that first hasty diremption; none have abandoned philosophy save those who have found what they sought, the religion in which they could rest. And when I come to think of it in an autobiographical way, it is strange I should ever have overlooked the philosophy I had learned from those who in precept or example most flouted its name; so that if this is to be a story of my philosophic education it cannot do better than begin arguing itself out from some very low beginnings.

I

A philosophy inspires confidence for what its sympathies take in, not for what they leave out. Austerity is a poverty; and one mistrusts either the experience or the reflection of the philosopher who can find no thought of religion in a love-song of Catullus or the wine-lilt from a *Copa*—

> pone merum et talos, pereat, qui crastina curat!

Why not, then? Why not, if one is aware?—

> Mors aurem vellens 'vivite,' ait, 'venio.'

You say, the *why not* is too plain to need giving: who takes no care for the morrow, let the morrow take care of him! Well, yes; that we all know and are agreed on, *provided there be a morrow*.

But need there be? For to let there be is a voluntary act, "and [as Hobbes remarks in another connection] of the voluntary acts of every man, the object is some good to himself." Say, then, of this *vivamus-amemus* philosophy not that it is foolish; but that its only wisdom is tragic. As a place to pass a holiday, the tavern is a poor place and Lesbia's arms no better; as a place to spend a last day, either will have scored life with one day too many. But is either worse than other more approved devices for "putting in one's days"—till some reason have approved itself for putting them in at all? Why not put them out? (*Mors aurem vellens* . . .)

A philosophy of forgetting is, then, a religious achievement, but it ends in the cult of death; and that it should ever have been sung in such gay numbers (only not so gay as they sound, perhaps— "ils n'ont pas l'air de croire à leur bonheur")—this only shows those who sang them to have been no true philosophers arrived at attainment, but just weary mortals tired of thought. Yet what more are the accepters of any religion that has come to terms with life? None but gives promise of rest to some manner of soul; but is it that thought shall find peace there, or that there one has peace from thought? All religions pretend the former; all philosophers suspect the latter—and toil on.

Which would seem to mean that philosophers are patient beyond all other men. And so they are and must needs be; yet they are impatient, too, in their own peculiar way. They resent being asked to retravel roads they have traveled before, over and over again. Of these ways, none more familiar than the old ways of hope deceived—let this story take for granted the cumulated pessimisms of the past. No need to follow anew the successive disillusionments of a noble mind as our Schopenhauer realized them: more beauty, fairer laws, gentler hearts, love with its genius for pity—these, we may well agree, could end in but one life, the life of The Man of Sorrows. As in what but sorrow could nobility end, having watched the hopes of life vanish one by one in a depth of understanding, while "life like a pendulum swings on, between desire unsatisfied which is pain, and desire satisfied which is ennui." Then, better to forget: the philosophy of surrender that began with a refrain from a wine-shop ends in a hymn to forgetting. Only, not in *askesis* lies the perfect forgetting.

One who has found identical reason in the "let us forget" of wine, love, asceticism; identical unreason in all "penultimate words," is not likely to have taken the sadness born of thought for a discovery of 1819. If he were, there is one, Schopenhauer, to prevent him; than whom no philosopher has been more anxious to feel all history at his back. But if Schopenhauer did not begin, neither did he end the world's education in despair: even while he was writing, unknown to him across the Alps one of another race and other muse was exhausting the tricks of hope. Of this poet a word later; for the moment I would no more than dwell on the historical significance of this word, *exhausting*, in whose suggestion lies the one quality I take to be modern in the story of pessimism following on the early eighteen hundreds. Anywhere in the literatures of Europe the religion of oblivion could be illustrated; but where in the tradition we inherit should we find alternative solutions of life so thoughtfully examined, so patiently analysed, so courageously rejected as in the whole art of the last hundred years? Or what higher tribute could be paid the increasing reflectiveness of these years than to note their gradual tolerance, their growing appreciation, their deepening understanding of the lives of a "Jack" and a "Jude," of the worlds of a Maupassant or a Chekhov? No longer is the portrayal in art of the grey and the dark, however unrelieved, taken for morbidity; nor should it ever have been, for nothing can be more wholesome than the discouragement of complacent optimisms, nothing more salutary than the lesson that hope in life, if it is to be had, is not to be had cheap.

However, in presence of such manifold disillusionment the mind is endangered of losing the one hope to which it has still a right, the hope that must outlive disillusionment itself, the hope, namely, of finding some reason for hoping. But before thought can turn to any fresh adventure in this sense, it must have simplified the bewildering display of lives-that-have-not-worked, by deducing their common collapse from a common principle of failure. Now, by nearly all this literature, the verdict of failure has been returned the moment a life has been brought to betray its unrest, inner and incurable; but, as no conscious life knows rest or can know, the verdict is always the same; whereon one by one all souls seeking peace are recommended to oblivion. To this, I say, most pessimism reduces its procedure; yet not all. For sometimes, and that where the thought goes deepest, our literature reveals a questioning self-critical wonder as to whether even this finding is the darkest thing we may find. Does the depth of tragedy rest indeed in a hopelessness of peace; does not a deeper lie in the horror of peace itself?——And as this question brings to its close the first period of my education, let so much of the story end, as it began, on a purely historical note.

In the year 1826, across the mountains from Schopenhauer that pale poet to whom I alluded was reading a traveler's tale newly brought from the East. One paragraph in particular caught him and held him: it sketched a scene from life, but life of a peace so perfect one can only liken its ways (as did our poet later) to the peaceful ways of heaven. Others than Leopardi may find matter for thought in this note, wherein the traveler narrates of a tribe of Asian shepherds how "plusieurs d'entre eux passent la nuit assis sur une pierre à regarder la lune, *et à improviser des paroles assez tristes sur des airs qui ne le sont pas moins.*"[1] What were these "sad words sung to tunes no less so," the traveler fails to note; but all the world knows how Leopardi found them, and to what melodies he put them:

> Che fai tu, luna, in ciel? dimmi, che fai,
> Silenziosa luna?
> Sorgi la sera, et vai,
> Contemplando i deserti; indi ti posi.
>
> Ancor non sei tu paga
> Di riandare i sempiterni calli?
> Ancor non prendi a schivo, ancor sei vaga
> Di mirar queste valli?
>
> Somiglia alla tua vita
> La vita del pastore.

[1] Baron de Meyerdorff, *Le Journal des savans*, 1826. Note furnished by G. Mestica, on authority of Leopardi, *G. Leopardi, poesie.*

II

The voice of the *Canto notturno* dies away on a question—

> Dimmi, o luna: a che vale
> Al pastor la sua vita,
> La vostra vita a voi? dimmi: ove tende
> Questo vagar . . .?

To this perfect voice of the twenties, when does that answer begin we have come to know so well—the answer pointing to *progress*? (Not that progress is new—a Lucretius could paint it, a Condorcet paint it well—but events of the sixties and on gave the conception an empire it could never have held before.) My retrospects, as has been seen, like to begin with *suspicions*; and a suspicion of things to come is surely to be caught in the fifties, in songs of *The Rolling Earth*, in songs of *The Open Road*—songs that had already come to know the universe as a road—

To know the universe itself as a road, as many roads, as roads for
    traveling souls.

All parts away for the progress of souls,
All religion, all solid things, arts, governments—all that was or is
    apparent upon this globe, or any globe, falls into niches and
Corners before the procession of souls along the grand roads
Of the universe.

Of the progress of the souls of men and women along the grand
Roads of the universe, all other progress is the needed
Emblem and sustenance.

Forever alive, forever forward,
Stately, solemn, sad, withdrawn, baffled, mad, turbulent, feeble,
    dissatisfied,
Desperate, proud, fond, sick, accepted by men, rejected by men,
They go! they go! I know that they go, but I know not where
They go,
But I know they go toward the best—toward something great.[1]

In 1859, comes the *Origin of Species*. Phrases gather round it: "the struggle for existence" (Spencer), "the survival of the fittest"

---

[1] Walt Whitman, *Leaves of Grass* (first edition, 1855), ed. McKay, 1894.

(Wallace). Evolution is upon us. At the end of the century, Nietzsche. The *Song of the Rolling Earth* has found words: "I sing to you the Superman, the Superman is the meaning of the earth." Evolution has evolved into Progress; Life has found a Goal.

After all this rush of history, one may afford a moment for reflection; and nothing feeds reflection as do the contrasts of history. But between those offerings of the past whose lessons have filled these first two chapters of an "education," the contrast is complete. From suspicions caught in a wine-shop developed that philosophy which seeking a religion of Peace found one of Forgetting. From a suspicion bred of the Open Road came an opposite motive which sought, not to end strife, but to give to strife *an end*. This end it found in the Superman; it made of this Goal its God. But no life wanted that Forgetting; can any want this God? What makes me think none can has been argued more fully elsewhere; but I may be allowed to resume it here by way of pointing the moral of my second lesson in failure.

One who has written *goal* for *god*, may have seized on an idea of real religious importance; but subject certainly to the condition that his god be at least a goal. And was Nietzsche's—though he said so? Let this Superman's relation to the present be all that Nietzsche would have it—a prevision of to-morrow's "fittest," if he will. Preparing the way for these a day may be planfully spent eliminating "the many too many"; but what shall we plan for the morrow? The same? And for the next day?——

> What is the ape to man? A jest and a bitter shame.
> And what is man to the Superman? A jest and a bitter shame.

Here Nietzsche's imagination stops; but yours and mine go on—

> And what is superman to the Supersuperman? . . . And what? . . .
> And what? . . .

There is a mathematician lurking in the soul of the most romantic of us, and that mathematician will at once grasp two things: first, the series our imagination here constructs is infinite; second, *there is nothing about this infinite series to make it converge*. That it is infinite is no matter; that it approaches no limiting conception is fatal to its defining a goal. Very likely (I should say quite certainly) a goal to be worth striving for has to be infinitely remote, essentially unattainable; but then with equal certainty, it has to be indefinitely approachable. There is inspiration in endless progress; there is none in endless change. To climb inexhaustible stairs which approach no conceivable landing to mark there *up* from their *down*—as lief be a caged squirrel busily turning its wheel. Or as lief be a Zarathustra, busily helping The Moment *to return*!——

For what of all things can come to pass, must they not again pass along this endless road that stretches before us?
And this slow spider crawling in the moonlight; aye, and this moonlight, and I and thou in the portal whispering of eternal things, must we not all have been before?
And must we not return again along that long road—must we not eternally return?
So spake he, and always lower and lower—afraid of his thoughts, and afterthoughts.

But, you say, never mind Nietzsche's lack of definition and the vagaries of Zarathustra; is there anything in the *meaning* of evolution to prevent it from defining a goal? I think there is indeed,——in "evolution" conceived as a struggle for existence with a survival of the fittest (to survive). Here is room for development if you please; but a development of means (weapons of warfare) to an end repeating itself in endless sameness. However, if not the Will-to-live, let us suppose a triumphant *Wille zur Macht* to evoke a limiting figure, the altogether lonely figure of a Conqueror of conquerors. Yet could I not call this goal a god. For a goal to be a god must be not only *goal*; it must also be *ideal*. Unattainable limit of approach, so much is every goal; the ideal adds one condition—it must be a goal *desirable*. But the way to the All-conqueror, does it add contentment to contentment, summing toward a limiting concept of *desire fulfilled*?

Among the many "influences" this autobiography has had no time to take count of, is one its hero seems to admire more than do some of his neighbours: it is the patient baffling wisdom of certain earlier chapters in which Hegel unfolds the *Phänomeno-*

logie des Geistes. There, for example, will be found that curious dialectic of *the master and the slave*; there, that apparent paradox of the dependence of man and god on recognition, on *acknowledgment by another. Anerkennung*—that is what we live by, and without it we are nothing. It is a deep thought, for *Anerkennung* is not applause, it is not adulation, it is nothing a slave could offer a master—not if the one were really slave, the other really master! But it is what the *nous* in the highest rational being might offer to the *Nous* that rolls the outer heaven. Rolls the outer heaven and the inner spheres, stirs the muddy depths of earth, all to produce—what? That highest rational being, the one being capable of recognizing his God. So much, from the most ancient times, has God effected that he might be acknowledged God by one who has knowledge of godhood. But our All-conqueror will not have become the All-conqueror till he shall have slain, or subjugated, the last of his own kind—the last who had been competent to know *power* from *success*, the last whose esteem had been of any value. Why, a champion prize-fighter reduced to such extremity could think of nothing better to do with his undisputed leisure than to devote it to the training of promising material, his heart meanwhile set on that distant day when he might once more share the world *with a fellow fit to prove him.* Then, and only then, will he recover that *Anerkennung*, which in destroying he had destroyed himself.

No; not if we can help it shall we ever climb those flights that mount from loneliness to loneliness, to heights where Cæsarian madness waits, peerless and alone.

III

"Lonely ambition—peaceful acquiescence in a common lot! The history of human relations is a struggle, more often than not a compromise, between these ideals. There is enough inspiring in each to make any man of understanding long for it; there is enough repulsive in each to turn any thoughtful soul against it. Wherefore the gruesome spectacle of world-war is but the outer and visible sign of the struggle that goes on every silent moment within the heart of each, as the volcano is but the overt violence of long sullen rumblings that have gone before. And so things must last if and so long as we really want two irreconcilable ideals: compromise must follow makeshift, war must punctuate peace, world without end."——To such melancholy purport did the foregoing lessons of an historic education once summarize themselves in the learner's mind.[1]

Then into a world so distraught, he imagined the advent of a new philosophy, which to mend the rift of historic thought began by rending the very thinker himself. If indeed this world were a house divided against itself in such wise that within it one desired war, another peace, then the manner of its fall were easily foreseen, as these two fought their difference to the death of all but one. Or if it were a world wherein all desired war and all desired peace but sought to alternate the *times*, then in endless rhythm we could see its epochs developing, evolving new weapons, progressing not at all. But conceive the truth to be (what our education must have taught us) that in this distracted humanity of ours all desire war, all desire peace, all desire both at once and always! Then may our new philosopher venture on the scene, as once my mind's eye saw him.——

"His cheerful gospel is that all men's ills are curable by taking thought, that men suffer only for their false philosophy. Now, of all philosophies none is so false as that which pretends one cannot have his penny and his cake. True it may be in the letter that I cannot keep a certain copper in my pocket and honestly entice a sweetmeat out of the baker's window. But I must be a sorry philosopher if I cannot keep all the potentiality of future enjoyment the penny stands for, and yet have all the actual satisfaction I happen for the moment to visualize in the form of cake. Or to put the thought in less poetic and more general terms, the heart that thinks itself torn by conflicting desires owes its plight to the failure of its imagination to realize that only the formulas in which it has so far expressed its desires are in contradiction; the desires themselves may well enough be reconciled in a larger world-view.

[1] *Modern Thinkers*, "Progress," English edition (Harrap).

"Take our present problem for example. It is impossible, you say, that I should deny the ambition to conquer for the sake of the love of my neighbour without killing what is most vital in myself. And it is equally impossible that I should give play to my ambition to conquer without losing my neighbour's love and living a lonely struggle. These things are indeed impossible in the world to which the imagination of the past has been fettered— this little finite earth the fulness whereof is so easily emptied. If to have all that I can win of such meagre fulness is the only meaning I can give to ambition, either I must kill ambition and love my neighbour across a fence, or I must tear down the fence and kill my neighbour. But what if the fault of all this lay not with the darkness of reality, but with the blindness of untrained imagination? What if we could set before ambition a boundless prospect, so that never, far as conquest might reach, could it find cause to weep for lack of more to conquer? What if, in the very conquering of such a world, the gain of one, so far from being another's loss, were the equal spoil of all; yes, and a weapon forged to the hand of all for new victories? Wherefore *then* should ambition yield or love be denied?

"But perhaps you will say this *is* but an imagining and a dream. Our humdrum world, the only real one, offers no such object of ambition; and if it did, our nature, just human nature, is not such as could understand, still less be fascinated and inspired by it.

"Does it sound ridiculous to say that our world *is* one that holds out just such a prospect to all who will but see? Aye, and that many a human eye has seen, and having seen remained single to this vision? I will call the promised land the Kingdom of Nature Subdued: I will call the vision the Vision of Science."

But to philosophers, this vision is in principle too familiar to invite reproduction here; one question only of those to which it leads can be critical for us. One recalls how the spacious eloquence of Winwood Reade once projected man's development "from martyrdom to mastery," into a future almost too magnificent for prose; but does he really mean to say, can anyone mean to say, that the potential conquest of nature by science knows no limit at all? No individual now breathing expects to breathe forever; and must not death forever put a term to life? Our solar system may well enough freeze to inanimation, or crash to annihilation; must not catastrophies of this order forever mock science's power to prevent? To these and all like questions (on the occasion here recalled) my philosopher's vision saw with Reade's and answered No. "Yes [he says] I know; the stars are rather big for our frail hands to play with even as all Nature once played with us. But how else am I to say that there is nothing [no *type* of thing] in Nature that can forever resist an onward march of science? What else am I to say when the same master equations hold in heaven as on the earth, and Arcturus with all his sons is but a falling pebble painted large?"

In no sense would our philosopher see in this famous "conquest of nature" a definition of that progress which justifies its goal. Such conquest can bring us (as Kant might have said) but hypothetical goods: good if the end be good. But in the search for a categorical good this "vision of science," though it define nothing, plays a most important rôle: it establishes a "universe" within which definition is possible; it offers a world-setting in which may be solved a hitherto insoluble problem, a problem whose solution *is* a definition of *the good*. This problem, already suggested, may now be formally worded: "How construct a world inhabited by many wills, in which each will pursuing its utmost desire shall to the utmost serve each other doing the same?"

As two small children of men, quarrelling over a penny, if warned that the ground whereon they fought was the entry to a treasure, would forget their penny-issue to help each other gather, so we, turned from cramped old world-views to live in the vision of science, must change our ways toward one another. In this new world wherein no manner of goodness can stand in permanent rebuke of desire, what real good there is must be that which leads to *the better*: wherewith the whole conception of goodness melts into that of progress. This progress may best define itself in terms of a definite measure, the measure of life's solution of the problem set by history, the measure in which wills shall have learned neither to deny themselves, nor yet deny each other.

By some such steps as these the "cheerful philosopher" of my vision was led to his final sentence, wherein progress is defined and measured by *the measure*:

(1) *of man's cooperation with man*
(2) *in the conquest of nature.*

IV

To have gathered long lessons of history in support of what new hopefulness their very discouragements encourage; then, having no more than presented this careful structure, to abandon it to its fate—this may seem a strange procedure. Strange, yes, and none too willing; for it must have been pleasant to linger with a moment of satisfaction before hurrying on to its sequel of discontent. But this is the story of a questioner whose life lies not in its pauses but in its motives of unrest—let his biographer, then, tell only of these. Nor, recalling the object of his quest, can these be far to seek; for there are motives enough in history, and no less felt in life, which would lead one to question the right of his "life of progress" to be called a *religious* life. Of these, the particular motive most disturbing our philosopher may not be at all the one coming first to the mind of the reader. It is not, for example, a fear lest this life could know no "heaven" to which its faithful might aspire; no more is it a doubt as to the manner and measure of their "heavenly reward"; least of all is it a hesitation as to the order of their "devotions." These are none of his fears, but rather among those satisfactions his story might not linger on; yet which, since they are brief, may have such mention here as will serve to explain their sequel.

First, as to the ordering of this "blessed life": He who knows the laboratory of science and the atelier of art has at hand a model (small and imperfect, to be sure) of a progressive world. Here indeed every ambition as it is fulfilled lays its triumph at every other's feet. Need one show in what measure discovery aids discovery, invention multiplies invention, art inspires art, and collaboration increases all? Yet here individualism may reign supreme; for what should duty find to bind, where each is self-bound to the common goal? In its leisures, this laborious house is a very Abbaye de Thélème, wherein scientist turns to artist for the refreshment of his soul; artist to scientist for the machinery of his ease. Their only common rule, "fais ce que voudras"; for where none can hamper any in any main ambition, who would control in his neighbour the spontaneities of taste, individualities of view-point, a fancy in selecting his personal share of the spoils? Need I say, the laboratory and atelier here depicted exist nowhere on earth as yet? But what of such workshops do exist come nearer to housing the ideal than does any other house built with hands. Of course, to accommodate all contributing lives our picture must be made quite roomy; and to house all that could if they would contribute, our shop must be built as wide as the world. It will then *be* "the world of progress."

There has been mention of "one's share in the spoils"; yet none who know the life-of-progress will suppose these bits of daily bread to constitute its "beatitudes." But just as our physiology gives us a sense of motion, so our psychology knows a sense of progress (or let me take this a little for granted)—"participation," some have called it, and felt they knew well what they meant. This sense becomes with reflection a clearer and clearer perception of the whole mental life, a knowledge of the moment's communion with the whole—or rather with the goal to which each well-directed moment tends. Those who know it (and who should know it better than the devoted philosopher), value this communion above all other values; it is for them their "heavenly reward." "Reward," do I say? A subtler mind has said better: truly this *beatitudo* "non est virtutis *præmium*, sed ipsa virtus."[1] Yet if this be the saying of a subtle mind, can none but the subtle experience its meaning? The like of this question has been asked before, and particularly by one who in his religion treasured most its treasure of the humble. His quaint form of answer is of its time; I like it best as it stands—the more literal may adapt it—

> If bliss had lien in art or strength,
> None but the wise and strong had gainèd it;
> Where now by faith all arms are of a length,
> One size doth all conditions fit.[2]

[1] Spinoza, *Ethica*, V, Prop. 42. [2] George Herbert, *Poems*, "Faith."

But indeed this "Faith" is most empirically founded; and the scientist who "belongs to the ages," and the *diener* who "belongs to the shop," may equally feel and know they feel a common confidence of belonging.

But to what, you ask, *do* they belong? (Which returns me to the beginning of my "satisfactions," for I see I have recalled them backward.) They belong, I should answer, to what gives the life-of-progress some right to be called in ancient sense religious; namely, the "heaven" which defines it. For who gives to progress only such meaning as lies in approach to the ideal has in this very ideal found for the pilgrim his heaven. And but for a greater remoteness, this heaven that is an ideal would seem little different in aspect from such as in the past have gladdened the eye and filled the thought of men devout. That goal toward which is set our pilgrim's progress is, as truly as any heaven, "another world"; and if its walls are not as of jasper, yet they hold a desirable vision, a city such as might be called "the city of harmonious wills." To this city are bound all who are of its faith—"ad unum Deum tendentes, et ei uni *religantes* animas"—quite as Augustine would have had the religious "bound" to their goal.[1] Or if one were to seek a wording in which the remote ideal might make itself present as a voice, what better words could he find than such as once à Kempis heard; saying, "My son, I ought to be thy supreme and ultimate end, if thou desire to be truly blessed."[2]

But here my "satisfactions" end. It may be that one who has made of the ideal his Heaven and his God, will have thought out in new fashion much of what is anciently felt to reside in "Heaven"; but will his thought have overlooked nothing of what once was felt to lie deep in "God"? At least on one point let our philosopher not deceive himself: he who ties his life to an ideal may be religious with all the thought of a Plato or a Boethius; yet can he not be religious with all the feeling of an Augustine or an à Kempis. Though he call his heaven *Deus*, though his ideal speak as *I*, though he address the universe as *Thou*, yet can he do none of these things without conscious poesy. But surely he will not pretend

---

[1] St. Augustine, *De vera religione*, 55; *Retractationes*, I, 13.
[2] *Imitation*, iii, 9.

Christian thought to have been poetic—not pretend it to have
been anything less than as literal as it knew how to be in letting
its religious discourse be of *I, Thou,* and *He*? "It is the essential
feature [writes a very sound historian] of the Christian conception
of the world that it regards the person and the relation of persons
to one another as the essence of reality."[1] And will a "religion"
have lost nothing but imaginings of the fathers, when, however
it may have affirmed man's bond to heaven, it has let slip from
its care the bond of man to man?

In songs of wine and love, in songs of the Open Road, lay
suspicions of meaning which when followed led to the depths;
and in the language of hymns, and in the language of prayers,
shall there be no suspicion of heights?

V

Thus are we come to those present questionings, to that
"lively discontent in all that has gone before," to which the
first pages of this story pointed as the burden of its last. True,
this unrest, could it offer no reason for its being other than an
unreasoned confidence in the depth of historic insights, might
communicate itself to few. Few would assume that every
strong suspicion history has entertained must find confirmation
among the maturities of thought; few would pretend that every
"demand of the heart" for being strong and old must therefore
be genuine and undeceived. No doubt humanity will have dreamt
its vivid dreams, suffered its persistent delusions; and perhaps
nowhere more than in its religious consolations has it been the
victim of "other worlds" born only of dreamers' hunger and
desire. But when this hunger and desire is as deep in the present
as in the past; when it is so part of one's self and one's familiar
kind, that had no historic religion taken it to heart, yet might
no future religion ignore it; when, in short, it is the clutching of
mortal for fellow-mortal—then indeed an ideal to which personalities are nothing can hardly pass unquestioned for a religion.
Not at least with us, for in these pages (it must by now have

[1] Windelband, *History of Philosophy*, tr. Tufts, 238.

306 CONTEMPORARY AMERICAN PHILOSOPHY

become clear) "religion" has had no other definition than the acknowledgment of some end in whose pursuit all desires are fulfilled. For one who so defines, an "austere" religion is none.

And so, of this old division between allegiance to things eternal and attachment to things ephemeral, how willingly would our "idealist" hope it might be mended by old devices! Is it not, after all, but a dilemma in the manner of all dilemmas wherein pennies vie with cakes and cakes with pennies? But a thousand experiences of life show how cake may be had and penny held for no more than a little thought on ways of having and holding. It was even by thus enlarging the "universe of possibilities" within which our thought might move that we brought under one ideal the demand for spoils unyielded and the demand for friendship held. Why not, then, set ourselves anew to the stretching of boundaries, till they shall have touched those generosities within which aspiration and attachment are equally at home? But alas, the imagination of him whose education these pages recall, has reached its limit; in stretching the world of its contemplation to make room for that last "vision of science" it has exhausted all it knows of its own elasticities. Wherefore, so far as it is concerned, if a world is to be thought of wherein (what have sometimes been called) "love of God" and "love of neighbour" are at one, this can be no "other world"—no other than the very one to which it last came and to which it feels itself confined. Hence the anxiety of its questionings!

But indeed, any who would know whether eternities and fleeting loves may be held in one desire has a right to his anxieties, if aught depend for him on wringing from ancient experience an affirmative advice. History is at one in its negative; divided only on the matter of which to choose and which to lose. Plato and Catullus are at one: "Ideals *or* Lesbias, not both." Only, then, Plato elects for the eternal Idea, rejecting other loves with their tortures. While Catullus, poor worldling, clings to this very torture (*odi*, he cries, *et amo*); for what so hurts is real as for him nothing else can be. But this—one of these—is the history of all the world. Of *nearly* all the world; for I think history may hold one exception, one lonely being who seems to gather in a same embrace the eternal and the fleeting. If of his wordless philosophy I have caught any suspicion, this may show in the sequel.

Meanwhile, with all the weight of history against it, how absurd must sound the suggestion that for man's advance along the way we have figured as "the heavenly" there is no condition more necessary than the one all reasoners have contemned—the attachment of person to person! Or if that be not the limit of absurdity, then perhaps this is (which might be called its converse); namely, that "to lose oneself in the moment" could have no other charm than such a charm as death has; but to have delight in the moment, one must be carried beyond it, beyond any "Verweile nur!" and on to a "Vergeh'!" But let these be the absurdities they seem, still do they bring to this winter of my discontent its first suspicion of spring; which though it prove deceptive may be a pleasanter deception to unfold than any other I might have chosen as end for this unended story. Let me unfold it, then, as I can.

Or rather, only the first riddle, for of the second all will have guessed the answer. Is there indeed any moment of joy to which one will say "Depart!" save a moment made joyful by its *promise*? But if here there is neither room nor need to expand this commonplace reflection, yet it seems wise not to have left it unnoticed. For in a sequel suggesting the dependence of progress (i.e. of the *promise* of life) on attachment to things of the moment, our thought might have come to lack balance had it allowed to escape it the equal force of the converse: no moment can hope to attach us, save a moment of promise.

And so, only of the first of our absurdities; only of that attachment to perishing things which, though it boast its spendthrift waste, must in just the measure of its genuine being, consent to serve the eternal!—— It is generally admitted that for any manner of thing to be made, the matter it is to be made of is of importance to the maker. "The artist must know his medium"; yes, but how much vaguer than paint and vaster than canvas must this medium be, if with the colourings of his soul he would colour the souls of men. Just so with that other artist, whom I imagine we may call "the religious," and who would form the common clay of which he and his fellows are made closer to a likeness of "the children of God." No doubt as a conqueror of nature, he is but a laboratory soldier serving with others like himself in the cold technique of science; and as with all soldiers the world over, when he falls his place in the ranks is taken by another, his function is continued, the disappearance of his person is nothing to *the cause*. So much, then, of progress as depends on subduing the mechanism of things to the manifold desires of men is no respecter of persons. But he who supposes the progress here defined to be no more than this conquest of nature, has missed our imperfect warnings; yet he may now recall progress to have been first of all measured by "the measure of man's cooperation with man." Of course, all cooperation must be *in* something; and the last clause of our definition does no more than specify that the cooperation measuring progress shall be *in* the conquest of nature. For his part in this collaboration your religious artist must know (or help him who knows) his instrument of exact science, just as painter must know pigments, brush, and surface. But must he not also know, just as the painter must know, the humanity on which he need work if he would persuade *it* to work —in harmony? Now that humanity in himself and others is heir to the warfare of "evolution": it is a most recalcitrant medium. How, then, should that part of the religious task wherein man is artist and medium of art dispense with any least bit of "worldly wisdom"? Never can it be furthered by the aloof; it is the work of *the knower of men*. But now, this knower of men—what manner of man is he?

Whether it be comic or tragic, it is always a stupid deception to suppose knowledge of men to be gathered from statistical study of (what is called) *humanity*. The humanitarian who cares for "cases," who measures his benefits in numbers, is a follower of that "cold statistical Christ" all human feeling mocks at. Quite other must have been that Friend of Man one feels back of all history; that "lonely being" whose wordless philosophy may have illumined these last pages with what dim light shows through them. Nor is this the Man of Sorrows whom Schopenhauer had accepted; for to know men with that knowledge which alone can help the religious artist in his art is not to feel through sympathy that in which all men are one, but to divine (through quite another organ of understanding) that in which all men differ and are forever held apart. This it is whose presence in reality makes "the person" to be of its "essence"; this it is we figure forth as "the personal point of view"; this it is makes the world look and feel one thing to you, another to me, the same to no two that ever were or shall be. It comprises all that unsharable loneliness in which the heart knoweth his own bitterness and by which the stranger is excluded from his joy. To penetrate to the heart of this individuality and never to ignore what is learned there; to keep individuals apart in understanding that they may be brought together in will—this is the knowledge of his medium without which your religious artist can be no great composer of the harmonies he dreams.

But since, you say, this individuality into whose interior understanding is invited, is exactly that loneliness in which the stranger doth not intermeddle, how shall the stranger enter? To be sure, the stranger may *not* enter there; the classifying humanitarian may not; only the friend and lover may. And only he, by virtue of no mere kindliness and inclination, but by strength of that attachment which makes its object irreplaceable, unique in the lover's world even as in its own; and only then, by the virtue of whatever genius it is lets one "love another as oneself." Such love, alone in all this world, has learned to say *Thou* to anything this world contains; such love alone, as all the world knows, has learned the language which has no tongue—to it alone can be delivered the secret which has no words. So (as nearly as our poor language reaches to describe a common enough experience) may "other worlds" be delivered to an understanding capable of seizing them. Naturally, a world so without double can be described in no generalities of speech; yet it is exactly of such incommunicable worlds *the world* consists. "The world"? That is, the very same "universe of discourse" in which was set the problem of progress. It is, then, in this world (which truly is not far from us) that any real aspiration toward the eternal must not only consist with but depend on real attachment to the ephemeral.

It may well be, then, that progressive lives, "ad unum Deum tendentes," will hardly be able to put their thought into deeds without feeling the depth of that "wordless philosophy," that philosophy Erasmus calls the *philosophia Christi*, that philosophy whose followers came to "regard the person and the relation of persons to one another as the essence of reality." For if not in the way here suggested, then in some other way this philosophy held in one embrace the eternal and the fleeting; and no less than this must any philosophy effect, that would make a religion of progress.

"If this be mysticism," I catch myself answering that part of me which stands guard against such treacheries of thought, "if this be treason, make the most of it!" But why should it be? Granted the genius for that "love which individuates" (as Royce so well characterizes the personal feeling we have here in mind)— granted this genius to be beyond all learning; yet is it so *only in its practice*. Its sudden seizing on things before they shall have vanished even as all life vanishes, *that* cannot be learned; that cannot be learned *in time*. But in after-thought, in late after-thought, is there not room for *this* reflection: Throughout the slow growth of science and of articulate discourse, just such incommunicable view-points as have been occupying our thought have painfully found a way to compose their independent findings into one space-time world: and shall the lonely griefs and joys of men for ever remain a pluralistic universe? Will they, if thought and will are bent in common religious interest on making this universe *one*?

PRINCIPAL PUBLICATIONS

Modern Thinkers and Present Problems. (New York: Henry Holt & Co., 1923; London: Harrap & Co., 1925.)
Mind as Behaviour. (Columbus, Ohio: R. G. Adams & Co., 1924.)
Fool's Advice. (New York: Henry Holt & Co., 1925.)

NATURE AND MIND

By CHARLES AUGUSTUS STRONG

Born 1862; Formerly Professor of Psychology, Columbia University, New York.

NATURE AND MIND

I AM the son of a Baptist minister conservative in his views, but admirable for energy, order, and exactness, and of a mother who joined keenness of vision with patience. In correcting the proofs of my father's work on theology I was so repelled by the unnaturalness of the suppositions which theologians made in order to reconcile the conflicting stories in the Gospels, that the foundations of my belief in Christianity began to crumble and I could not become a minister myself as I had intended. At about this time I had the good fortune to study under William James. The questions debated in his classes, beginning with the infinity of time and space, interested me so much that, free at last from a false position and able to follow my natural bent, I chose philosophy as a calling.

James was a finitist and looked to some form of idealism as an escape from the actual infinite. But I could not see how space could have limits, or time a beginning and an end. I submitted to him a paper maintaining their infinity; and I well remember how, when he returned it to me with the margins filled out with comments in the opposite sense in his beautiful handwriting, I felt at first like sinking through the floor; but on second thoughts came to the conclusion that I was right after all.

I had previously sat under a sturdy Scotchman, who proved the truth of Hamiltonian realism by pounding on the table. The mind, located in the nerves, he told us, came in contact with external matter and knew its existence directly. It occurred to me that the intervening cuticle must prevent the contact and knowledge from being absolutely direct; but, when I urged this difficulty, he told me not to ask silly, hair-splitting questions. This was my first glimpse of the problems of philosophy.

James was the most responsive and open-minded of teachers. Perplexed in his thinking, but simple, honest, and deeply interested himself, he was a cause of thought in his pupils. We read Locke, Berkeley, and Hume, and I heard his lectures on Herbert Spencer. The problem of perception unfolded itself before me. From the stimulating conversation of a friend I learned the importance in this connection of physiological and what I may call medical considerations, and began to study anatomy and physiology. I turned for further light to psychology, and for a time looked at philosophical questions from a narrowly psychological point of view, ignoring the logical and epistemological refinements which, as I was later to learn, were necessary to their accurate solution. The relation of mind and body became my especial problem.

I studied in Berlin under Paulsen, whose sober, judicious mind seemed and seems to me still the model for a philosopher. Philosophy, to Paulsen, was completed science—"*das einheitliche System aller Wissenschaften.*" His panpsychism, derived from Fechner, promised an explanation of the connection of mind and body, to me still the only intelligible one. The key to their connection was to be found in perception, as I shall explain in a moment. At this time I held that the stuff of all things was "consciousness"—little suspecting the ambiguities hidden under that obscure word. My doctrine of perception was subjectivist: I said to myself that what we *mean* by an object is something possessing colour and other secondary qualities; and it was easy to show that these depend for their appearing on an intra-organic process. But I also believed in a real thing, of which the phenomenal object was the representative—a thing in itself: and, as the intra-organic process referred to was one taking place in this world of real things, supposed myself to have attained to a satisfactory realism. It was long before I became aware of the contradiction that may be said to lie in such a complete denial of the identity of phenomenon and thing in itself. The truth, I now think, is that phenomenal thing and real thing are always identical in the view of the naïve percipient and for his intent, but, in fact, are in some respects identical and in other respects not so, according as perception is veridical or erroneous.

My views at this period are contained in my first book, *Why the Mind has a Body*. I had the doubtful notion that it was desirable to make the title of a book convey its doctrine; and as the bodiliness of things was, on my theory, due wholly to perception—a thing which in itself is consciousness (or, as I should now say, something midway between mind and matter) appearing to the senses as material—I thought that my doctrine explained intelligibly the *why* of the connection. It did not, of course, explain why the psychical existent appearing as the brain is connected with the outlying existents that appear as the rest of the body. Every conception in that book—consciousness, perception, the relation of phenomenon to thing in itself—I have since subjected to revision and materially altered, as indeed was necessary; but in substance I still regard the solution offered as sound, and even know of no other suggested solution, alternative views seeming to me to consist in suppression of the problem.

I take some credit to myself for having changed my opinions in philosophy from time to time, and feel more respect for a philosopher who thinks differently to-day from what he did yesterday than for one whose position remains always the same. Of course when a man is right he does well to remain so. But the opinions even of philosophers are partly the result of circumstances, as is evident in my own case; and, to free oneself from the control of accident, discussion with men of other ways of thinking is requisite.

I have been singularly fortunate in the opponents with whom it has been my privilege to discuss philosophy; chief among whom—though I can hardly call him an opponent!—is Mr. Santayana. We were students together at Harvard and Berlin, and then for a time saw little of each other; but, meeting again in the middle years of life, we had long conversations about fundamental matters, and I owe it to these that the neglected logical side of philosophical problems was brought to my attention. At a certain date I had come to the conclusion that intelligent discussion of perception required the recognition of three categories: the object or existent thing, the subject or self, and the form in which the thing appears to the self. Santayana's conception of "essence" seemed to me to be the right definition of this form, this third category. I also made at this time a correction of my view as to the relation of phenomenon and thing in itself, a correction destined in time to free me from the fallacy of representationism. It consisted in recognising that, since the real thing is that concerning which perception brings knowledge, it, and not the phenomenon, is really entitled to be called the "object." The phenomenon, in other words, is not an object, but only the form (perhaps correct, perhaps incorrect) in which the object appears. The thing in itself is thus no longer an unknowable—a *Ding an sich* in the bad sense—but is that which is known; and only capable of being known falsely as well as truly. These two changes mark an epoch in my thinking.

I had also come to perceive the ambiguity of the word "consciousness," and to see the need of distinguishing between awareness and the subject which is aware. James, with whom I had some useful discussions, now published his important article, "Does 'Consciousness' Exist?" I had never believed in a "Soul," distinct from the existent that appears as the body and antithetical to it in nature; and I readily agreed that awareness, if conceived as such an immaterial existent, is "the last faint breath left by the Soul." On the other hand, I could not accept James's view that the only consciousness or awareness we need recognise is the phenomenon re-baptised. For I considered that subject and object—whose relation, in perception, corresponds to that between the organism and a thing in its environment—are *two* existents and not one, and I held that each of these existents is, in its own nature, psychical rather than material. All existence is material as well as psychical, if by "material" you mean not in time only but also in space; but perception (being a view of an existent from without) does not show us what is the nature of the existents that occupy space, while introspection in my opinion does show us what is the nature of the self—namely, that it consists of feeling. The phenomenon arises by the use of feeling to bring before the subject the existence of objects; it is a product of a highly complicated situation occurring in the life of animals, and the last thing that can be properly looked to as constituting in its own being the stuff of which reality is made. And yet the phenomenon, in so far as it is veridical, correctly reveals the outlines of the external object.

While thus rejecting James's view of the unity of subject and object (if "object" means real thing) in the moment of perception, I heartily agreed with it in so far as it was a doctrine of the substantial unity of subject and *phenomenon*. For the phenomenon, as I have just explained, arises by a portion of the feelings constituting the subject being used to mirror real things external to him. James's view that in "experience" (if by that term we mean the subject's life, not his mirroring of objects) there is no inner duplicity, and that of this life feeling is the nature—thus dispensing with an entity which feels—seemed to me sound and an important advance; indeed, I had been led to it by my own thought. The neo-realistic doctrine that the subject is the object looked at from a new point of view, or taken in a different context, really expresses the same insight as my doctrine that phenomenon is produced by the use of the subject's life to mirror objects; but my doctrine avoids that attribution of existence to the phenomenon as such, that complete identification of the phenomenal with the real, which, I must hold, is the fallacy of neo-realism. In his *Psychology* James speaks of "an undertow drawing us back to the Soul": the soul to which I have been drawn back (or led forward) is one made of psychical atoms, which appear or might appear as the atoms of matter.

I want to take this opportunity of acknowledging my great indebtedness to James. From the first I felt the concrete, empirical quality of his mind, so different from the confident rationalism of his Hegelian colleagues; their views seemed in some respects more logical, but he was more cautious and alive to facts. It was only later that I awoke to the originality and vigour of his thought. I could never accept his pragmatism, nor one-half of his radical empiricism (the phenomenalistic side of it), nor his indeterminism. His "will to believe" still seems to me the makeshift of a mind not free from credulity. Yet it was from him (from his article in *Mind* on "The Function of Cognition") that I got my mechanical explanation of awareness—as a mirroring effected through behaviour, in a certain causal setting; from him or with his aid, the view that the core of the self lies in feeling, not in a Soul or in awareness; from him, encouragement to a pluralistic or—to use a term which I remember his quoting from Charles Peirce—*synechist* view of things.

Unfortunately James was too much under the spell of the Hegelism he detested and of the British philosophy in which he

318 CONTEMPORARY AMERICAN PHILOSOPHY

had been brought up. Shadworth Hodgson had convinced him that things were "what they are experienced as being." The phrase covers a fatal confusion. True as it is that we can learn of existents only through experience, and are dependent on experience for our knowledge of what they are, to say that they *consist* of experience (ours, that is, not their own) is, in effect, to say that they exist by our seeing, hearing, and touching them. In truth, sight, hearing, and touch are, as Berkeley saw, a language which conveys the presence of things, but does not deliver them over bodily. In Santayana's apt phrase, perception is "a salutation, not an embrace." We are put in touch with reality by what he calls *intent*, not by an infallible intuition. The trouble with the empiricist philosophies now so much in vogue is that, when they analyse perception, they begin by dropping the intent.

What is intent? It is the inevitable implication of the active side of our nature, by which, when an object produces an impression on us, we are moved to behave not with reference to the impression, but to the object which is its cause. When a light strikes the eyes, they automatically direct themselves upon the source from which the light proceeds; and all the rest of the body follows suit. This direction upon an object—or "reference to an object," in the consecrated phrase—is the uniform characteristic of all our cognitive experiences; it depends on behaviour, or the readiness to behave; and the object upon which the experiences are directed is evidently distinct both from the experiences themselves (the impressions or sensations, that is, which it has produced in us) and from the use of these experiences to convey it, and only not distinct from that which we, who have the experiences, intend. The thing as experienced may *differ* from the thing as it is, if the impressions produced chance to be such as to convey the latter falsely (as in the case of projected after-images or of double vision), but what is experienced is always meant to be identical both in being and in quality with the real thing; and must be supposed really to be so to some extent, if we are ever to attain to knowledge at all. The assumption of their identity is what Santayana calls *animal faith*.

The strong point of current neo-realism is its insistence on the necessity of this identity. But, owing to its lack of a satisfactory doctrine of consciousness—its ignorance of the manner in which phenomena are brought into being—it is led to deny, in the face of fact, that appearances can ever be erroneous, and to conceive perception, in the old naïve way, as infallible intuition of the real. This is the last faint breath, or rather, still strong breeze, left in the air of philosophy by British empiricism, with its doctrine that objects are "impressions" (not that which impresses), "sensations" (not the external source of sensations); and by German transcendental idealism, with its extravagant thesis that Nature (not our awareness of Nature) is a creation of thought. Kant was the eater of sour grapes when, instead of replying to Hume by pointing out the activity and consequent intent that underlies our cognitive experiences, he continued Hume's sceptical slumber by declaring that we cannot by means of our eyes, ears, and hands, or rather, of the trustful intent which the use of these implies, know the existence and nature of things outside our bodies. I say "outside our bodies," for the things that are there are also outside our minds.

The antidote to this error lies in seeing that there is no awareness or intuition except so far as the subject behaves as if there were a real thing, and so has intent. Doubt is psychologically secondary; it can arise only by a subsequent questioning of the intent and assertion in which we engage by instinct. The reply to Hume is that, unless one acts as if things were real, one has nothing before one's mind at all. The cases in which we repute things, such as winged horses, to be imaginary, or think of abstractions, such as virtue, are late artificial products, impossible except by the complex exercise of a function which, in its original use, involves the belief that objects seen and touched are real. But philosophers have imagined that knowing and acting were quite separate—that we could first barely contemplate without any bodily activity being involved in the contemplation, and then proceed to act. This is not the case. There is no knowledge without attention, and no attention without some sort of bodily response, which is what gives direction upon an object and converts mere feeling into awareness.

Philosophers would not have fallen into this error if they had concerned themselves less exclusively with knowing, and paid more attention to feeling and will. For in these we have states of mind which cannot be treated as mere data of intuition. How often do epistemologists seem to be looking at perception solely from the point of view of vision, and forgetting that the same real thing may be given at once in terms of sight, hearing, and touch! How rarely do they ask what is the nature of the occurrences in the nervous system with which knowing is immediately connected! Physiological psychology, to be sure, is a creation of the last sixty years, and Kant and Hume cannot be blamed for non-acquaintance with its results.

A word must now be said about introspection. A person seeing or hearing is usually aware only of the object seen or heard, and unaware that he sees or hears; yet at any moment he may become aware of this. Epistemologists often suppose that what he then becomes aware of is *his awareness*—that is, the relation of seeing or hearing between himself and the object. That this is not the correct account of the matter may be seen from the fact that, in becoming thus aware, he ceases wholly to be aware of the seen or heard object, and therefore cannot be aware of a relation or a cognitive function connecting him with it. As James has shown, there is no such datum of experience as awareness. Awareness is a functional relation between self and object inferred by the mind after the fact, and that can be inferred only when the self has already been cognised. What the introspecting person has really apprehended is *a state of himself*. He has become aware that the light or the sound is not merely an external object, but at the same time a mode of his own being. And he has learned this, not, as James supposed, by considering it in a different context, but by altering the direction of his attention so that the light or sound, which at first was viewed solely as an external object, is now viewed as internal to him and as a state of his being. What he has mistaken for awareness is the sentient or psychical nature of this state of himself. In this state, the *what* and the *that* stand on exactly the same footing: there is no awareness of one by the other—or, in James's phrase, no inner duplicity. And when this state is projected outward and used to bring an external light or sound before him, there is again no inner duplicity, or at least subject-object relation, between its aspects: the quality is taken as the quality of the object, and the sentient being as the apparent being of the object.

Introspection, then, is self-awareness. It is made possible by a new direction of the attention, supervening upon the old sensuous matter; attention involves reaction, which is as necessary to awareness of the self as it is to awareness of external things; by behaving with reference to what is within our bodies we are enabled to take notice of the state by means of which we see or hear.

The existent of which we thus become aware is just as truly other than our awareness of it, and just as much brought before us by a phenomenon not necessarily coincident in all respects with the real thing known, as in the case of external perception. The feelings composing the self are not given to awareness merely by existing; visual sensations exist in us whenever we see, but what we are ordinarily aware of is not they but only the objects seen. The sensations become our objects only by our actively making them so. Thus I differ from most contemporary thinkers in holding that Kant was right in his belief in an "internal sense," however erroneously he may have conceived it. Introspection lost its credit with philosophers only as a result of the general substitution of phenomena for real things, of the transcendental for the transcendent; and a thoroughgoing realism should recognise introspection and apply realistic principles to it, among these the distinction of the real and the phenomenal, no less than to perception.

A philosopher so full of animal faith and so generous in the assumption of reals as I am is bound to give an answer to the ultimate question concerning all knowing, namely, this: What security have we that, in any case whatever, the real thing is as it is experienced as being? To this question I have a special and a general answer. The general answer is that, as we know only by animal faith *that* anything exists, so we can know *what* things are only by the exercise of more animal faith. If you haven't it in you to exercise animal faith, cease to know altogether. But then do not philosophise. For myself, my animal faith is so great that I feel perfectly sure that all existents are in space as well as in time. I do not think that they are coloured, because physics g ves a colourless account of the nature of the different wave-lengths of light, and because psychologically I can conceive colour arising as a quality in phenomena through the "simplifica-tion" of psychical elements which have it not. As for those who, with Kant, imagine that external reality may be non-spatial and non-temporal, it may be said of them that if they had animal faith as a grain of mustard-seed they would not try to remove mountains.

The special answer is a complex deduction from the whole of the preceding theory. According to this theory, phenomena arise through the use of psychical states as signs, and the real things must therefore be supposed to differ from one another much as their phenomenal presentments do. The phenomenal presentment of a psychical state, to perception, is an event in the nervous system; and nervous events differ so widely from events outside the body that such psychical states as visual sensations—even when modified by "projection"—cannot be supposed to reveal more than the true outlines of external things. In introspection, on the contrary, a psychical state is used as the sign of another just preceding psychical state (in phenomenal terms, a nervous event as the sign of another nervous event). In this case, accord-ingly, the real thing and the vehicle by means of which it is presented are alike. We may **therefore** reasonably assume that the nature which introspection shows us—namely, feeling—is the true nature of the existent cognised. The fact that in all our feelings, not in visual sensations only, traces of "extensity" are detectible confirms me in the belief that feeling, or something which by integration gives rise to it, is the reality that is spread out in space.

We are witnessing at present, as a result of the astonishingly successful labours of physicists, a substitution of the notion of energy for the traditional conception of matter. It is one of my greatest regrets that, owing to my small knowledge of mathematics,

I am unable to enter into the details of their reasoning and understand fully the processes by which such marvellous results have been reached. I am obliged here to fall back on authority; and I confess to a certain satisfaction in finding that better qualified thinkers, such as Bergson and Whitehead, consider Einstein's presumably correct mathematics to be capable of an interpretation more in harmony with common-sense ideas of space and time, and that so profound a physicist as Larmor declares Newtonian time to be essential to astronomy—so that we need not, as at present advised, regard a universal cosmic time as an exploded superstition, or cease to believe in a strict simultaneity between events distant from each other in space.

Panpsychism would, of course, be a futile philosophy if it were inconsistent with these great advances in physics. But the contrary, I think, is the case. Since physics has abandoned the conception of matter as ultimate and substituted for it that of energy, without professing to explain what energy is in itself, and since the progress of my own thought has led me to discard my early notion that the stuff of things is "consciousness" and to conceive feelings as not even necessarily coincident with the data of introspection, it seems to me that physics and my philosophy have been approaching the truth from opposite sides. I remember how inept it seemed to me, in the early days, of Spencer to derive consciousness from purely physical being by saying that it first became "nascent" and then effectively real. I still believe that one cannot get feelings by a continuous process out of energy unless one conceives energy in a very particular way; yet my fundamental conviction is that all things, even consciousness, do arise by continuous process, and I think that the evolution of mind out of the apparently non-mental is a problem which philosophers must now take in hand.

My epistemology, it will be seen, is a combination of sensationalism with behaviourism. Behaviourism without feeling seems to me ridiculous (does anybody really hold it?), and sensationalism has been often enough denounced; but, together, I believe them capable of giving a satisfactory explanation of the psychology of knowing. The view of knowing to which they lead is such that what appears to us as material may quite well, in itself, be sentience, or a raw material out of which animal sentience is made.

But how, the reader unaccustomed to the paradoxes of philosophy may ask, can we possibly believe that mountains, and white-hot stars, and the electrons of physics, are one and all made of feeling? The answer is (1) that feeling, as it exists in human beings, is a tremendously complex integration of elementary units, permitting them to mirror external things and one another for the better regulation of conduct; (2) that the first essential of a sound psychology is to distinguish between *phenomena*, which are creations of intent, and among which feelings appear when they are made objects of awareness, and *feelings themselves*, such as exist in us when we see or hear and are lost in the object—which latter are states of the self, and no more self-transcendent in their own nature than nervous processes are; (3) that, since careful introspection reveals traces of spatiality in our feelings, these must be composed of parts, and may be composed of parts *ad infinitum*; (4) that these parts (like the nervous parts that reveal them to the eye) are *active* in their nature—since feelings do in fact prompt to action—and thus as truly forces as the existents in the physical world. I can accept Professor Montague's thesis that consciousness is the same thing as potential energy, if by "consciousness" be meant feelings divorced from awareness.

Thus I share the view of Leibniz that the only point at which we have what amounts to intuition of real being, and are able truly to apprehend its nature, is in our introspective knowledge of ourselves. I do not, to be sure, agree with Leibniz that the characteristics we find real being to possess are perception and appetition, or that it consists of monads. I think that its characteristics are feeling and impulse, and that it consists of what he calls metaphysical points. Unscientific views of the mind inevitably led earlier philosophers to exalt its functions and unity, to the neglect of the simple elements on which these functions and this functional unity depend.

Of late I have occupied myself again with the question that first attracted me—the infinity of time and space—in the endeavour to understand the nature of continuity. Logicians would perhaps have been more likely to reach sound views in this matter if they had considered first the continuity of time, and not allowed their analysis to be deflected by prior consideration of space. Time must be so conceived as to provide a real *present*. Philosophers have been singularly neglectful, I think, in not supplying us with a tenable account of this primary fact. They too often suppose that the present can be a little bit of duration. The most extravagant conclusions are drawn from this view as a premiss—as that the past is equally real with the present, and the future, in comparison with the past, wholly unreal. But every duration is composed of parts, which follow each other in succession, and cannot be the present together but only separately. It follows that *no* duration, however short, can be the present—that the present can only be an instant. This was quite clear to Leibniz.

But an instant, it will be replied, is a nothing of time, and can contain no reality. This is an error. It is a nothing only of *duration*, and can contain no *change*; but change is not reality—it is the passage from one state of reality to another. Nothing ever exists but the states. Change is, in its essence, always either prospective or retrospective.

There is no possible doubt as to the conclusion that must be drawn. *Time is composed of instants.* It is the infinite number of these that give to it duration.

The parallel argument in regard to space shows it to be composed of points. Let me state this argument. Whatever exists must be some*where*. But every extension is a multiplicity of wheres; when you look into it, you find it to consist of parts *ad infinitum*. A simple where, a single place, must be one not consisting of parts—and this can only be a point.

What becomes, on this analysis, of the relations which join points into extension, instants into duration?

Time and space are not existent frames that can be objectively without having anything in them: they are the most general orders in which existents are arranged. These existents reside in points, at instants. Change is the rearrangement of these metaphysical units (if units they be) occurring from instant to instant. It does not occur *between* the instants—as it were, in an intervening time; the ultimate fact is the annihilation of one instant, or rather of the arrangement of units in it, and the immediate creation of another instant in which the units are differently arranged; which latter, because it is born out of the former, is the *next* instant. Thus there is something that lies deeper, or nearer to the substance of things, than time; and that is causality. Causality is the necessity, in reality existing at an instant, by which it gives birth to reality at the next instant.

For the sake of simplicity I have spoken in the preceding of what exists in a point as a "unit." But, with the substitution of the conception of energy for that of matter, it becomes possible that what resides in a point at an instant is not a simple unit, but a variable amount of energy. The units of energy, if such there be, may not be impenetrable to each other. In this way "fields of force" with varying levels would arise. The physical world would not be either a plenum or a partial vacuum, but would be more or less full at different points and in different regions. Newton thought that the interstellar spaces were very full indeed, and "fed" the sun and the stars; this was his guess as to the cause of gravitation. Tension or intensity, if the present notion is correct, would be a fourth dimension in the instant, additional to the three spatial dimensions. This seems to permit an answer to the obvious objection to my doctrine of time as composed of instants, that the instant affords no room for velocity, acceleration, and momentum. These may exist in the instant in the form of the relative height of different waves, and the ultimate solution of physical problems may be furnished by wave-mechanics.

Continuity, both temporal and spatial, depends, according to this analysis, on the causal relations by which adjacent reals co-operate to produce the redistribution of energy at the next instant. Energy is conserved, and there is therefore an identity of the energies in successive instants, at least as to quantity. It is important now to take note of the negative as well as of the positive side of continuity. The connection between adjoining portions of energy, by which they are able to co-operate and modify each other's position at the next instant, is balanced by a complete absence of connection between portions of energy at a distance from each other, and by a complete inability on their part to affect each other causally. All causal action proceeds by spatial and temporal continuity. Newton, Clerk Maxwell, and Einstein agree that there is no such thing as action at a distance.

Moreover, the subdivision of energies is infinitely fine, and there is no place too small for action to proceed from it—not even an inextended point. This enables us to admit a measure of truth in Leibniz's theory that space and time are subjective. If all action proceeds ultimately from points (though with more force from some points than from others), and if the only real connections in Nature are the causal relations by which the energies in adjacent points co-operate, either resisting or supporting each other, then Nature is a continuum but not a whole. This is the essential thesis of my synechism. Space and time as wholes, and the lesser wholes consisting of portions of space and time or what is in them, are one and all made by the mind, in so far as it considers things together which in Nature are disconnected.

The reader will now be able to perceive the true sense of my panpsychism. It is not the view that nothing exists but souls, nor is it the view that nothing exists but awareness; it is only the view that if energy were not in its own being soulful, or capable of awareness, no such things as minds could ever arise. This is only a revised materialism, if you like; at least, it is as near as I can come to the truth of things.

Nor is it inconsistent with a belief in "spirit," as the writings of Mr. Santayana show. Spirit is that supersensible function, dependent on sensation and behaviour, by which we contemplate the past and the future, the absent as well as the present, the feelings and acts of our fellow-men and likewise our own, and perceive (or are capable of perceiving) all things in their true relations. Spirit, as James says of consciousness, though non-existent as an entity, is very real as a function. And the relations it perceives may be not the less true because they are reached by summation of the immediate connections which alone are present in Nature. The unity of apprehension is a functional unity, arising through the use of feelings as signs, and not justifying the inference of existential unity in the self. No philosopher who understands the meanings of words can deny the reality and importance of spirit. *Im Innern ist ein Universum auch.* . . .

What acts in us is not consciousness or awareness, which is only a mirroring of things external and internal, but the self, composed of feelings which (being identical in their substance with energy) are at the same time impulses. This makes it possible for a philosopher holding my views to be at once an interactionist and a parallelist. Parallelism is true, because the existent called self and its physical manifestation (to an anatomist looking on at the brain, or to you looking on at my body) never interact. Interactionism is true, because there is interaction between the self and the contiguous parts of the real world—the physiological processes, first of all, surrounding the brain-process. And, further-more, even the much reprobated "conscious automaton theory" is true, since awareness is a supersensible relation, a function of intending and having to do with, which, not being an existent but only a function, is no more capable of producing physical effects than is my resemblance to my image in the glass. Yet, for all that, the self is efficacious.

In the short span allotted me for reflection I have paid but little attention to the higher logical questions, and made no systematic study of ethics and religion, because I felt that the problem of perception and that of the relation of mind and body were more fundamental, and that one's solution of these must largely determine one's attitude on the great cosmic questions. I will only say, as regards these, that it seems to me plain matter of fact that Nature is morally indifferent—caring not for our human goods and ills. On the other hand, of course Nature is far from tolerant of bad conduct; and even ordinary men are aware that wisdom—primary wisdom—lies in correctly knowing Nature's laws. Philosophy therefore is still on the side of the angels when it endeavours to establish, on solid grounds, that Nature is real and knowable.

The ground of morality, I am convinced, lies not in Nature

but in human nature. At most times we are but half awake—failing to enter imaginatively and fully into the events about us, to read the feelings of other people, to foresee the consequences of our own acts: in a word, to perceive our circumstances in their truth. But moments come when the veil is lifted, and the human drama stands before our inner vision with more completeness. Religion consists in living as nearly as possible in this sense of the reality of things. It is independent of any view as to the nature of the world.

There is another, but not lower, wisdom which lies in correctly knowing the laws of human nature; and if I had another life to live, I would gladly devote myself to acquiring more of this second kind of wisdom.

PRINCIPAL PUBLICATIONS

Why the Mind has a Body (1903).
The Origin of Consciousness (1918).
The Wisdom of the Beasts (1921).
A Theory of Knowledge (1923).
Essays on the Natural Origin of the Mind (in preparation).

WHAT I BELIEVE

By JAMES HAYDEN TUFTS

Born 1862; Professor of Philosophy, The University of Chicago.

WHAT I BELIEVE

My generation has seen the passing of systems of thought which had reigned since Augustine. The conception of the world as a kingdom ruled by God, subject to his laws and their penalties, which had been undisturbed by the Protestant Reformation, has dissolved. We watch the process, but as yet are scarcely awake to its possible outcome. The sanctions of our inherited morality have gone. Principles and standards which had stood for nearly two thousand years are questioned. The process goes on among us in methods which are perhaps no less radical because they are not violent. In Russia the change is both radical and violent. It is seen at work in our great institutions of law, politics, business, industry, and philanthropy. To understand and interpret the origins of moral life and the complex relationships between moral ideas and the great social institutions has seemed to me a fascinating field of work. I began my work in philosophy with studies in its history. I changed to ethics because, as I came to gain a clearer view of the important tendencies of the time, I thought the ethical changes the most significant.

I was born and received my early education in western Massachusetts. My ancestry along all its various lines, with the exception of the paternal Tufts strain, had come to Massachusetts in the Puritan migration of 1630 or shortly afterwards. My great-great-grandfather, John Tufts, had come to western Massachusetts in the considerable company of Scotch-Irish about a hundred years later. One of the emigrant ancestors, the Reverend Ralph Wheelock, is said to have been enrolled in Clare College, Cambridge; but with this exception all my ancestors in both lines were farmers until my grandfather, James Tufts, went to Brown University (then Providence College) as a preparation for the ministry, graduating in 1789; and my maternal grandfather fitted himself for the practice of medicine by attendance upon lectures in Dartmouth College. Both settled in a pioneer town of southern Vermont, high on the Green Mountains. My clerical ancestor remained in this, his first parish, until his death, and in accord with what seems to have been a not uncommon usage, was known as "Priest" Tufts through all the county, and indeed beyond. He was in his theology a follower of Nathaniel Emmons, with whom he had studied after graduation from college. It was a stern doctrine which he preached; yet for forty years he was a commanding influence as the spiritual ruler of the community. Very probably it was the ambition of the alert-planning mother, who was quite as influential in family decisions as the more formally educated father, that encouraged the second James Tufts, my father, to set out from home across the mountain, forty miles on foot, his outfit in a small satchel, to begin preparation for Yale College. My father never lost the atmosphere of this Green Mountain town in which the church was the centre and circumference of the community life, and in which no one thought of questioning the minister's declaration of the counsels of God. The Yale College of that day was a group of very serious young men, many of them expecting to enter the ministry. The atmosphere of the parsonage was repeated in New Haven and further found in Andover Theological Seminary, to which my father went from Yale. Sudden loss of voice prevented my father from preaching as he had intended, but he maintained throughout his long life his theological interest, and this was an element in the environment of my early years.

My father was fond of discussion. On week days the morning newspaper, on Sunday the subjects of the morning sermon were invariably discussed, and the boys of our family were expected to remember at least the minister's text and to state the principal "heads" of the discourse.

My mother was also an important influence in my education, although during the formative years of my childhood she was a nearly helpless invalid. She had received a good education according to the standards of that day for women, and had been a successful teacher previous to her marriage. She had inherited from both father and mother a refinement of spirit; her religious experience of conversion had given scope and purpose to her life. To meet her ambitions and standards was a goal to be striven for.

My early education was of a somewhat irregular sort. After my father had remained for some years without definite occupation, owing to the loss of his voice, he was induced by his old college friend to become principal of one of the New England academies. After a few years he resigned from this position and took into his home a small number of boys for private instruction. Some of these boys were fitting for college, and my own preparation was hitched on somewhat casually to the work which chanced to be under way. If a boy came along who wished to begin algebra, I began or reviewed algebra, and when other boys began Latin or Greek, I formed one of the beginning class in that subject. My father was an excellent drill master, and I had thorough preparation in the classics with a minimum of hours devoted to study. It was a relatively easy and enjoyable journey that I traversed through Caesar and Cicero and Virgil, Xenophon and Homer. At fourteen I had covered the ground prescribed for college entrance, although in many other lines my education was grossly deficient.

Meanwhile, I was getting another sort of education for which I have always been thankful. My father's homestead included a small farm whose dairy and garden supplied the family table with a large share of what hungry boys ate and drank. The manual labour was in the charge of a capable hired man, but there seemed to be a large amount of work which was within the powers and duties of a boy. In the winter, the care of the cattle after the morning's milking; in the summer, the work of planting and haying and harvesting—all offered strength and health and fellowship with other workers. From being a rather delicate young child I became well and strong. I acquired a constitution that knew little fatigue and seemingly no limits of endurance, during my years of study and early teaching. What was, perhaps, almost equally valuable was my acquaintance with the point of view of the man who works with his hands, and my ability to meet many sorts and conditions of men on common terms. During the four years after I had traversed the preparatory studies for admission to college, and before the actual date of my entrance upon my college course, I had read a considerable amount of history, had reviewed and extended my reading of the classics, and had (unwisely) taught a district school for two years. I had also become a member of the Congregational Church. So far as I can recall, I accepted even the somewhat comprehensive creed. While I do not think that doctrines relating to the future life occupied relatively a large part in actual worship and preaching, I presume that if asked I should have given them assent. At eighteen I entered college and a new stage of my intellectual life began.

The New England college of those days has now completely vanished. The curriculum, indeed, had been partially liberalized by the introduction of a considerable number of elective courses. But the spirit of the college remained much as it had been in the days of its founders, sixty years earlier. We studied the Classics, mathematics, the basal natural sciences, the modern languages and literatures. In the senior year, all students had the course in philosophy. But the outstanding feature of the college, as I now picture its atmosphere and its influence, was the religious seriousness. The impressive figure of President Seelye made morning chapel and Sunday church service the most characteristic exercises of the week. I elected typical courses in language, literature, natural science, and philosophy. Professor Garman began his work as teacher in our freshman year, as our instructor in mathematics. In our senior year he taught us philosophy, but he had not yet worked out the course which gave him such a conspicuous position among American teachers of philosophy. Yet even so, his sympathetic grasp of the undergraduates' somewhat bewildered state of mind in traversing Hickok's texts and his illumination of the deeper issues in religion and society left a leaven at work.

A conviction of the influence of ideas was one of the chief reasons for the selection of a career. The atmosphere of my home was almost compelling. I recall vividly my mother's report of a conversation which she had with the mother of a classmate at the time of my graduation from college. The two mothers were comparing notes as to the plans and prospects of their sons. The mother of the classmate said, "I don't know what X will do, but his mind is filled with plans for making money." She spoke in a tone of disappointment, and my mother repeated the conversation as though such disappointment was the most natural thing in the world. For women of their antecedents some professional career was the only thinkable line of work. I had never discussed seriously the question of a career, but my own interest in this case coincided with the expectations of my parents. My father, although he had himself expected to enter the ministry, until loss of health compelled him to change to the allied profession of teaching, was more scrupulous than might have been expected in attempting to influence my choice, although I knew he would be greatly disappointed if I did not choose a career which had in it the opportunity for useful work of some sort. In the Amherst College of the 'eighties a transition was in progress. Until that period a large proportion of the able students among the graduates had entered the ministry. In the 'eighties and 'nineties the profession of college or university teacher began to be increasingly effective. President Seelye and Professor Garman did much to encourage this tendency. President Seelye spoke frequently and with pride of the numbers of Amherst men upon the faculty of Columbia and of the recently organized Johns Hopkins. It was the conviction of President Seelye and Professor Garman that in the days of transition in religious and political views which was then in progress, the opportunity of the thoroughly trained teacher was greatest of all. He seemed to embody in concrete form the power of ideas. It was hard for one who had passed four years in the study of ideas and their relationships to life and institutions to think in any other terms than in those of the opportunity for influence thus afforded. Reports reached us, through Garman's course, of new industrial organizations, of the beginnings of the struggle of the Government with corporate wealth. But to all except a few of the students of the college these reports seemed to be from a world which did not concern us. If we took them seriously we thought of our function in society as that of understanding and discussing rather than of actually plunging into the world of affairs. At any rate, to understand what was going on and to teach young people seemed to many of us at that time one of the genuinely worth-while lines of effort.

Two years spent in the college as an instructor in mathematics helped to define my problem further. I was still somewhat hesitant between teaching philosophy, as advised by President Seelye and Professor Garman on the one hand, and entering the ministry. During my college course I had taken an active part in student activities from football to debating. I enjoyed speaking to an audience, and thought it probable that the executive opportunities in the ministry might appeal to my interests in that direction. I entered Yale Divinity School with the question still undecided, and divided my time nearly equally between the divinity course, on the one hand, and studies in philosophy with Professor Ladd and anthropology under William G. Sumner on the other. It was an invitation from President Angell to become an instructor in the University of Michigan, coming in the summer after my graduation from the Divinity School, which was the decisive factor in my career. Henceforward I gave myself to the life of the scholar, although at intervals I have taken on administrative work as Dean of the Colleges; and when in 1925 President Burton, of the University of Chicago, felt the need of assistance in his large plans for a new creative epoch, I found a fascinating though extremely difficult field in the office of Vice-President.

The University of Michigan in 1889 was a stimulating place. President Angell was surrounded by a faculty comprising some of the older generation, and some men fresh from Johns Hopkins and other schools of graduate work. Many who have since achieved the highest eminence in their fields were then on the staff. The University was undoubtedly the most active centre of research west of the Alleghanies. Professor Dewey had already made himself known by his Psychology and his Leibniz. The tradition of philosophy, as this had been built by Professor George Morris, was that of a commanding and enriching subject. The ablest students elected it. A young instructor could have had no more favourable conditions.

But at Yale I had studied with Professor W. R. Harper and had been greatly impressed by his tireless energy and far-reaching ideas. When, therefore, he invited me to join the faculty which he was assembling for the new University of Chicago I reluctantly decided to leave my attractive position at Ann Arbor and to cast in my lot with the new enterprise. Believing that study in Europe would be important for effective work in the new institution, I spent a year at Berlin and Freiburg, taking my doctor's degree at the latter university under Aloys Riehl with a thesis upon Kant's Teleology. My years of academic training had reached an end. I was eager to join the body of scholars which assembled on October 1, 1892, and with the exception of the year 1920–21, spent as visiting professor in Columbia University, I have continued in my position in the University of Chicago.

Stimulating and absorbing as it was to take part in the making of a new university, I can now see that this was, perhaps, less crucial for my development in the long run than the contacts with the City of Chicago, and the challenge to all my previous philosophy which the unaccustomed conflicts of forces presented. At the outset I devoted myself to the history of philosophy, and during the first year translated Windelband's *History*. But I began almost from the first to feel the impact of an environment very different from that of my New England scheme of the political and economic order. On the one hand, Chicago was then, and continued to be, a city of power. The centre of marketing, transportation, finance, for the great Middle West, it had been a school for forceful leaders. In the building of vast industries, of establishments for wholesale and retail trade, and of substantial banking organizations, it was a city of opportunity. It was a city still in the making, and with ambitions not limited by ordinary bounds. The beauty of its World's Fair augured well for its future support of a university.

Power and the attitude of brooking no resistance to great plans gave rise in some cases to a disposition which, if not arrogant, was at any rate little disposed to submit to restraint or dictation from any opposing body of opinion, whether from labour unions, or from politicians, or from courts. Least of all, perhaps, was it inclined to seek wisdom from academic opinion or social reformer. The tendency was rather toward fighting out controversies than toward compromise. The contrast between dwellings upon the Lake front and those back of the Yards, or in South Chicago, evidenced the sharp division of wealth from poverty.

What place could the University be expected to fill in such a turbulent, swift-moving stream? Would the City dominate the University? Would the University in time supply new interests and contribute toward new standards of individual and civic life? Coming closer to my own field, the many threads which had been thus far weaving no definite pattern beyond that of the traditional systems and methods seemed gradually to fit into an order which for me, at least, was a new structure. The making of ideas and the reaction of ideas upon the forming and reforming of moral and civic trends became a focus of attention.

Ethics must begin by understanding our ethical conceptions. It came home to me that these could not be adequately understood by purely intellectual analysis. Justice, I found, meant different things to different persons and different groups. Perhaps similar ambiguities lurked beneath other concepts. I determined to ask whether history would throw any light upon their formation. I was not definitely challenging Lotze's distinction between origin and validity. In fact, I had been taken by it when I had first heard it applied to the field of religion. Rather I was following a line which had always been fascinating to me and which had been strongly reinforced by my studies in anthropology and folkways under Professor William G. Sumner. But as time went on I came incidentally upon difference in ethical premises, in what we like to think of as our common morality, which could apparently be accounted for only by the attitudes of mind begotten by status or occupation. I found myself impelled in the direction of the thesis: (1) Moral ideas are shaped under the influence of economic, social, and religious forces; (2) and ideas in turn do not remain as objects of contemplation or scientific analysis only, but become patterns for action, emerging, it may be, in a Russian revolution.

Opportunities for more specific testing of both phases of the above thesis were not wanting. For example, I found myself Chairman of a committee of the social agencies of the City, which had been appointed to keep track of all legislation, proposed or enacted, that might concern the civic, philanthropic, and protective work of these agencies. We framed a number of bills, some of which passed the legislature and became laws. The subsequent fate of a proposal for providing health insurance by the

State was very instructive. A commission was authorized for the investigation of the proposal, a competent expert was engaged, and an excellent study made, but the report which came from the committee to the legislature bore no relation to the data of the experts' inquiry. The combined opposition of labour unionists, physicians, and those opposed to any new and unusual plan killed the measure. It is not easy to pass a law which is likely to interfere with a vested interest.

My closest contact was made possible through an invitation to act as Chairman of the Board of Arbitration in the Hart Schaffner & Marx clothing industry—a responsibility which later came to cover the clothing industry in Chicago. It was of the essence of this function that the arbitration was a continuous process. The Board was like a court in that it recorded all its decisions and followed precedents if these seemed to be the best ways of meeting changing situations, but differed from a court in having no necessary rules except those jointly agreed upon by the firm and the union. As the Board of Arbitration met, not as is frequently the case in arbitration proceedings, to settle a particular strike, but rather as a permanent body to make a substitution of reason for force and determine such policies as would promote peace and efficiency in the industry, the conditions called for adjustment, not on the basis of compromise, but rather on the basis of finding, so far as is humanly possible, what was the right thing and what would give permanent satisfaction.

I served for two years in this work and found it very difficult, but also very much worth while. For nearly every moral principle which I had been reaching by study of industry from the outside was called upon in the settlement of the questions which were presented to the Board. Fortunately, my predecessor had laid well the foundations for subsequent procedure, but every contest for appeal tested the method which I had been following. I repeatedly found that to know the whole history of the situation put a controversy in a different light. I learned at first hand how certain of our basal conceptions are affected by origins.

The thesis that moral ideas are subtly coloured or infected by particular circumstances is opposed to the doctrine that such ideas are independent of time and place and human bias; that right is right, and may be discovered and fixed by rational intuition unaided and unaffected by feeling or non-rational factors. In the study of this thesis, I had been particularly struck with the obvious derivation of many moral concepts from class distinctions. "Honour," "nobility," are obviously the qualities required or found in a superior class; "mean" and "villain" are correlates. The military class, the sporting class, the trading class, the working class, each has its term of class approval, and some of these ultimately get recognition as good ethical concepts. But with some of the fundamental ethical concepts, the subtle influence of class is less commonly recognized. Let us examine certain influences that work in fixing the meaning of honesty and justice. These are conceptions which Sidgwick treats as lacking in clearness and certainty, when used by common sense.

One day, as Chairman of the Board of Arbitration in a local industry, I had been listening to a rather severe complaint on the part of the management. The charge was made that in a certain workroom the standard of efficiency was low. The particular part of the manufacturing process which was performed in this room had not been placed upon a piece-work basis, nor yet had it been so thoroughly standardized as to give a fairly accurate measure of the work of each man. It was claimed by the management that some of the workers took advantage of the situation and shirked or slacked. "We pay a fair wage; these men do not give a fair day's work in return; they are not honest." Whereupon one of the workers' representatives, not so much in reply to the charge as in genuine uncertainty, exclaimed half under his breath, "What is 'honest'?" I thus had forcibly presented the doubt of the worker as to the standard employed. For when one considers the process of gradual speeding up which has been the accompaniment of constantly improved machinery and constant division of labour, one is forced to recall that the wage cost per hour of product has greatly diminished, while the wage, although increasing, has often increased far less than the total gain from improved processes would seem to warrant. How can we determine what would be the honest share of labour in the increased efficiency

of the machine process? Should all the profit go to the manu-
facturer, or should a part go to the workman? And if the latter,
then how much will be an honest share? Can we say that the
bargaining of the market will yield a standard of division which
can claim moral sanction, or are we forced to say that if the
standard is set purely by the market, then the amount of labour
given in return should be set likewise by a purely market pace?
In other words, honesty under such circumstances is no longer
an unambiguously moral conception.

A slightly different aspect of the ambiguity in the conception
of honesty is presented by the so-called double-standard of
business and industry. The workman in industry is expected to
perform some service and to receive a wage which represents as
nearly as can be determined a fair payment therefor. But in
many business transactions the only limit of profit is what you
can get. The successful business man is he who can reap the largest
profit with the least expenditure of effort. It is, of course, not
unknown to the worker that profit is justified on the basis of risk
which is a feature of speculation. Nevertheless the obstinate fact
remains that in many specific cases huge profits are the result
of accident, or of sudden demands for real estate, or to general
business trends, and do not imply any useful service on the part
of the man who profits. The less expenditure in time and effort
which he makes the greater the praise for his shrewdness and
business capacity. Certainly it is somewhat awkward to have
these two standards side by side, especially since it has been
customary to shift a considerable part of risk to the shoulders of
employees by reducing the force when times are slack.

Conceptions of justice afford a peculiarly complex example of
the mingling of rational and non-rational factors. Justice, together
with its allied conceptions of what is fair, or equitable, or reasonable, may plausibly claim to be a conception reached by rational
analysis. It seems to disclaim any sociological, or economic, or
political warping. The appeal of the Hebrew prophet to do justly,
no less than the philosophic conception of the Roman Jurisconsult,
to live honourably, to injure none, and to give every man his own,
or the principles of natural law laid down by Blackstone, may

plausibly claim to be a fixed standard. From the prophetic revival in ancient Egypt unto the present day the scales have been the symbol of justice, and the cry of the "eloquent peasant": "Can the scales weigh falsely?" seems to deserve but one answer. Nevertheless to one who traces the history of the concept in law and morals two strands are evident: on the one hand justice seeks equality through its principle of equality before the law; on the other it is tender to vested interests or existing status; on the one hand it magnifies permanence and fixity; on the other it leans toward giving some place for change; on the one hand it is the ideal of reason; on the other it is the decree of authority. And according as this authority takes the form of precedent or that of the will of the sovereign or of the people, we have the basis for the divided attitude of our poets and the divided conceptions of justice which prevail among our different social classes. Or if we take the mode of defining justice which conceives it as securing and protecting rights, we have still more apparent the influence of class and status. To the property-owning class, rights of property seem fundamental to the established order and good of society. On the other hand, the alleged right of a workman to his job seems a fantastic and fully unjustifiable claim. And a second article in the creed of Union labour, "Thou shalt not take a fellow-workman's job," is likewise incomprehensible to an employer, for whom labour is a commodity to be bought and sold in the open market as is any other unit necessary for production. The thinking of the workman naturally starts from what seems to him the most fundamental of all rights—namely, the right to live. How can one live unless he can get a living? And how can he get a living except as he has a job? And to the man who knows but one craft, what job can he claim if not the one which he has learned and practised?

To the employer, on the other hand, especially if he has built up a business largely through his own organizing ability, the workman has no claims beyond the close of the day or week or month for which he is hired. There may be a place for kindness to the workman who is ill, but there is no requirement of justice.

A head-on collision between conceptions of justice is presented by recent controversy between mine-owners and miners. In the Hitchman cases the mine-owner required the applicant for a job to sign a contract by which he agrees not to join any labour union while working for the company. On the basis of prohibiting interference with these contracts, the Miners' Union is enjoined by the court from inducing or persuading any of the contracting miners to join the union.

Here, then, is a conflict of fundamental rights which to each party respectively appear absolute. The workman regards the contracts, the signing of which is a necessary condition of getting a job, as depriving him of his natural rights to combine with others in order to improve his conditions. If he is deprived of all help from association, what is left to him? The fact that he has signed a contract does not, in his view, alter the main fact, viz. that he has signed away his one phase of freedom which was most important to him. On the other hand, the mine-owner conceives the business as his business and his property. In his view the union is an outside organization which is interfering with the conduct of his business. He does not ask anyone to work for him. He accepts men who apply. He requires a contract which prevents them from joining a union, but he places no coercion upon any man to compel him to sign this contract. The right of property and the right to combine are here in flat contradiction. Which set of rights is favoured by courts will evidently depend upon which, in the opinion of the court, are most important to preserve.

In other words, justice is in certain hard cases dependent upon the standard set by the court.

The theory is, of course, that the courts decide cases according to law and not according to bias. No doubt this is true in many types of cases, but in the cases which involve fundamental conceptions, where it is often the decision of the court that will make the law and not *vice versa*, we see the complex influences at work.

The conclusive evidence that the judges are expected to make the law in a given direction is seen in the weight attached in a presidential campaign to the appointing power of the President. When a strong argument for the election of a given candidate for the presidency is found in the probability that he will appoint safe or radical members of the court, no further evidence is needed that the Supreme Court is expected to follow the elections.

The logic which underlies such facts as we have quoted is highly instructive for the procedure in pronouncing judgments in new situations. On the one hand, we attack a situation, bringing to bear previous judgments, which have been more or less consolidated into a rule. But the new situation presents stubborn facts which are not easily brought under the rule. To abide by the rule as a definite standard satisfies one demand; it yields the formula for equality of treatment which is certainly one of the factors in justice. But as Professor Pound has so clearly shown, the opposing demand is equally strong, viz. that we should not be influenced by abstract reasoning in such fashion as to lead us to ignore the actual circumstances of the specific case. "General propositions," says Mr. Justice Holmes, in his famous dissenting opinion in the case of Lochner v. New York, "do not determine concrete cases." The logic of the whole process of idea formation and reconstruction could scarcely be better suggested than by the above statement and its implication.

The uncertainty which Sidgwick found in the concept of justice as it functions in the morality of common sense is not surprising when we consider the origins and developments of court rulings. The standard will swing this way or that according as influences of class, or profession, or individual temperament come in to decide which rights ought to prevail.

If, now, it be asked what effect this habitual mode of seeing problems in their concrete and institutional settings has had upon my attitude toward the great historical problems of philosophy, I think I should answer somewhat as follows: I had been easily persuaded by the many arguments by which Plato endeavoured to prove that pleasure could not be considered as the only good. A health of the soul, a life guided by reason, and fulfilling a function in society, a balanced or measured life in which thought and feeling, intelligence and pure pleasures, should all have a place—this seemed and still seems a fair picture. It appeals to the young, it has a permanent message for each new generation.

Nevertheless the picture does not include the greater issues of our day. To interpret these Kant had projected his concepts of duty, universal law, worth of personality, freedom through autonomy. It was an interpretation which sought to include the sacredness of the Hebrew-Christian divine law to which had been added the rational basis of the Stoic-Roman conception of law of nature. When the authority of this universal law was transferred from external power to the legislative self, and when such a self was declared to have ultimate worth, it might appear that Kant summed up the twofold outcome of the process which culminated in the American and French Revolutions. At least, it presented an approach to a moral problem which had a fair claim to be set beside the Greek picture.

As I sought to adjust these two rival systems, centering respectively in the concepts of the good and of right and duty, I thought I found in my genetic studies a more valuable clue to the problem as to which concept should be taken as primary and which made subordinate, than an attempt to solve the problem by analysis. For if we look at the origins of these ideas we find they are distinct. The idea of good is the correlate of desire. It finds its birth in a civilization in which values of various kinds—economic, political, religious, æsthetic—are present; in which wealth, power, delight of sense, or imagination, at once stimulate and satisfy. Wherever, through competition and comparison, the various impulses and suggested objects of desire, which give promise of satisfying some urge or interest, come into a field of intelligent choice, choice that involves in the last analysis the determination of a new self at the same time with the preference of the object, we have the category of the good emerging.

The categories of right and duty belong rather to a world of personal relations. Both right and duty speak the language of a principle emerging with the dawning consciousness of personalities in relationship to one another, of a social order which speaks of both permanence and change. It is not strange that a culture, such as that of Greece, made the conception of good central. It was not strange that the interpreter of religion, law, and freedom, should make the conceptions of right and duty fundamental.

But the great ethical question of to-day is not precisely that of Plato, nor that of Kant. It is the question of the ethical principles which are now on trial in our social-economic-political system. It is not a question of imagining a perfect state laid up in heaven, but rather of watching the forces and ideas at work in the societies of America, of Europe, and in the not distant future of Asia. If anything was needed to sharpen our interest, Russia has supplied the lack. Capitalism and communism stand over against each other, while Facism holds itself proudly above both.

Capitalism, as interpreted by Adam Smith, combines three ethical principles. It was based on freedom—freedom to do what one likes; freedom to control one's own property; freedom to buy and sell and exchange as one pleases; freedom to adjust prices by bargaining rather than have them adjusted by guild or government. It was opposed to the medieval doctrine of status. Such a doctrine was welcomed in Europe, but it seemed even more at home in America, for it had no vested rights to fetter it.

In the second place, capitalism made strong appeal to self-interest. The natural right of property, or of the pursuit of happiness, seemed already to put the individual into the centre of his world of affairs. Adam Smith held that a man could look after his own affairs better than another. If each man could look forward to profit from his activity he would have the strongest motive to production. The whole motivation of capitalism has its focus in self-interest. In other words, capitalism rests for its second support upon egoism.

In the third place, however, the egoism of capitalism is harmonized with the universal and democratic principle of utilitarianism. If everyone sought his own good, he would contribute in the most effective way toward the happiness of all. Certainly a system which could combine egoism with general welfare, freedom with equality, might claim to be the work of divine wisdom and divine benevolence as Smith declared. But as the system developed in full force, as it employed not merely the new forces of steam and machines, but the co-operation of great numbers of men, the accumulation of credit, the control over transportation, the fixing of prices, it created huge organizations of capital and threatened complete control over the laws of debt and credit, of supply and demand, of price and valuation. On the one hand, the power of wealth with its extraordinary inequality of distribution, on the other, the power of the people expressed through legislation. On the one hand, the masters of our economic life, selected by the competition of the market; on the other hand, the masters of our political life, selected by votes. It is a conflict upon a grand scale. On the one hand, capitalism is immensely profitable; it makes possible a general level of comfort such as had not been known before. On the other hand, is it not probable that to rely upon egoism as the great motive for the world's work is to foster a certain hardness of temper on the part of masters of industry, and to make material wealth the highest value in the scheme of life? I fear that it is. I believe that we have, on the whole, reason to be content with our culture and civilization in proportion as we have found a balance for the naked principle of capitalism. This balance is found, not so much in the attempted legislative control of trusts and monopolies, of huge fortunes, of railroads and banks, as in the policy of public education for all children and young people, which has become increasingly the pride and the serious enterprise of American life. The equality of opportunity, which is afforded in education, stands over against the inequality of property and income, and is in the long run likely to be at least equally significant for liberty of soul.

Capitalism is on trial as to its ability to secure decent living conditions for all members of society. It is worth while to have an experiment which seeks to make sure of a minimum of necessities for all its citizens. Brutal as the rule of the Bolshevik has been in its methods of control, it has one principle which it may be well for the world to see tried under fair terms. The principle that all should share in at least the necessities is worth trying. At any rate, it is likely to have a considerable trial. The philosopher may be permitted to watch it, although he may expect in some quarters condemnation for his temerity. When the great world conducts a gigantic experiment, the philosopher may at least watch and learn.

My experience in college teaching, which will complete its

fortieth year this coming spring, has been highly fortunate in the contacts which I have made with young men and young women. Very few of them, so far as I have been able to follow their careers, have failed to be useful men and women, and many of them have become distinguished in the world of scholarship and the world of affairs. I differ strongly from the opinion of many writers upon educational subjects who condemn our American system of college education and would confine the work of universities to graduate and professional schools, and who regret the increased tendency on the part of young people to seek a college education.

With the highest respect for men in the professions, they are not, on the whole, the most influential members of the commonwealth. If the college and the university fail to give education to the men of affairs who are the strongest power in American life, they are missing a great opportunity and forsaking a trust. With all due respect to the importance of devoting time and funds to research, through which the causes of natural and social processes can be brought to light, it may be questioned whether any process is more important than the process of education, and whether college and university can afford to omit from their programme the education of those who are probably for some generations still to come likely to be the leaders in the commonwealth. It may well be that a different college system may give better results than the apparently wasteful methods now in vogue. It seems that our colleges, like our cities, have outgrown the village form of organization and government which gives rise to grossly defective administration. Yet it ought to be possible to maintain for college students the ideals of scholarship and the union of freedom with responsibility which have marked our best institutions. Having taught in an endowed small college for men, in a co-educational state university, and finally for most of my life in an endowed university in which research has been a prominent feature, I believe that the small college will continue to have a place in education; that the State universities in the greater states will probably be forced to divide their numbers in some fashion, especially their undergraduates, or else find in the organization of junior colleges a measure of relief; and that endowed universities may wisely experiment along a variety of types of organization, but will, in my judgment, make a mistake if they disclaim all interest in the education of men of affairs. At present, one of the most serious questions is the somewhat mediocre type of student who presents himself for graduate work. It is a common complaint that numbers of candidates for the master's degree are increasing in quantity without any corresponding improvement in quality, and that even a considerable proportion of those who receive the doctor's degree prove unable or disinclined to carry on scholarly production after their doctor's thesis. In other words, the calibre of those who are candidates for positions as college and university teachers is by no means what is to be desired, if American scholarship is to occupy an appropriate place in the field of world scholarship.

So much concerning the general problem of education I have ventured to put forth as an article of faith to which I have come to subscribe during my administrative experience as Dean and Vice-President.

Thus far my more reasoned beliefs. I add certain reflections—perhaps they do not merit the term beliefs—which have a place in my total attitude. These concern art and religion.

My early life was not particularly adapted to cultivate a taste for art. A country village provided no art except music, and Amherst in the 'eighties, although one of the world's choice places for its natural beauty, offered likewise meagre opportunities in the Fine Arts other than literature. Yet in this college period two windows were opened which have never ceased to afford calm and refreshment—namely, Greek tragedy and modern literature, especially English and German. Travel has enabled me to enter into the ideals and constructions of Western Europe, and I have found much material for instruction and appreciation in the cultures and products of our American Indians. I have found in the teaching of æsthetics to successive classes of young people an opportunity to afford some aid in appreciating both natural beauty and the forms through which the human spirit has found expression. I believe strongly that our young people need in their lives at just the college age the control and poise and sublimation which are found in the best types of art and literature. I have found interest and satisfaction in aiding them to see nature and art and to listen to music with more intelligent appreciation, and to recognize that the values of life are not exhausted by knowing and doing. I look at the decorations, patterned from the lotus flower, which beautify many of our buildings, and wonder whether anything which we are now thinking or doing or creating will last five thousand years and find itself as perennially a source of joy. I believe that it helps to give students a juster view of the worth of different cultures and the capacities of other peoples, to become familiar with the patterns which these folk of past ages and wide areas of earth have devised. To follow sympathetically the expressions of beauty, to be lifted by the sublime, to confront calamity and catastrophe with tragic depth of comprehension, and to look upon all human efforts and good or ill fortune with the sympathy and detachment of friendly good humour—all this belongs to the philosophy of life.

I began this sketch with a reference to the changes in religious doctrines which I have seen and in a sense felt to be vital. The religious community of to-day is beginning to be aware of the gap between the facts which early religion sought to interpret and the symbolism which was used in this effort at interpretation. But no new symbolism has yet proved adequate to embody the profounder experiences which religion has included. Liberally minded members of the great community are seeking new imagery, but to find an imagery for spiritual needs and values, comparable in power and tenderness with the symbolism of the ages, is not easy. Meanwhile, those for whom religion is a spirit rather than a doctrine may at least find themselves united in the desire to bring about a better order in human society, and as such may feel, if they cannot know, a unity with whatever makes for good.

More than most, perhaps, who have aimed to think through these problems honestly, I have continued a relationship with the Church, for I have considered the common purpose and the common feeling more important than the credo. The Church has, on the whole, and in spite of its failures, borne witness to the exist-

ence of other than material aims. How the future will meet the
change in symbolism and preserve the spirit which has declared
the abiding values to be faith, hope, and love, I am content to
leave for coming generations to disclose.

PRINCIPAL PUBLICATIONS

Windelband's History of Philosophy (Translator and Editor). New
York. Macmillan, 1893, 1901.
Ethics (jointly with John Dewey). New York. Henry Holt, 1908.
The Ethics of Co-operation. Boston. Houghton Miflin, 1917.
"The Moral Life and the Creation of Values and Standards," in
Creative Intelligence. New York. Henry Holt, 1917, pp. 354–408.
The Real Business of Living. New York. Henry Holt, 1918.
Education and Training for Social Work. New York. The Russell Sage
Foundation, 1923.

METAPHYSICS AND VALUE

By WILBUR M. URBAN

Born 1873 ; Stone Professor of Philosophy in Dartmouth College, Hanover, New Hampshire.

BIOGRAPHICAL

I WAS born in 1873, the son of Rev. A. L. Urban, a clergyman of the Protestant Episcopal Church, from whose essentially philosophical and mystical mind I received most of my philosophical interests and impulses. I was educated at the William Penn Charter School, Philadelphia, and at Princeton University, receiving from the latter the A.B. degree in 1895. In the same year I was appointed Chancellor Green Fellow in Mental Science at Princeton. I studied at different times in the Universities of Jena, Leipzig, Munich, and Graz, passing the examinations for the doctorate at Leipzig in 1897.

METAPHYSICS AND VALUE

I

Any man's *apologia pro sua vita* has its own interest—often as we have come to feel in this age of human documents, the more insignificant the life, the more significant the apology. This is perhaps all the more true in the life of thought. All serious thought, however inept and however limited, has not only its own little dignity, but also, perhaps, its own claim, however slight, to the interest of one's fellow-thinkers. It is only on some such assumption as this that I have dared to accept the invitation of the Committee to write "an intellectual autobiography, in which the psychological causes as well as the logical reasons" for my "philosophical creed" are set forth. It is only because I believe that the way my own thought has gone in the last quarter-century may throw some light on the problems of this interesting epoch that I feel at all justified in displaying it.[1]

I cannot but envy those who are studying philosophy for the first time at the present moment. It was my own evil fortune to begin that fascinating study in what was in some respects the most unphilosophical atmosphere the world has ever seen—that period of scientific positivism that began about 1850 and lasted on into the twentieth century. It was necessary historically that the offence should come, but it was rather unfortunate for those of us who had to suffer the offence. I do not mean, of course, that there were not strong influences working in the opposite direction. In my own case, for instance, under the teaching of such men as A. T. Ormond at Princeton and later Rudolf Eucken at Jena, I learned the significance of the great speculative systems. In my heart I knew that they were right, but the form of presentation was somehow not such as appealed to

[1] The request for a statement of my philosophical creed at this time is in my case singularly inopportune, for the reason that much that I should like to presuppose in this statement has only recently appeared in a book that represents the thought of a decade or more. This book, entitled *The Intelligible World: Metaphysics and Value*, is from the press of George Allen & Unwin, Ltd., London.

358 CONTEMPORARY AMERICAN PHILOSOPHY

me at that time. The chief sources of my inspiration came rather from J. M. Baldwin at Princeton, with his genetic psychology and evolutionary naturalism; from Otto Liebmann at Jena, with his cry "back to Kant"; and later from Wundt (in whose laboratory I worked in Leipzig), with his ideal of scientific method in philosophy. In the anti-metaphysical atmosphere which then prevailed it was only natural that we felt it to be almost a sacred duty to suppress all the spiritual initiatives, all the natural metaphysics of the human soul, and the intellectual and moral scars left by these inhibitions will probably never be completely removed.

This was all the more unfortunate for me in that, although I did not know it fully then, I am one of those whom *Metaphysik allein macht selig*. As a youth I could apparently have devoted myself with equal pleasure to literature, religion, or philosophy. As I look back now, I can see what it was that drove me on to philosophy—that metaphysical instinct which, in one aspect at least, is only the highest sublimation of the will to live. Philosophy, metaphysic—what you will—is for me life itself, or at least the interpretation of the meaning of life. How bring the light of thought to play upon this meaning without, so to speak, drying it up, without turning it into the desiccated preparations of theory? How understand the meaning of life without turning it into that which it is not? How shall philosophy remain knowledge without being subject to all the prejudices and limitations of the theoretical point of view? In these few sentences is expressed, I think, all that needs to be stated specifically about the psychological motives, as well as the philosophical ideals, that have determined all my thinking.

II

For convenience, I shall date my self-conscious purposive thinking from the summer of 1897. It happened at that time— in the second year of my graduate study in Germany—that I came upon, almost simultaneously, two books, the ideas of which were, by a kind of chemical combination, to start all that was individual in my thinking. The first of these was Nietzsche's *Genealogy of Morals*, the second Meinong's *Psychologische-ethische Untersuchungen zur Werttheorie* (1894), both of which I picked up almost by accident in the bookshops of Jena and Eisenach.

I shall never forget the long night in which I read through the *Genealogy of Morals*. It was, I believe, the greatest single spiritual adventure of my life. In the grey light of the morning I found myself surveying the wreckage of my beliefs in a curious mood— one in which a profound sense of loss was not unmixed with that unholy *Schaden-freude* in which the naturally destructive instincts of youth so often find satisfaction. Enough that I knew from that moment that, not only was the problem of values my problem, but also that it was destined to be the key problem of the epoch in which I was to live. So far as the immediate problem—of the proposed transvaluation of our *moral* values— is concerned, my personal solution is here of no interest. The important point is that the problem widened out for me, as it did for Nietzsche himself—and for many others—into the problem of values at large, including the values of knowledge and logic. In all these matters Nietzsche has always been for me a sort of *advocatus diaboli*, as it were. In this *enfant terrible* of modernism I have found, not only the most incisive intellect of our time, but the epitome of all that I have come to recognize as the spirit of modernism. But of this more later. The immediate effect of the *Genealogy* was to create in me the desire to investigate the whole field of human values.

At this time my entire thinking was determined by what is called the "scientific point of view." Not only had I adopted the "protective colouring" of scientific method, but like many at that stage of development I really knew no categories except the existential and the causal. Between explaining a thing and understanding it I saw no difference, and a genetic account of the origin of a thing was the same thing as its interpretation. It was natural, therefore, that Meinong's little book should have much to say to me. "The value problem before the forum of psychology," as he described it, was precisely what I wanted at that time.

I saw in Meinong's little book many things. First of all, of course, an unusually keen application of scientific method to the problems that fascinated me. But as I look back, I now see that there were certain germinal ideas which, although I did not fully appreciate their implications then, were to be progressively more and more influential. For one thing, I saw that, even before the forum of psychology, value must be clearly distinguished from "pleasure-causation"; that value, while feeling, is the content of feeling only when it is mediated by judgments and assumptions. This was my first inkling of the possible limitations of a causal, genetic point of view, and a fuller realization of the implications of this thesis led me into the entire problem of the relation of knowing and valuing, and ultimately to the question of the relation of value to reality. In the meantime, however, the studies of Ehrenfels served rather to confirm me in the psycho-biological point of view. Value appeared as "a biological phenomenon appearing in a psychological form," and this conception started me on an analysis and interpretation that was essentially genetic and evolutionary in character, and which served to raise the question of the relation of genesis to value and validity in an acute form.

The thought of this period naturally found expression in many papers, largely psychological in character, and in a book, *Valuation : Its Nature and Laws.* What I had in mind in the latter was, of course, a kind of phenomenology of valuing. My object was to explore all the different fields of value, to connect fields hitherto unrelated, to discover, if possible, any laws or principles that might be found to be common to these different fields, and to explain or interpret, if possible, the levels of value and preferences between these levels. How successful I was in accomplishing this object is here wholly beside the mark. The only thing of interest here is the place of this work as a stage in the forming of my own philosophical creed. From this point of view the book has always been a source of real embarrassment to me. For it turned out, as is often the case, that its completion marked the passing beyond the stage which the book itself represented.

As to what happened to me in the course of the writing of this book, I can merely suggest it in the barest outline. What I wanted was really to *understand* human values. To this end I had developed what I called the *Presuppositional Method* which, as I defined it, should stand midway between the method of interpretation of the normative sciences and the causal method of explanation which abstracts from all meaning and its interpretation. I can only say that when I came to the fundamental problems of the last chapters I found the method breaking apart in my hands. I now realize that what I was feeling after was such a phenomenology as was much later developed by Spranger and Jasper, but which was possible only after value theory had developed far beyond the point which it had reached at that time. The immediate result for me was the practical abandonment of the psycho-biological approach to value, and the development of the *axiological* standpoint and method.[1] It led ultimately, of course, to a denial of the prevenience of scientific method and to a recasting of my entire conception and ideal of philosophy.

The attainment of this standpoint—which I have called the "axiological point of view"—had important consequences for my general philosophical position, of which I shall speak presently. It will be enough to mention here three important positions to which the working out of this standpoint led me. I came to see, for one thing, that value is ultimately indefinable in the sense that it cannot be understood through other things; it is rather an ultimate category through which other things (including

[1] The term "axiological" was coined by me wholly independently, and, so far as I know, it occurs in no earlier literature on Value. I mention this fact, not because of any special pride in the invention itself, but rather because I wish to show by mention of the fact that the same necessities of thought that led to its creation elsewhere were equally present in my own thinking. It is, however, something of a pleasure to remember the fun that some of the reviewers of *Valuation* had over the coining of this new term. As to the neo-Kantian literature on Value, especially the writings of Windelband and Rickert, my indebtedness to them is, of course, immeasurable, but rather in the way of helping me to find expression for my standpoint than in determining that standpoint itself. My own position was determined rather by reaction against the pragmatic and neo-realistic theories of value.

truth and existence themselves) are to be understood. The conception of value as a quality which underlay most of the current theories of value I found to be, not only the result of a faulty analysis of the "value judgment," but the source of most of the perplexities and artificialities of these theories. I came to see that knowing and valuing—fact and value—are inseparable. Reality, as we live it and know it, is our reality only as the stuff of experience is formed by the categories of value. We orient ourselves in the world by the relations of over and under, right and left, more and less, but not less necessarily by the relations of higher and lower, better and worse. It was one of Kant's peculiar limitations that while he recognized that the knowledge of nature is determined by certain forms immanent in mind, to the equally necessary forms of interpretation of life and the world he allowed merely the character of practical postulates. Though a necessary stage in the restoration of the objectivity of value, this was only a temporary position. I sought, therefore, to work out the *a priori* elements in value and valuation. Finally, I came to see that the fundamental problem of all philosophy is the relation of value and existence in a total "world-view." This involves the question of the ontological *status* of value. I had to admit that when one asks *what* and *where* value *is*, one is led into what are apparently almost insoluble problems. On one point alone was I quite clear at this stage—namely, that value is not an "existent" nor "subsistent" in any intelligible meaning of those terms—that its being is its validity. In a very significant sense "value is above all ontology," and the full realization of the implications of this fact was bound, I felt, to lead to a reformulation of the entire philosophical problem.

It is not necessary here to recount either the stages by which this general standpoint was reached or the arguments for the specific positions which it includes. They constitute a well-trodden path over which many have gone, and constitute part of the history of thought of the last decades. It is worth while, however, to single out one aspect of my thought for special comment. It concerns the gradual development in my thinking of what I later came to call the principle of *philosophical intelligibility*.

In the working out of my position I had come to see the insufficiency of what I have called the psycho-biological foundation of values. But I had also come to see in it a way of thinking that involves a circle so vicious as to constitute a veritable scandal in philosophic thought. We wish to *understand* values (and understanding involves validation) by carrying them back to life. But in this it is already assumed that life and its continuance have value. We have already acknowledged value as something known. The recognition that value is a logically primitive concept that can be neither defined nor validated in terms of anything else, came to me to be the first condition of any intelligible discourse about values at all. But this circle, apparent in connection with the alogical values, is *a fortiori* present when we consider the values of knowledge and truth. For if knowledge and the logical values, upon the acknowledgment of which knowledge rests, get their significance solely from their teleological relation to life, surely life must get its significance from absolute values which it embodies, or knowledge itself loses all genuine significance. I should put it this way. *Mere* intelligibility—at least *philosophical* intelligibility—necessitates a doctrine of absolute values. In all meaningful discourse about values acknowledgment of absolute values is already presupposed.

The philosophy of absolute values thus became, so to speak, my philosophical creed. And it is in a very real sense a *credo*. Not without a logic of its own, which to its holder seems not only a very cogent but an inescapable logic, it may seem to those who do not hold it one of those cases of giving bad reasons for things we hold on instinct.

In a sense there is something instinctive in it—the fundamental metaphysical instinct itself. The doctrine of absolute values is, in fact, the revenge which the suppressed and violated metaphysical instinct took upon the positivism of the nineteenth century. As such, there is a certain fanaticism in it—if you will. The affirmation of absolute values which do not exist in any intelligible sense of that word, but whose objectivity is precisely their validity—absolute values that can but be acknowledged, but whose acknowledgment is the condition of any meaningful existential or truth judgment—has, indeed, something in it both of the sophistication and the wilfulness inseparable from our epoch. I had a feeling from the first that this creed, while a necessary stage in thought, could not be final. The self that holds these absolute values, that acknowledges their validity, must also, so to speak, push out into life and reality. The desert of *mere* validity is unbearable. About this very notion of validity I realized certain difficulties. I came to see that while we must learn to breathe this somewhat rarefied air, we could not remain very long in it. Or, to change the figure, while we must learn to talk the language of validity, plain man and philosopher alike must in the end speak an ontological language. By this I mean that while the philosophy of absolute values must be a necessary stage in any intelligible philosophy, it cannot be final; it must ultimately pass into a metaphysic. But of this more later.

III

It is now time to say something of the wider ramifications of my thought—to which, as I have suggested, the theory of value could in a sense be only a prelude. And first of all I find it necessary to speak of the way in which this particular approach to philosophy caused me to envisage the knowledge problem, that problem which, whether we like it or not, we have been forced to make central in our thinking. I can do this best, perhaps, by indicating my reactions to certain major movements in philosophy in the last quarter-century.

It is easy to see that on a mind thus oriented from the beginning, and fertilized in the way described, the pragmatic movement could not fail to have a real influence. I was never for one moment really a pragmatist, but there were long periods when I thought that perhaps I ought to be one, just as there have been long periods when I thought I ought to be a "realist." Some kindly instinct prevented me from committing myself to either position, and I am now able to see why I was preserved. So far as Pragmatism was concerned, the persuasiveness of

William James was almost irresistible. That which appealed to me primarily, of course, was his clear recognition that the problem of knowledge is part of the problem of values at large. The phase of this general position which had most influence on my thought was, however, his very brilliant and original chapter on "Metaphysical Problems Pragmatically Considered."

Under this heading he takes up successively the alternatives, materialism and spiritualism, mechanism and teleology, determinism and free will. On his pragmatic principles, it will be remembered, he argues that these alternatives are irrelevant from the retrospective, scientific point of view. Any decision or preference, for spirit, free will, purpose, monism, have as their *sole* meaning a better promise for the world's outcome, "be they false or be they true, the meaning of them is their meliorism." Of course this original and fascinating reinterpretation of traditional metaphysical problems soon disclosed itself to me as the rather violent *tour de force* it really is. But I also felt that the realization of this fact should not obscure the important half-truth in the conception. The complete truth of these metaphysical conceptions does not, it is true, lie in their meliorism, their practical value, but an important part does. A still more important part of their meaning lies in their value, if value be understood as I had come to understand it. In a world in which certain values were not already acknowledged, it would be immaterial whether the world had its origin in matter or spirit, whether there were freedom or determinism. In a word, these conceptions are really significant only for interpretation, and interpretation presupposes communication with its acknowledgment of values.

For this partial recognition on the part of James of the real nature and meaning of metaphysical problems, I owe him much. If in the enthusiasm of his genial insight he was led to extravagances of thought we now realize, we may perhaps think of them as necessary incidents of a new way of thinking. But the *tour de force* was patent to me. In attempting to separate questions of value from questions of ultimate being—more particularly to separate questions of destiny from questions of origin—he was simply attempting one of those impossible things so beloved of the modern mind—that combination of incompatibles which, as Ferrero has well said, is one of its chief characteristics.

In indicating one of the important contributions of Pragmatism to the development of my philosophical creed, I have also indicated what prevented me from ever becoming a pragmatist. What was it that held me back? Many things, of course. What I have elsewhere called the essential incoherence of the pragmatic theory of value, which is, of course, but a form of that vicious circle that I have already indicated. Then there is its instability as a theory of knowledge, its vacillation between a naturalistic realism and a subjective idealism. But what chiefly held me back was the inescapable feeling that there was a curious process of *denaturing* going on. Everything it touched with its "pragmatic value," whether knowledge, truth, freedom, God— what not, by a curious fatality seemed to have all its meaning taken out of it. It was something like Midas's golden touch. I seemed to sense from the beginning its predestined end—the pan-fictionism of Vaihinger and the pan-illusionism of Gaultier. An article entitled "The Will to Make Believe," which I intended to be an ironical comment on *The Will to Believe*, signalized at once my experiences with Pragmatism and my deliverance from it.

As I have never been a pragmatist, so I have never really been a realist, although here also there have been times when I felt that I ought to be one. But here I am afraid I shall have difficulty in making myself clear, for the very simple, but what will seem to many curious, reason that I am not an idealist either, in the sense in which the term is often used in current epistemological controversy. My position is "beyond realism and idealism."

With the various "new" realisms I have never been able to come to an understanding at all. For one thing, their "refutations of idealism" seem to me to be based either on an impossible attempt to reduce historic idealism to the Berkeleyan formula, or else on an unintelligent application of a theory of relations, developed in modern mathematical logic, to the knowledge relation where it does not apply. The attempt on the part of New Realism proper to restore a naïve realism by a paradoxical theory of illusions seems to me to be a violent *tour de force* possible only to a philosophy at its wits' end. With what is called Critical Realism I find myself little better able to come to an understanding. Are universals to be given a purely psychological interpretation, or must subsistents be assumed that have a wholly non-psychological status? Such a divergence of opinion seems to me to be not merely one incidental to developing theory, but one which, when consistently thought out, leads to wholly divergent results. But, after all, it is none of these things—important as they may be in a way—that really determines my attitude towards realism in either of its modern forms. It is rather what I consider the fundamental misconception—on the part of both—of the nature of the knowledge problem.

From this point of view, whatever their differences, they represent the same standpoint and the same point of departure. Naturalism is the keynote of both. For both mind is conceived organically in terms of responses of higher nervous centres. Thus the setting of both is psycho-biological, and to my mind this setting is fundamentally false. It is true that even here there are differences between the two types of realism. Neo-realism tends towards an extreme Behaviorism, and is sceptical of any subjective realm, while the "critical realist" accepts such a realm and holds it to be intrinsic to the total "organic response." But from my point of view these are minor differences. Both involve a peculiarly vicious circular movement of thought which, to me at least, means philosophical unintelligibility. First, various natural sciences are taken as premises for the conclusion that the objects or contents of consciousness occur within the organism as part of its response to stimulation by physical objects other than it. Then we are told that these intra-organic contents have a cognitive function. But how invest them with a function which by their very definition and characterization they do not have and are patently incapable of discharging? The fact that so many modern minds do not feel difficulties of this sort is one of the things I have the greatest difficulty in understanding. I can only explain it by surmising that our extreme empiricism has robbed us of a certain sense for logicality, or for what I should call the finer, inner harmonies of thought—in other words, the sense for philosophical intelligibility.

Nevertheless, as I have said, there have been many times when I have felt that I ought to be a realist. In my perplexity I turned to certain forms of realism which have been developed in Germany. In this connection I may perhaps refer to an experience in the year 1913, part of which I spent with A. Meinong in Graz. Ostensibly there for the study of value problems, I was secretly hoping that I should be converted to realism. Our specific problem was whether values should be considered *Gegenstände* in the sense of some form of subsistence or whether their being is their validity. As we spent many afternoons reading Rickert's *Gegenstand der Erkentniss* and Husserl's *Phenomeno-logie*, we were led into all the questions of realism and idealism. With the general standpoint of *Gegenstand-theorie* and *Pheno-menologie* (for in fundamentals they are the same movement), I found myself in very real sympathy. Here the setting of the epistemological problem is not psycho-biological; the realism of the phenomenological point of view is not tied to naturalism. But it is precisely this study that led me to go the way of Husserl rather than that of Meinong. When Husserl finds that the very condition or presupposition of the phenomenological point of view itself is "a transcendental sociology having reference to a manifest multiplicity of conscious subjects communicating with each other"—a transcendental monadology, as he calls it, I can only agree with him. *This communication is the ultimate fact to which all analysis of knowledge must come.* If this is idealism, as most of his critics say that it is, then I am an idealist. For my own part, I think that it is a position that transcends the opposition of realism and idealism.

I should like to take the present opportunity to develop this position which I describe as "beyond realism and idealism," but space will not permit. I have already published a preliminary sketch of my solution of the problem, and am now developing it in fuller form. I can merely suggest here in the most general way the lines along which my mind is moving.

I have come to believe, with many of both parties to the

dispute, that the opposition is not fundamental, but one that can be transcended. I believe that the developments of modern science have done away with many of the extrinsic motives that have kept alive the opposition; and also that the increasing agreement of realists and idealists as to the over-individual and over-social nature of values is creating a standpoint from which the opposition becomes greatly softened and takes on a new and different meaning. Of determinative importance, however, is my present conception of the nature of the problem itself. I have come to believe that in this dispute we are not concerned with a problem of knowledge in the ordinary empirical sense at all, but with a matter of *dialectic*, wholly within the realm of discourse. Neither idealist nor realist can *prove* his own position, and neither can really *refute* the other, as indeed Fichte long ago saw. The arguments of either position are cogent only for one who has already acknowledged the ideal of "genuine knowledge" or of "*bonâ fide* logic" already postulated. In other words, the epistemological problem is part of the problem of values at large. If, then, we change the form of our question and ask what ideals of knowledge must be postulated, what logical values must be assumed, if genuine knowledge is to be possible, we shall find, I think, that in the end both of the values for which idealists and realists have stood must be acknowledged. Otherwise stated, a problem that has proved wholly insoluble from the existential point of view is fully capable of solution if we take the *axiological* standpoint; the two positions which are in complete opposition from the point of view of the exclusive logics of realism and idealism are entirely compatible from the standpoint of values. For these and other reasons I am coming to believe that a proposal, such as that of Professor Kemp-Smith, "to formulate an idealist theory of knowledge on realist lines," is not paradoxical but fully capable of being carried out.

In any case, my own epistemological creed contains three articles which seem, to me at least, to be essential to any enlightened theory of knowledge. First, the activity of knowing cannot be the object of "science" in any intelligible sense of that word, for science presupposes it. Secondly, all genuine knowledge presupposes that the object of our knowledge is different from our thinking, but it also presupposes communication from mind to mind, and such communication, to be intelligible, presupposes mutual acknowledgment of values. Thirdly, the standpoint of a theory of knowledge is above the distinction of realism and idealism, for both must presuppose communication and the realm of meanings and values, the acknowledgment of which alone makes communication possible.

IV

I suppose that one of the most trying problems of my entire intellectual life has been to find a name for my philosophical position. For a long time the term neo-Kantian would perhaps have fitted it better than any other. My indurated metaphysical scepticism was gradually yielding, but I was for a long time under the dominance of the notion that ontology or metaphysics is merely a roundabout way of solving the value problem, and that the solution of this problem *is* philosophy. My creed of absolute values, arrived at in the manner described, and my view of the nature of the knowledge problem, had led me to the position that the farthest point to which philosophy can go is the recognition of the ultimate inseparability of fact and value, value and existence, and that any step beyond that point must necessarily involve a trenching on the mythical or the mystical.

My philosophical conversion to metaphysics really came from something deeper than "logic." I did not so much change my beliefs as wake up to find them changed. Perhaps the change may be described in the following way. I found myself almost insensibly doing something I had not done for a long time— namely, re-reading the great philosophers of the past, not as grist for my technical mill, so to speak, but rather, if I am to be frank about it, as a means of edification. What I wanted was *Weltanschauung*, and none of the moderns had anything to offer. The metaphysical instinct in me, that which alone makes blessed, found satisfaction only in these.

This philosophical conversion, it should be said, was part

of a larger movement of my entire spiritual life. I had come to see that I was living in a period in which the break with the past was immensely more far-reaching than I had realized—that the novel developments in philosophy to which I had sought to adjust my thought were but expressions in the form of reflection of those tendencies in art, religion, and science which we have come to call modernistic. I began to seek to understand this, especially as I found myself more and more out of sympathy both with the mood of modernism and with the premises on which that mood seemed to be based. To my surprise I found it tremendously difficult to really understand my time. It is doubtful whether there has ever been a period in which man has understood himself so little, in which man has at the same time been so knowing and so unaware, so burdened with purposes and yet at bottom so purposeless, so disillusioned and yet feeling himself so completely the victim of illusion. This contradiction pervades our entire modern culture, our science and our philosophy, our literature and our art. What is the meaning of this? I asked myself. Well, I came to the conclusion that we are trying to decide whether we are really merely high-grade simians or whether we are sons of God—in more philosophical terms, whether our intelligence, reason, and all that these terms connote, are really merely biological adaptations or have also a transcendental meaning and *status*. This indecision of the modern mind did not at first seem to bother us, but it is now beginning to get under our skins. We are finding it increasingly difficult to talk about such things as "ideals" and "values," yes, even of truth—the very truth of science itself—without sticking our tongues in our cheeks. Such talk somehow sounds ridiculous in the mouth of a high-grade simian.

In all this some may think to catch a note of fanaticism, and yet it seems to me to express the universal and fundamental problem of our epoch, and our indecision regarding it to be the key to all our incoherence and contradictions. The way the problem presented itself to me was, of course, determined by my own special approach to philosophy and by the terms in which I had been working. From the beginning I had felt, not only that the problem of values was my problem, but that it was the distinctive problem of the epoch to which I belonged. This epoch, I felt, had now come quite universally to this point: the values are there—in some fashion—irrespective of a mechanistic science, of a devastating *psychologism*, or of a merely biological conception of the mind. But it does not do for the *philosopher* merely to assert that they are there; he must face the question of where they are and how they are there. In some obscure, but very real, way their *very being as values* depends upon the answer to this question.

Hitherto these values had been connected with great traditional systems of philosophy and theology. Gone, we are told, gone completely is this metaphysic. The values must now be transferred to the foundations of modern realism and naturalism. But is this possible? Now it was entirely clear to me from my studies of value that this is not possible. The entire attempt of the modern mind to do this seemed to me but one of the many indications of its loss of the sense of essential intelligibility and of that readiness to combine incompatibles which is one of its chief characteristics. Still less possible seemed to me that other *tour de force* of the modern mind, according to which it finds itself able to talk of values as immediately "enjoyed," but in their essence completely divorced from existence. This seemed to me, not only the height of sophistication, but, as James says, "the perfection of rottenness." Enough that searchings of mind and heart such as these led me to review afresh the whole field of traditional philosophy with which the values had been bound up, and to face again the whole way of thinking which had led modernism to turn its back on this *philosophia perennis*. I came to the conclusion that the great tradition is not dead, but that its restatement must constitute the next great step in philosophical development.

In the recasting of my thinking at this point the study of Nietzsche and Bergson was of outstanding importance. In his chapter on "The Prejudices of the Philosophers" I found Nietzsche stating much more clearly than the "technical" philosophers the inmost driving-force of this tradition. He made it clear to me that there are certain things "common to the metaphysicians of all time." All subscribe to that "mythical philosophy," as the moderns now call it, which connects the values of things in some way with their origin and their end. Bergson also made it clear to me, not only that there is a continuous tradition from Plato and Aristotle to the present time, but that this tradition is really the "natural metaphysic of the human mind." Not only is it the metaphysic to which every mind will come that follows the natural bent of the reason, but it is natural precisely because, as he points out, it is oriented towards value. He sees also that it refuses to separate the meaning and value of things from their origin and their end.

Now it is on this tradition that both Nietzsche and Bergson turn their backs. And why do they thus turn their backs upon it? For the same reason that actuates all the other typical modernist philosophies—for the reason, namely, that the intellect or reason of man, for which this metaphysic is the natural expression, is conceived as a merely biological product, developed on the service of the biological life. All the categories—the logic and the language—in which this natural metaphysics expresses itself, are infected with error and relativity at their very source, and constitute a mythology, amiable or otherwise, according to our mood or standpoint.

Here, then, was finally a clean-cut issue to which my mind was gradually being forced. Between the premises of this tradition and the premises of modernism there is no common ground. The whole question resolves itself into one of those fundamental issues which Fichte analysed so knowingly—one in which the matter is in a sense ultimately one of free choice. Faced with such an issue there could be for me only one choice, for while in a sense it was free, in another sense the option was forced. It is quite possible to say that it is a matter of temperament, of psychological rather than logical reasons, and to such an *ad hominem* there is really no wholly satisfactory answer. In any case, the option was forced for me by what I call the demands of philosophical intelligibility.

What I understand by philosophical intelligibility has been

suggested in a general way at a number of points. I find it wholly unintelligible to seek to validate values by carrying them back to life and at the same time to refuse to acknowledge the absolute values that alone give life meaning, and without which it cannot be interpreted. I find it unintelligible—to the point of being suicidal—to ascribe to knowledge a cognitive function and then so to describe knowledge, naturalistically, as to make the events of which it is composed, by their very nature, incapable of discharging that function. But the climax is reached when we assert that the values are there, are valid, and then divorce them from the only metaphysic that makes their validity intelligible.

It was then by ways of thinking such as these that my creed of absolute values became a transition to metaphysics and to the development of a metaphysical creed. I had already learned one important lesson from William James—namely, that questions of origin and destiny are irrelevant and meaningless if abstracted from questions of value. I now came to see, even more clearly, that questions regarding the validity of values are meaningless if values are divorced from questions of origin and destiny. The temporary effort of the modern mind to do this could be understood only as a necessary, though desperate, resort in the face of an overpowering evolutionary naturalism. I now came to see that the *axiological* point of view, the standpoint of absolute values, not only might be, but must be a transition to metaphysics. I found myself coming to agree with Lotze in his memorable statement that "the apodictic character of experience itself can be ascribed only to the good (or value). Everything depends upon the fact that an *ought* is there, that sets the play of thoughts, of ground, cause purpose, in movement." I came to see that the entire body of traditional metaphysic was essentially a value-charged scheme of thought and must be interpreted from this point of view. Precisely because to separate value and reality is unintelligible, such a value charged scheme of thought is the necessary form of an intelligible world.

Here again I can simply state the metaphysical creed to which I have arrived, confident, however, that it is not only that to which one is inevitably driven by conscious lines of argument such as I have suggested, but that it also represents the deeper convictions to which the less conscious thinking of the period has driven most of those who have approached the philosophical problem in my way.

I hold that there can be no existence without value and no value without existence. Reality is neither mental nor material, but a realm in which thought and thing, fact and value, are inseparable. The acknowledgment of this relation is the condition of philosophical intelligibility. To separate value and reality leads to contradiction and unintelligibility. To this first article I add a second. This inseparability of value and existence means that value cannot be separated from origin and destiny. These are "time-forms" of value, and no interpretation of the temporal is possible without them. Some conception of *intelligible causation* and of *intelligible finality* must enter into any intelligible philosophy. These categories—together with the categories of substance and totality with which they are closely connected—are very flexible. If one form is refuted, they will immediately take another; but no logic, nor conception of logic, whether atomistic or idealistic—has either the power or the right to turn them into appearance, nor to inhibit the fundamental spiritual initiatives out of which they arise. Thirdly, any intelligible philosophy must be a system—and ultimately a system of values. It is all very well for the modernist to say that system in philosophy is a "rationalization," or that logically a completed system is a self-contradictory notion. The fact remains that without system there is no philosophy, and it is our business to form an intelligible concept of system. Such a system must in the last analysis be a system of values and validities, and must be able in some way to embody or interpret the "form of philosophical intelligibility" which belongs to the innate metaphysic of the human mind.

In thus describing my return to the metaphysic that the moderns have called "mythical," I should perhaps add two further comments. I am not, of course, unaware of the element of symbolism in it. Metaphysic is for me, not as Bergson supposes, the science that seeks to dispense with symbols, but rather that which develops the symbolism inherent in language to its highest pitch, that which seeks language for the expression of the meaning of reality in its totality. It follows, then, that while this metaphysic, with its concepts of ultimate origin and ultimate destiny, will never be refuted, it is very flexible and capable of ever new restatement and reinterpretation. It is the function of value philosophy to understand its symbolic character and to interpret it.

In the second place, the conception here developed determines my conception of religion and of its philosophy. For me the religious problem has always been the fundamental problem of philosophy. I am, I suppose, what would be called religiously minded. For one thing, when I meet a really religious man I am conscious of a type of personality that I immediately understand —one who has a certain grasp of life and reality that irreligious men have not. In the latter I find a certain leanness of soul that is to me frankly repellent. In any case, this will perhaps explain why, for me at least, religion has always been, to use a term applied by Coleridge to poetry, "covert metaphysics," and I am unable to distinguish ultimately between philosophy and religion. Both have as their ultimate problem the relation of value to reality, and any religion divorced from metaphysics is a *contradictio in adjecto.* It will also be understood why for me Theism in some form is the only intelligible philosophy of religion. For the reason that there cannot be any intelligible metaphysics without intelligible causation and intelligible finality, the form of thinking about God is the same as the form of thinking about ultimate reality; the arguments from first cause and teleology are essentially sound. They are simply special applications of the principle that origin and value and value and destiny are inseparable. Finally, it will doubtless be understood when I say that modernism in religion—with its irresistible drift to a merely naturalistic humanism—is for me wholly unintelligible. If one speaks to me of a "god in the making," I simply throw up my hands. It is simply incomprehensible to me how thinkers of this type should take so long to learn their lesson from Nietzsche —that for them God should have long since been dead.

V

The constant use of the terms "philosophical intelligibility" and "intelligible world" in my later thinking and writing indicates both the standpoint from which I am now viewing all philosophical problems and also the end towards which all my philosophical investigations are now directed. I have come to feel that the basal problem of all science and philosophy is the problem of a philosophy of language and symbolism, and I hope ultimately to contribute something toward the solution of that problem.

The way this has come about is something like this. I find myself in a world of thought and expression in which the language used is in many respects very different from that of the past. So great is this "divide" that some of the more enthusiastic moderns inform us that "our mental nature has so changed that we now have entirely new notions of what facts are and of what standards of thought are." This new mentality is so different that we speak a new idiom, and "we could scarcely now hope to make ourselves understood by minds of an older age." As a corollary of this, I am told that the traditional language of philosophy, in which all the philosophers of the past have held high converse, must now be abandoned because it is bound up with a form of logic which the labours of certain modern logicians have rendered obsolete.

All this, of course, throws me into a state of great bewilderment. For one thing, a large part of what the moderns are saying in this new idiom is to me wholly unintelligible. I understand the words, of course, but I do not understand the sense. When they speak of Socrates as a "collection," or tell me that there is no such thing as consciousness in their language, or that it is no longer good form to use the words, substance, cause, purpose, because science does not use them in its language, I am of course puzzled. But I am even more bewildered when I am told that because our natural language is infected with error, the ideal would be a logic that abstained from all use of natural language, and to develop a Volapük in which there would be no subjects and predicates any more. I am bewildered because I cannot see any outcome to this except a complete paralysis of speech. I don't see how we can go on talking at all unless there are subjects to talk about and predicates to apply to them.

Again, all this naturally leads me to ask the question: how they could possibly "get that way?" I find that it is fairly easy to see how men can say such things if one understands their premises. I find all these moderns, whether they are pragmatists, atomistic logicians, or intuitional mystics, have much the same things to say about language—and for much the same reasons. They all think of thought, and therefore of language, in a purely biological context. Language being "but the cries of the forests, corrupted and complicated by arrogant anthropoid apes," it is unfitted either to grasp or express the true nature of being: it is not "moulded on reality." Whatever may be said of the premises, the consequences are astounding. The modern mind seems to find itself suspended between two contradictory positions, both of which it is trying to accept at the same time. In one mood it is flirting with an extreme Behaviorism which defines science as language well-made, and then views language as a merely biological adaptation to environment—the only result of which is a pan-fictionism that swallows up science itself. At another moment it dreams of an absolute logic which can become so only by a complete divorce from language. In the first case language can say nothing true, in the latter nothing that really interests anybody.

This is what I call neo-nominalism, and is the key to all modernistic tendencies in philosophy. Now I agree that on such premises the language of traditional metaphysics is "either nonsense or a sorry sort of poetry." But I also think, with Chesterton, that such nominalism is the deepest of all heresies. It is, surely, a dreadful thing to be told that there is no Socrates, or that when we use such terms as life, soul, God, personality, beauty, truth, etc., we are using words for which there is no "referent." It is a dreadful thing to be told that all these are "pseudo-simples," and that all the categories of substance, cause, purpose, with which philosophy has operated in the past, must be eliminated from the polite discourse of the moderns. But that is not the most dreadful thing about this heresy; it is rather the thought that, if I am to be logical in this sophisticated sense, I must turn my back entirely on the natural logic and metaphysics of the great minds of the past, and in the end confine my communication wholly to these moderns.

The outlook is really too dreadful to contemplate! For myself, the whole thing seems to me to be one of the most monstrous thoughts that it has ever entered into the mind of man to conceive. I am sure that there must be something terribly wrong with it, and for my part I am determined to find out what is wrong. In any case, I am convinced that this whole question of language and logic will have to be gone over again—and from the beginning. I think that we shall have to take again as basal certain things that are now everywhere impugned: (1) that communication, and a certain trust in natural language necessary for communication, are presupposed by knowledge and science, and cannot in any intelligible sense be explained by science; (2) that the potentiality of logical form in natural language is the necessary postulate of such communication, and therefore of any intelligible logic; (3) finally, that the natural metaphysics which has developed out of natural language in man's efforts to express the meaning of life, and of the world in which that life is lived, cannot be fundamentally invalidated by any later developments of language and logic created for certain specific purposes.

I cannot, of course, argue in detail for these positions here. I can only say that to work on the opposite assumptions means, if the consequences are carried out consistently, not only that philosophy is ultimately shorn of all the concepts that have hitherto made communication possible, not only that most of the things about which philosophy has hitherto talked must be put in the class of "those things that cannot be expressed," but ultimately that complete paralysis of speech to which I have referred. This seems to me to be a veritable *reductio ad absurdum*, and merely part of the general philosophical unintelligibility of which I have spoken.

VI

At the beginning of this attempt to state my philosophical creed, I referred to it as an *apologia*. For reasons that are now apparent, it is perhaps of necessity more of an apology than many of the other papers in this series. To be a fundamentalist and traditionalist in philosophy requires, to be sure, more justification than any reasons I have been able to bring forward in this context; I shall be content if I have been able to suggest some of the more compelling motives that have actuated my thinking.

There is one point that I feel that I must add in conclusion. A philosophical *creed*, like any other—religious, social, artistic, scientific—involves always in a sense, and to a degree, "believing where we cannot see." There are many things that I cannot see, and in all probability never shall see clearly. I cannot quite see, for instance, just how fact and value, value and existence, are related (there are many perplexities here), although I do see perfectly that to separate them means ultimately unintelligibility. All attempts to state that relation leave something to be desired; I cannot deny an element of mystery here. Again I cannot quite see how the absolute values are to be grasped as a totality. There are many things that argue for their autonomy, and no attempt to organize these values in a system has been satisfactory. But I do see clearly that they do constitute a totality, and that system is the condition of intelligibility. And so it is with all my major beliefs. Thus, for me it is true—both psychologically and philosophically—that "the soul possesses God in so far as it participates in the absolute," but a complete indentification of the religious with the metaphysical notion I have never found possible.

I do not see these things, I say, and yet this is not quite the truth. I see many of these things in certain moments of insight, and these moments are sufficient to bear the weight of a great deal of rationalizing. I must therefore admit a certain element of mysticism into my creed and, like James Ward, acknowledge that the most fundamental things in philosophy cannot be expressed without "trenching on the mystical." But this does not disturb me, for it is the one thing that above all else proves to me the inseparability of philosophy and life. In any case, I am not a mystic in the sense that my mysticism involves either a negative metaphysic or a negative theology. I find myself akin to those who have found it possible to live with comfort in the great systems in which *philosophia perennis* has continually expressed itself. These systems are in a sense houses (man-made houses, if you will) in which men dwell. Even so I for one am content to dwell in such a house, for I am sure that in some way which I cannot quite express, back of it, or in it, is "a house not made with hands, eternal in the heavens."

PRINCIPAL PUBLICATIONS

Valuation: Its Nature and Laws. (Library of Philosophy.) George Allen & Unwin, Ltd. (1909).
The Intelligible World: Metaphysics and Value. (Library of Philosophy.) George Allen & Unwin, Ltd. (1929).
"Value Theory and Æsthetics," in *Philosophy To-day.* Open Court Publishing Co. (1928).

ARTICLES

(Pertinent to the foregoing discussion.)

"Value and Existence," *Journal of Philosophy, Psychology, Etc.,* Vol. XIII, No. 17 (1916).
"Knowledge of Value, Etc.," *Journal of Philosophy, Psychology, Etc.,* Vol. XIII, No. 24 (1916).
"Ontological Problems of Value," *Journal of Philosophy, Psychology, Etc.,* Vol. XIV, No. 12 (1917).
"Beyond Realism and Idealism," *Philosophical Review,* Vol. XXVII, No. 1 (1917).
"Origin and Value: The Unintelligibility of Philosophic Modernism," *Philosophical Review,* Vol. XXXII, No. 5 (1923).
"The Philosophy of Language," *Psychological Bulletin,* Vol. XXVI, No. 5 (1929).
"Progress in Philosophy in the Last Quarter-Century" (Presidential Address before the American Philosophical Association), *Philosophical Review,* Vol. XXXV, No. 2 (1926).

AN UNBORN IDEALISM

By ROBERT MARK WENLEY [1]

[1] Died March 29, 1929.

Born Edinburgh, 1861; Head of the Department of Philosophy and Psychology in the University of Michigan since 1896.

AN UNBORN IDEALISM

THE courteous invitation to appear in this volume asks, among other things, that the article "should embody its author's philosophical creed." Good omen or bad, I am still in search of one! Fortunately the sentence continues, "together with the circumstances in his life history which have influenced him in reaching it." So, my creedlessness may be mitigated somewhat by the fact that the conditions of my nurture and education, far away and long ago, cannot but be in sharp contrast to those of my colleagues. This creates a diversion which seems to compel a fuller account than would be advisable otherwise. It may be apposite to recall that I did not appear upon the American scene till I had turned thirty-five, and to add, that nobody escapes these formative years. What came before 1896 is of paramount importance, so far as I can judge, and I offer no apology for intruding it.

The same interval has sped since F. H. Bradley wrote: "The present generation is learning that to gain education a man must study in more than one school." [1] Well, it goes without saying that America furnished abundant opportunities for a second education, to use Gibbon's phrase. More to the point, probably, when a youngster I was cast unwitting into the vortex of a definite "school" at its liveliest. With praiseworthy intent, my father wished me to complete the Arts course at Glasgow ere adopting the profession he recommended. His selection was the fruit of intimate knowledge of feasible careers, to put it mildly. The vortex whirled me from a secure, not to say profitable, berth with a solid firm of Scots "writers" (*more Americano*, lawyers)— manifest proof of its coercive effect, the counter-attraction considered. As a sequel, I found very much to learn and unlearn in the school of a life, precarious and unremunerative by comparison. Moreover, the influence of a system, despite harsh experience, convicted me, if not of gullibility, then of unwisdom; so my father's circle judged emphatically. Thus, the sympathetic or benevolent optimism of teachers, to whom ties of scholastic respect and personal affection bound me, was shaken by know-

---

[1] Preface to *Appearance and Reality*, p. xiii (1893).

ledge of evils in their proportion—nay, beyond all proportion, as it seemed to me more than once.

I

Like kindred institutions everywhere, the Scottish Universities, especially the two larger, Glasgow and Edinburgh, have undergone profound changes since my graduation forty-four years ago. So much so, that contemporary teachers and students could scarce reconstruct the situation in my time; Americans would be wholly at sea. The reason is not far to seek. It has been well said that, till the Act of 1889, the Scottish Universities preserved the mediæval tradition more closely than any of their European sisters. When I matriculated, a bare decade had passed since migration to the present spacious buildings (1870) from the cramped seventeenth-century quarters (1640), themselves the third home since the original charter (1451). Our professors, with one exception, having taught in the old place for years, kept touch with an age strange even to my generation.[1] More important, the *Trivium* and *Quadrivium* remained strongly vestigial in the curriculum for the Arts degree. Choice there was none. Two years of Latin, Greek, and Mathematics; one year of Logic, Moral Philosophy, English Literature, and Natural Philosophy (physics) were obligatory upon every candidate for a "Pass"; an admirable discipline, which had everything to do with that typical product of the "old" Scots' training, the polymath. (Perhaps I ought to interject at this point, that I sometimes think of myself as nigh the last of the line!) For "Honours," one had the choice of the "Departments" of Classics, or Mathematics and Natural Philosophy, or Mental Philosophy (including English Literature). If one cared to fare farther afield, a B.Sc., or Honours in Natural Science, might be achieved. Consequently, specialization involved preparatory contact with various fields of knowledge. "Men who went conscientiously through that

[1] For an earlier generation see Professor Knight, *Memoir of John Nichol*, pp. 114 f. (1896); David Murray, *Memories of the Old College of Glasgow* (1927).

course carried with them in after-life, for the most part, an intellectual mark that was unmistakable." [1] Its flexibility notwithstanding, I doubt whether the "new" scheme can pretend to the former basic thoroughness. As may be inferred, too, a majority of the students were headed for future careers in the church, law, medicine, the secondary schools, the civil services, or politics; a small minority, destined to commerce, took a "Pass" for cultural purposes. Such, then, was the educational and social perspective.

Seven subjects (the "sacred seven"), therefore seven professors in chief; we at Glasgow were in luck, the university being midmost one of those "golden ages," intermittent at all universities, I suppose. Latin was in charge of G. G. Ramsay, a first-rate teacher; Jebb, already of European repute, decorated Greek; Blackburn, in mathematics, did not count, despite his record as editor of Newton—his classes rioted joyously; Veitch, in Logic and Rhetoric, a "character" full of Aristotelian and Scots Border lore, represented the national philosophy, of which more anon; Sir William Thomson (afterwards Lord Kelvin) needs no comment; Nichol, in English literature, the best lecturer I ever heard, exerted broad and, no less, broadening influence, the more that he did not suffer fools gladly. Even so, the *genius loci* was Edward Caird, Professor of Moral Philosophy, the most ingratiating teacher it has been my fortune to encounter anywhere; and he was seconded powerfully by his older brother John, Principal of the University, foremost British preacher of the time.[2] The brothers, together with Nichol, had made the university a "veritable seething-pot of ideas." [3] Nor were the junior staff, although, in the position of "assistants" quite subordinate then, unworthy their seniors. J. H. Muirhead and Henry Jones (later Sir Henry) cannot escape mention here. The raw material was excellent. James Bonar, *Golden Bough* Frazer, and John MacCunn had graduated recently, together with not a few others

[1] The late Professor George Chrystal in *Proceedings R.S.E.*, vol. xxxii, p. 479. Cf. John Theodore Merz, *A History of European Thought in the Nineteenth Century*, vol. i, pp. 267 f. (1896).

[2] Cf. *The Spectator* (London), vol. lxxxi, p. 174 (August 6, 1898).

[3] Cf. My article "Edward Caird," *Harvard Theological Review*, vol. ii, pp. 115 f. (1909).

destined to future fame. Francis Anderson, who was to leave his impress upon Australian thought, and J. S. Mackenzie, to name two of at least a dozen lights, were still in residence. Little wonder that study ranked the "major sport," and that intense emulation—too intense mayhap—gave tone to the place. Moreover, numbers were small enough to favour intimate contacts— my class graduated seventy-seven. Then, too, the new buildings had been erected on Gilmorehill, an eminence overlooking and marching with Kelvingrove Park of some 120 acres in the West End, giving us a kind of *rus in urbe*, seeing that the population of the city (1,100,000 to-day), then about 350,000, clustered to the east and south. Westward, green fields, reminders of the country houses affected by Virginian merchants till the commercial disaster of the American Revolution, lay almost within a stone's throw; indeed, the old mansion of Gilmorehill stood its ground inside the quadrangles, finding use as an administrative office. Such, then, was the immediate *milieu*.

II

But, after all, no matter what the apparent, because present, authority of institutions and persons, national imponderables lay in wait to take toll—a most decisive feature in Scotland after the Disruption (1843).[1] The cultural tradition preserved vigour, being comparatively recent; the ferment arose soon after Francis Hutcheson's lectures at Glasgow (1730–46). He "disputed no dogma, and taught no heresy as he discussed the beauty of moral virtue, descanted on the harmony of the passions and the dignity of human nature; all this, not in dull obscure Latin like his colleagues, but in eloquent English." By the same sign, he inaugurated "Moderatism" in the Kirk, rendering the Five Points of Knox "strangely unreal." [2] Subsequent to Hume, also a "moderate," the Scottish School, "keeping to its own field, that of inductive psychology, allowed the students to follow their

[1] Cf. John Sutherland Black and George Chrystal, *The Life of William Robertson Smith*, pp. 1 f., 444 f. (1912), for the Disruption and "Moderatism."
[2] Cf. Henry Grey Graham, *The Social Life of Scotland in the Eighteenth Century*, pp. 352 f. (1906).

own convictions, evangelical or rationalistic, but training all to a habit of skilful arrangement and exposition."[1] Metaphysical presuppositions being relegated to the theologians by silent agreement, tacit norms did not come under fire.[2] The ecclesiastical cataclysm of 1843, upthrusting evangelical convictions, tended to preserve this division of labour by stress upon a practical piety masterful enough to recall the activist certainties of the Covenanters.[3] In workshop, store, and office, common life was sustained by an uncommon quality savouring of commerce with an Absolute. Hence everything ran back to mysteries too grave for discussion, yet intimating definite suggestions which forbade, not scepticism merely, but even inquiry. It is not surprising, then, that Scotland was fated to exhibit noteworthy symptoms of distress on the entrance of "modern thought" with Darwin (1859) and *Essays and Reviews* (1860).[4]

[1] James M'Cosh, *The Scottish Philosophy from Hutcheson to Hamilton*, p. 268 (1875).

[2] I have tried to outline this in Donald Macmillan, *The Life of Flint*, chap. viii (1914); cf. Henry Grey Graham, *Scottish Men of Letters in the Eighteenth Century*, pp. 425 f. (1908).

[3] For other aspects of the picture, cf. H. C. Graham, *Literary and Historical Essays*, pp. 233 f. (1908); Black and Chrystal, *op. cit.*, pp. 414 f.

[4] Sufficient time has elapsed now to make it abundantly evident that this state of affairs deflected the fortunes of Philosophy, thanks to the preconceptions swaying patrons of academic chairs. One cannot fail to remark the refusals to appoint J. F. Ferrier, at Edinburgh in 1856; John Nichol, at Glasgow in 1864 ("I know that some people are afraid of his theological views," *Memoir*, p. 189); T. H. Green, at St. Andrews in 1864 ("I have been told that, though not a monster otherwise, I carry Comtism and Materialism to a degree hitherto unknown at Oxford," *Works*, vol. iii, p. xli); J. Hutchison Stirling, and even Robert Flint, at Edinburgh in 1868 (cf. Amelia Hutchison Stirling, *James Hutchison Stirling, His Life and Works* (1912), *Life of Flint*, pp. 172 f.); and A. M. Fairbairn, at Aberdeen in 1876 (cf. W. B. Selbie, *The Life of Andrew Martin Fairbairn*, pp. 73 f., 1893); to say nothing of others still alive. Edward Caird's appointment at Glasgow (1866) presupposed favourable local conditions—he had "done nothing," as he told me—that is, had not committed himself to his harm (cf. Sir Henry Jones and J. H. Muirhead, *Life and Work of Edward Caird*, pp. 46 f., 1921). So late as the eighties, the rumour gained ready currency that Sir Ray Lankester, who resigned the Chair of Natural History at Edinburgh ere induction (1882), had bowed to an anti-Darwin storm. He has been kind enough to inform me that the report lacks all foundation. This may serve to hint that the "controversy over Darwin"

Be details as they may, a transition, slow at first, accelerating through the seventies, governed the quarter-century (1860–85) that saw my schooling. Prudent guidance and "formation of character," rather than intellectual discipline for its own sake, were featured from many professorial chairs. In any case, the conspicuous events took a practical turn, and the youth, shepherded carefully, could not sense the commonplace limits of the moral or ecclesiastico-political questions enlisting their

never became acute in Scotland; the scientific leaders, Sir William Thomson, P. G. Tait, and Clerk Maxwell, to name three, were believers in revealed religion (cf. *The Unseen Universe, or Physical Speculations on a Future State* (1875); published anonymously; the authors were Tait and Balfour Stewart). By the time it might have raised trouble, other events occupied the foreground, arousing the motion and absorbing the intellect of the nation. They were: (1) the "great mission" of the American evangelists, Moody and Sankey, 1873–75 (cf. George Adam Smith, *The Life of Henry Drummond*, chap. iv, 1898); (2) Flint's Baird Lectures (*Theism*, 1876; *Anti-Theistic Theories*, 1877); (3) the prosecution of Robertson Smith for heresy (higher criticism of the Old Testament), leading to suspension and, finally, to deposition from his Chair at the Aberdeen Theological College of the Free Church (1875–81), but to eventual victory over the narrow view of the inspiration of the Scriptures held hitherto (cf. Black and Chrystal, *op. cit.*, chaps. v–viii, xiv); (4) Henry Drummond's *Natural Law in the Spiritual World* (1883) (cf. G. A. Smith, *op. cit.*, pp. 148 f., 228 f.) The Smith case kept Scotland in turmoil for a decade. *Theism* ran through thirteen editions in a few years—extraordinary for so technical a book; Drummond sold 123,000 copies quickly, and kept on selling into the nineties. Briefly, not Darwin, but the general relations between science and religion, with special reference to theological and quasi-philosophical principles, were "a topic of most acute personal interest to thousands." Notice, moreover, that something had happened in Scotland by 1883. "The hostile criticism, which the main idea of Drummond's book had received from the Glasgow Club to which it was first communicated, was repeated nowhere more persistently than in Scotland, and by none with greater conviction than by a few of the author's closest companions" (G. A. Smith, *op. cit.*, p. 229). Edward Caird's influence told here. In addition, the fact was that Drummond had no hold upon philosophy. Further, those who were moved strongly by the *practical* religious movements of the day, tended to abandon philosophy as taught from very different standpoints by the three most powerful professors (Bain at Aberdeen, Campbell Fraser at Edinburgh, and E. Caird at Glasgow), substituting the *testimonium Spiritus Sancti*. On the other hand, and inevitably, those of us who were undergraduates could not escape the national preoccupation in ecclesiastical and theological controversy, whether we liked it or not.

enthusiasm. No doubt the relentless tide of industrialism was overtaking the middle and lower middle classes, but "social reform" had not acquired sufficient momentum to be ominous. Accordingly, the clamant problems, as men saw them then, loomed up in a theological or, as too often, ecclesiastical perspective; even Carlyle, the gleam followed by the generation of the fifties, lay in partial shadow.

My contacts with the disturbance happened to be unusual, possibly unique; for this reason my future career was profoundly influenced. My paternal grandparents, who immigrated from East Anglia in the late twenties, were Anglican by nurture. Due to circumstances irrecoverable now, ante-Disruption struggles seized them and, so far as children by adoption could, they shared the evangelical "revival," which thus gave my father his youthful outlook. On the contrary, my mother's people, scions of an old Border stock, held the "moderate" tradition (semi-Deistic), and viewed the "supreme consciousness of special election" with detachment, not to say cynical amusement. Although I never gave the matter thought as a schoolboy, it is plain to me now that I favoured the maternal strain. Moreover, my father's early contact with scientific circles, and his excellent library, led to suggestions hardly consonant with "pure" evangelical doctrine! He had certain relations with David Livingstone, of a financial character, I take it. He was greatly interested in arctic exploration, and, more than likely, this accounted for his friendship with Sir John Murray in the late sixties and, afterwards, for his connection with the *Challenger* expeditions. At all events, he rendered service sufficient to justify election as Fellow of the Royal Society of Edinburgh. This aspect of the home (a makeweight for my loss in not being sent to one of the great Public Schools, disapproved by my father) was rendered more vital by frequent visits, in the seventies, from my mother's kinsman, George John Romanes. I played *Diener* to him when he was gathering material for his *Jelly-Fishes* at our seaside cottage. As he was then in *A Candid Examination of Theism* (1878) stage, many discussions occurred whose purport would have horrified the "decent" evangelical Scot of the moment.

Then, too, the library furnished windows upon a larger world. I read Rénan's *Vie de Jesus*, Draper's *The Intellectual Development of Europe*, stretches of Grote's *Greece*, Sir Walter Scott, and, needless to recount, Paley. A first edition of Darwin's *Origin* and Jowett's *Plato* (1871) are among my early recollections— they remain among my cherished possessions. From my mother's brother, who lived near by and was something of a collector, I had news of recent books, often discoloured theologically! An English cousin, far-flung as secretary to a diplomat, and my father's brother, who had returned (1872) from a long sojourn in Malaya, brought strange tales of other lands, well calculated to stimulate curiosity, if nothing else. Hence, as a lad with some Greek, more Latin, and most French, I had boxed a bit of the compass, and believed myself a sceptic (Hume), only to be sat upon severely by Veitch and Denney (the winsome evangelical leader of after-days), with whom I began philosophical study. They riled me—nothing else! I little foresaw that the crucial years were very nigh at hand.

III

Unusual contacts despite, it is plain enough that an adolescent cannot have given hostages to thought. It is scarce less plain that, if he had reached categories, habituations were likely to have played substitute for reflection, with the result that contingencies would tend to rate important. Now, the persistence of eighteenth-century modes in Britain—the Pre-Raphaelite movement (*c.* 1860), an *early* symptom of discontent—favoured the survival of neat oppositions, which governed even those who sat in the seats of the mighty. Without more ado, then, I deem it evident that I had never encountered "the real thing" by eighteen or thereby; above all, the idea of development had not arisen for judgment. Take the political sphere as an example: I was quite unaware that, as Professor Cappon says admirably, "Carlyle's universal is far deeper than any optimistic or pessimistic, Conservative or Radical theory of life."[1] Accordingly,

---

[1] *Philosophical Essays Presented to John Watson*, p. 30 (1922).

there was every reason why I should succumb to the "seething zymosis"[1] of Caird's teaching.

To begin with, one was removed from the arena of fragmentary polemics to a region where the torrid onsets of current opinion fell flat. Professor MacCunn may testify for me, because he conveys the *ictus* exactly: "The effect produced on the majority of the class was as if we were witnessing the creation of a new world. The dead-weight of custom and tradition was insensibly lifted, and we felt that for the first time we had begun to see things as they are."[2] This is the unanimous testimony of pupils. And the secret? In the first place, a negative answer may serve to disperse dusty cobwebs spun since. It was not discipular Hegelianism! As I have said elsewhere, "attempt to range him with Hegel's pupils and colleagues, in the attractive rows of Right, Left, or Centre, and you find at once that he eludes your complacent attentions. The national temper and traditions of the Scot vary so fundamentally from those of the Swabian, the philosophical situation in Britain during the rule of Gladstone was so different from the speculative excitement in the Prussia of Stein and Hardenberg, that simple reproduction of the one spirit by the other is an idea too naïve for serious consideration."[3] Positively, Bosanquet has conveyed the secret in a phrase—it was "the sense of an exalted quest."[4] The breadth and significance of Philosophy were brought home to us through persistent use of the historical method backed by encyclopaedic humanism. Unyielding distinctions "subject" and "object," *a priori* and *a posteriori*, "finite" and "infinite," and the rest—vanished; the several doctrines whereof we had been making hard-shell finalities took their *relative* places in a developing whole. Venerable convictions might be modified or justified or condemned; be the consequence what it might, one must face the task of inquiry. Agglomerative or anachronistic theories must give way to forthright interpretation guided by the sense of a whole informing the

---

[1] Cf. Sir Henry Jones and J. H. Muirhead, *The Life and Philosophy of Edward Caird*, pp. 89 f.

[2] *Op. cit.*, p. 249. [3] *Ut sup.*, p. 130.

[4] *Proceedings British Academy*, 1907–08, p. 383.

parts. We learned that silent, transforming influences alter and, at length, bring to light the internal significance of particular events—whether "ideas" or "things"—in a continuous process. Aught worth the names "science" or "philosophy" is an expression of the nature of those who think and, no less, of the objects of their thought. Portions of experience set over against one another mark stages, so interwoven that we proceed from relations in "reality" to comprehension of these relations by "thought." Most startling—and beneficial—for the theologically minded Scot, "any necessity for an irruption of the spiritual into the natural world would seem inconsistent with the idea that the latter is spiritual in its own right."[1] It were superfluous to elaborate further, for the revolution wrought subtly by a seminal teacher cannot be conveyed verbally to those who never knew him in the flesh. Suffice it to say that the stress of readjustment, coupled with the drudgery incident to the competitive academic system, broke my physical strength, and my *Wanderung* began.

Familiarity with French headed me for Paris, where, finding no philosophical stimulus, I gave myself to study, of the origins of Christianity especially, to mastering the spoken tongue, and, later, to reading scholastic philosophy with a Jesuit father. Four months in Rome, the ancient rather than the mediaeval city casting the spell, a couple of months in Florence, with a natural change to the story of the Renaissance, and return to Paris over a summer, completed the tale of my first wanderings. So far as I can judge, France and Italy left no mark on my thought, although they did much to broaden my equipment. Still unable for full work on return to Glasgow, but compelled to keep Terms, I heard Caird again. He was busy with the sad task of preparing Green's *Prolegomena to Ethics* for publication, and giving a new set of lectures suggested in part by this work. Due, no doubt, to the narrower scope of the subject, the first fine rapture hardly recurred. Moreover, I had diverged into philosophy of religion, and was beginning to feel that the exultant confidence in reason which had enchanted at the first blush, might be less invulnerable

[1] Jones and Muirhead, *op. cit.*, p. 181.

than I had suspected. Believing that philosophy of religion demands acquaintance with technical theology, I heard the theological professors regularly. Three were scholars of large acquirement; indeed, William Purdie Dickson, *the* polymath of the university, was resorted to by foreign investigators frequently. I garnered a great deal from them, but, seeing that none possessed what, for want of a better phrase, one may call transitive personality, I was able to pursue my inquiries in my own way, free from the romanticism of discipleship. Individualistic by temperament, I imagine this was just what I desired; in any case, it has been my habit ever since. I am unaware that my long association with Veitch, whose assistant I became on graduation (1884), left definite mark; it did compel me to give instruction in logic for a decade—no bad thing. I resided twice in Germany for some months. Lotze's massive caution and gracious manner wrought upon me for a moment; his philosophy left me cold. So far as I could make out, he joined Being to Thought ethically and, for this reason, was never comfortable with Nature. Hence, I was more affected by the example of his magnificent equipment than by his irenical temper. I continued along my own path, getting numerous knocks for my pains, but discovering that, in the things of the mind, the price paid is a large portion of value received. Possibly I was civilized enough to sacrifice immediate desires to future benefits—I trust so. In any case, I held fast to one idea which I owed to Caird—that the world is a unit, and that distinctions are artifices of convenience. For this reason and, unquestionably, because of my intellectual experience otherwise, I came to labour in border-line subjects, becoming more and more convinced that (1) "a true and valuable idealism can be reached only through the interpretation of the data of experience by the special sciences, and the reinterpretation of the results of these by philosophy"[1]; and that (2) special attention must be given to "history as ideas," with consequent elaboration of the human sciences. In other words, the more one rationalizes nature and history by research, the more one finds unsolved

[1] E. Caird in *The Progress of the Century* (American edition), p. 170 (1901).

problems. Initiation, whatever its seductive delights, deceives if it be mistaken for culmination. The inner process binding the whole is "the real thing"; and progress depends upon penetration of the symbols known to us as "events." Truth is to be found in the history of human experience or—not at all. In short, philosophy is no pseudo-science, but the temper of mind which attempts to think things together. Accordingly, if premature syntheses are to be avoided, it must wait upon "things," wait, particularly, till the sciences, human and natural, have reached a point where the philosophical implications can be dodged no longer. I presume that the practical facts of life from 1884 till 1906, say, served to confirm this attitude.

In 1886 I was appointed to the independent lectureship at Queen Margaret College (the Glasgow college for women). The double duties incident to this and to my assistantship, together with the necessity for supplementing a meagre salary, interfered with publication; on the other hand, elapsing time enabled me to conserve my spiritual independence—the main issue. After long negotiations, I succeeded Professor Dewey at Michigan in 1896. Adjustment to the enormous changes, while most stimulating, took heavy toll of ten years, during which, moreover, I became immersed in encyclopaedic work, particularly in the anxious consultations preliminary to the *Encyclopaedia of Religion and Ethics*. In this period, likewise, the deaths of my father and mother within a few months shook me profoundly.

Through thick and thin, I have striven to keep my skirts clear of all cliques, and to ensure that no pupils of mine should ever band themselves into a "school," proliferating manifestos designed to put outsiders "in their proper places." The petty world of local lights, admiring friends and, by contrast, depreciatory enemies, gets between men and their wits. Not thus, but by quiet work alone, can advances come. Another facet from my angular tradition, and I have done. Universities crave men of good will who give themselves unsparingly to pupils. Paraphrasing Goethe, the teacher who has life in him feels himself to be here for their sakes, not for the public. In our present mood, we have something to emulate in—nay, to divine from—-the British on this score.

Better a mature, serene spirit than a superfluous volume. The immediate job is to persuade the youth that one's subject really matters, and, this done, the intangible reward of souls to one's hire rather than of tangible pages to one's name more than suffices. For "production" of human relations between teacher and taught happens to be the sole defence of universities against a common type of criticism. Accomplish it even in a measure, and "recognition," the itch of those who lack moral stamina, can be foregone cheerfully.

IV

Knowledge of the pit whence I was digged may help others to realize my disabilities, to forecast my spiritual voyage of discovery, not yet ended. Let me confess to a lifelong, insatiable curiosity, still strong upon me, and that, thanks to it probably, I have been and am attracted to philosophy for the light shed upon the mental and cultural experience of men. But "philosophy" and "experience" are dubious terms; the more they evade definition, the more they need to be humanized. By "experience," then, I understand everything covered by the clumsy word "mentality," which includes much besides bare intelligence or reason, a feeble though yeasty element. We must take account of temperament, character, and socialized adjustments, indeed of all factors and qualities, no matter how elusive, hidden under the deceitful label "personality." Again, your philosopher cannot divest himself of the personal equation. So, I confess impenitence regarding "philosophy." If it does not mean metaphysics, then it is hardly worth while; any "human science" might masquerade for it, contemporary fashion furnishing proof. Perhaps a little specification might be advantageous.

The confession, that one has no philosophy of his own, happens to be compatible with the circumstance that any philosophy demands individual effort and singular outlook. It is easy to say that philosophy embodies a search for first principles, or a fundamental view of things, or a general theory of reality, and so forth. If these phrases intimate that it must take all knowledge for province, the impracticable side of the case emerges; if they hint the theoretical nature of the quest as an issue of intellectual urge, then one can echo Goethe:

> Das weit Zerstreute sammelt sein Gemüth,
> Und sein Gefühl belebt das Unbelebte.

Nevertheless, perils beset this function, and, seeing they arise precisely from the Whole or, if you please, Absolute, clamorous temptations ensue. Examples may serve to underline the point. One may agree with Mr. James Stephens that "in most poems there is an intellectual content, an emotional content, and a third content for which we have no name: what Keats meant when he said, 'Heard melodies are sweet, but those unheard are sweeter.' . . . It is that unheard rhythm which is the poetry in the poem." Similarly, in Gothic architecture, calculable statics furnish the intellectual content, the willing suspension of the stone the emotional; beyond these, however, lies the mystical "yearning to create a supersensuous world of spiritual expression."[1] Now, it is customary to affirm that the average man has a philosophy; in other words, he does adjust his affairs to a world where stable recurrences maintain themselves, and he does obey or break the controls of a socio-ethical order, sharing or antagonizing current norms. So, too, on a higher because more deliberate level, the investigator assumes and, in experiment, tries to guarantee the "thisness" of his objects, that he may generalize; in like manner, the patriot or partisan sacrifices self for "the cause." The intellectual and emotional contents are plain enough. But a Whole of some sort lurks near by "unheard"—let us admit the mystery. Dangers multiply forthwith. The pervasive something beckons, inviting capture. Hence the specious insinuation of its homogeneousness with us, and of our consequent capacity to deploy ultimate intelligibility at a word of command. Intuition, if not imagination, syncopates labour *ex datis*, and complexities are apt to be dealt short shrift. Of course, I am well aware that emphasis upon the Infinite, Absolute, Self-consciousness, Logos, or what you will, may favour desirable elasticity of thought,

---

[1] Cf. Wilhelm Worringer, *Formprobleme der Gothik* (1920).

tending to break down conventional distinctions with their attractive, if commonplace, simplifications. Notwithstanding, a bland suspicion lingers that lapses into rhetoric of the unutterable may occur, more comforting than illuminative. Sober reflection is in duty bound to stand them off; nay, it has so striven these last thirty years.

The insurrection against the Locke-Mill-Spencer tradition, already at high tide in my youth, presupposed this dynasty, historically remote to-day. A later generation may judge it to have overshot the mark, like all revolts. Hence, the "decisive rejection of representative ideas in favour of directly apprehended unities" bred a fresh revolt, often termed "new"—a recommendation, I presume. As a matter of fact, some of us, being recalcitrant pupils, felt its undertow forty years ago. I recognize the difficulty of dealing with a past marked by extraordinary discontinuity, but plead that I am asked to make my confession. Well, I felt in particular that the opposition between an external "material" world and an internal "spiritual" world might have been overcome too cavalierly; that formulæ and true categories might have been imposed upon phenomena arbitrarily; that refractory events might have been pigeon-holed when not neglected. I knew that in the name of *geistliche* order, a vast web of deduction had been spun whence escape, however embarrassing, had become imperative. Be this as it may, the quest of the *Epigoni* for unity was not immune to change; no cause for wonder, when the numerous discoveries and hypotheses in the physical, biological, and social sciences, to say nothing of psychology, are recalled. Nor is this by any means the whole tale, for we dare not omit reckoning with the progressive secularization of life, which has played a rôle of greater magnitude than is recognized in some quarters. Consider that "whatever the implication of it may be, it is true that almost any sixty-year-old [i.e. till *circa* 1860] collection of letters deals very largely with theology, whereas any similar modern collection does not do so at all"; or, going into a very different gallery, con again the "Concluding Remarks" to Bradley's *Ethical Studies* (1876). And, if you care to jump a long century, take a Statute of the Seatonian Prize (1738) at Newton's university: "Which subject shall, for the first year, be one or other of the perfections or attributes of the Supreme Being, and so the succeeding years, till the subject be exhausted." With such prepossessions, it was altogether explicable that the intelligibility of the universe should have been taken for granted, if not baldly, then with grateful optimism; that the natural inference to a regnant intelligence should have proven congenial; and that, with this temper abroad, the doctrine of the "subjection of all things to the Divine Logos" should have been held to vindicate the "witness" of the thought of man to the thought of God. Briefly, a faith, the more vital that it was itself a protest, blossomed forth as a consistent, rational account of the ultimate. Thus, a very ancient temptation gained new lease on life; the presence of the Logos overshadowing, changes shrunk into their shell abashed, and human spontaneity seemed to receive undue chastening. Accordingly, despite powerful contrary influences, I was prepared to consider objections with an open mind, if not altogether to see to it that criticism, however unavoidable, might be sympathetic, even generous, to its own gain. In a word, natural dialectic was bound to take its ironical course. What more natural than a reversion to Hume! It was evident that many developments were conspiring to resuscitate his caution: "So narrow are the bounds of human understanding, that little satisfaction can be hoped for in this regard. . . . Indulge your passion for science [says nature], but let your science be human, and such as may have a direct reference to action and society. . . . Be a philosopher, but, amidst all your philosophy, be still a man."

The persistent diremption of experience favours "half-and-half" standpoints. An eminent physiologist said to me once, "If only our science were like physics, we would get somewhere." He had in mind rationalistic completion dependent upon an "absolute" *terminus a quo*: a substantive something, proof against human fallibility, furnishes the firm foundation. In like manner, the doctrine that "Truth" belongs to a non-human universe, whence it is thrust upon mundane events, derived warrant, if not authority, from the opposition between Appearance and Reality

Demurrers were in order forthwith on both counts. To begin with, when one comes to "matters of fact," are indubitable necessary and universal truths possible? Psychology drifted toward the negative, and the denial had been accentuated by the tendency of evolution to obliterate distinctions held inviolable by classical science and philosophy. "The sciences are coming together" and, as an accompaniment of their synthesis, the continuity of man with "external" things, with other organic beings, and with society was blazing fresh trails. The One and the Many, Flux and Being, returned from a dim past to confrontation by stern judges who said that, as perdurable forms beyond experience, they are so much moonshine. Emerging from severe discipline in history of philosophy, and from the deliquescencies of *religionsgeschichtliche* theology, one was receptive to the American suggestion that "the brain often runs away with the heart's best blood." Moreover, these were the brave days when Schopenhauer seemed to merit serious attention, when Nietzsche swung scintillating athwart the horizon, when William James's *The Principles of Psychology* aroused joyous, if unholy, glee in the natural man. Perhaps a valid, because concrete, order might be descried did one bethink him of actual human activities. Influences unfavourable to systematic philosophy were telling their tale, the emotional was asserting its rights, and romanticism attracted, allowing room for idiosyncrasy. The soul had starved on the rich food offered to the mind. "Die Scheidewand zwischen Fabel und Wahrheit, zwischen Vergangenheit und Gegenwart ist eingefallen: Glauben, Phantasie und Poesie schliessen die innerste Welt auf." Problems that admit neither solution nor escape held the foreground for a time, spiritual and practical freedom having been set by the ears. In vain: once more the suspicion would not down, that the scale of man's universe was being missed. Dodging Nietzsche's "spiritual rat-catchers," one had merely wandered into a world where Nature makes nothing but leaps. To wit, our world is "on the make," in so far forth it *is* a world where practice spells betterment, if scarcely perfection; in any case, adaptations supervene. Hence, whatever our hypothesis about the relations between *sensa* and thought, our concern is with empirical particulars, never with alleged universals, and, fitness being the test, truth reduces to economic grip of the opportune. A prudential relativism may compound for and with the sins of the whole people. To make a long story short, your adventure among the workaday will amount to achievement of truth. This gained, you need not care if you substitute a nostrum compounded of moralizing, scolding and, be it said, gossip for the spacious *afflatus* of perplexed Teutons; if your utilitarian diligence, cumbered about much serving, lacks distinction; if your contempt for history runs to the new for novelty's sake; if you handle high issues crudely, intent upon temporary advantage. As a romantic Dionysus playing hob with the eternal verities, you cut a fine figure—but, after all, are you more than a successful functionary, shouting *solvitur crambo*? Truly, grave misgivings perturbed. Admitting to the full timely reminders loosed by the "moderns," the fact remains that a point of reference, a universe, will not down. Definite rejection of one theory of knowledge, the copy theory, say, removes no ultimate problem, and the thin air of individual consciousness proves too rarified for persistent norms. The humanization of knowledge, genial though it be, may have cost too much. For a world "more meant against than meaning" has its revenge in the reduction of values to mere approvals or disapprovals.

Approaching from the human side, it is natural to conceive experience as the sphere of desire and, mayhap, perfection—a full-orbed world in miniature, entrancing its immediate denizens. But queazy moods follow when, psychological deliverances seeming arbitrary, we scent victimization by vague, perhaps irrelevant, opinion. Thereupon dialectic swings away from

> A doctrinal and witty hieroglyphic
> Of a blessed kingdom

to the rigid outlines associated with substantiality. Granted that accident produced social arrangements, and that the sciences of society linger in the rudimentary stage, are we not driven by cautious opportunism itself to seek securer footing? Profuseness, chaos, even anarchy, may be masked by "working conceptions";

but a reliable vehicle independent of Mind or minds, with principles of its own unaffected by psychological states, portends deliverance from arbitrariness. Concrete realities replace discontinuity and dependence here, and this not by any rationalizing magic in the temper of eighteenth-century materialistic utopianism. Betide contingencies how they may, Science progresses, and can be drafted to furnish stability. Things are not amorphous, and "natural law," thanks to the wonderful extension of the inherently calculable, bestows a "closed system" promising certainty. The weary generation of the nineties, having had its fill of disconcerting men of to-morrow, sought relief from flinging "sentience," "ideas," "actions," "values," and what not into the pot for luck. The reign of law might be risked for the benefits of practicable limitation—*in der Beschränkung zeigt sich erst der Meister.* Moreover, once safe within the laboratory, a succession of engrossing technicalities will ward off delusions of grandeur. We even dare be fussy, and yet remain admirable in modest veracity about emergent discoveries. To what purpose?

Great as are the satisfactions to be derived from progress in "natural knowledge," they nevertheless leave *the* problem unsolved, both ends out of sight, never out of mind. For, if one abandon the major general questions in favour of mastery over special cases—one merely abandons them! If conclusions commanding universal assent be obtainable, the more tenuous the content which the assent supports. "Laws" of cycles (e.g. conservation of mass, gravitation), like statistical laws of, say, gases, avoid, and properly avoid, the "will-o'-the-wisp" of ultimates; indeed, I understand that they throw no light even upon *quanta.* If biological investigation be stabilized by adoption of the physico-chemical hypothesis, mind still eludes. If attention be concentrated upon *systems* of particulars, evidently objects which, as inferred, are at least as important as those perceived, remain for judgment. If we "progress backwards," referring every phenomenon to a lower-grade predecessor as sufficient explanation, what becomes of our Evolution, which involves "new" consequents? If categories themselves be "non-mental," what *can* be said of mind? Then, too, must one reduce human history to a mere succession, on the *schillrend* ground that it does not repeat itself; or are we at the old game of appeal to a simple transcendent? Are we pleading preoccupation with method or, if not, just indulging hardy conjecture? In sum, then, we *are* limiting ourselves to white and black, to light and shade, neglectful of deeper perspective. And this turns out unsatisfactory, for, after all, modern science seems fertile in broad hints that the universe depends much more upon mind than we had dared to suppose. In any case, insistence that attainment of truth must precede every other aim is a two-edged proposition—entirely outside scientific inquiry, on the one hand, and, in addition, itself an open question, on the other. Thus, the "appeal to fact" threw me back upon the "second remove from fact," warned, however, against some dangers of traffic

> With the land that produced one Kant with a K,
> And many a Cant with a C.

This synoptic retrospect no doubt points a moral plainer to veterans than to recruits, for it savours of the doubts and despondencies which, the age controlling, have assailed one for forty years, and led to numerous blunders. The perfervid expectations characteristic of the great post-Kantians, equivalent almost to an evangel, had faded; challenges like the *Aufklärung*, or common sense, or "Force," or "Matter" were no more. In fine, the dynamic prospect of a fresh era consorted ill with a period of disintegration. The attraction of spiritual things, diminished by the allurements of political, industrial, and naturalistic concerns, seemed a philosophical hindrance to some. Preliminary, if not quite subsidiary puzzles, hypostatized in special disciplines, were preempting the foreground. Avid for "new material," we had bogged ourselves in erudition (*mea culpa*). Fragmental systems, relevant, of course, to portions wrenched from experience, eclipsed the system of the Whole, and we pawed over sensibilities, especially the sensibilities of our abnormal neighbours, in place of trying to understand life. We all belonged with the Afterborn— not that we were *laudatores temporis acti*, much less disciples; rather because, in explicable bewilderment, we played King Log to fundamental problems. Habituation to specific spheres, fenced off as private claims by "expert" groups, tended to discourage bold demand for harmony between the warring factors of experience resultant upon constant analysis. Above all, sense of ignorance in face of unsuspected complexities manifest alike in thought and nature, enfeebled will to synthesis. A "subjective" and a "natural" unity appeared compossible, but larger integration abashed—perhaps it was beyond reach.

Nevertheless, it would be folly to sit down and cry over spilt milk, as if the recent past had been resultless, mistaken, or even fatuous. Agreed, there is nothing like general acceptance of any philosophy as true and, till a common doctrine disengages itself from the present welter (as has happened before), this confusion may or must persist. On the other hand, the diremption of experience has been accentuated, masses of information have come to light, which await the process of rethinking, and flat uniformity is out of the question. Stated otherwise, the departmentalizing of the world is serving a purpose in so far as it renders organic to experience many things hitherto held "external" or non-significant or negligible. As a result, we are bound to read the immanent cypher on a broader, profounder scale when and if the general spirit moves. As always, perspective will take care of itself. Some bemoan the emphasis upon science. Well, the "scientific period" is not new, seeing it dates from the seventeenth century, when Galileo, Kepler, Harvey, and Descartes seized the torch for transmission to Newton and Locke, whose profound influence upon Leibniz and Kant made the "reign of law" a vital issue. Popular estimate notwithstanding, Darwinism left things where they were. Generalization of "law" raised interesting queries about evident gaps and possible exceptions; the essential problem loomed up the same, if vaster and more complex in detail as sciences displaced Science. Nay, while speculative thought petrified on the convenient level of this or that naturalism, the ultimate difficulty posed itself the more in the old way. Opposites crystallized in separation, their mutual entanglement missed amid manifold "research," and heaping information, impressive in itself, melodramatic in its practical applications, took the place swept and garnished by historical criticism. Competing types of naturalism united, however, by the dogma of an "objective" order alien from yet determining all human activities, held the field for a moment; whereupon valuation theories arose to conserve a *punctum stans* whence, brandishing his ideals, man might hurl defiance at the inimical or heedless march of nature. Our temptations and, at a pinch, recourses were subordination of thought to the stream of things, with relief in exploiting curiosities, always in the naïve hope of getting knowledge; or postulation of a law for man—his very own— with appeal to "axiology" where Worths, whatever their pretensions to universality, could be "explained" as accompaniments of local or temporary conditions, and could therefore be conscripted as further proofs of the naturalism they were designed to offset! No matter how suggestive, nay, comforting for the nonce, they merely served to cloud the fundamental issue—that of παντελῶς ὂν παντελῶς γνωστόν or, better, of the Νοῦς considered as ἀρχή and τέλος alike. The very terms hint the age-old, insistent scope of the philosophical quest. Not that philosophy must "go back," but that it must surmount its timidity toward a process and attitude far different from those of science.

V

This recital, more engrossing doubtless to the writer than to the reader, may close with a few tentative remarks.

The notion of "progress," especially of continuous progress, is abandoned, for the simple reason that man progresses by deepening of spiritual insight. Besides, paradox though it be, the means devised to guard results often get between men and their real selves. To take a case. Since 1840, we have been reproducing, if on a larger scale, the ferment of the period from Ficino to Hooker. Similar tendencies toward "naturalism," similar confusions, and a similar disposition to slur, if not minimize, the problem presented by man's double nature, have prevailed. The need for a synthesis such as the post-Kantians formulated, but freed from their soaring romanticism, has come full circle.

As concerns dominant ideas, there would seem to have been but two epochs: Greece, with culmination in Plato and, for certain aspects, in Aristotle; Mediaevalism, with culmination in the Scholastic system and Dante. To say that the two were mutually exclusive would be to strain the truth; still it is clear that the "pagan" underlined what the Roman Christian depressed, and vice versa. We have now reached the stage of a reinterpretation, where the chief interests of each confront one another, their respective implications more fully evident. The Greeks founded science. As with us, so with them, the determined attack upon empirical questions developed outside, possibly beyond, the sanctions of organized religion. A recoil was to be anticipated, and it is full-throated early in the millenarianism of "the day of the Lord," due "to come as a thief in the night."[1] This universe of discourse, with every bound and aspiration, finds final expression in the *Divine Comedy*. Human curiosity has been trying to recapture Greek objectivity ever since, aided yet hampered by wealth of detail and consequent acute consciousness of difficulties unknown to the ancients. We still yearn for a synthesis in their temper, not rejecting succour from the Ages of Faith, our deep disturbance by the sense of an "unexplored remainder" impelling. Reverting to our wider knowledge: "The lifetime of a fixed star is estimated at approximately one million million . . . years, a period so long that the whole duration of the world's history from the days of the ancient Egyptians down to our own time amounts to not even one per cent. of the millionth part of the life-history of our solar system."[2] This granted, we can but agree with Lotze, "how universal but, at the same time, how subordinate is the part which mechanism plays in nature."[3] "Objective" reality is evidently mixed, and no part torn from relation to the Whole satisfies, however unitary. Your star-history, vastly homogeneous and quantitative, cannot say to your Egyptian-American history, minutely heterogeneous and qualitative, "I have no need of thee." "Matter" may be "everlasting," but so are the rules

[1] 2 Pet. iii. 10.
[2] A. Haas in *The Scientific Monthly*, February 1928, p. 145.
[3] Cf. *Metaphysic*, Book II, chap. viii.

enabling this predication; indeed, as man interprets them, they attract him because they furnish a simple or "closed" universe of *Erhaltung*. Seductive as immanence on this wise may be, it remains thoroughly abstract. The post-Kantian doctrine of a transcendental power internal to history, whereby the individual is transmuted by the presence of the universal, posed the metaphysical problem, concrete by comparison because revealing the possibilities of *Entfaltung*. Far from external adjustment or composition, we have another issue—"creative," if you like—in any event, commanding recognition of fresh imponderables.

Following upon the double-entry philosophy of the seventeenth and eighteenth centuries, the question of synthesis became so urgent as to overwhelm other considerations between 1795 and 1840. Thereafter, Lotze the single serious exception, this was deserted, then flouted through two generations. The "claims" of the mechanical and the spiritual aspects of experience, having taken their several ways separately, are upon us again, with the result that the task attempted by Aristotle, Kant, and Hegel has developed new urgency. It is necessary to set forth some defensible scheme embodying the irreducible attitudes of thought whereby men overleap the limits set by common sense and the particular sciences. We have shirked the metaphysical presuppositions incident to moral and religious conviction, postponing them in favour of study of the phenomena of nature, of history, and of psychological process, to the exclusion of *Geist*— or whatever you care to term the most inclusive order knowable by man. Symptomatic of this, there has been much uncritical employment of fundamental general ideas when dealing with individuation of "natural facts"; so, too, in psychology, in the human sciences and, we may as well confess, in epistemology. What avails it to treat the "subject," and even the "object" analytically approached, as if they were merely *continua* and nothing more? Why should we cozen ourselves into supposing that endless composition and concrete organization *are* identical universes, presented under identical categories? Partial systems, excellent prefaces as they may be, deceive when they masquerade as complete or, worse luck, the sole totalities. Let information proliferate as it may, philosophy cannot forgo assault upon the primary difficulty. Itself a stage bound to change and pass, it bids us rest content with nothing less than the boldest application of an immanent principle which, no matter how intimative of an "unexplored margin," is not antagonistic to, because rooted in knowledge of the muddy vesture. But, imagination and faith suggesting, it would urge inclusive vision, seeing that spiritual things are as veritably part of man's reach as the commonest details recognizable by irreflective sight. The reaction against science, as it has been called—whether "idealistic" or other boots little—brings the two types of system to confrontation; not without hope of advance beyond dour opposition, seeing there is a mutual emphasis upon immanent principle, whether the object examined be the "natural" or the "human" world. Under the circumstances, quest is the sole path to truth; its *stadia* are Truth: in so far forth we *have* it. Solution of the problem must be correlative to comprehension of it; we can but seek soberly for coherence, eschewing confident remarks on "ultimate" reality.

The untidiness and unpredictableness of life persist; but so do human ideals. Consider ordinary folk, especially those who know how to keep their heads and tempers, betide what may. Faithful to an ideal, they have attained just what philosophy would compass—serene rationality. Their mastery bears intimation, for it hints a region beyond the changeful fashions of theory, yet undisturbed by distant profundities. Face to face with the permanent in them, we admit that we know neither whence nor how comes the insight capable of saving man from his dire predicament as a feeble or, in moments of rude strength, ferine mortal. For this very reason, one is suspicious of all, sceptical about most systems promising immediate realization of the philosophical aim—explanation of *our* universe (never *the* universe) in terms of human consciousness, and implying that personality on its "creative" side provides the best clue. Such a view may well be true or, again, it may be illusory. But these judgments miss the mark if the position defies outflanking.

Contemporary Manichaeism, overborne by the "large injustice" of Nature, forgetful of the Great Mother, serves to warn that "creative" personality may not be identified offhand with the God of religion. In a realistic age, the host of heaven, earth an inconsiderable partner, play the leads, puny mortals momentary and powerless by contrast. Admirable, even platitudinous, this view happens to be off focus when one elicits the ideal dimension present even in human triviality, whence the commonplace derives splendour. Philosophy seeks atmosphere and perspective in this quarter, because only thus can it escape "reality" become a *caput mortuum*. Taking manifest human discontinuities into account, the formidable and persistent problems concern unification of knowledge and its relation to faith. The key lies in the nature of the ideal. What factors are to be designated "bodily," what referred to "mentality," is a preliminary, mayhap a minor question of information. Information, with the practical applications resultant upon it, may effect much to mitigate our earthly lot; they cannot save us from ourselves, because powerless to save in the right way. We are just learning this as our material civilization speeds its headlong course. We are beginning to ask, Are we, then, in any respects better or wiser than our "slow" ancestors? More changes are said to have occurred since 1840 than in the preceding millennium; at what price? Be all these as they may, the most inclusive Whole conceivable belongs in the region of the ideal. If you project a theory of reality, the ideals embraced and subserved by men will surely confute it, unless you have allowed for their dynamic centrality. The more certain —and abstract—your "system," the less significance it is likely to bear in a final summation. From this point of view, ideals constitute the fundamental problems, and relevant statement, alterable though it may be by accumulation of contingent *data*, is more than half the battle. Quite probably, greed for "new" angles of approach, pervasive in a time of confusion, makes too many concessions to various temporary attitudes posing as "common sense." Nevertheless, the helpful or apposite angle sifts itself out from time to time. The saint does evoke things of good report, the artist does evoke loveliness; less fortunate, the philosopher attempts to evoke truth. None of these evocations are susceptible of proof, proof being superfluous! In the beginning and at the end, the thinker imposes belief upon himself. Idealistic in the sense suggested, his idealism is always *aborning*, never altogether born. Seeing that ideals are polymorphic, the quest after unity never ceases, and it never needs to begin. Partial unity being an eternal present, disillusion takes to flight before authoritative, tenable conviction. Approximation is afoot and, to this extent, the ideal manifests inherent objectivity—a satisfying prevision. The prevalent immanence dictates the condition of any possible transcendence, the one actual, the other ever actualizing, both together attesting a definite nature, which happens to be the only Whole that can furnish all the terms indispensable to a rounded interpretation.

PRINCIPAL PUBLICATIONS

Socrates and Christ: a Study in the Philosophy of Religion (Edinburgh and London, 1889).
Aspects of Pessimism (Edinburgh and London, 1894).
Contemporary Theology and Theism (Edinburgh and New York, 1897).
Outline Introductory to Kant's "Critique of Pure Reason" (New York, 1897).
Kant and his Philosophical Revolution (Edinburgh and New York, 1910).
The Anarchist Ideal, and other Essays (Boston and Ann Arbor, 1913).
The Life of Robert Flint (with Donald Macmillan and others) (London, 1914).
The Life and Work of George Sylvester Morris: a Chapter in the History of American Thought in the Nineteenth Century (New York, 1917).
Stoicism and Its Influence (Boston and New York, 1924).

Editorial and Contributor's Work: *The Dictionary of Philosophy and Psychology* (edited by J. Mark Baldwin); and *Encyclopaedia of Religion and Ethics* (edited by James Hastings), 1898–1908.

CONFESSIONS

By FREDERICK J. E. WOODBRIDGE

Born 1867; Johnsonian Professor of Philosophy, Columbia
University, New York.

CONFESSIONS

As I review the course of my philosophical studies and attempt to express the conclusions to which they have led, I am conscious of special indebtedness to Aristotle, Spinoza, and Locke among the dead and to Santayana among the living. It is to them that I repeatedly turn both for refreshment and discipline. They represent, I may say, a selection or survival from the forces that have influenced me rather than a sequence which my own thinking has followed. I cannot name a date when they were first recognized as controlling. I know, however, that when I began teaching at Columbia University in 1902 Aristotle, Spinoza, and Locke had already become the philosophers in whom I was most interested, and Santayana appeared to me as a brilliant and provoking writer. After reading his *Life of Reason*, which I reviewed for the New York *Nation*, I felt that I had found in it a matchless commentary on our human thinking. Since the contributions to this volume of essays are admittedly personal and egotistic, I may as well say now that the *Life of Reason* is a book I wish I could have written myself. I do not ask Santayana to take this as a compliment, for it is a doubtful one. I make the confession to indicate that his book is the kind of book which appeals to me as genuinely philosophical. For as I understand the *Life of Reason*, it makes no attempt to explain why the life of man should be intellectual. It attempts, rather, simply to tell the truth about that life. And telling the truth about the life of reason and trying to discover what that truth implies seem to me to be the business of philosophy. I had reached this conviction before I read the *Life of Reason*, but after reading it the conviction had received a force and an illumination which it had not had before.

And more than this; my understanding of the history of philosophy seemed to be enhanced. I felt that I could enter into the thoughts of others with a keener and more sympathetic appreciation. Indeed, if I may use a chemical figure, the reading of Santayana has acted upon my own thoughts like a catalysing agent, dissolving them and recombining them in ways better

suited to my own satisfaction at least. Two examples may serve
as illustrative. When I read, "With Aristotle the conception of
human life is perfectly sound, for with him everything ideal has
a natural basis and everything natural an ideal fulfilment"—
when I read this, not only did the disorderly writings of the
Stagerite combine together to produce one impressive effect,
but what I myself had been clumsily feeling for received a
clarified and satisfactory expression. In that one sentence was
revealed what certainly seems to be one of the major tasks of
philosophy: to exhibit the passage from the natural to the ideal;
from common sense to reason; from animal love to ideal love;
from gregarious association to free society; from practice and
invention to liberal art; from mythology to enlightened religion;
and from crude cosmologies to that impersonal objectivity found
in science. In that one sentence, too, I found an acceptable
standard of criticism, for it seemed to me that ideals are significant as they round out and complete some natural function, and
that the natural, when cut off from the ideal, must not be looked
upon as affording by itself any standard of conduct or reason for
its existence; it is brutally impersonal. And when I read, "Knowledge is not eating and we cannot be expected to devour what
we mean," I found the vanities of epistemology exposed more
conclusively than any laboured exposition of my own had exposed
them. I could have insisted that "knowing a world" and "having
a world to know" are never the same condition, but I could see
it better with the metaphor to help. To these illustrations I may
add that reading and re-reading the *Dialogues in Limbo* has
become a prized experience in the clarification of my own ideas.
I must rate that book very high in the philosophical literature
I have read.

I have dwelt on my indebtedness to Santayana first because of
its especial character. The basic ideas of "my philosophy"—I use
the phrase conscious of the egotistical privileges of this essay—
were laid before I read him. Perhaps it would be more modest
and even more truthful to say that I think they were. The thing,
however, of which I am acutely conscious is, that through reading
him I seem to have won for myself greater freedom and clarity

in the handling of my ideas. I think I know better what I am about. The scheme which was forming itself in my own mind through the study of Aristotle, Spinoza, and Locke in particular, became more definite, and it became easier, for myself at least, to formulate the chief conviction to which that study had led. A synthesis of Aristotle and Spinoza, tempered by the uncompromising, yet compromised, empiricism of Locke, became something which I thought I clearly conceived and which I believed to be useful in removing some of the confusion for which modern philosophy seemed to be clearly responsible. Aristotle's thoroughgoing naturalism and his conception of productivity, Spinoza's rigid insistence on structure, and Locke's doctrine of the acquisition of ideas through experience, seemed to afford, when taken together, a means of backing up the philosophical enterprise with a metaphysics which would be analytical instead of controversial. If effective ideas are really acquired through experience, an analysis of these ideas should reveal something about the world in which that experience occurs; and the chief revelations seem to be a limiting structure or structures for all events and a genuinely productive activity within these limits. The structure determines what is possible and the activity determines what exists. But this result should not be taken as an absurd dualism which starts with two gods and then produces a world through their co-operation. Structure and activity are things implied by the fact that the world is known and controlled by getting ideas through experience. They are arrived at analytically and are not invoked as demiurges to account for the world we live in. The development of a germ into thoughtful consideration of its habitat and of the manner and incidents of its development, is the basal fact for every philosopher. He can never get behind it. He can only tell the truth about it and try to find out what that truth implies. He may explore his world and control it in some measure, but he can never find originals which brought it into being.

All this at the age of sixty seems to me to be so simple as to need no elaboration. One's familiarity with one's own line of thought begets this illusion. I have to confess—like every other worker in these mazes of thought—that I have entertained in the past, with entire conviction, opinions which I can hold no longer. This, if nothing else, should make me recognize that what now seems so clear to me may not seem clear at all to others, and that I myself may be among those others at a later date. Yet I venture to think, even if so thinking savours of contradiction and dialectic, that the principle of hesitation which I have just expressed is an essential part of the position to which I have been led. Hesitation, doubt, perplexity, uncertainty, the sense of incompleteness and of more to be done, the prospect and probability that one will change one's mind—all these things are as real as anything else. The doubtful man is as much a product of nature as the confident. Indeed, nothing that happens can be convicted of impossibility. There must, consequently, be room in one's metaphysics for anything that may happen. This I take to be a very solid principle. We may condemn philosophies as false, but we cannot impugn their existence. It is easy to claim that men ought not to think in certain ways and forget that they do think in those ways. Their thinking may be improper, but it is clearly not improper from the point of view of its existence or as an illustration of nature's productivity. From the point of view of existence one might as well accuse the diversified flora and fauna of the earth of impropriety. The principle, therefore, that there must be room in one's metaphysics for whatever may happen or that nothing that happens can be convicted of impossibility, seems clearly to imply that our distinctions are distinctions within one common field and not between two fields which the distinctions make incompatible. Rather clumsily expressed, they are distinctions "within" and not distinctions between "within and without." Appearance and reality, truth and error, good and evil, beautiful and ugly, are all correlative. An existence which did not own them would not be our existence. A metaphysics which abolished them would not be a true metaphysics, but it would demonstrate them. Even in being false it would have a claim on existence. I could boast that my metaphysics recognizes this, making it a cardinal principle. Rather than boast, however, I would make this the first step in metaphysics—the recognition that existence is primarily what it is and can neither be explained nor explained away. The most that can be done is to find out what it implies. And the great error of metaphysicians is the supposition that the implications of existence are its causes and lead us to something more fundamental than existence, or prior to it, or in itself irrelevant to it.

I have, consequently, often called myself a realist, and one of a very naïve sort. But calling names seems to have parallel consequences, whether oneself or others be the object. One is not always comfortable with one's associates. The linking name is not a marriage ring symbolizing community of bed and board. Yet I confess a sympathy with all realists of whatever stripe, even the mediaeval and the literary. They are evidently trying to see things as they are, even when what they see is selected. Novelists often tell us what real life is by telling us about some unfamiliar life, and philosophers also often discern real existence in the unfamiliar. The realism I would urge is one of principle rather than one of selection. As a principle it does not dichotomize existence. There is, for example, an ancient question, whether a rose is red when it is not seen. The answer always has seemed to me to be: a red rose is. The colours of roses are not like guesses in Blind Man's Buff, and many a rose is born to blush unseen. I can attach no meaning to the question: *Is* the colour of a rose what it is? I am too sensible of the fact that I have bought bushes of a nurseryman who—nor I—have not as yet seen the roses they will bear. Such experiences may drive us back on the general fact of colour and lead us to ask: Do colours exist when they are not perceived? It is hard for me to attach a meaning even to this question. A dark room may exclude all colours save black when the eyes are open, and a similar effect may be produced by binding the eyes in a lighted room. And this simple experiment forces me to conclude that colour is as much something with the existence of which I have nothing to do as it is something with the existence of which I have something to do. When I try to find out how much I have to do with it, I find that much very little— no more than the fact that if I did not exist, I would never ask such curious questions. I would not ask any questions at all. And I cannot possibly conceive what a world is like about which no questions whatever are asked. Furthermore, it seems monstrous to me to conclude that *the* world is only *my* world, for "my" world means nothing unless distinguished from a world not mine. I may distinguish such a world just as I distinguish houses which are not mine. A metaphysical distinction, if made at all, must be of a similar kind, or it is meaningless. This is what I mean by a realism of principle rather than of selection. As I am fond of saying, the only universe relevant to inquiry, the only universe that exists for purposes of observation, experiment, and ratiocination, is the universe of discourse. Any other universe is meaningless. If I am challenged to prove this, I point out such obvious facts as this: we do not proceed originally from the implications of colour to colour, but from colour to its implications. The subject-matter of inquiry cannot be called in question. Individual existences may be related to one another and compared, but "the whole of existence" can be related to nothing or compared with nothing.

This is the basic dogma of metaphysics. I cannot remember when it first gained possession of me. I am tempted to think that I always thought that way. I remember quite distinctly that when I first read Berkeley, which was in my college days at Amherst, I was troubled over the conflict between the incredibility of his doctrine and the obvious truth of its foundation. Looking back now at the experience, I can formulate it as I could not have formulated it then: I was conscious that he converted a definition of subject-matter into the cause of its existence. He saw clearly enough that existence implies mind in some objective sense, but he made mind the creator of what exists. In those same days, I had a similar experience with Kant, but it was many years before I could say that this synthetic philosophy was anything more than a definition of subject-matter converted into a wholly incredible explanation of experience. And the little I had then of Hegel—getting his ideas, not through reading but through the fascinating exposition of Professor Garman—fired my imagination as a little of Hegel did that of many of my contemporaries. Glimpses of the organic unity of experience were inspiring for minds distracted by an associationist psychology on the one hand and the artificiality of the "critical philosophy" on the other. We read no Aristotle in those days, and it was only later that I saw that Hegel had done little more than turn Aristotle upside down and done it clumsily. I am conscious of such early experiences and such later formulations, but conscious of them as a pretty steady and natural development of my thinking unmarked by a sense of violent conversion. This development seems to be a line along which I have been led rather than a programme ever deliberately adopted. This seeming may be one of the illusions which I egotistically cherish, but I set it down with the frankness which confessions like these inspire.

I could cite other things more casual, perhaps, than those already mentioned. A remark in a cherished copy of Jevons' *Lessons in Logic* stands pencilled with a question mark: "We cannot suppose, and there is no reason to suppose, that by the constitution of the mind we are obliged to think of things differently from the manner in which they are." There is a note to the remark: "Discuss light, colour, sound, etc." The book is a heritage from college days and carries the name of a class-mate. I must have purloined it. The question mark and the note were put there when I taught logic at the University of Minnesota. I was very conscious of the hopelessness of an obligation to think of things differently from the manner in which they are, and ended a contribution to the *Essays Philosophical and Psychological in Honour of William James* with the remark of Jevons. When I read, shamelessly, as youth is wont to do, the *Essays* of Matthew Arnold while Professor Shedd lectured on Dogmatic Theology at the Union Theological Seminary, there was tucked away in my memory one of Arnold's favourite quotations: "Things are what they are and the consequences of them will be what they will be; why then should we wish to be deceived?" So I take the principle of realism as something pretty well ingrained and constitutional in me. Like everybody else, I pride myself on a sense of fact.

I have tried to support this pride by teaching and by the little I have written. The principle of realism seems so important to

422 CONTEMPORARY AMERICAN PHILOSOPHY

me for metaphysics and philosophy that I have been more busy with championing it than with developing it. Yet to keep insisting on it seems worth while. It helps me not to wish to be deceived. If this world were *explained* as so many of us philosophers try to explain it, it wouldn't be this world at all. It may cry for an explanation, but a metaphysician in his wish not to be deceived will set that down as one interesting fact about it. He will see poetry and religion, and art and society, and morals and science and philosophy even, as responses to that cry and be glad and not contemptuous of them. He will recognize them *as* responses, confident that when they cease to be such, there will be no more world. The cry is essential to what existence is. Nature has generated and supports it. With Aristotle we may make it the evocation of God's bare presence and rest content with that, for God is a rather final explanation of things. But if we do not wish to be deceived we will not make him the creator of the world, responsible for microbes and men, or try to deduce from his nature the way of a man with a maid. We may insist with theology that he must be incarnated, born of a virgin, even, to be as effective with men as he is with the stars, but we will recognize in that insistence a supreme illustration of the cry. The appeal of existence will not have ceased. First and fundamentally it is an appeal.

To find it first and fundamentally something else is to acknowledge oneself a selective realist rather than a realist in principle and to have chosen one instance of the natural kinesis instead of the character of them all. Matter, atoms, space and time, ions, electrical charges, the stable bodies and rhythmic motions of the physical world, the microscope's revelations of the mutations of the seeds and carriers of subsequent developments, and the natural evolution of living organisms, must bulk large in one's thinking. They make an imposing spectacle, suited to arouse both the admiration of a poet and the curiosity of a scientist. It is trivial to ask which treats them the more adequately unless one specifies the purpose for which they are treated. The heavens declare both the glory of God and an opportunity for astronomers. They declare neither exclusively. If we look for an exclusive declaration, it is found, not by selecting one from a number, calling the one real and the others illusion; it is found rather in the steady recognition of the fact that something is declared. This is but saying again that existence *is* what it reveals itself to be to a seeker, without addition or subtraction. And this may be turned around. It is the seeking of what existence reveals that defines the unity in existence and discovers the manifoldness of its revelations. This shows again how metaphysics is realistic in principle. At the risk of seeming to talk nonsense, I may say that the question, What is existence? is an existing question, one thrown up in the operations of nature, an event in the world fully as much as an eclipse of the sun, but more conspicuous than the latter. Familiarity with it may breed contempt. It is not, however, to be set aside and neglected. For man does not stand outside of nature and ask her questions. He stands inside. His questions well up within him, form on his lips as naturally as his smiles, and are as much a revelation of existence as his answers are. They are more. They are the final revelation of existence, declaring it to be—for metaphysics at least—first and foremost a question. When this is seen, the metaphysician need not hesitate to see a question answered in the growth of an acorn into an oak or the revolution of a planet about the sun. He may even go so far, running the risk of being laughed at as a poet or lover of metaphors, and say that acorn and planet have asked questions and found answers. At any rate, existence seeking will be for him a more impressive fact than existence found. That is why he will not put the inquisitive mind outside of nature and suppose that it is obliged to think of things different from the manner in which they are. He will keep it inside as the sure indication of what natural processes are, and if he finds an atom, he will not let the little thing drive mind out of nature and make of mind a problem never to be solved. He will gladly be something of an Hegelian and more of an Aristotelian to avoid that disaster.

All this, as I have said, seems very simple to me. I have been told that it is too obvious, too much bare matter of fact, and that a philosopher, if he accepted it, would have nothing left to do. He would lose his profession. I might answer that, if this were true, humanity might profit by the loss. But I do not believe it to be true. There is something still left for the philosopher. He can at least keep on asking questions and seeking their answers, and do this with the added consciousness of knowing what he is about. His questions may be less foolish than they were. He may find that he has to give up many cherished problems, like that of the red rose, the doubled moon, the vanished star, the bent stick, the presence of evil, the ubiquity of error, the clash of freedom and necessity, the reconciliation of mechanism and teleology, the possibility of knowledge, and the relation of soul to body, but he ought to thank God for it. He ought to be glad to be rid of appendages, sloughing them off, as nature seems to do, when they become useless or a hindrance. Even then he will have plenty to do in making confession to the world and, by his teaching, warning others from a sad employment of their time, using the history of philosophy as a text. And then, if he has sympathy, he may do some good.

These remarks are a further confession of my own thoughts. I have never been interested in the "problems" of philosophy. That is, perhaps, not strictly true. Yet I cannot remember ever having been seriously worried about them. This fact, rather than the problems, has often worried me, for it convicts me, even to myself, of a lack of sympathy and stimulates my natural egotism unduly. These problems have been very important things in history and have had serious consequences. To be cold to them is not to be wholly comfortable in the society of others or in the quiet reading in one's study. I have known souls desperate in the clutches of necessity and I have read about Erasmus and Luther. The cry for a just God in a naughty world I have heard. But it all seems to me, speaking quite frankly, unfortunate and absurd, and sometimes abominable. I know, of course, that these worries are quite real and very important. I have had enough practical experience, enough of that sort of dealing with others which acutely exposes the conflicts which go on in men's souls, to know how real these things are, to be stirred with deep concern and to be prompted to be resolute in action.

Yet I could never translate the practical conflicts of life into problems which philosophy must solve in order that these conflicts may be reduced. This may be in me what is often called temperamental, or it may be a consequence of my father's influence on my education. He was one of the justest and fairest men I have ever known, unselfishly solicitous about others, but he never worried about the world. Its make-up and that distribution of good and evil which marks the life of man were never problems crying for a theoretical solution. He was a devout Christian and a devoted Churchman, but he never worried over any doctrine. I was early heretical and brought back Herbert Spencer from college. His serenity was undisturbed. He was serene. I can think of no better adjective. To borrow Matthew Arnold's words about Wordsworth—the cloud of mortal destiny he put by. His constant prayer was: "We know not what a day may bring forth; we only know that the hour for serving Thee is always present." We were intimate companions. And it may well be that living from childhood in the shadow of his unruffled confidence, I early grew to be indifferent to much that otherwise might have disturbed me. There have been times when the evident indifference of the order of nature to human concerns has been emotionally shocking and the sense of estrangement acute, but it is rare indeed that I have felt that such experiences implied a theoretical problem to be solved. In this sense, I was early, without knowing it, something of a pragmatist, asking myself what difference does it make to-morrow whether I am fated or free. And in my student days in Berlin, in 1893, I wrote a never-published and now-lost paper to prove that it made no difference. I wish I could read it now to see how well reminiscence is confirmed.

Yet I have been and am interested in the problems of philosophy as excursions of the human mind. The history of ideas is one of the most absorbing and fascinating subjects in which I have ever engaged. Of all the great philosophers, Leibniz is the only one I could willingly eliminate. Here I confess to a prejudice. I know its origin. When I heard Ebbinghaus lecture on Leibniz in Berlin, he remarked: "Leibniz went about introducing himself to prominent people as a promising young man." That remark stuck. I always see Leibniz that way first and, consequently, come at his ideas with amusement. Yet, as I forget this, I can enjoy some enthusiasm in seeing how the differential calculus and the doctrine of pre-established harmony admirably work together, the monads reflecting the function of one equation, each with its own little differential. It is, generally, such congruences in ideas that I find more fascinating than any concern about their validity. Here I confess a greater debt to Ebbinghaus than amusement over Leibniz. He had the habit, every now and then, of brushing aside his notes, which followed a rather stupid method of classification, and running his fingers through his hair, exclaiming: "Aber nun, meine Herrn, wir mussen ein bischen interpretieren. Was *will* der Mensch?" Then, there was a lecture indeed. Yes; what would a man have? How does he go about having it? Whither is he led? Into the grip of what ideas does he fall? Where does he arrive, with or against his will?—like Hobbes sending Christian souls to martyrdom in a heathen state as the only allowable escape from the absolute sovereignty of a king who orders them to renounce their faith. There is an inevitability to which ideas bow. They are gotten of experience, as Locke so abundantly shows, but once gotten, they lead experience instead of following it. And that to which they lead may send them back to clarify or mock their source. It is so with the problems of philosophy. They are born of ideas which experience generates. Once born, they run their course and then come back to clear or muddy their origin. They exercise a function rather than lead to a solution. The exercise of that function seems to me to be better displayed in the thinking of the great than it is displayed in introductions to philosophy, like Paulsen's for example, where the problems are systematically detached and rendered as the outgivings of a universal experience which no man ever had. *Was der Mensch will* is then entirely forgotten, although it is always what some man would, what he would in his day and generation, moved by the forces that played upon him, which has generated these problems with vitality. Deprived of individual and social backing, they are little more than formal

exercises, good for discipline in ratiocination, but poor substitutes
for the vitality of Plato or of Hume.

While I have been writing, a rather cryptic saying of Professor
Garman's has been claiming attention: "A man never *thinks*
wrong; his danger lies in *not* thinking." It was a perplexing
utterance and mixed up, as I remember, with some Hegelianism.
Errors of thought seemed to be all too frequent and familiar
things to be swept aside with an aphorism. The maxim did
pedagogical service in his classroom. I will not say that he made
us think right, but he made us think fatally. I well remember a
class-mate, one of the best students in the college, who, after a
thrice-repeated perfect analysis of Hume on causation, was made
to swallow the doctrine much against his will, because he found
no fault with it besides his own dislike. I cannot say what
"Garman's philosophy" was. He certainly left me with no system
of philosophy and no consciousness of one. He did leave me
with an immense respect for the thinking mind. Its wanderings
and where it would go next became more alluring than stopping
at some comfortable inn along the way. And I remember another
class-mate, a partner of the Berlin days, who asked me what
system of philosophy I had decided on to teach when I returned
to America. The question struck me as preposterous. I was
diffident about admitting that I had no system, but I had heard
the phrase "the Odyssey of the spirit," and was more interested in
what that phrase implied than in indoctrinating youth with any
system, whether borrowed or egotistically thought to be original.
I fear I may have changed in this respect, although I still boast
of a contempt of discipleship. These things are said, however,
not to praise my character but rather to illustrate my education
and its bearing on my attitude toward the problems of philosophy
and the history of ideas. The mind, like the body, has its excursions. The profit of them is the traveller's profit.

I have already hinted that the travelling has a consequence.
With me it has become a major one. Ideas, as Locke urged, are
born of experience, of the body's contact with the body's world.
He thought that God could—although he believed that God did
not—have made the body think without the addition of a soul to

help it. There was a beautiful courage in that honest Englishman who, like some other philosophers, came near to being a clergyman. Yet he seems to have been a little afraid of the soul, a little afraid of "ideas" and used the term abominably. They ran away with him at times, as is well illustrated in his chapter on "Solidity." In this chapter Locke makes two statements which deserve critical attention: "That which hinders the approach of two bodies when they are moved one towards another, I call solidity"; and "If anyone asks me what this solidity is, I send him to his senses to inform him." Who will forbid the sending? But who can deny that the effect of it is a definition? Solidity turns out to be more than something at the tips of our fingers; it turns out to be something characteristic of the system of things in which our fingers move. Going to the senses opens the door to definable relationships. A man thereby enters a realm of being in which ideas enlarge and fructuate and from which he may return to his senses with a different touch. He is on his way to knowledge. This is not a matter of comparing our ideas to see whether they agree or differ as one might compare a sound and a colour. It is not a matter of compounding them as one might compound the tastes of water, sugar, and lemons and get the taste of lemonade. Locke's illustration is "gold," but his examples of knowledge are pitiful. When he is through with knowledge, he throws most of it over in favour of what he calls judgment, leaving the remnant as a foretaste of future bliss. It can all be made very ridiculous. Yet he was fundamentally sound. We must go to our senses, not our souls, if we are ever to enter the realm of mind. Far less acute than Descartes and far less subtle than Hume or Kant, he was far more solid than any of them. We enter the realm of mind through our senses, but it is a realm we enter. There a different authority rules than the porter who let us in. There one travels among ideas which are forced to acknowledge a controlling fate.

And so, to continue this apology for my life, I have leaned on Locke as on a sure support. I have ridiculed before my classes what has seemed to me to be ridiculous in him, and I have forced him to exhibit the fate to which his own ideas were committed.

If, however, I am at all sane, I thank him from the bottom of my heart, I thank him for sending me to my senses to find the mind rather than to Descartes to find it in doubt. For this "sending to the senses" when thoroughly worked out, reveals that what the senses define is not a discrete series of isolated contacts on which some synthesis must be superimposed. Locke so supposed, and his working out of the supposition amply demonstrates its futility. He was forced to define *real knowledge* as something no man could ever attain and make it, consequently, a conception of no use whatever in this mortal life. He should have paid more attention to what he had left, to those sciences he would free from the dictation of philosophers. We can never *know* whether our ideas agree with things, but we have to *proceed* as if they did! But if we cannot know the former, what possible sense is there in saying the latter? What is the sense of saying that we must proceed on the basis of something we know nothing about? What is the sense of trying to reduce knowledge to psychology, when psychology must be a branch of knowledge or not worth the paper on which it is written? Is psychology, too, the taking of ideas to agree with something without any knowledge whether they do or what that something is? Is the "science of knowledge" the same sort of thing? I must protest. The doctrine of the "association of ideas" in some form or other has remarkable vitality. The reason is, I suppose, that they *are* associated. When, however, we turn the fact of their association into an explanation of knowledge, we have to make a number of assumptions for which association cannot account. Chief of these is the great assumption which Locke himself made: that there is, to begin with, an order in things to which the mind tries to conform, sometimes succeeding, perhaps, but more often failing. This makes "the order in things" the crucial thing for the whole doctrine. If there is no such order, it is senseless to suppose that the association of ideas conforms to it or reveals it. If there is such an order, and if it is helpful to explain the association of ideas, then the association of ideas does not explain it or our knowledge of it. If we try to escape these alternatives by concluding that we have *only* an association of *ideas* to deal with, we may, perhaps, understand what we mean by "association" in this conclusion, but we ask in vain for an answer to the question, What do "only" and "ideas" distinguish? What are "ideas" contrasted with and what does "only" exclude? The conclusion excludes an answer, and is, therefore, meaningless. It is much better to go to one's senses, to go to what even Locke too much neglected, to the enterprises in which men are engaged in discovering order and not in supposing it exists or in trying to account for its existence—to the hope of getting knowledge, not to the hopelessness of explaining it. Then order imposes itself upon us. It is found to be, not an assumption which we make, but a discovery which we welcome and fear. On it our happiness and misery depend. The better we know it, the more we can modify our destiny; and we are in its hands as in the hands of fate. We go to touch for solidity to discover it to be that which keeps bodies apart, something more than an isolated sense datum, something in an order of things.

So I once wrote an article on "Structure" and, later, the *Realm of Mind*. The principle of realism, carried out, seems to me to lead repeatedly to at least the implication of structure. I have frequently hinted at this in what I have here written. Even the attempt to write something like one's philosophical biography, calling the past to remembrance and probably distorting it for effect, involves the attempt to find a framework into which events, readings, and reflections fit and thereby own some relation to one another. Whatever our account may be of, it is an account with some order or structure that is aimed at and expected. Without it the account cannot be understood; we call it unintelligible. If it is of the world or of nature that we would give an account, the same implication holds; we must discover or invent an order or structure. We are often deceived by invented orders when they are brilliant and tightly knit. They may impose on mankind for centuries. Even when we reject them, we admire them, and we more readily believe a man who tells us lies in an orderly fashion than one who tells us the truth in disorder. The reason for this is not our credulity. Invented orders are rarely pure inventions or wholly arbitrary. I doubt if they ever are. One lie forces a man to tell another, but this other must be a supporting lie, one which fits into a structure, the structure which the first implies, so that with the first lie a man is doomed to go on inevitably, if he goes on at all in its support. Even Fairyland and Nowhere soon rob their explorers of freedom. Premises freely or conventionally accepted lead to conclusions which their acceptance never suspected. Mathematics is the crowning example. Counting by tens is a convention, but Kant made a good deal of the fact that $7 + 5 = 12$ is not. He belaboured the fact with astute phraseology which ought not, however, because of a dislike of words, to obscure the leaning of the proposition on an order and not on its subject. Mathematics *is* the crowning example, and with its many applications is powerful enough to prove that order is not a human bias or an imposition on reluctant material. It is an implication of all existence, something to be set down as metaphysical, something which we creatures of a day never made—for if we did, why do we rebel against it, cry over it, and yet seek it with our whole heart in the belief that it is the final answer to every question that we ask? It, and not our minds, is responsible for the intelligibility of the world, and we have minds because our bodies are in contact with other bodies which jointly with it are in an order enmeshed. That is why I wrote the *Realm of Mind*.

And that is why I have joined Spinoza to Locke in my affections. Few philosophers have had the sense of order as supremely as Spinoza had it. It overpowered him and set him all atremble. Ostracized by society and ill with consumption, he could rest in it as in the embrace of God's love. The beauty of it in him for a modern reader lies in his freedom from epistemology and the confusions of subjectivism. He is astonishingly free from empiricism also. This, I find, is a matter of offence with students. It is difficult to get them to put, with him, the empirical world aside or take it for granted as something acknowledged but not allowed to interfere with the fatality of thought. They expect him to show why, as a consequence of God's nature, the seasons change and the clouds drop down their dew. That he is wise about men and has a profound knowledge of human nature seems clear

from many a penetrating remark, but to affirm that whatever is—
even in this matter of human nature—is in God and without God
can neither be nor be conceived, is a queer sort of psychology.
They often look at him as a juggler, who presents to them an
apparently empty hat in the shape of definitions and axioms
and then proceeds to draw out of it astonishing things. They
rarely fail in the end to be impressed by an inevitability, august,
sublime, and possibly tender. The empirical world is somehow
caught in it and illustrates it just as *this* circle is caught in and
illustrates *the* circle. The question why, if *the* circle exists, *this*
circle should also exist, remains unanswered, but it tends to
become unimportant, for there seems to be some sense, even if
an obscure and baffling sense, in saying that without *the* circle, *this*
circle could neither be nor be conceived. Quite possibly, Spinoza,
like the rest of us, was a man who thought he proved more than
he did. There is abundant evidence of it; and his method of
exhibiting his thoughts leaves much to be desired. He was a
very interesting person and a baffling one. People found him
that. They thought he had said something important which they
did not understand and which seemed to violate cherished
beliefs and obvious facts, and when they asked him about it, he
had the habit of telling them that they did not understand,
that they knew nothing of God and the human mind. A psycho-
analyst can readily find in him an inferiority complex and a
defensive mechanism. It may be ungrudgingly admitted that he
had both, and fled to God because the world rejected him or
because he was too weak to accommodate himself to the world.
The fact of him, however, and what he did are more important
than any analysis of his personality. The *Ethics* is a book which,
like Euclid, should be read with no curiosity about its author.
It is a book in which personal opinions and prejudices should not
be allowed to count. They are as irrelevant to the reader as
Euclid, the man, is irrelevant to the boy studying geometry. For
it is a geometrical effect one comes away with. In the light of
this effect, the language can be discounted. The mediaeval
terminology, all the apparent jugglery with essence, existence,
idea, and power, is an instrument to impress upon the reader

an overwhelming sense of the fact of order and structure. He must get *substance* before he gets anything else. He must begin philosophy with God and not with Locke. Unless he begins in this way, he can never understand anything; he may go to touch for solidity, but if he stops there he can never understand what he is saying when he says: By solidity, I mean this or that. For knowledge is not eating and we cannot be expected to devour what we mean.

And so I lean on Spinoza as well as on Locke. To touch the world or experience it is very far from knowing it. Experience and knowledge seem to me to be very different things. I quote Santayana again, from memory: "I have often wondered at those philosophers who have said that all our ideas are derived from experience. They could never have been poets and must have forgotten that they were ever children; for the great problem of education is how to get experience out of ideas." It is the great problem of life and science: how to fit oneself into an order, how to get out of the idea of Relativity white marks on a photographic plate. Doing these things is knowledge. Bumping one's head against a wall is experience and a poor substitute. There is joy in going to the senses—to experience—if one does not stay there. They open the door to the realm of mind, to order, to structure, to the inevitable, to freedom, to substance, to God—if God is that in view of which our destinies are shaped.

It is with one of those unreasonable enthusiasms which we often have that I turn to Aristotle. He has said everything that I have ever said or shall ever say. He tells me that that is continuous which, when cut, has common boundaries, and I find it unnecessary to go to Dedekind. This is quite stupid, I know, but I may as well confess it. He tells me that A is the cause of B, and B the cause of C, and so on for ever, but that B is not the cause of C because A is the cause of B; and the weight of an infinite series is lifted from my mind for ever. Everything begins when it does, and there is no need to search the past for a first cause or origin of things. Existence begins now fully as much as it ever began. A road begins at this end, but it also begins at the other end, even if it began at this end before it began at the other; for nothing ever begins before or after it does begin. I admire this cool insistence on such simple and obvious things—taking the beginning of a road as a first illustration of "principle" and then going to the keel of a ship, the axioms of geometry and the rules of a city. The principle of a thing is found where the thing begins, and we must never forget that in searching for principles. The tenses of the verb are the carriers of time. One thing may begin before or after another or may so have begun. Things may be and are arranged that way. But to arrange principles themselves in temporal order is to forget that we are always dealing with a dynamic world. Form, matter, efficacy, and end (purpose) are just as much now as they have ever been, but this particular case of them—this man, this house, this stone—never was or is, or will be again. It is this particular case which is interesting and important and the object of our questions. What is it? Out of what did it come? What effected its coming out? What purpose does it serve? A complete answer to these questions would tell us everything about the case. It would help us to the formulation of conditions which are "catholic," which hold good "on the whole" or for the most part; and so help us to arrange our knowledge in bodies of knowledge appropriate to this or that particular subject-matter. While we must always remember that we are dealing with a dynamic world and recognize that it is only some particular, individual case, not something in general, that raises the question of the "four causes," we may address ourselves to this very fact and discover that particular field of inquiry which was later called metaphysics. What we must remember and recognize and what questions we ask when dealing with a stone or a house or a man, ought to give some indication of what it is *to be*, whether it is a stone, a house, or a man—or even a god—that *is*. The implications of being something are the implications of being anything, if "things will not be governed ill"—τά δε ὄντα οὐ βούλεται πολιτεύεσθαι κακῶς.

I owe to Aristotle my conception of metaphysics and the love of it. His errors and omissions—I can point them out as con-

fidently as the next man. I know how history has distorted him
and what a tyrant he became over the minds of men. That was
because few really read and studied him, or because they read
and studied him with a mental set previously determined by their
own language and ideas. I had to tell a very brilliant student
once that the word "cause" never occurs in Aristotle, before I
could make him see that his contention that Aristotle was not
justified in the use of the term was amusing rather than critical.
Students who go to his text often forget that his writings are not
translations of English. Even so, he has a gripping power and,
when read attentively, is still the great intellectual force he has
always been. Compared with that, his errors, omissions, and
tyranny are now trivial. From him I learned that metaphysics is
a special interest and not a super-science which should dictate
to others and criticize them. They can get on without it, although
it cannot get on very well without them. Yet it admits no servile
dependence. It does not wait on their permission or advice any
more than they wait upon its. It would share with them mutually
in the interests of the mind. But it frequently has to protest
against the substitution of them in its place. It dares to be as
egotistical as they are and be thankful. If Aristotle could try to
keep them all together in happy companionship, why not keep
on trying? For metaphysics would never aim at usurping their
place. It would not boast, even if it boasted perfection, that it
could solve a single problem in physics, chemistry, or biology,
and it would not expect them to do its own work of analysis.
Yet it would claim to be a very human enterprise without which
a man may be easily intellectually warped and deficient in sympathy with the great episodes of human life. Aristotle, with all
his errors, is immune to that.

And, more technically, I have learned from him that metaphysics is analytic. It produces nothing out of a juggler's hat,
and certainly not God and the world. It takes things as they are,
in all their obvious plurality, and never supposes that they can
be reduced to ultimates from which they sprang by miracle or
evolution. It leaves the history of existence to historians and its
evolution to evolutionists. Its interest is in what it is to be a

history and what it is to be an evolution. That there are space
and time, and matter and energy, and life and death and thought
—a world to know and minds to know it—it admits beyond
question. Faced with these things, it has no interest in why they
are as they are—why the body has a mind or the mind a body.
It does not try to justify the ways of God or matter. Since nature
produces many things, it is content to take her productivity as a
fact without asking for a reason for it, knowing that the only
possible reason would be "something that produces." But metaphysics would analyse productivity to see what it implies,
without supposing that the results of its analysis disclose factors
which once, in some far-away time, conspired together to make
a world.

One further debt I must acknowledge to Aristotle—an appreciation of language which I never had until I studied him. I was
early impressed with his use of the verb "to say" and his insistence
that truth is not a matter of things but of propositions. Knowledge, with him, is largely a matter of *saying* what things are.
This gives a dominant *logical* note to all his writings, noticeable
even in his descriptions and illustrations. It would seem, at times,
as if a coherent system of sayings in a given field was of more
importance to him than its subject-matter. He points out how
certain common uses and turns of speech vary as they are used
in varying connections. τὸ ὄν λέγεται πολλαχῶς. The principle
is generalized almost to the roots of being. What is said is
relevant to the occasions of saying it, so that the same expression may exercise quite different functions in different connections. He made common words and phrases do unexpected
service. He made, one might say, the Greek language conscious
of itself as an instrument rather than as a language different from
that of barbarians. And although truth is not a matter of nature,
the *saying* of things is. When Socrates is said to be a man, something has happened to him of which he may be unaware, but he
has provoked conversation fully as much as he provoked the
resentment of Athens. Existence is provocative. Its being so is
one instance of its kinetic character, for speech is a motion fully
as much as the movements of the spheres. What a saying effects

is consequently more important than the way of saying it, although a scrupulous nicety about expression is to be commended highly. From all this I hope I have learned a respect for language and been made aware that alarmingly different expressions in the same language and in different languages may convey the same idea. I have often told my classes that when Jonathan Edwards called his sweetheart "a handmaid of the Lord" he was not very far removed from the modern youth, who might call his "a damn fine girl." The different expressions connote a different culture and different proprieties, but should a metaphysician quarrel with either of them? The maid was provocative. I should not be surprised, therefore, if I found out that Thomas Aquinas and Immanuel Kant were saying the same thing; or John Calvin and Charles Darwin—the many are called and the few chosen. It is again "Was *will* der Mensch"; and, perhaps, when a man thinks, he does not think wrong. The language he speaks may be unintelligible or sound absurd, but there is at least the suspicion that it is humanly vernacular. We all live in the same world of sunrise and sunset, but talk about it in languages which are diverse; and what our differing utterances are relevant to is more important than their relevances to one another. Since they are relevant to something, I have been led to consider language as an instance of that give and take in nature which discovers ideas.

And so I end, conscious that I have left unsaid things that might have been said and not as sure as I should like to be that I have fulfilled the purpose of this volume. I have taken the opportunity to be one which permits and encourages a freedom of expression and intimacy which one ordinarily might prefer to avoid. Confession is said to be good for the soul. I think I have had some good of it. Receivers of confessions—one leaves the priest a little worried about what has been told. I think of David Hume: "I cannot say there is no vanity in making this funeral oration of myself, but I hope it is not a misplaced one; and this is a matter of fact which is easily clensed and ascertained."

PRINCIPAL PUBLICATIONS

The Philosophy of Hobbes (H. W. Wilson Co., 1903).

The Purpose of History (Columbia University Press, 1916).

The Realm of Mind (Columbia University Press, 1926).

Contrasts in Education (Teachers' College, Columbia University, 1929).

The Son of Apollo: The Themes of Plato (Houghton, Mifflin Co., 1929).

Editor (with W. T. Bush and H. W. Schneider) of the *Journal of Philosophy*.

INDEX

DATE DUE

MAR 3 1 1993			